# CALIFORNIA GUN LAWS

## A guide to state and federal firearm regulations

**COLDAW**
PUBLISHING

COLDAW
PUBLISHING

COLDAW PUBLISHING
C. D. Michel
180 E. Ocean Blvd., Suite 200
Long Beach, CA 90802
562-216-4444 Office ~ 562-216-4445 Fax
www.calgunlawsbook.com
www.michellawyers.com

MICHEL & ASSOCIATES, P.C.
Attorneys at Law

Cover Design: Matthew Navoa
Editing: Jason O. Crye
Layout: Sarah Hinman
Project Manager/Agent: Penny Callmeyer, Tiger Lilly Enterprises

ISBN 978-0-9884602-0-1
Library of Congress Control Number: 2012950983

ATTENTION
Contact the publisher for information on quantity discounts!

Printed and bound in the United States of America
at Color House Graphics, Grand Rapids, Michigan

First Edition

# TABLE OF CONTENTS

# ACKNOWLEDGMENTS

I would first like to extend my gratitude to Tamara Rider, Sean Brady, Joe Silvoso, and Hillary Green. Tamara, without you this project would have come off the rails. Thank you for your dedication to this multiple-year endeavor. This book could not have been published without your commitment to seeing it finished. Sean and Joe, the breadth of your knowledge of state and federal firearm laws far exceeds your years. Without you this book would not be as detailed and specific as it is. Hillary, without your contributions this book would not be accessible to the wide audience it is intended to reach.

I also wish to thank all of the Michel & Associates, P.C. staffers and attorneys who work or worked for Michel & Associates, P.C., or have contributed to the firm's body of firearms law knowledge and resources over the years. These contributors include Anna Barvir, Scott Franklin, Tom Maciejewski, Glenn McRoberts, Clint Monfort, Claudia Nuñez, Haydee Villegas-Aguilar, and many others.

I also owe a debt of gratitude to the firearm, constitutional, and other lawyers throughout the country who have mentored, counseled, employed, worked for, or worked with me over the years. These include Eric Archer, Jim Baker, Mark Barnes, Chris Chiafullo, Bruce Colodny, Chris Conte, Jason Davis, John Eastman, Eric Epstein, John Frazer, Steve Halbrook, David Hardy, Matthew Horeczko, Judge Eleanor Hunter, Burt Jacobson, Don Kates, Larry Keane, Don Kilmer, David Kopel, David Lehman, Judge J.D. Lord, John Machtinger, Pat O'Malley, Al Peacock, and Judge Jesse Rodriguez.

I am particularly grateful to civil rights activists and leaders George Barr, Tom Boyer, Clayton Cramer, Paul Dougherty, Jim Erdman, John Fields, Joel Friedman, Hayden Heal, Steve Helsley, Dwight Van Horn, Ed Hunt, John Lott, Tanya Metaksa, Tony Montanarella, Sam Parades, Paul Payne, Senator H.L. Richardson (ret.), Jerry Upholt, Gene Wolberg, and Ed Worley and for their support and insight over the years. And all the individual plaintiffs in the various lawsuits who volunteered to stand up for all of our self-defense civil rights deserve special thanks.

Activist and Bloomfield Press publisher Alan Korwin and Tiger Lilly Enterprises Publishing Consultant Penny Callmeyer also deserve special mention for their patience and help in making this book happen.

Cooperation or information has been gratefully received from the California Department of Justice Firearms Bureau, Los Angeles District Attorney Steve Cooley and the Los Angeles County District Attorney's Office, the Los Angeles County Public Defender's Office, officers with the Long Beach and Sacramento Police Departments, Redondo Beach City Attorney Mike Webb and the Redondo Beach City Attorney's Office, San Francisco Public Defender Jeff Adachi and the San Francisco Public Defender's Office, and Turner's Outdoorsman Vice President of Operations Bill Ortiz.

My wife Sydne and my sons Colton and Dawson have also been particularly patient with me as I worked the long hours finalizing this project.

Last, but certainly not least, I thank my clients the National Rifle Association and the California Rifle and Pistol Association Foundation for the meaningful, challenging, and fulfilling legal work that those associations have allowed me to perform on behalf of NRA and CRPA members over the past almost twenty years and for the knowledge base that legal work created, much of which was put to use in writing this book.

# DEDICATION

To my father, Carl Robert Michel,
a volunteer NRA Instructor who taught his three sons how to shoot.
And to my mother, Joan Hancock Michel,
who loved us enough to put up with it,
and to occasionally plink a can off the back stoop
with the Crosman 760 herself.

# DISCLAIMER

This book is not "the law," and it is not a substitute for "the law." "The law" includes all of the legal obligations imposed on you as a gun owner and involves a much greater volume of work and opinion than the coverage of firearm statutes and regulations contained in this book. No book can cover everything or replace a competent and experienced lawyer's advice. This book is only a guide, designed to provide general information regarding California gun laws and to provide references to seek additional information. It is not intended to be a legal treatise or a summary of the entire body of law covering firearms.

I expressly disclaim any liability for errors or omissions that may be in this book. There are many legal and technical "gray area" questions about firearms law that have not been decided by the courts yet, and may never be. Although I do my best to identify the gray areas of which I am aware and provide *my* analysis and likely or *possible* interpretations as to how courts *may* decide certain issues, by no means should my analysis or interpretations be taken as the law. Despite my efforts in researching, collecting, organizing, writing, and preparing this book, I do not make any claims, promises, or guarantees about the absolute accuracy, completeness, or adequacy of the contents of this book. The opinions of other attorneys, and particularly prosecuting attorneys or judges, may be different from mine.

Many people find laws hard to understand, and gathering all the relevant ones, let alone explaining them, is a lot of work. This book helps you with these chores. Again, while great care has been taken to accomplish this with a high degree of accuracy, *no guarantee of accuracy is expressed or implied, and the explanatory sections of this book are not to be considered legal advice or a restatement of law.*

The exact language of the principal state laws controlling gun use in California are generally not reprinted verbatim in this book. Typically only edited pieces of laws are included here. The laws and other regulations are expressed in conversational terms for your convenience and cross-reference statutes or published court cases. In using plain English to explain the general meanings of the laws, differences inevitably arise, so *you must always check the actual laws.*

You are fully accountable under the exact words and current official interpretations of all applicable laws, regulations, court precedents, executive orders, and more when you deal with firearms under any circumstances. You are responsible for researching the applicable federal, state, and/or local law(s) applicable to your particular inquiry or circumstance, or for hiring an attorney to advise you on your particular question given your particular circumstances. For guidance on how to find a competent attorney, review the "How to Judge a Lawyer" memorandum published on my website www.calgunlaws.com.

As the author, even though I am an attorney, I am not providing legal advice nor am I rendering other professional services. The use of this book does *not* create an attorney-client relationship. Please do not send me or my law firm any confidential or sensitive information until you speak with one of my attorneys and obtain prior written authorization to send that information to my law office. Guidance on how to communicate with my office so that confidentiality can be preserved is available through my website. Communication of information by, in, to, or through this book and your receipt *or* use of it (1) is *not* provided in the course of and does not create or constitute an attorney-client relationship, (2) is *not* intended as a solicitation, (3) is *not* intended to convey or constitute legal advice, and (4) is *not* a substitute for obtaining legal advice from a qualified attorney. You should not act upon any such information without first seeking qualified professional counsel on your specific matter. The hiring of an attorney is an important decision that should not be based solely upon this book or its promotional materials.

For the most part, local ordinances, rules, regulations, and policies are not covered by this book. This book concerns the general gun laws as they apply to law-abiding private residents in the state of California only. Though this book touches on certain aspects of these topics, it is not intended to and does not describe most situations relating to licensed gun dealers; museums or educational institutions; local or federal military personnel; American Indians; hunting; foreign nationals; the police or other peace officers; other government employees summoned by a peace officer to help in the performance of official duties; people with special licenses, authorizations or permits; non-residents; bequests or intestate succession; persons under indictment; felons; prisoners; escapees; dangerous or repetitive offenders; criminal street gang members; incorrigible juvenile delinquents; or unsupervised juveniles.

While this book discusses possible criminal consequences of improper gun use, it avoids most issues related to deliberate gun crimes, particularly violent ones. This means certain laws are excluded or not explained in the text. Some examples are: 1ˢᵗ degree murder, 2ⁿᵈ degree murder, homicide, manslaughter, gun theft, gunrunning, concealment of stolen firearms, enhanced penalties for commission of crimes with firearms (including armed robbery, burglary, theft, kidnapping, drug offenses, assault, and priors), smuggling firearms into public aircraft, threatening flight attendants with firearms, possession of contraband, possession of a firearm in a prison by a prisoner, false application for a firearm, shooting at a building as part of a criminal street gang, removal of a body after a shooting, drive-by shooting, and retaliation. This is only a partial list.

New laws and regulations may be enacted at any time by federal, state, and local authorities. The author and publisher make no representation that this book includes all requirements and prohibitions that may exist. Be aware that firearm laws are subject to change without notice. You are strongly urged to consult with a qualified attorney and local authorities to determine the current status and applicability of the law to specific situations you may encounter.

You are accepting this book, and the contents thereof, "as is" without any warranty of any kind, express or implied, including but not limited to the implied warranty of merchantability or fitness for a particular purpose. All liability and/or resulting damages from this book's use are disclaimed. Again, the author and publisher expressly disclaim any liability whatsoever arising out of reliance on information contained in this book. *The Author and the Publisher Shall Not Be Liable for Any Direct, Indirect, Incidental, Special, Exemplary, or Consequential Damages However Caused and on Any Theory of Liability, Whether in Contract, Strict Liability, or Tort, Arising in Any Way out of the Use of this Book.* Damages disclaimed include, but are not limited to, direct, indirect, incidental, compensatory, equitable, exemplary, special, and/or consequential damages, regardless of any cause of action by which the damages may arise.

Again, the information contained in this book is not a substitute for professional advice and does not constitute professional advice, nor is the information contained in this book conveyed or intended to be conveyed as professional advice. Under no circumstances shall you hold the author responsible for any acts you decide to take or not to take. Any decisions you make, and any subsequent consequences, are your own. If you need legal advice or other expert assistance, hire a lawyer familiar with firearms law.

# INTRODUCTION

## I.  GUN SAFETY IS YOUR RESPONSIBILITY

Firearm ownership, possession, and use are individual rights that carry extraordinary responsibility, both morally and legally. Firearms are potentially deadly. Possessing and using them demands the highest level of responsibility from you. Depending on your individual circumstances, accepting that responsibility may require you to do more than the law requires to avoid accidents.

The overwhelming majority of gun owners are extremely responsible. Gun accidents claim far fewer lives than most people are made to think. Typically less than 40 children under age 10 die from gun accidents each year. With over 90 million adults owning a gun and almost 40 million children under age 10, the improper use of guns causes proportionally few accidental deaths. Meanwhile, thousands more tragically die from car accidents, residential fires, bathtub drownings, accidental poisonings, and household hazards. In fact, homes where gun accidents occur usually are not typical homes. Alcoholism and criminal histories are common, as is disproportionate involvement in automobile accidents and driver's license suspensions. All of this reflects individual irresponsibility in homes where accidents happen.

The only foolproof way to avoid gun accidents is to educate people. If everyone obeyed the four simple rules of firearm safety, accidents would not happen. The four rules of firearm safety are: 1) treat all firearms as if they are always loaded – no exceptions, 2) never allow the muzzle of your firearm to point toward anything you do not intend to destroy, 3) keep your finger off the trigger until your sights are aligned with the target and you have made a conscious mental decision to shoot, and 4) be sure of your target and its surroundings, especially what is behind it.

The gun-ban lobby typically distorts facts and resists efforts to promote real gun-safety instruction or offer gun owners more opportunities to learn. They fear that merely mentioning a firearm in an educational context would tacitly endorse the concept that firearms have social utility. But firearms do have social utility as self-defense tools and for their crime deterrent effect. Firearms are used at least four times more often to prevent a crime than to commit one. Nonetheless, instead of education, gun-ban lobbyists have pushed one-size-fits-all legislation such as mechanical lock mandates that, while potentially one part of an individualized safety system, often are inappropriate or create a false sense of security that can actually increase carelessness and accidents.

Thanks to the efforts of over 35,000 certified gun-safety instructors who teach gun safety to law enforcement and civilians across the country, as well as the award-winning, time-proven, and law enforcement–endorsed safety programs being used nationally, firearm accident rates are at their lowest levels ever recorded. To do your part, you can learn those guidelines, live by them, and teach them to others. Taking classes in firearms handling is an excellent way to do this. Free materials concerning firearm safety are available in almost every gun store and from the National Rifle Association and the California Rifle and Pistol Association websites.

## II. HOW TO USE THIS BOOK

Along with your responsibility to know and follow safety procedures, you also have increasing legal responsibilities. The goal of this book is to educate those who are subject to California's complex firearms laws so that they can avoid inadvertently violating them, as well as to educate those tasked with enforcing those laws so they avoid causing innocent people unnecessary legal problems.

This book discusses how to legally buy, own, transport, and possess firearms, how to legally use deadly force, and how you may be able to get your firearms, or firearm rights, back if they are taken away. This book also explores, explains, and summarizes the major firearm laws affecting firearm owners in California and particularly warns about legal "traps" that California firearm owners often unintentionally fall into.

As the Disclaimer makes clear, this book only serves as a general guide. It is not a complete legal treatise of firearm law. Since firearm laws frequently change, only constant study and legal analysis will keep you informed about their current status and applicability. As always, it is strongly encouraged you seek an experienced firearm attorney's advice if you have additional questions or concerns about firearm laws and how they apply to your personal circumstances.

While reading this book, keep in mind that the exact language from many code sections and court decisions has been shortened and/or paraphrased to highlight the particular point being made. For exact statutory language, and when analyzing the cited cases, the particular statute, code, and/or specific case(s) can and should be consulted directly.

Because this book is intended for a wide audience, including firearms owners, firearms consumers, law enforcement, and lawyers, exact legal "Bluebook" citation format is not used. For example, "*id's*" and "*supra's*," (terms used by lawyers to denote preceding or subsequent authority), do not appear in this book. However, *general* Bluebook citation format is utilized for consistency. For the exact and proper legal citations, please refer to the specific case, statute, or website you are interested in.

## A. The Materials Posted at www.calgunlaws.com Compliment This Book

I will try to the make the complete current text of all codes and court decisions, as well as an index for this book and supplemental authorities, available at www.calgunlaws.com. This book is designed to be complimented by that website, and vise versa. Updates to this book, more detailed legal memoranda elaborating on particular subjects covered in each chapter of this book, and additional helpful materials will also be posted at www.calgunlaws.com.

If you have firearm law questions, or would like to make suggestions for topics to be included in upcoming editions, email gunlawquestion@calgunlaws.com. To receive email news bulletins on cutting-edge self-defense issues, civil rights issues, cases, court rulings, and other legal developments, subscribe to receive these bulletins at www.calgunlaws.com.

# III. HOW TO READ LAWS AND DETERMINE WHETHER THEY APPLY

## A. Federal Laws, State Laws, and Local Laws

This book covers both federal and state firearm laws. Local laws, however, are beyond the scope of this book. Federal law is made up of the "United States Constitution, federal statutes and regulations, U.S. treatises, and federal [case] law[,]" *i.e.*, court opinions.[1] State law consists of the "state's constitution, statutes, regulations," and state court law cases.[2] Local laws are statutes or ordinances that are applicable to a particular locality rather

---

[1] BLACK'S LAW DICTIONARY 645 (8th. ed. 2004).
[2] BLACK'S LAW DICTIONARY 1444 (8th. ed. 2004).

than the entire state.[3] This book discusses both California and federal law under the main topic or heading, pointing out where most people run into problems with law enforcement. Even though this book does not discuss every local law in California, you are always obligated to comply with federal, state, and local law.

## B. Statutory Interpretation Techniques

Regardless of whether you or a court is examining a federal or state law, the following rules governing statutory interpretation apply.

As the United States Supreme Court explained, "in interpreting a statute a court should always turn first to one, cardinal canon before all others ...[C]ourts must presume that a legislature says in a statute what it means and means in a statute what it says there. [] When the words of a statute are unambiguous, then, this first canon is also the last: 'judicial inquiry is complete.'"[4] "Congress is presumed to act intentionally and purposely when it includes language in one section but omits it in another."[5]

If a statute's plain language is ambiguous, courts then look to the legislature's intent and give it "a reasonable and common sense interpretation consistent with the apparent purpose, which will result in wise policy rather than mischief and absurdity."[6] If necessary, courts will break down the words of the statute and compare their placement within the statute as a whole. Courts will also consider its context, purpose, evils to be remedied, other legislation, and public policy.[7] For example, in *People v. Squier*, the California Appellate Court said that "[t]he rule of strict interpretation of penal statutes does not apply in California[]" and "where two interpretations of a penal statute are possible, that construction which favors the defendant is preferred unless such a construction is contrary to public interest, sound sense, and wise policy."[8] Therefore, according to the rule of lenity, when a statute is susceptible to two reasonable interpretations, the court should prefer the interpretation that most favors a defendant. In reality, it rarely works to a defendant's advantage.

Courts are also permitted to review secondary sources like legal treatises and law review articles to see what experts in a particular field say about the statute. These secondary sources are not binding, however, and serve merely as persuasive authority.

---

[3] BLACK'S LAW DICTIONARY 957 (8th. ed. 2004).
[4] *Connecticut Nat. Bank v. Germain*, 503 U.S. 249, 253-254 (1992) (internal citations omitted).
[5] *Estate of Bell v. C.I.R.*, 928 F.2d 901, 904 (9th Cir. 1991).
[6] 7 Witkin, Summary of Cal. Law (10th) *Const. Law* § 115 (2012).
[7] *See* 7 Witkin, Summary of Cal. Law (10th) *Const. Law* § 115 (2012).
[8] *People v. Squier*, 15 Cal.App.4th 235, 241 (1993).

## C. How to Read Court Opinions

When a dispute results in a lawsuit, the court's rulings in the lawsuit will usually be issued through a court "opinion." These court opinions can be issued by either trial or appellate court judges. A court's opinion typically lays out the facts of the case and the laws governing the facts and then applies the governing laws to each of the relevant fact patterns.[9]

When reading a court opinion, the first thing to look at is the case name, or caption. This will identify the parties to the case. The party bringing the lawsuit is the plaintiff. The one defending against the lawsuit is the defendant. If the case is a criminal case, the state or federal prosecutor will bring a lawsuit on behalf of the government. The plaintiff in a criminal case is typically the "United States" or the "People of the State of California."

After the case name you will see a legal "citation." This tells you where you can locate the actual opinion of the case. Many court opinions are now available for free online. I will try to get all of the opinions cited in this book posted on www.calgunlaws.com. The case citation can tell you which court rendered the decision and when the opinion was rendered. For example, *District of Columbia v. Heller,* the 2008 United States Supreme Court case that determined there is an individual right to keep and bear arms for self-defense, is cited as *Dist. of Columbia v. Heller,* 554 U.S. 570 (2008). The citation of "554" is the volume of the United States Reports, "U.S." is the abbreviation of the United States Reports, and "570" is the page number where this opinion begins. The final "2008" represents the year in which the opinion was rendered.

Under the case name there is a courthouse case number, dates indicating when the lawsuit was filed and when it was decided, and the names of the attorneys who represented the parties (if any). The judge who rendered the opinion will also be identified.

In most opinions the judge first discusses the facts of the case, then the procedural history of the case (*i.e.,* how the case has progressed through the court system), and then the ultimate legal or factual issue(s) the judge had to resolve.

After discussing the governing law and doing a statutory analysis, if the meaning of a law is subject to dispute (as it often is), then the judge will discuss how the law applies to the facts. By weaving the governing laws into the facts of the case, the judge will reach an ultimate ruling, a decision or opinion, on the issue(s) of the case.

Since not all cases are factually the same, lawyers either try to distinguish their facts from the facts that formed the basis of any earlier adverse

---

[9] For a more substantive analysis on how to read court opinions, *see* Orin S. Kerr, *How to Read A Legal Opinion: A Guide for New Law Students,* 11 GREEN BAG 2d 51 (2007) *available at* www.calgunlaws.com.

court opinion(s) so the court does not adopt that opinion as its rationale, or the lawyers try to show why the earlier court opinion(s) should be legal "precedent" that the court should follow and adopt. This can be a difficult task. It is one of the things lawyers really earn their money doing.

# IV. HOW TO JUDGE A LAWYER

If you ever need a lawyer, regardless of whether it is a firearms attorney or an attorney in another practice area, it is important that you properly evaluate the attorney before you retain him or her for your case. There are a lot of bad lawyers out there. Meaningful factors to consider when evaluating an attorney are years of experience, cases actually tried to a jury, practice area(s), specializations, and competence in the particular area in which you need assistance.

There is a lot of helpful information about lawyers on the internet. But do not be fooled by slick internet marketing techniques, inflated website "ratings," and meaningless "awards." These days, a lawyer's reputation can be manipulated online. Just because the attorney claims to be "the best attorney" in a particular area or shows up first on a Google or Yahoo search, does not necessarily mean that attorney is the right or best one for you. There are ways attorneys can manipulate their marketing profiles and endorsements so that it looks like they are accomplished in a particular field when, in actuality, they refer those cases out or are themselves novice attorneys.

For more guidance on how to evaluate and select an attorney who is right for you, see the "How to Judge a Lawyer" memorandum located at www.calgunlaws.com.

# ABBREVIATIONS USED
# THROUGHOUT THIS BOOK

Numerous laws from various sources are discussed, quoted, or paraphrased throughout this book. Additionally, common firearm language is discussed as well. Important laws or language will be fully listed when discussed for the first time but then will be subsequently abbreviated. Below is a list of commonly used terms and their corresponding abbreviations that are consistently used throughout the book:

| | |
|---|---|
| Armed Prohibited Persons System | APPS |
| Assault Weapon Identification Guide | AWIG |
| Assault Weapons Control Act | AWCA |
| Attorney General | AG |
| Automated Firearms System | AFS |
| Bureau of Alcohol, Tobacco, Firearms, and Explosives | ATF |
| Bureau of Land Management | BLM |
| Business and Professions Code | Bus. & Prof. Code |
| California Civil Code | Cal. Civ. Code |
| California Code of Civil Procedure | C.C.P. |
| California Code of Regulations | Cal. Code Regs. |
| California Department of Justice | Cal. DOJ |
| California Elections Code | Cal. Elections Code |
| California Government Code | Cal. Gov't Code |
| California Health and Safety Code | Cal. Health & Saf. Code |
| California Law Revision Commission | CLRC |
| California Rifle and Pistol Association | CRPA |
| California Vehicle Code | Cal. Veh. Code |
| California Welfare and Institutions Code | W.I.C. |
| Carry Concealed Weapon | CCW |

| | |
|---|---|
| Certificate of Eligibility | COE |
| Code of Federal Regulations | C.F.R. |
| Code of Public Resources | C. Pub. Res. |
| Dangerous Weapons Control Act | DWCA |
| Dealer's Record of Sale | DROS |
| Department of Justice | DOJ |
| Entertainment Firearms Permit | EFP |
| Environmental Protection Agency | EPA |
| Exclusive Economic Zone | EEZ |
| Family Code | Fam. Code |
| Federal Aviation Administration | FAA |
| Federal Bureau of Investigation | FBI |
| Federal Firearms Licensee | FFL |
| Firearm Owners' Protection Act | FOPA |
| Gun Control Act | GCA |
| Handgun Safety Certificate | HSC |
| Immigration and Nationality Act | INA |
| Law Enforcement Gun Release | LEGR |
| Law Enforcement Gun Release – Firearms Eligibility Clearance Letter | LEGR Letter |
| Law Enforcement Officer Safety Act | LEOSA |
| Misdemeanor Crime of Domestic Violence | MCDV |
| National Firearms Act | NFA |
| National Instant Criminal Background Check System | NICS |
| National Rifle Association | NRA |
| National Shooting Sports Foundation | NSSF |
| Peace Officer Standards and Training | POST |
| Penal Code | P.C. |
| Personal Firearms Eligibility Check Application | PFEC |
| Private Party Transfer | PPT |
| Qualified Law Enforcement Officer | QLEO |
| Qualified Retired Law Enforcement Officer | QRLEO |
| Transportation Security Administration | TSA |
| United Nations Convention on the Law of the Sea | UNCLOS |
| United States | U.S. |
| United States Code | U.S.C. |

## CHAPTER 1:

# THE CALIFORNIA REGULATORY ENVIRONMENT

## I. THE UGLY PROCESS OF GUN LAW POLITICS

### A. The Legislative Process

The California State Legislature is currently controlled by a liberal-Democratic majority, and has been for years. Control is unlikely to shift in the foreseeable future. As the party in control, the Democrats control the agenda and will not allow anything to pass that might make Republicans look good. Although gun control laws are generally favored by the Democratic party, many Democratic legislators from rural areas of the state, like the central valley, (so-called "Blue Dog" Democrats) are not big gun control supporters. That is why things are not worse than they are for gun owners in California.

Although technically any legislator can author a bill on any subject, when it comes to gun control laws there are certain Democratic legislators who lead the gun ban movement amongst their colleagues. Depending on the demographics of a legislator's district, gun control can translate to press coverage, and press coverage translates to name recognition. Having name recognition is critical to getting elected or reelected. When a group like the National Rifle Association (NRA) is pulled into the debate, it can actually serve the purposes of an anti-gun legislator because it increases the level of conflict for the media to cover.

A comprehensive treatment of the California legislative process, and just how corrupt it is, is beyond the scope of this book. But for the purposes of this chapter, suffice it to say that legislators often vote for or against a bill for reasons having nothing to do with its merits, and frequently do not read the bills they are voting on.

Over the years I have had a number of private conversations with anti-gun politicians who were candid enough to admit that their agenda was to ban all civilian gun ownership, or at least civilian ownership of handguns. This undisclosed agenda makes it tough to debate the merits of specific gun laws. I once lobbied a Los Angeles City Councilman to vote against a ban on affordable self-defense handguns that they demonized by calling them "Saturday Night Specials." When I pointed out that by the way the proposed ordinance defined that term, the Glock handguns used by the LAPD would be deemed "junk guns," the politician replied that it did not matter since all they really wanted to do was take another step toward banning all handguns. At a luncheon with another anti-gun politician, I established that a ban on .50 caliber target rifles was unnecessary since these rifles were never used in crime. The politician, who had not known this, then justified her position by arguing that it was important to "make people *feel* safe." That one floored me. Do we really want our legislators to make us *feel* safe? Particularly, do we want to be fooled into *feeling* safe if we are not *actually* safe? This strikes me as a patronizing approach to governing, one that keeps placated citizens blissfully ignorant of reality while politicians get credit for passing complicated "feel good" laws that actually do nothing – except, too often, turn good people into accidental criminals.

Unfortunately the reality is that firearm laws are rarely based on technical knowledge, rational principle, or a genuine need for regulation. Rather, politics drives the process, not logic. A retired Department of Justice (DOJ) official has explained that when meeting with the authors of significant gun legislation, the authors have displayed a level of ignorance about firearms that shows they do not even understand what their proposed laws do. For example, the legislator who authored the "Unsafe Handgun Act" had to ask the DOJ official, "Where is the barrel?"

For an eye-opening account from a retired Sacramento politician about how laws are created and made, read "What Makes You Think We Read the Bills?" by California State Senator H.L. Richardson (ret.). Senator Richardson deserves special recognition because he founded Gun Owners of California and sponsored California's preemption statute, which prohibits local governments from over-regulating firearms, as discussed below.

## B. The Gun Ban Lobby

Anti-gun groups have spent millions of dollars on public relations consultants and efforts to demonize guns, exaggerate their dangers, make it politically incorrect to choose to own one, and "spin" pending legislation to appeal to legislators and unsophisticated constituents. Common platitudes include "talk concept not content," meaning do not get into a debate about the actual language of a bill or what it actually does. Bills often do much more that their emotionally appealing title would reveal. Instead, gun ban lobbyists focus on the seemingly benign concepts of a bill, like some notion of public safety, often "for the children." If they can be pulled into a discussion of what the specific language of a bill actually does, they argue, "don't let the perfect be the enemy of the good." This, to me, is another way of saying "close enough for government work."

Regardless, the gun ban lobby has been quite successful in getting most of their anti-gun-owner agenda passed in California. And they have not given up. But despite their efforts, polls show an increasing recognition and appreciation of the right to choose to own a gun to defend yourself or your loved ones, and record-setting gun sales figures prove an increasing number of people are choosing to exercise that right.

Perhaps in recognition of this trend and what appears to be a disturbing new approach, the gun ban lobby has been pushing laws that actually compel otherwise law-abiding gun owners to report themselves to the police, which forces gun owners into a position where they should decline to cooperate. For example, several cities have passed ordinances that require gun owners to report the theft or loss of their firearms within 48 hours. The gun ban lobby claims the ordinances help prevent unlawful "straw sales," and that persons engaged in illegal firearm transfers falsely claim that a "crime gun" traced to the owner is "stolen" or "lost" when in fact the firearm was supplied to a criminal. But these ordinances often further victimize crime victims and are *frustrating* police investigations. If you do not report a gun's loss or theft and you are then contacted by police investigating after the gun is recovered at a crime scene, you face possible criminal prosecution for failing to report the missing gun. Although most gun owners would ordinarily be happy to assist the police with their investigation, in such a situation the prudent thing to do would be to hire a lawyer, who will almost certainly advise you to remain silent while immunity is negotiated. As a result, police cannot quickly get the information they need to investigate the crime. Legal representation is appropriate not only when the firearm is found by the police, but also when it is first discovered missing. You can be prosecuted if the missing gun was not reported within 48 or 72 hours of when you "should have known" the gun was gone, and the gun ban lobby maintains that "responsible" gun owners know where their gun is at every single moment. Therefore, according to them, you "should know" a gun is gone *immediately.* Some anti-gun prosecutors may adopt this mistaken philosophy. And the penalty will encourage those who miss the 48-hour window *to not report their loss at all* for fear of prosecution.

Gun owners generally have no desire to frustrate police investigations and would usually be happy to help the police. Unfortunately these types of ordinances put gun owners in jeopardy of prosecution for becoming a victim of a crime. As a gun owner, you are now in the position of having to involve an attorney before offering information about your stolen firearm to the police because you could be incriminating yourself by offering information about how the firearm came to be stolen.

Aside from indecipherable laws and laws making criminals out of crime victims, federal, state, and local law enforcement authorities are continuing their stepped-up efforts to conduct "stings" at gun shows and against licensed gun dealers, particularly throughout California and in neighboring states. Increasingly those facing gun-related charges are being turned into confidential civilian informants who try to work off their criminal charges by luring other gun owners to violate the law. These informants and undercover plain clothes law enforcement officers often try to entice gun owners to forego the California legal requirement that all gun sales be processed through a licensed gun dealer, or offer to sell an "assault weapon" (which may not appear to be one). Rare or "almost legal" guns are sometimes offered at "too good to be true" prices in order to seduce the "stingee." Police also monitor Shotgun News, Gun List, Gunbroker.com, and other trade magazines, and even run fake ads themselves. Suspects who fall for these "stings" typically have their businesses and residences searched and all of their firearms seized.

While many of the efforts of these agencies are laudable, far too often the people being arrested are not violent felons. They typically have no prior criminal record and are solid citizens. Some police agencies simply go for the "easy meat" to bolster their prosecution and gun seizure statistics, regardless of whether violent crime actually gets reduced in the process.

Every violation of the law, however inadvertent, is politicized and ultimately used by the gun ban lobby to advance its cultural and political war against civilian firearm ownership in general, and to urge closure of gun stores or an end to gun shows in particular. Sadly caution must increasingly be exercised before cooperating with authorities. Your attempt at cooperation could easily lead to making an incriminating admission that results in criminal charges for an inadvertent violation. If you are approached about a possibly illegal transaction, remember: Do not equivocate – refuse to participate!

Ronald Reagan was right when he said, "there are two things the public should never watch being made, sausage and laws." Lawmaking in Sacramento is not pretty. Gun-law-making is especially ugly.

## C. The Pro-Gun Lobby

There are a number of pro-Second Amendment groups working in Sacramento, including the National Shooting Sports Foundation, Gun Owners of California, and the *FFLGuard* service. The NRA, the California Rifle and Pistol Association (CRPA), and the Gun Owners of California are the only ones with a full-time lobbyist in the California Capital.

The NRA and CRPA deserve special mention because I have represented them for many years.

### 1. The National Rifle Association (NRA) and California Rifle and Pistol Association (CRPA)

Dismayed by the lack of marksmanship shown by their troops, Union veterans Col. William C. Church and Gen. George Wingate formed the NRA in 1871. That makes it the oldest civil rights organization in the country. In response to repeated attacks on Second Amendment rights, the NRA formed the Legislative Affairs Division in 1934. While the NRA did not lobby directly at first, it did mail out legislative facts and analyses to members, whereby they could take action on their own. In 1975, recognizing the critical need for political defense of the Second Amendment, the NRA formed the Institute for Legislative Action, or ILA. Meanwhile, the NRA continued its commitment to training, education, and marksmanship.

While widely recognized today as a major political force and as America's foremost defender of Second Amendment rights, the NRA has, since its inception, been the premier firearms education organization in the world. But the NRA's successes would not be possible without the tireless efforts and countless hours of service the NRA's nearly four million members have given to champion Second Amendment rights and support NRA programs. As former Clinton spokesman George Stephanopoulos said, "Let me make one small vote for the NRA. They're good citizens. They call their congressmen. They write. They vote. They contribute. And they get what they want over time."

As mentioned, the NRA employs a much needed full-time employee as a lobbyist in Sacramento. But given California's politics, the NRA's power in Washington, D.C. does not translate to the same extent in Sacramento.

Founded in 1875, the CRPA is the official state association of the NRA. CRPA is dedicated to protecting firearm freedoms and promoting shooting sports solely in the State of California. CRPA's full time lobbyist in Sacramento also fights adverse firearm legislation and works to promote laws that protect your right to choose to own a gun to protect yourself or your family. CRPA Foundation is the 501(c)(3) sibling of the CRPA and funds some of the Second Amendment litigation and other litigation in which I am often involved.

As you read this book, I hope becoming educated about some of the problems with California's gun laws will cause you to consider getting involved in California's political process.

## II. THE RIGHT TO KEEP AND BEAR ARMS AND TO SELF-DEFENSE

This book is primarily a practical guide to California and federal laws regulating firearms. But that body of law is evolving at an increased pace because of two Supreme Court decisions that addressed the meaning and application of the Second Amendment to the United States Constitution. This section addresses some of the recent developments in Second Amendment jurisprudence and will give you a constitutional context when reading the laws discussed in the following chapters. It also addresses some of the other legal doctrines that limit the expansion of laws that restrict your civil right to self-defense.

So if you just want to get a question answered about whether a law applies to a situation, you can skip this section. But if you are interested in how the Second Amendment may change the legal playing field in the future and how your life, your children's lives, notions of freedom, and perhaps the very way our government interacts with citizens may be changed by how the Second Amendment is interpreted and applied by courts in the future, read on.

In my view, we as a society are at a turning point. The country is diametrically divided ideologically to a perhaps greater extent than at almost any other time in our history – except during the Civil War. So it is an understatement to say that the issue seems pretty important to me, and I think it will be to most of you.

### A. The United States and California Constitutions

The Second Amendment provides: "A well regulated Militia, being necessary to the security of a free State, the right of the people to keep and bear Arms, shall not be infringed."[1]

In 2008, the Supreme Court confirmed in *District of Columbia v. Heller*[2] that the Second Amendment protects an *individual's* right to keep and

---

[1] U.S. CONST. amend. II.
[2] *Dist. of Columbia v. Heller*, 554 U.S. 570, 634-635 (2008).

bear arms for self-defense – contrary to gun control advocates' claims for decades that the Second Amendment only provided collective rights for state militias.

In 2010, in *McDonald v. Chicago*,[3] the Supreme Court confirmed that an *individual's* right to keep and bear arms is fundamental and is thus "incorporated" into the Bill of Rights through the 14th Amendment. This means that federal, state, and local governments cannot infringe upon your Second Amendment rights to keep and bear arms and to self-defense.

After these decisions came down, hundreds of cases raised the Second Amendment as an issue, and hundreds of courts have addressed the scope of the Second Amendment's protections. Unfortunately the issue was most often raised as a defense in criminal cases, where the chances of success are decreased by court overcrowding, and by lawyers who are insufficiently prepared to properly present such novel and complicated issues to the court.

Even in the fewer civil cases that have been brought challenging firearm regulations, or that would serve as precedent to challenge some of California's ill-conceived laws, the lawyers bringing the claims are often inexperienced and lack the resources needed to do the job right. The NRA and the CRPA, along with several other Second Amendment advocacy groups, have brought a few dozen cases, with mixed success. Those cases, and others that have yet to be filed, are making their way inexorably toward the Supreme Court.

As of this book's publication date, I have already seen several petitions asking the Supreme Court to address cases raising Second Amendment-related issues. Though the high court has expressed some heightened interest in hearing a Second Amendment case, it has so far rejected all Second Amendment-related petitions.

The high court will inevitably have to address the foundational issues that have been raised regarding the scope and application of the *Heller* and *McDonald* decisions, and then subsequently address the additional issues that will inevitably arise in cases brought thereafter. But this will be a dynamic and rapidly changing legal landscape. To keep up to date on these developments, subscribe to my free newsletters at www.calgunlaws.com.

Most states have their own version of the Second Amendment right to keep and bear arms in their respective constitutions.[4] Unlike other states, however, California does not have an express right to keep and bear arms in its constitution.

---

[3] *McDonald v. Chicago*, 561 U.S. __, 130 S. Ct. 3020 (2010).
[4] *See* Eugene Volokh, *State Constitutional Right to Keep and Bear Arms*, 11 Tex. Rev. L. & Pol. 191 (2006).

It has been argued though that one provision of the California constitution *does* implicate the right to self-defense: "All people are by nature free and independent and have inalienable rights. Among these are enjoying and defending life and liberty, acquiring, possessing, and protecting property, and pursuing and obtaining safety, happiness, and privacy."[5] Unfortunately the California Supreme Court has rejected this notion.[6] Thus, despite the promise of the Supreme Court's *Heller* and *McDonald* decisions, many courts and politicians still remain opposed to fundamental Second Amendment rights.

## B. Primary Issues Being Addressed in Current Second Amendment Litigation

Laws regulating firearms typically fall into one of several categories. There are laws that regulate where and how firearms can be possessed, which types of firearms or firearms accessories can be possessed, and whether certain people can possess firearms.

So far there has been reluctance by most lower courts to recognize that Second Amendment rights go beyond the specific issues in *Heller* and *McDonald* (handguns in the home for self-defense). While a few courts have recognized a right to carry a firearm outside of the home, most have refused to accept any right outside the home. But those types of cases are making their way to the various circuit Courts of Appeal, and the Supreme Court will inevitably be compelled to consider the questions they raise.

In a Second Amendment case, the judge has to decide whether the individual conduct being legislatively restricted even implicates the Second Amendment rights in the first place. Some cases should be relatively easy, such as possessing a handgun in the home for self-defense. That conduct was at issue in *District of Columbia v. Heller*, and the Supreme Court ruled 5-4 that Mr. Heller did have a Second Amendment right to own a handgun for self-defense.

But if a person wanted to own his own operable tank, a court would certainly rule that the person has no Second Amendment right to do so. The Second Amendment's language of "keep and bear arms" implies that the Amendment protects weapons that a person can "bear" or carry. A tank "bears" the driver. The individual does not bear the tank.

But how about possessing a rifle or shotgun in the home for self-defense? Or carrying a handgun outside the home for self-defense? Gun-free

---

[5] CAL. CONST. art. I, § 1.

[6] *Kasler v. Lockyer*, 23 Cal.4th 472, 481 (2000) ("If plaintiffs are implying that a right to bear arms is one of the rights recognized in the California Constitution's declaration of rights, they are simply wrong.").

zones? What rights do we have to possess a firearm for things other than self-defense? What about target shooting, hunting, or collecting? What kinds of people can have their Second Amendment rights taken away, and for how long? Felons? Yes. Forever? Not so clear. People with misdemeanor convictions? Which ones?

What about air guns? Knives, clubs, swords, or bows? Electronic devices such as tasers? Chemical self-defense sprays? Are any of these within the scope of the Second Amendment?

Once an activity is acknowledged as being within the scope of a constitutional right, does that mean that any restrictions on the right are unconstitutional? Definitely not. Courts use several tests, or "standards of review," to determine if something violates a right. Which test a court utilizes may depend on the particular right and how close something is to the core of that right.

Notably the *Heller* Court did not formally announce a standard of review for Second Amendment cases, so lower courts have been figuring out the proper analysis by drawing implications from *Heller*. Of course many judges have taken very different approaches.

Some, including this author, believe no formulaic standard of review is necessary. A court should merely look at history to determine whether the challenged law has been traditionally accepted.

Before *Heller* many courts upheld all firearm laws because they believed that ordinary citizens had no Second Amendment rights. So a firearm ban or other harsh restriction was deemed proper because legislators could have had a "rational" belief that preventing ordinary citizens from having firearms would reduce firearm misuse.

For all the three major standards of review (strict scrutiny, intermediate scrutiny, and rational basis), there are variants, special situations, and so on to consider, but I will skip those. In practice, intermediate scrutiny is the standard that gives the judge the most discretion in deciding a case.

As of this book's publication date, the big questions that the courts are wrestling with are whether the Second Amendment protects anything other than the possession of a handgun in the home and the appropriate "standard of review" or level of court scrutiny that gun control laws should be subjected to by a court. Courts are also wrestling with the extent to which legislative "findings" should be considered or accepted as justification for a gun control law.

Historically two other standards for right-to-arms cases have been important for state courts interpreting state constitutions. These two could be used by courts analyzing the Second Amendment. The "frustration" test asks whether a law "frustrates" the exercise of the right to keep and bear arms or "perfects" the exercise of the right. The classic 19th century application of the test was to uphold bans on carrying a *concealed* firearm. Courts reasoned that a ban on defensive carry would "frustrate" the right to keep and bear arms. However, a law that allowed the carrying of a firearm openly but banned carrying a concealed firearm would "perfect" the manner of exercising the right.

Especially in the latter part of the 20th century, many state courts used a "reasonableness" standard. How courts applied the standard varied tremendously. Some courts used "reasonable" as basically a synonym for "rational basis" so that even complete bans on handguns could be upheld – as in the 1984 Illinois Supreme Court's *Kalodimos v. Village of Morton Grove*.[7]

Other courts conducted a much more searching inquiry and struck down laws which did not genuinely and realistically promote public safety, or which "unreasonably" infringed upon the right to arms.

The Brady Center has been busy urging courts to use "reasonableness" in reviewing Second Amendment claims. According to the Brady Center, every possible gun control and gun prohibition is "reasonable," except for what *Heller* explicitly forbade (banning all handguns in the home). Serious judicial protection of the Second Amendment right is relatively new. Although state courts have nearly two centuries of experience in protecting the right to arms under state constitutions, many courts have ignored the Second Amendment until recently. Similarly, from 1791 until the 1930s, most courts did almost nothing to protect First Amendment rights. Now the right to free speech is sacred.

The scope of the Second Amendment's protection is, and will continue to be, defined through litigation. Certain cases and examples are therefore highlighted throughout this book to help you understand the different ways firearm laws are being interpreted and applied. These lawsuits encompass a variety of issues, ranging from accessibility of carry licenses to defining what constitutes a "sensitive place" where firearms may lawfully be prohibited.

Again, to stay updated on the status of Second Amendment litigation and other firearms-related litigation and issues, sign up for free alerts at www.calgunlaws.com.

---

[7] *See Kalodimos v. Village of Morton Grove*, 103 Ill.2d 483 (1984).

# III.   THE PREEMPTION DOCTRINE

## A. Federal Law Preemption Doctrine

Setting California's constitution and politicians aside, it is helpful to address federal and state law preemption before diving into California's firearm laws and their various nuances.

The idea of federal preemption is found in the supremacy clause of the United States Constitution:

> This Constitution, and the Laws of the United States which shall be made in Pursuance thereof; and all Treaties made, or which shall be made, under the Authority of the United States, shall be the supreme Law of the Land; and the Judges in every State shall be bound thereby, any Thing in the Constitution or Laws of any State to the Contrary notwithstanding.[8]

The supremacy clause means that if a conflict exists between state and federal law, "the federal law controls and the state law is invalidated because federal law is supreme."[9]

Because federal law can preempt California law in many ways, this book addresses both state and federal firearm laws, though the emphasis is on California law.

## B. California Law Preemption Doctrine

Just as federal law can supersede (or preempt) conflicting state laws, state laws likewise preempt conflicting local (i.e., city and county) laws.

California's statutory scheme preempts certain firearm laws, either expressly or implicitly. Where state laws expressly preempt local laws, the preemptive effect is generally clear. But there are some cases where the scope of that effect can be disputed.[10] Under California's implied preemption doctrine, a local regulation is implicitly preempted where it conflicts with

---

[8] U.S. Const. art. VI, cl. 2.

[9] Erwin Chemerinsky, Constitutional Law Principles and Policies 376 (Erwin Chemerinsky et al. eds., 2d ed. 2002). See also Gade v. Nat'l Solid Wastes Mgmt. Ass'n, 505 U.S. 88, 108 (1992) (stating "any state law, however clearly within a State's acknowledged power, which interferes with or is contrary to federal law, must yield.").

[10] See, e.g., Fiscal v. City & County of San Francisco, 158 Cal.App.4th 895, 910 (2008) (where the City of San Francisco argued that California Government Code section 53071's express preemption of local laws "related to" firearm licensing did not stop it from prohibiting all handguns within its borders. Fortunately the Fiscal court disagreed, finding that such a ban is expressly preempted by section 53071).

state law, *i.e.*, duplicates it, contradicts it, or enters into a field fully occupied by[11] it to the exclusion of local regulation.[12]

It is not clear what local laws are preempted, whether expressly or implicitly, by California's legal scheme. But it is certain that localities cannot ban firearms outright, require their registration, or require licenses to own them.

For a more in-depth analysis of California's preemption doctrine, see the law review article I co-authored: *Local Gun Bans in California: A Futile Exercise.*[13]

# IV. THE CALIFORNIA LEGAL SCHEME

## A. The Dangerous Weapons Control Act (DWCA)

California's Penal Code § 16000 *et seq.* is collectively referred to as the Dangerous Weapons Control Act (DWCA), the reorganization of which is further discussed below. These Penal Code sections are home to most of California's firearm laws. But some firearm laws are also found in the Fish and Game Code, Welfare and Institutions Code, Vehicle Code, Business and Professions Code, Health and Safety Code, Government Code, and other parts of the Penal Code and California Code of Regulations. California is somewhat unique in that some municipal governments have also passed extensive local gun control ordinances.

Of course federal firearm laws apply in California and are contained in federal statutes and regulations.

## B. Confusion Runs Rampant

There are thousands of federal laws and regulations covering firearms. California state statutes regulating the manufacture, distribution, sale, possession, and use of firearms now number over 800! That does not include administrative regulations, local ordinances, or the California De-

---

[11] A local ordinance "enters a field fully occupied" by state law either expressly or implicitly. A law implicitly occupies a field when: " '(1) the subject matter has been so fully and completely covered by general law as to clearly indicate that it has become exclusively a matter of state concern; (2) the subject matter has been partially covered by general law couched in such terms as to indicate clearly that a paramount state concern will not tolerate further or additional local action; or (3) the subject matter has been partially covered by general law, and the subject is of such a nature that the adverse effect of a local ordinance on the transient citizens of the state outweighs the possible benefit to the' locality[.]" *Sherwin-Williams Co. v. City of Los Angeles,* 4 Cal.4th 893, 898 (1993).

[12] *Fiscal v. City & County of San Francisco,* 158 Cal.App.4th 895, 909 (2008).

[13] Don B. Kates & C.D. Michel, *Local Gun Bans in California: A Futile Exercise,* 41 U.S.F. L. Rev. 333 (2007).

partment of Justice Firearms Bureau's written and unwritten policies. As former California Attorney General Dan Lungren once noted, thanks to politicians, California firearm laws are now as complex as the state's byzantine environmental and tax laws. And the politicians are not backing off. Unfortunately, unlike corporations with lawyers on retainer to answer legal questions and ensure compliance with the environmental and tax laws, gun owners typically have no expert lawyers on retainer to advise them on what the increasingly complex gun laws require.

With all the overlapping rules, it is no wonder confusion is rampant among California gun owners. Not surprisingly, inadvertent gun law violations by well-intentioned good people have become increasingly common. And in the politicized environment of California firearm laws, the consequences of even an inadvertent violation can be severe.

Because firearms are so extensively regulated, it is understandable that there is great confusion about what the law requires among those who are responsible for enforcing it, as well as among those who choose to own a gun for work, hunting, sport, or to defend themselves and their families.

In commenting on a proposed anti-gun bill in September of 2004, Governor Schwarzenegger acknowledged:

...Such ambiguity in the law invites arbitrary enforcement and judicial review ... Before a government exercises its power to take away one's liberty, it should be clear to every person what actions will cause them to forfeit their freedom. Instead of adding to the lengthy and complex area of firearm laws, a reorganization of the current laws should be undertaken to ensure that statutes that impose criminal penalties are easily understandable.[14]

Judges are equally confused. California Appeals Court Justice Bedsworth, writing about firearm law, said it best: "At first blush, the statutes seem impenetrable. Reading them is hard, writing about them arduous, reading about them probably downright painful. The [complexity] makes for tough sledding. As Alfred North Whitehead wrote of rationalism, the effort is, itself, 'an adventure in the clarification of thought.'"[15]

The California Assault Weapons Control Act (AWCA) is perhaps the most complicated of all California firearm laws. Not only do ordinary citizens find it difficult – if not impossible – to determine whether a semiautomatic firearm should be considered an "assault weapon," trained law enforcement officers, prosecutors, and judges have similar difficulty.

---

[14] *SB 1140, Senate Bill Veto*, Official California Legislative Information, ftp://leginfo.public.ca.gov/ pub/03-04/bill/sen/sb_1101-1150/sb_1140_vt_20040920.html (last visited Aug. 3, 2012).

[15] *Rash v. Lungen*, 59 Cal.App.4th 1233, 1235 (1997).

The author of the legislation that required the Attorney General to produce the Assault Weapon Identification Guide (AWIG) recognized this difficulty:

> I am writing to request your signature on SB 2444 which would enable law enforcement personnel in the field the means to be able to recognize what actually is or is not an "assault weapon," as defined under state law ... Unfortunately, a great many law enforcement officers who deal directly with the public are not experts in specific firearms identification ... There are numerous makes and models of civilian military-looking semi-automatic firearms which are not listed by California as "assault weapons" but which are very similar in external appearance. This situation sets the stage for honest law-enforcement mistakes resulting in unjustified confiscations of non-assault weapon firearms. Such mistakes, although innocently made, could easily result in unnecessary, time consuming, and costly legal actions both for law enforcement and for the lawful firearms owners affected.[16]

## C. 2012 Reorganization of the Dangerous Weapons Control Act (DWCA)

To improve the California Penal Code's organization and understandability, and in recognition of the tremendous confusion surrounding the interpretation and enforcement of California firearm laws, the Dangerous Weapons Recodification Act of 2010 was adopted. It took effect on January 1, 2012. Under this recodification, the California Law Revision Commission (CLRC) completely renumbered the DWCA, as well as parts of some other California codes, to "improve the organization and accessibility of the deadly weapons statutes, without making any change to criminal liability under those statutes."[17]

The Recodification Act was adopted pursuant to ACR 73[18] in 2006, which directed the CLRC to study, report on, and prepare recommended legislation to simplify and reorganize the portions of the Penal Code

---

[16] *See Harrott v. County of Kings*, 25 Cal.4th 1138, 1147 n.4 (2001) (citing Sen. Don Rogers' letter to Governor Deukmejian re: Sen. Bill No. 2444 (1989-1990 Reg. Sess.) Aug. 23, 1990).

[17] *Nonsubstantive Reorganization of Deadly Weapons Statutes*, 38 CAL. L. REVISION COMM'N REPORTS 217, 219 (2009) (letter from Chairwoman Pamela L. Hemminger to Gov. Arnold Schwarzenegger); *Nonsubstantive Reorganization of Deadly Weapon Statutes*, CALIFORNIA LAW REVISION COMMISSION, http://clrc.ca.gov/pub/Printed-Reports/Pub233.pdf (last visited Aug. 3, 2012).

[18] Assembly Concurrent Resolution authored by McCarthy, enacted as Resolution Chapter 128 of the Statutes of 2006.

relating to the control of deadly weapons, without making any substantive change to the scope of criminal liability under those provisions. The CLRC's report on the matter was due by July 1, 2009.

The author of ACR 73 said:

> In addition to the criminal storage laws, *many other provisions of the Penal Code are very confusing. In particular, the laws relating to the transfers of firearms are lengthy, with numerous cross-references, highly fact-specific exemptions, and complex provisions.* For example, Penal Code Section 12078 is 5880 words long and occupies 11 pages if printed in a 12-point font with conventional margins. The section has cross-references to many scattered sections of other firearms provisions, some of them hundreds of sections away. *The firearms laws occupy over 100 pages of an unannotated version of the Penal Code when printed in dual column in tiny print.*
>
> *These areas of the law are not for legal experts only. Firearms owners, licensed dealers, and law enforcement need to be able to interpret these provisions in order to comply with the law and avoid criminal liability. Ambiguity and confusion do not promote the public policy goals that those laws were designated to accomplish.*

ACR 73 was designed to have the CLRC, a neutral body of legal experts, simplify and reorganize these laws.[19]

The CLRC completed their task in 2009, and the Dangerous Weapons Recodification Act was adopted in 2010. It took effect on January 1, 2012.

To assist persons using those laws, I have posted a disposition table on the www.calgunlaws.com website showing where each provision was relocated. Visit the site for that and additional information on the reorganization.

The reorganization is generally a welcome change, but it will take some getting used to – making this book particularly timely for firearm owners, law enforcement, judges, and lawyers.

## D. "Gray Areas" and Test Cases

Despite my best efforts to explain the gun laws in California, as is the case with most any legal scheme as convoluted as California's firearm laws, there are some unanswered questions. I may have my own personal beliefs as to how law enforcement would likely interpret these. My purpose in addressing these legal "gray areas" is not to provide my position on what the law

---

[19] *ACR 73 Assembly Concurrent Resolution - Bill Analysis*, OFFICIAL CALIFORNIA LEGISLATIVE INFORMATION, ftp://www.leginfo.ca.gov/pub/05-06/bill/asm/ab_0051-0100/acr_73_cfa_20060822_195816_sen_floor.html (last visited Aug. 3, 2012) (emphasis added).

actually is or should be, nor to persuade or dissuade you from deciding to engage in activities falling in a "gray area" category. But as an attorney I believe part of my obligation is to make you aware of the uncertainty about what some of the laws allow and that there are potential risks associated with certain activities. I will let you decide what makes sense for your personal situation. When these legal "gray areas" arise in the book, I have tried to indicate them as such and remind the reader of the admonition in this chapter.

Some people choose to push the legal "envelope" by engaging in activities that would fall in these legal "gray areas." And some even insist that certain activities are not "gray" at all, but are clearly legal, and that their interpretation precludes law enforcement from causing you any legal problems. This overly academic mind-set is driven by wishful thinking, a misunderstanding of the context of California firearm laws, and the practically oriented judicial system in which they are typically applied.

## E. Government Bias in Applying Gun Laws

People just cannot count on logic or reasonableness alone in deciphering California's firearm laws in a way that protects them. If that were the case, there would be little need for this book; at least, it would be much shorter.

In my many years of handling thousands of criminal and civil matters involving firearms, it is my experience that some law enforcement officers, many prosecutors, and most California courts are not sympathetic toward civilian firearm ownership. They have repeatedly gone, and likely will continue to go, out of their way to interpret a questionable practice as unlawful. This is the case even if a technical reading of a statute or regulation suggests the practice is legal. Once your defense depends on parsing the language of statutes and/or explaining technical discrepancies, you are fighting an uphill battle. And the cost of taking that proverbial "hill" can often be costly. I do not need to warn you that lawyers cost money.

A prime example of the troublesome nature of interpreting firearm laws is the fact that the preeminent case from the United States Supreme Court interpreting the Second Amendment right to keep and bear arms as an individual right, *District of Columbia v. Heller,* was decided by a vote of 5-4. That means four justices disagree that there is even an individual right to firearm possession. The same vote count was repeated in the following Supreme Court ruling on whether the Second Amendment applied to the states and local governments in *McDonald v. Chicago.*

Unfortunately *what the law says and what authorities and courts do are not always an exact match.* You must remember that each legal case is different and may lack prior court precedents. A decision to prosecute a case and what charges are brought may involve a degree of discretion from the authorities involved. Sometimes, there is not a plain or clear-cut answer you can rely upon. Abuses, ignorance, carelessness, human frailties, and plain fate subject you to legal risks, which can be exacerbated when firearms are involved. Take nothing for granted, recognize that legal risk is attached to everything you do with a firearm, and unless you are ready to be a test case or have a life and death need, my recommendation is that you err on the side of compliance. My law firm has been fighting and will continue to fight bad gun laws in courthouses every day, and we have no shortage of test cases, and unfortunate gun owners, now.

## CHAPTER 2:

# WHAT IS LEGALLY CONSIDERED A "FIREARM" AND "AMMUNITION"?

**W**hat is a firearm? What is ammunition? These may seem like dumb questions. You probably think you already know what a "firearm" is and what constitutes "ammunition." But for regulatory purposes, firearm and ammunition definitions can be tricky. In the eyes of the law, not only things formally called "guns" are regulated as "firearms." Items like flare launchers can be "firearms." And sometimes only *part* of a firearm is actually a "firearm under the law." Then there are differences between federal and state law definitions of "firearm" and "ammunition," and even different definitions *within* those federal and state laws. Misunderstanding these definitions causes legal trouble for some firearm owners. In the highly politicized legal environment of gun control laws, the consequences of an innocent mistake can be severe.

Understanding these legal terms will help you avoid problems with things like flare guns, tear gas guns, certain air and BB guns, and other types of "guns" that might be regulated as "firearms." Knowing these definitions will also help you understand this book's later discussion relating to restrictions on firearm and ammunition possession, as well as provide you with the information to lawfully acquire "firearms" and "ammunition."

## I. "FIREARM" DEFINITIONS

### A. California Law "Firearm" Definitions

Under the previous version of the DWCA – the portion of the California Penal Code with most of the "Deadly Weapon Statutes"[1] – some statutes

---

[1] Formerly California Penal Code § 12000 *et seq.* All further section references are to the California Penal Code unless otherwise indicated and will be abbreviated as "P.C." Also, certain Penal Code statutes have been summarized and/or paraphrased. For exact statute wording, please reference the California Penal Code directly.

had specific definitions for firearm terms,[2] while others cross-referenced definitions in separate sections. This caused a lot of confusion.

In the current and revised version of the "Deadly Weapon Statutes," P.C. § 16520(a) generally defines the term "firearm" as it is used within other California statutes.

'[Firearm]' means any [1] device, [2] designed to be used as a weapon, [3] from which is expelled through a barrel, [4] a projectile by the force of any explosion or other form of combustion.

This definition of "firearm" is more narrow and does not include a bare frame or receiver.[3] But the definition of "firearm" in P.C. §16520(b) does include the frame or receiver. This means that when the P.C. §16520(b) definition applies, the frame or receiver is considered a "firearm" all by itself even though it cannot function as a firearm without additional parts.

## 1. History of California's "Firearm" Definition

To understand the reasoning behind P.C. § 16520 and why some code sections treat frames and receivers as "firearms" while others do not, you need to understand the definition's history and how it developed from former P.C. § 12001.

Before 1969 former P.C. § 12001 only defined a "firearm" as a " 'pistol,' 'revolver,' and 'firearm capable of being concealed upon the person' … [including] any device, designed to be used as a weapon, from which is expelled a projectile by the force of any explosion, or other form of combustion, and which has a barrel less than 12 inches in length."[4]

In 1968 a California court said that if a firearm was unable to fire because its firing pin was broken and another firing pin was unavailable to make the firearm work, the other parts alone were insufficient to be considered a "firearm." In other words, a firearm that is missing a piece of equipment necessary to make it fire (like a firing pin) is not a "firearm" until that part is replaced.[5] This means that if someone did not technically possess a functioning "firearm," he or she could not be convicted of feloniously possessing a firearm.

---

[2] For example, some definitions like that for "machinegun" include frames and receivers, the parts that can be used to convert a firearm into a "machinegun," or a complete firearm that shoots more than one shot per single pull of the trigger. P.C. § 16880.

[3] A "receiver" is " 'the metal frame in which the action of a firearm is fitted and to which the breech end of the barrel is attached.' " *Harrott v. County of Kings*, 25 Cal.4th 1138, 1147 (2001) (citing Webster's New Internat. Dict. 1894 (3d ed. 1965)). An "action" is "[t]he mechanism of a gun, usually breechloading, by which it is loaded, fired, and unloaded." John Quick, *Dictionary of Weapons & Military Terms* 3 (Harold B. Crawford et al. 1973).

[4] *See People v. Thompson,* 72 Cal.App.3d 1, 4 (1977) (quoting former P.C. § 12001 as it existed in 1968).

[5] *People v. Jackson,* 266 Cal.App.2d 341, 349 (1968).

To avoid the result of *Jackson*, a broader "firearm" definition was subsequently added to the Penal Code, but it only applied to certain statutes.[6] This broader definition of "firearm" included some of a firearm's *parts* – which are not functional firearms by themselves.

## 2. When Is a Frame or Receiver Considered a "Firearm"?

Although P.C. § 16520(b)[7] sets forth a broader "firearm" definition, which includes frames and receivers, that definition should only apply in certain contexts, usually relating to transfers and illegal possession.[8]

The rationale behind certain firearm *parts* being considered "firearms" themselves is to prevent those who are legally prohibited from possessing firearms (see Chapter 3) from having access to the operating parts of a firearm that could then be put together and made into functional firearms. By defining "firearm" to include frames or receivers and regulating them as functional firearms, California law seeks to ensure that no one can lawfully sell or transfer these essential parts to such prohibited people.[9] It also closes a loophole for prohibited persons who might try to avoid criminal liability by keeping their firearms disassembled in separate parts.

## B. Federal Law "Firearm" Definitions

To confuse matters more, federal law defines a "firearm" in two different sections for different purposes. The Gun Control Act (GCA) defines "firearm" generally with respect to transferring firearms and restricting who can possess them.[10] On the other hand, the National Firearms Act (NFA) defines "firearm" by specifically listing highly restricted items (some of which are not "guns"), making it easier to further explain the detailed re-

---

[6] Former P.C. § 12001 was later codified as P.C. § 12001(c).

[7] Formerly P.C. § 12001(c).

[8] *See* P.C. § 16550 (Firearm transaction records); P.C. § 16730 ("Infrequent" firearm transactions); P.C. § 16960 ("Operation of law" transfers); P.C. § 16990 (Taking firearm title or possession by operation of law); P.C. § 17070 ("Responsible adult"); P.C. § 17310 ("Used firearm"); P.C. §§ 26500 - 26588 (License requirements to sell, lease, or transfer and exceptions); P.C. §§ 26600 - 27140 (Exceptions for sale, lease or transfer to law enforcement); P.C. §§ 27400 - 28000 (Exceptions for law enforcement at gun shows or events); P.C. § 28100 (Electronic and telephonic transfer register or record); P.C. §§ 28400 - 28415 (Exceptions for law enforcement record keeping, background checks, and fees for firearm sale, lease, or transfer); P.C. §§ 29010 - 29150 (License requirements for firearm manufacturer); P.C. §§ 29610 - 29750 (Illegal firearm possession); P.C. §§ 29800 - 29905 (Firearm access prohibitions); P.C. §§ 30150 - 30165 (Exceptions for law enforcement firearm eligibility checks); P.C. § 31615 ("Handgun safety certificate" requirement); P.C. §§ 31705 - 31830 (Exceptions for sale, delivery, or transfer to authorized law enforcement representatives for "handgun safety certificate"); P.C. §§ 34355 - 34370 (Exceptions for the sale, delivery or transfer to authorized law enforcement representatives for ballistics identification system); Cal. Welf. & Inst. Code §§ 8100, 8101, 8103 and P.C. § 16520(b) (Mental health restriction prohibitions). California Welfare and Institutions Code is hereafter referred to as "W.I.C."

[9] *See* P.C. §§ 26500 *et seq.*, 26700.

[10] 18 U.S.C. § 921 *et seq.*

quirements to lawfully possess, import, and transfer those items by having them all in one category.[11]

## 1. Gun Control Act (GCA)

The GCA defines a "firearm" as:

(A) any weapon (including a starter gun) which will or is designed to or may readily be converted to expel a projectile by the action of an explosive;

(B) the frame or receiver of any such weapon;

(C) any firearm muffler or firearm silencer; or

(D) any destructive device.

But an "antique firearm" is not included in the GCA's definition of "firearm."[12]

## 2. National Firearms Act (NFA)

Under the NFA, the term "firearm" means:

- A shotgun with a barrel or barrels of less than 18 inches in length;
- A weapon made from a shotgun if, as modified, has an overall length of less than 26 inches or a barrel or barrels of less than 18 inches in length;
- A rifle with a barrel or barrels of less than 16 inches in length;
- A weapon made from a rifle if, as modified, has an overall length of less than 26 inches or a barrel or barrels of less than 16 inches in length;
- "Any other weapon" as defined in subsection (e) of 26 U.S.C. § 5845;
- A machinegun;
- A silencer; and
- A destructive device.[13]

As mentioned, this definition simply lists several highly restricted items. These restrictions came about as a result of the NFA's passage in the 1930s when the government sought to curtail gangland violence by restricting weapons generally associated with gangs in that era, like machineguns and

---

[11] 26 U.S.C. § 5801 *et seq.*

[12] 18 U.S.C. § 921(a)(3). The definitions of "firearm silencer," "firearm muffler," and "destructive device" are discussed in Chapter 9.

[13] 26 U.S.C. § 5845(a).

grenades. Though the government wanted a comprehensive legal scheme to deal with these items, it did not ban them because it believed doing so would violate the Second Amendment. Instead, the government heavily taxed possession and transfer of these items and required they be registered to assure the tax was paid if they were ever transferred again.[14]

The specific characteristics of these "firearms," along with their respective restrictions, are further discussed in Chapter 9. The Bureau of Alcohol, Tobacco, Firearms, and Explosives (ATF) has opined that an item may lose its "firearm" status under the NFA if it is modified in a way that permanently removes the characteristics that make it an NFA firearm or that completely destroys the item.[15]

Like most others, the NFA's definition of "firearm" does not include "antique firearms." Nor does the NFA consider a "firearm" any device that the Secretary of Treasury finds is "primarily a collector's item" and thus unlikely to be used as a weapon.[16]

Federal "firearm" definitions are as complex as those in California, if not more so. If you are interested in finding out more about the federal definitions, Stephen Halbrook's *Firearms Law Deskbook* is a great reference and deals specifically with federal firearm laws.[17]

## II. FIREARM SUBGROUP DEFINITIONS

Certain items meeting the general "firearm" definition are further classified into groups based on their characteristics and have more specific definitions under both California law and the GCA. The most common of these groups are handguns, rifles, and shotguns. But even these groups are further divided into subgroups with more specific definitions, as explained in Chapters 8 and 9. Knowing what classification a firearm belongs to is crucial to knowing what regulations apply and can mean the difference between an activity being perfectly legal or a jailable offense.

---

[14] *National Firearms Act: History of the National Firearms Act*, ATF, http://www.atf.gov/firearms/nfa/ (last visited July 25, 2012).

[15] Order 3310.45 (ATF 1989).

[16] 26 U.S.C. § 5845(a). The NFA definition for "antique firearm," as explained further in this chapter below, is slightly different than the definition used in the GCA.

[17] Stephen P. Halbrook, *Firearms Law Deskbook* (West 2011-2012 ed. 2011).

## A. "Handguns"

Under California law a "handgun" is "any pistol, revolver, or firearm capable of being concealed upon the person."[18] The terms "firearm capable of being concealed upon the person," "pistol," and "revolver" apply to and include:

[A]ny device designed to be used as a weapon, from which is expelled a projectile by the force of any explosion, or other form of combustion, and that has a barrel less than 16 inches in length. These terms also include any device that has a barrel 16 inches or more in length which is designed to be interchanged with a barrel less than 16 inches in length.[19]

Under the federal GCA a "handgun" is:

"(A) a firearm which has a short stock and is designed to be held and fired by the use of a single hand; and

(B) any combination of parts from which [such] a firearm ... can be assembled."[20]

## B. "Rifles" and "Shotguns"[21]

California law does not provide a general definition for "rifle." It does define "rifle" in the context of "short-barreled rifles" as being "a weapon designed or redesigned, made or remade, and intended to be fired from the shoulder and designed or redesigned and made or remade to use the energy of the explosive in a fixed cartridge to fire only a single projectile through a rifled bore for each single pull of the trigger."[22]

Though the federal GCA's definition for "rifle" is practically identical to California's, the GCA omits the "in a fixed cartridge" qualifier.[23] This means that, regardless of its form, a muzzle-loading-only "firearm" can certainly not be a "short-barreled rifle" and maybe not a "rifle" under California law, but it can be one under federal law.

As with rifles California law does not provide a general definition for "shotgun" either. It does define "shotgun" in the context of "short-barreled

---

[18] P.C. § 16640(a).

[19] P.C. § 16530(a).

[20] 18 U.S.C. § 921(a)(29).

[21] Shotguns and rifles are commonly referred to collectively as "long guns," and will be referred to this way throughout this book when the distinction is not relevant.

[22] P.C. § 17090.

[23] 18 U.S.C. § 921(a)(7).

shotguns" as being "a weapon designed or redesigned, made or remade, and intended to be fired from the shoulder and designed or redesigned and made or remade to use the energy of the explosive in a fixed shotgun shell to fire through a smooth bore either a number of projectiles (ball shot) or a single projectile for each pull of the trigger."[24] The qualifier "in a fixed shotgun shell" suggests that a firearm cannot be a "short-barreled shotgun" and maybe not a "shotgun" unless it fires fixed shotgun shells.

Again, though the federal GCA's "shotgun" definition is practically identical to California's "shotgun" definition, the GCA omits the "in a fixed shotgun shell" qualifier.[25] Thus it appears an item like a blunderbuss could be a "shotgun" under federal law, but likely is not one under California law.

Note that even if a firearm of legal length looks like something you would informally call a "shotgun" or "rifle," it is not one unless it is intended to be fired from the shoulder, *i.e.*, if no stock, then likely not a "shotgun" or "rifle."[26]

## C. Other "Firearms"

Like receivers, certain other items do not fit neatly into the "handgun," "rifle," or "shotgun" categories but still meet the legal definition of, and are treated as, "firearms." For example, a stockless firearm of legal length that shoots shotgun shells is not a "shotgun" because it does not have a stock and thus cannot be fired from the shoulder. It is also not a "short-barreled shotgun" because of its length. It nevertheless is a "firearm" because it is a "device, designed to be used as a weapon, from which is expelled through a barrel, a projectile by the force of any explosion or other form of combustion."[27]

"Machineguns" and the NFA's "any other weapons" are also firearm subgroups with specific definitions, which are further discussed in Chapter 9. Moreover, modifying a "handgun," "rifle," or "shotgun" may cause it to move from one category to another or fall outside of one of those categories.

As discussed below, issues sometimes arise as to whether an item actually meets the applicable "firearm" definition, which is important as to whether it is regulated or not.

---

[24] P.C. § 17190.

[25] 18 U.S.C. § 921(a)(5).

[26] Note, however, as explained in Chapter 9, such a firearm could still be considered a "short-barreled shotgun" if not long enough.

[27] P.C. § 16520(a).

## D. Definition of "Weapon"

An element included in all of the above definitions of "firearm" is the word "weapon." This means that to be a "firearm" an item must first be a "weapon." But neither state nor federal law specifically define what a "weapon" is. California courts do, however, instruct that "[a] weapon may be broadly defined as an instrument of offensive or defensive combat."[28]

Certain items will indisputably meet any reasonable "weapon" definition, e.g., standard firearms, dirks, and daggers.[29] But whether an item is actually a "weapon" is not always so clear when its uses for "combat" are uncertain or untraditional, e.g., pen guns (discussed below). California courts have held that one must know an object *is* a "weapon," may be *used* as a weapon, or must possess the object "as a weapon" for it to legally be considered a weapon.[30] Knowledge of an item's use can, of course, be proved by circumstantial evidence.[31]

In *People v. Fannin* the California Appellate Court considered whether a bicycle chain with a lock at the end was a "slungshot" – a prohibited "dangerous weapon" under the Penal Code. The court held that "if the object is not a weapon per se, but an instrument with ordinary innocent uses, the prosecution must prove that the object was possessed as a *weapon*."[32]

In short, though no set legal definition for "weapon" exists, there are items, like certain standard firearms, that are likely "weapons per se." Items not falling in that "weapons per se" category are analyzed with respect to the persons' knowledge of the items' uses or their actual use or intended use as a weapon to determine whether the items will legally be considered "weapons."[33]

## E. "Antique Firearms"

Because items meeting the definition of an "antique firearm" are not regulated as "firearms" for most purposes, it is important to know the California and federal definitions for "antique firearms."

---

[28] 63 Cal. Jur. 3d Weapons § 1 (*citing* Am. Jur. 2d, Weapons and Firearms § 1).

[29] *See People v. Reid*, 133 Cal.App.3d 354, 365 (1982).

[30] *People v. Gaitan*, 92 Cal.App.4th 540, 547 (2001); *People v. Taylor*, 93 Cal.App.4th 933, 941 (2001); *People v. Fannin*, 91 Cal.App.4th 1399, 1401 (2001).

[31] *People v. King*, 38 Cal.4th 617, 627 (2006). The prosecution need not prove that the defendant knew there was a law against possessing the item, nor that the defendant intended to break or violate the law, just that the defendant knew of the item's uses.

[32] *People v. Fannin*, 91 Cal.App.4th 1399, 1404 (2001) (emphasis in original); *see also People v. Grubb*, 63 Cal.2d 614, 621 (1965) (possession of modified baseball bat).

[33] See discussion on penguns, coyote catchers, and potato guns below for application of this rule.

## 1. California Law Definition

"Antique firearm" has a different definition in different contexts under California law. For firearm transactions, "antique firearm" means the same as it does in the federal GCA provided below.[34] And for "generally prohibited weapons,"[35] "antique firearm" means either:

(1) Any firearm not designed or redesigned for using rim fire or conventional centerfire ignition with fixed ammunition and manufactured in or before 1898. This includes any matchlock, flintlock, percussion cap, or similar type of ignition system or replica thereof, whether actually manufactured before or after the year 1898[; or]

(2) Any firearm using fixed ammunition manufactured in or before 1898, for which ammunition is no longer manufactured in the United States and is not readily available in the ordinary channels of commercial trade.[36]

With almost anything available on the internet, previously rare rimfire and centerfire cartridges have become more easily available. So the question of what ammunition is "not readily available" in subsection (2) above becomes obscured.[37]

Finally, as it relates to "assault weapons" and ".50 BMG rifles," the term "antique firearm" means "any firearm manufactured before January 1, 1899."[38]

---

[34] *See* P.C. § 16170(b). For GCA's definition, *see* 18 U.S.C. § 921(a)(16). *See also* Chapter 4 for "antique firearm" transactions.

[35] Discussed in Chapter 9.

[36] P.C. § 16170(c).

[37] For further analysis of this issue, *see Gun Ammo Googling: Does Internet Access to Rare Ammunition Calibers Limit the Availability of "Replicas" to Qualify as "Antique Firearms?"*, http://www.calgunlaws. com/wp-content/uploads/2012/07/Gun-Anno-Googling.pdf (last visited Sept. 13, 2012). The ATF also discusses this issue in the NFA Handbook, stating "[c]oncerning ammunition availability, it is important to note that a specific type of fixed ammunition that has been out of production for many years may again become available due to increasing interest in older firearms. Therefore, the classification of a specific NFA firearm as an antique can change if ammunition for the weapon becomes readily available in the ordinary channels of commercial trade." *See* U.S. DEPT. OF JUSTICE, BUREAU OF ALCOHOL, TOBACCO, FIREARMS, AND EXPLOSIVES, ATF NATIONAL FIREARMS ACT HANDBOOK 21 (2009).

[38] P.C. § 16170(a); *see also* Chapter 8.

## 2. Federal Law Definitions

### a. Gun Control Act (GCA)

As mentioned above, the GCA "firearm" definition does not include "antique firearms."[39] An "antique firearm" under the GCA is defined in 18 U.S.C. § 921(a)(16):

- any firearm (including any firearm with a matchlock, flintlock, percussion cap, or similar type of ignition system) manufactured in or before 1898;

[OR]

- any replica of ... [such a] firearm ... if such replica:
  i)  is not designed or redesigned for using rimfire or conventional centerfire fixed ammunition, or
  ii) uses rimfire or conventional centerfire fixed ammunition which is no longer manufactured in the United States and which is not readily available in the ordinary channels of commercial trade;[40]

[OR]

- any muzzle loading rifle, muzzle loading shotgun, or muzzle loading pistol, which is designed to use black powder, or a black powder substitute, and which cannot use fixed ammunition[, but does] ... not include any weapon which incorporates a firearm frame or receiver, any firearm which is converted into a muzzle loading weapon, or any muzzle loading weapon which can be readily converted to fire fixed ammunition by replacing the barrel, bolt, breechblock, or any combination thereof.[41]

---

[39] 18 U.S.C. § 921(a)(3).
[40] Like California's "antique firearm" definition, this federal category is affected by the internet making previously rare cartridges more available.
[41] 18 U.S.C. § 921(a)(16).

Items not meeting any of these definitions are regulated as "firearms" under the GCA.[42]

By excluding "antique firearms" from the GCA's "firearm" definition, its requirements and restrictions (discussed in Chapters 3 and 4) do not apply to those items meeting the "antique firearm" definition.

### b. National Firearms Act (NFA)

The NFA has a slightly different definition for "antique firearms" than does the GCA, which includes:

Any firearm not designed or redesigned for using rim fire or conventional centerfire ignition with fixed ammunition and manufactured in or before 1898 (including any matchlock, flintlock, percussion cap, or similar type of ignition system or replica thereof, whether actually manufactured before or after the year 1898) and also any firearm using fixed ammunition manufactured in or before 1898, for which ammunition is no longer manufactured in the United States and is not readily available in the ordinary channels of commercial trade.[43]

The main difference between the GCA and the NFA definitions is that the NFA definition does not expressly include muzzle loading firearms that use black powder and that *cannot* use fixed ammunition, although such firearms appear to fall within the definition regardless.

## F. "Curios or Relics"

"Curios or relics" have the same definition under California law as they do under federal law.[44]

---

[42] Additionally the ATF maintains a list – which it warns is *not* exhaustive and frequently changes – of certain weapons that load from the muzzle that it considers to be "firearms" under the GCA, which includes:
1. "Savage Model 10ML (early, 1st version).
2. Mossberg 500 shotgun with muzzle loading barrel.
3. Remington 870 shotgun with muzzle loading barrel.
4. Mauser 98 rifle with muzzle loading barrel.
5. SKS rifle with muzzle loading barrel.
6. RPB sM10 pistol with muzzle loading barrel.
7. H&R/New England Firearm Huntsman.
8. Thompson Center Encore/Contender.
9. Rossi .50 muzzle loading rifle." *Frequently Asked Questions – Collectors*, ATF, http://www.atf.gov/firearms/faq/collectors.html#antique-definition (last visited July 25, 2012).
[43] 26 U.S.C. § 5845(g).
[44] P.C. § 17705(a).

The Code of Federal Regulations[45] provides that "curios or relics" are firearms "of special interest to collectors by reason of some quality other than is associated with firearms intended for sporting use or as offensive or defensive weapons." To be "curios or relics," firearms must either be:

- manufactured at least 50 years prior to the current date, but not including replicas thereof;

[OR]

- certified by the curator of a municipal, State, or Federal museum which exhibits firearms to be curios or relics of museum interest;

[OR]

- derive a substantial part of their monetary value from the fact that they are novel, rare, bizarre, or because of their association with some historical figure, period, or event. Proof of qualification of a particular firearm under this category may be established by evidence of present value and evidence that like firearms are not available except as collector's items, or that the value of like firearms available in ordinary commercial channels is substantially less.[46]

The ATF has opined that a "receiver" is not a "curio or relic" item, and that a firearm must be in its original configuration to qualify as a "curio or relic." Minor alterations to a "curio or relic" firearm, however, such as adding scope mounts or sling swivels, are not likely to remove it from its "curio or relic" status.[47]

# III. IS THAT THING CONSIDERED A "FIREARM"?

The doctrine of Constitutional due process requires that to be convicted of a firearm violation, each element of the pertinent "firearm" definition must be proven beyond a reasonable doubt to a jury.[48]

Whether an item meets the applicable "firearm" definition is sometimes unclear. For example, toy guns, pellet guns, and BB guns are not considered "firearms" "because, instead of [using] explosion or other com-

---

[45] The Code of Federal Regulations is a compilation of rules adopted by federal agencies in furtherance of implementing federal laws enacted by Congress and is hereafter abbreviated as "C.F.R."

[46] 27 C.F.R. § 478.11.

[47] Ruling 85-10 (ATF 1985); see Firearms – Frequently Asked Questions – Curios & Relics, ATF, http://www.atf.gov/firearms/faq/curios-relics.html#modifications (last visited July 25, 2012).

[48] See Medley v. Runnels, 506 F.3d 857, 863-864 (9th Cir. 2007).

bustion, they use the force of air pressure, gas pressure, or spring action to expel a projectile."[49]

The "projectile" does not need to be traditional ammunition either. One court found a crude device made by a prison inmate – consisting of a tube sealed at one end packed with around 30 match heads with a hole to light them – to be a "firearm" even though no projectiles were found with it. An officer testified that such devices are often used to shoot melted or broken plastic and tinfoil balls.[50] Another court found taser "barbs" that make contact with the target to be "projectiles" within the "firearm" definition. That same court, in holding that a taser *is* a "firearm,"[51] also found the plastic, squared chambers holding the barbs to be "barrels" because "there appears no reason logically or semantically to insist that a gun's barrel must be made of metal or that it be cylindrical."[52]

In another example a defendant was charged with unlawfully possessing an "unconventional pistol," which, as explained in Chapter 9, is an illegal "firearm." The defendant had a Penguin Tear Gas Pen Gun designed for launching flares or tear gas canisters – not firing ammunition – though it was shown that ammunition *could be* fired from it (with a likelihood of causing injury to the shooter). Because ammunition *could* be fired from it, there was an issue about whether it was actually "*designed* to be used as a weapon." The state needed to prove it was "designed" to be used as a weapon in order to prove the pen gun was a "firearm," and to prove the owner *knew* it could be used in this way.

There was also an issue as to whether the tear gas pen gun even had a "barrel" through which a projectile was expelled because the tear gas canisters and flares were designed to screw on to the end of it.[53]

## A. Bang Sticks/Shark Killers

Sometimes an item that would not generally be referred to as a firearm still meets the legal definition of one. A relatively common example is a "bang stick," a shaft or pole carried by divers with a "power head" (a device containing a cartridge that has a fixed firing pin) attached at the end that will

---

[49] *People v. Law*, 195 Cal.App.4th 976, 983 (2011) (citing *People v. Monjaras*, 164 Cal.App.4th 1432, 1435 (2008)).

[50] *People v. Talkington*, 140 Cal.App.3d 557, 562 (1983).

[51] *People v. Heffner*, 70 Cal.App.3d 643, 652 (1977). As an aside, older model tasers used primers to launch the barbs while modern tasers use compressed air and, thus, are not considered "firearms."

[52] *People v. Heffner*, 70 Cal.App.3d 643, 648-649 (1977) (noting that the taser in question discharged the barbs using combustion). Modern tasers are discharged using air pressure and do not meet the definition of "firearm" for that reason.

[53] I litigated this case in Ventura County and ultimately obtained a dismissal of charges for the defendant, but that does not mean the same result is guaranteed for everyone.

discharge the cartridge when thrust forcefully in a linear motion, usually toward a shark. No trigger or sophisticated mechanics are involved, and it looks more like a boat antenna than a traditional firearm. But since it is a device designed to be a weapon (albeit against sharks, and although blanks can be used just as effectively) and its projectile is still expelled by explosive force, the only real question is whether the "power head" where the cartridge is contained constitutes a "barrel." Though it is unclear, because the cartridge is fully contained and even set back from the opening of the "power head," it is arguably a barrel – especially since a court has considered tasers to have a barrel – likely making a "bang stick" a "firearm" and subject to all applicable restrictions.

## B. Coyote Booby Traps

Sometimes, even when the item may technically meet the "firearm" definition, courts will conclude the item is *not* one. For example, a Colorado court decided a "coyote getter" – a device with a hollow tube of light metal, crimped at one end, and a spring-loaded firing pin that propels cyanide into a coyote's mouth when it pulls on the bait – was not a "firearm" under the NFA because it lacked practical use as a weapon, and because the ATF's expert refused to fire one using live ammunition.[54]

## C. Potato Guns a.k.a. "Spud Guns"

A potato gun or "spud gun" is a device that, as its name implies, shoots potatoes, typically using some form of flammable aerosol or liquid. The flammable material is stored in the device that is attached to the barrel. The potato (or piece of potato) is crammed into the barrel, and a well-built potato gun can shoot a potato 100 yards or more.

Since a potato gun is obviously a device that expels a projectile through a barrel by combustive force, the question of whether it is a "firearm" turns on whether it is a "weapon." As explained above, no exact legal definition exists for the term "weapon." But, given the above "weapon" definition and its subsequent analysis, it seems unlikely that a potato gun would be considered a "weapon" unless it was intentionally used as one. An argument could be made, however, that a person need only know that it *could* be used to injure or kill for it to be considered a "weapon."

---

[54] *United States v. Brady*, 710 F. Supp. 290, 293 (D. Colo. 1989) (the court noted that the expert would not fire the coyote getter using live ammunition because it was possible that the catcher would explode. The court concluded that the getter was not considered "any other weapon" under the federal law definition of firearm because "[r]esearch ha[d] found no cases in which a court or administrative agency found that a device which was likely to explode if used with normal ammunition was any other weapon.").

If potato guns *are* considered "weapons," a question also exists about whether these devices are illegal "destructive devices" under state and/or federal law (see Chapter 9). In California, these devices may be considered a launching device for a bomb, grenade, explosive missile, or similar device – though they usually cannot shoot anything as dense as a bomb or grenade. And some designs or building materials are so flimsy that launching anything heavier than a potato may result in catastrophic failure. Nevertheless, criminal cases have been and will continue to be filed alleging "spud guns" are "firearms," "destructive devices," or "zip guns," (see Chapter 9).

Under federal law a potato gun can be considered an illegal "destructive device" that expels a projectile by explosive force with a barrel diameter of more than half an inch. And even if it is not considered a "firearm," it may still meet the definition of some other prohibited item.

It is strongly advised you proceed cautiously before deciding to make a potato gun because of the confusion about their legality.

## D. Items Meeting the "Firearm" Definition, but Expressly Exempted

Even if an item forming the basis of a crime is a "firearm," it may still be exempt from certain restrictions based on the *type* of "firearm" it is. For example, as explained above, "antique firearms" are usually exempt, and firearms considered "curios or relics" may be as well.

It is your responsibility to know whether or not the device you own is a "firearm" and to know what restrictions do and do not apply to it. The examples listed are just some of the types of considerations courts make in determining whether something is a "firearm."

# IV.  "AMMUNITION"

## A. California Law "Ammunition" Definitions

The word "ammunition" is undefined throughout most of the Penal Code, but is given a specific definition in certain sections.[55] Pay close attention because these specific definitions often include items you would not commonly consider "ammunition."

For those prohibited from possessing firearms and "ammunition," (see Chapter 3), "ammunition" includes, but is not limited to, "any bullet, cartridge, magazine, clip, speed loader, autoloader, or projectile capable of be-

---

[55] P.C. §§ 16150, 16650. Certain prohibited ammunition and ammunition containing lead projectiles are discussed in Chapter 9.

ing fired from a firearm with a deadly consequence. 'Ammunition' does not include blanks."[56] In other words, mere components of ammunition like bullets and ammunition feeding devices like magazines are themselves considered "ammunition" in this context.

"*Handgun* ammunition" means ammunition principally for use in handguns, even if it can be used in some rifles.[57] "Handgun ammunition" does *not* include ammunition for "antique firearms" or blanks.[58]

## B. "Ammunition" Parts

California does not regulate possessing ammunition parts, other than for those persons prohibited from possessing firearms and ammunition. But it does regulate possessing ammunition *powder*. So, reloaders, beware.

Even though smokeless powder does not technically explode, it is still considered an "explosive" in California because an "explosive" includes, but is not limited to:

- "any substance, or combination of substances, the primary or common purpose of which is detonation or rapid combustion, and which is capable of a relatively instantaneous or rapid release of gas and heat, or any substance, the primary purpose of which, when combined with others, is to form a substance capable of a relatively instantaneous or rapid release of gas and heat;"
- any "explosive" as defined in 18 U.S.C. § 841 and published per 27 Code Fed. Regs. § 555.23;
- "dynamite, nitroglycerine, picric acid, lead azide, fulminate of mercury, *black powder, smokeless powder,* propellant explosives, detonating primers, blasting caps, or commercial boosters;"[59]
- certain substances classified by the Department of Transportation;[60] and
- any material designated by the Fire Marshal pursuant to regulations in accordance with Department of Transportation standards.[61]

---

[56] P.C. § 16150(b).

[57] P.C. § 16650(a). The standard "principally for use in a handgun" has been found in at least one context to be unconstitutionally vague, because it is impossible to know whether any given cartridge is used more often in a handgun or a rifle. *See Parker v. State of California,* No. 10CECG02116 (Super. Ct. Fresno Jan. 31, 2011), *appeal docketed,* No. F062490 (Cal. App. May 20, 2011), which I litigated. For this reason, most ammunition vendors ask the purchaser what type of firearm the ammunition will be used in to meet this standard.

[58] P.C. § 16650(b).

[59] P.C. § 16510(a) (emphasis added).

[60] P.C. §§ 16510(b)-(c).

[61] P.C. § 16510(d).

The term "explosive" does "not include any destructive device, [or] ammunition or small arms primers manufactured for use in shotguns, rifles, and pistols."[62]

No one may possess an "explosive" without a permit.[63] However, you can possess black powder in quantities of five pounds or less and smokeless powder in quantities of 20 pounds or less without a permit.[64]

## C. Federal Law "Ammunition" Definition

For purposes of the GCA, "ammunition" is "ammunition or cartridge cases, primers, bullets, or propellant powder designed for use in any firearm."[65] Also, in the Code of Federal Regulations, "ammunition" is defined as "[a]mmunition or cartridge cases, primers, bullets, or propellent powder designed for use in any firearm other than an antique firearm. The term [does] not include (a) any shotgun shot or pellet not designed for use as the single, complete projectile load for one shotgun hull or casing, nor (b) any unloaded, non-metallic shotgun hull or casing not having a primer."[66]

---

[62] P.C. § 16510(f). "Destructive devices" are discussed in Chapter 9.

[63] Cal. Health & Saf. Code § 12101(a)(3).

[64] Cal. Health & Saf. Code § 12001(f)(1).

[65] 18 U.S.C. § 921(a)(17)(A). This definition also applies to those federally prohibited from possessing firearms and ammunition as discussed in Chapter 3.

[66] 27 C.F.R. § 478.11.

## CHAPTER 3:
# WHO CAN OWN AND POSSESS FIREARMS AND AMMUNITION?

**B**oth California and federal laws place restrictions on firearms and ammunition[1] for certain classes of people. Depending on the type of restriction, these laws can prohibit you from owning, possessing, receiving, purchasing, shipping, and/or transporting firearms.

Aside from age restrictions, there are several situations where your right to own and/or possess firearms can be restricted, either temporarily or permanently. For example, you may be prohibited because of a criminal conviction, restraining order, or mental health commitment.

How long you may be prohibited, and from what specific activities, depends on which class you are in and whether state and/or federal prohibitions apply. It is possible, for example, to be prohibited under *both* state and federal law or under only one of them. The prohibition may also only be temporary under one set of laws and last a lifetime under the other.

One general distinction between California and federal firearm restrictions is that California bars prohibited persons[2] from even owning firearms,[3] while federal law does not ban firearm ownership but rather merely possession (and certain other activities).[4] As explained below, this

---

[1] What constitutes a "firearm" or "ammunition" is different under California and federal law (see Chapter 2). All firearm restrictions listed in this chapter also include "ammunition" unless specifically stated otherwise.

[2] "Prohibited person" as used hereafter means an individual who is subject to one or more legal restrictions relating to the person's legal ability to own and/or possess firearms.

[3] The California firearm and ammunition prohibition generally restricts owning, purchasing, receiving, and possessing firearms, or having firearms under your custody or control. *See* P.C. §§ 29800, 29805, 29815, 29820, 29825, 29900, 30305 and W.I.C §§ 8100, 8103. A person with California firearm and ammunition prohibitions is precluded from all of these activities. In the interests of brevity this book only mentions the prohibition on "possessing" firearms, but remember that all of these activities are precluded for a person prohibited from "possessing" firearms and ammunition.

[4] 18 U.S.C. § 922(g) makes it illegal for those with a firearm restriction "to ship or transport in interstate or foreign commerce, or possess in or affecting commerce, any firearm or ammunition; or to receive any firearm or ammunition which has been shipped or transported in interstate or foreign commerce." *See* 18 U.S.C. § 922(n) for restrictions on shipment, transportation, and acquisition, discussed at the end of this chapter.

distinction can be significant as to what activities someone with such a prohibition may lawfully participate in.

# I. WHAT DOES "POSSESSION" MEAN?

Most state and federal violations occur when a prohibited person is found in "possession" of a firearm. Whether you "possess" a firearm is not always easy to determine. There are two kinds of legal possession: "actual possession" and "constructive possession."

"Actual possession" means you knowingly have direct physical control of an object.[5] You may have "actual possession" of an object in your hand, clothes, purse, bag, or other container. Knowingly having the object for even a limited time and purpose can constitute "actual possession."[6]

"Constructive possession" means you knowingly have control of, or have *the right to* control the object, either directly or through another person.[7] More than one person can possess the same object at the same time.[8] Whether you could direct the object's movement or whether it would be reasonable to think you had such control are factors in determining whether you have "constructive possession."[9] But, you must also, in fact, *know* that you have this control over the object to legally be considered to constructively "possess" it.[10]

The idea of "possession" can be problematic if you live with someone (*e.g.*, a family member or roommate) who owns firearms or if you want to give your firearms to someone you live with while you are prohibited, because you may still be considered to "possess" any firearm that is under your roof if you have access to it, even if you do not own it. The bottom line is that firearms and ammunition should not remain in your residence while you are prohibited from owning and possessing firearms. If you have police or probation officers coming to your residence for any reason, you should seriously consider whether you may be considered to "possess" firearms. If any firearm or ammunition in your residence belongs to someone else, you should find another place to live unless that other person is willing to remove it from the residence. If you have firearms or ammunition in

---

[5] *People v. Scott*, 45 Cal.4th 743, 748 (2009) (citing CALJIC No. 1.24).

[6] *People v. Neese*, 272 Cal.App.2d 235, 244-245 (1969).

[7] *People v. Neese*, 272 Cal.App.2d 235, 244-247 (1969); *see also People v. Rogers*, 5 Cal.3d 129, 134 (1971).

[8] *See People v. Azevedo*, 161 Cal.App.3d 235, 243 (1984), *overruled on other grounds by People v. King*, 38 Cal.4th 617 (2006) (holding knowledge of a weapon's prohibited character is a necessary element that the prosecution must prove); *see also* CALCRIM 2510.

[9] *Armstrong v. Superior Court*, 217 Cal.App.3d 535, 539 (1990); *see also People v. Scott*, 45 Cal.4th 743, 757 (2009).

[10] CALJIC No. 1.24.

your residence while you are prohibited, you should contact an attorney to discuss how to dispose of them.

## II. WHAT DOES "OWN" MEAN?

While the California Penal Code does not define what it means to "own" a firearm, the California Civil Code states that "ownership of a thing is the right of one or more persons to possess and use it to the exclusion of others."[11] The California Civil Code further says that all inanimate things, such as property, which can be appropriated or manually delivered can be owned.[12] Since firearms are personal property that can be appropriated or manually delivered, they may be "owned" pursuant to the above definition.[13] Therefore, to "own" a firearm, you have to have *the right to* possess or use it (not necessarily be in possession of it).

## III. DETERMINING WHEN FIREARM POSSESSION PROHIBITIONS APPLY

California is a "point of contact" state, meaning the California DOJ does the background checks to determine your eligibility to purchase or receive firearms when you try to buy a firearm, rather than the federal National Instant Criminal Background Check System (NICS) operated by the Federal Bureau of Investigation (FBI). The California DOJ looks for criminal convictions, restraining orders, and mental health records. If your background information does not meet any of the firearm restriction criteria explained below, your name is not "flagged." On the other hand, if you have a conviction, are subject to a restraining order, or had a mental health commitment, the California DOJ will investigate it to see if it triggers a firearm restriction.[14]

If you are incorrectly considered prohibited by the California DOJ, you can try to correct the error with them or request an "NICS Appeal" through the FBI.[15] However, unless the government clearly made an error

---

[11] Cal. Civ. Code § 654.

[12] Cal. Civ. Code § 655.

[13] This "ownership" definition is similar to that used in criminal law as well. *See, e.g., People v. Kozlowski,* 96 Cal.App.4th 853, 866 (2002).

[14] For example, convictions for felonies, offenses designated as "violent" pursuant to P.C. § 29905, and misdemeanor crimes of domestic violence will prohibit you from possessing a firearm for life. Other offenses, such as those misdemeanor convictions listed within P.C. § 29805, will prohibit you from possessing firearms for a 10-year period.

[15] A NICS Appeal brochure may be downloaded at: *nics-guide-for-appealing,* FBI, http://www.fbi.gov/about-us/cjis/nics/appeals/nics-guide-for-appealing (last visited July 26, 2012). Additional information concerning NICS may be found at: *FBI - Gun Checks/NICS,* FBI, http://www.fbi.gov/about-us/cjis/nics (last visited July 26, 2012).

or evidence is available to prove the error, the FBI or DOJ will consider you as a prohibited person until proof is shown that you should *not* be prohibited. Unfortunately, since some cases are years, if not decades, old, no proof may be available to successfully restore your firearm rights. At this point you should contact an attorney.

## IV. CALIFORNIA'S ARMED PROHIBITED PERSON SYSTEM

Once you are denied a firearm or fall under one of the categories of persons prohibited from possessing firearms under California or federal law, your name is entered into the Automated Criminal History System. Once that happens, the California DOJ is required to check to see if you have any firearms, including registered "assault weapons" or .50 BMG rifles in your name.[16] If it is discovered that you possess or own firearms, your name and information will be placed on a list accessible to law enforcement via the Armed Prohibited Persons System (APPS).

As a result of Senate Bill 819 that was introduced by Senator Leno and became law in 2012,[17] money collected from DROS fees can be used to pay for the APPS program, allowing for law enforcement to go after more people on the APPS list. Consequently there has been a rise in law enforcement visiting and arresting people who have firearms registered in their name and who have a potentially prohibiting event in their past.

If you are prohibited from possessing firearms and ammunition but still possess or have firearms registered in your name, you should speak with an attorney and transfer them as soon as possible, as discussed below.

## V. DISPOSSESSION BY TRANSFERRING FIREARMS/AMMUNITION TO SPOUSE OR OTHERS

Because firearms and ammunition should generally not be in your home while you are prohibited, continuing to possess firearms and/or ammunition is problematic. If you become prohibited from possessing firearms, however, you may still have certain rights concerning how the firearms and ammunition you own are disposed of. In *People v. Beck* the court held "it is [the] defendant, not the state, who has the right to designate disposition

---

[16] P.C. § 30005(a).

[17] *SB 819 Senate Bill - Chaptered*, OFFICIAL CALIFORNIA LEGISLATIVE INFORMATION, http://leginfo.ca.gov/pub/11-12/bill/sen/sb_0801-0850/sb_819_bill_20111009_chaptered.html (last visited July 26, 2012).

of the title. The successor owner, if qualified, may obtain possession of the firearms."[18] This means that a person who legally owned a firearm before becoming prohibited from possessing firearms has the right to sell the firearm to a non-prohibited person and collect the revenue. But if the firearm was used in the crime that resulted in the firearm prohibition, this option may not be available (see Chapter 10).

California has several forms designed to encourage and facilitate transferring firearms from prohibited persons to non-prohibited persons. One option is the California DOJ's Prohibited Persons Notice Form, which allows you to give power of attorney to someone to transfer your firearms on your behalf if you are prohibited.[19] Attorneys should be aware of this form in any case where their client pleads to an offense that results in a firearm restriction and their client owns or has firearms in his or her residence at the time of the plea. Courts and attorneys sometimes do not immediately realize that someone is prohibited the moment their plea and sentence are entered, meaning that once they return home where firearms are present, they could be violating the law.

In these cases, firearms may also be transferred to an "immediate family member" or spouse because the transfer can be done right away without going through a dealer.[20] But the firearms should still not be kept where you can access them. However, as explained below, if you are prohibited because of a restraining order, you *cannot* give your firearms to an "immediate family member," spouse, or to anyone else. Your options are limited to surrendering the firearms to law enforcement or selling them to a Federal Firearms Licensee (FFL).

It is worth pointing out again that if you become prohibited and you still have the right to dispose of your firearms, you should *not* transfer them to someone where you will still have access to them.

---

[18] *People v. Beck*, 25 Cal.App.4th 1095, 1106 (1994); *see also Hibbard v. City of Anaheim*, 162 Cal.App.3d 270, 275-276 (1984).

[19] The Prohibited Persons Notice Form and Power of Attorney for Transfer and Disposal Form facilitates immediately transferring firearms to a third party to dispose of them on behalf of the prohibited person. The California DOJ Firearms Division has these forms on its website. *See Forms and Publications*, Office of the Attorney General, http://caag.state.ca.us/firearms/forms/ (last visited July 26, 2012).

[20] P.C. §§ 27870(a)-(b). Note handguns transferred in this manner must be reported to the DOJ (*see* Chapter 4) and "assault weapons" cannot be transferred at all (*see* Chapter 8).

# VI. FIREARM AND AMMUNITION POSSESSION RESTRICTIONS FOR PEOPLE UNDER 21

## A. Restrictions for Minors (under age 18)

### 1. Shotguns, Rifles, and Transferring Firearms to Minors

Neither California nor federal law regulates minors *possessing* rifles and shotguns, but under California law it is illegal to *give possession of* any firearm (handgun or long gun) to a minor without the parent or legal guardian's express permission. Federal law prohibits the transfer of handguns to minors except for certain situations.[21]

### 2. Handguns

In California those under age 18 may not generally *possess* handguns[22] unless they are actively engaged in, or are going directly to or from, a lawful activity that involves using a handgun, and are either:

- With their parent or legal guardian;
- With a "responsible adult"[23] and have prior *written* consent from their parent or legal guardian;
- At least age 16 with prior *written* consent from their parent or legal guardian; or
- On lands owned or lawfully possessed by their parent or legal guardian and they have their parent or legal guardian's prior *written* consent.[24]

Under federal law minors are prohibited from possessing handguns unless the handgun is possessed temporarily:

(A)

"(i) in the course of employment, in the course of ranching or farming related to activities at the residence of the juvenile (or on property used for ranching or farming at which the juvenile, with the permission of the property owner or lessee, is performing activities related to the operation of the farm or ranch), target practice, hunting, or a course of instruction in the safe and lawful use of a handgun;

---

[21] *See* Chapter 4 concerning the laws relating to transferring firearms to minors.

[22] P.C. § 29610.

[23] "Responsible adult" means someone "at least age 21 who is not prohibited by state or federal law from possessing, receiving, owning, or purchasing a firearm." P.C. § 17070.

[24] P.C. §§ 29610, 29615.

(ii) with the prior written consent of the juvenile's parent or guardian who is not prohibited by Federal, State, or local law from possessing a firearm, except –

(I) during transportation by the juvenile of an unloaded handgun in a locked container directly from the place of transfer to a place at which an activity described in clause (i) is to take place and transportation by the juvenile of that handgun, unloaded and in a locked container, directly from the place at which such an activity took place to the transferor; or

(II) with respect to ranching or farming activities as described in clause (i), a juvenile may possess and use a handgun or ammunition with the prior written approval of the juvenile's parent or legal guardian and at the direction of an adult who is not prohibited by Federal, State or local law from possessing a firearm;

(iii) the juvenile has the prior *written* consent in the juvenile's possession at all times when a handgun is in the possession of the juvenile; and

(iv) in accordance with State and local law;

(B) by a juvenile who is a member of the Armed Forces of the United States or the National Guard who possesses or is armed with a handgun in the line of duty;

(C) as a result of a transfer by inheritance of title (but not possession) of a handgun or ammunition to a juvenile; or

(D) if possession of the handgun or ammunition is taken in defense of the juvenile or other persons against an intruder into the residence of the juvenile or a residence in which the juvenile is an invited guest."[25]

In general, by complying with California laws concerning loaning firearms to a minor, you should also be in compliance with federal laws.

## 3. Ammunition

Under California law minors cannot *possess* any kind of live ammunition[26] unless one of the following conditions is met:

- They have *written* consent from their parent or legal guardian.
- They are with their parent or legal guardian.
- They are "actively engaged in, or [are] going to or from, a lawful,

---

[25] 18 U.S.C. § 922(x)(3) (emphasis added).
[26] P.C. § 29650.

recreational sport, including, but not limited to, competitive shooting, or agricultural, ranching, or hunting activity, the nature of which involves the use of a firearm."[27]

Minors who violate this law can be charged with a crime.[28] Unlike California, federal law does not prohibit minors from possessing *all* ammunition, just ammunition that is suitable for use only in a handgun.[29] And all the exceptions to the general federal prohibition on minors possessing handguns also apply to their possession of the ammunition.

## B. Restrictions for 18 to 21-Year-Olds

Under both California and federal law, you may buy "complete" rifles and shotguns from an FFL once you turn 18.[30] Under federal law, frames and receivers (see Chapter 2) cannot be purchased until the purchaser reaches age 21. Federal law specifies only "rifles" and "shotguns" can be purchased by 18 to 21-year-olds, and the ATF interprets this rule to mean "complete" firearms.[31]

# VII. CRIMINAL CONVICTIONS RESULTING IN LOSS OF FIREARM POSSESSION RIGHTS

Felony and certain misdemeanor convictions cause most firearm restrictions. You can also be prohibited under certain probation terms. California and federal law sometimes differ as to what convictions trigger restrictions and to what extent. It is crucial that you know what restrictions, if any, apply to any conviction you have so you know how to comply with them. In general, California restrictions based on criminal convictions are set out

---

[27] P.C. § 29655.

[28] P.C. § 29700.

[29] 18 U.S.C. § 922(x)(2). It is doubtful that a prosecutor can convict a juvenile of this offense because there really is no such thing as ammunition "suitable for use *only* in a handgun." Some non-handguns can safely discharge virtually any cartridge in existence. But the California restriction still applies and could result in a conviction.

[30] *See* P.C. § 27510; *see* 18 U.S.C. § 922(b)(1).

[31] *Open Letter to All Federal Firearms Licensees*, U.S. DEPT. OF JUSTICE – BUREAU OF ALCOHOL, TOBACCO, FIREARMS AND EXPLOSIVES, http://www.atf.gov/press/releases/2009/07/070709-openletter-ffl-gca.pdf (last visited July 27, 2012); *see* 18 U.S.C. § 922(b)(1); *see also ATF Form 4473 - Firearm Transaction Record*, U.S. DEPT. OF JUSTICE – BUREAU OF ALCOHOL, TOBACCO, FIREARMS AND EXPLOSIVES, http://www.atf.gov/press/releases/2009/07/070709-openletter-ffl-gca.pdf (last visited July 27, 2012) and Chapter 4 for further explanation.

in P.C. §§ 29800-29875, and 29900 *et seq.*[32] while federal prohibitions are listed in 18 U.S.C. § 922(g).

## A. California Restrictions for Felony Convictions

In California, anyone who has been convicted of a felony under California or federal law, or another state or country's law,[33] may not own, purchase, receive, or possess a firearm or ammunition.[34]

This California prohibition does *not* apply to felony convictions under federal law unless *either* of the following two things happened:

- The conviction was for an offense that would only result in felony punishment under California law, or
- You were sentenced to a federal correctional facility for more than 30 days, and/or were fined more than $1,000.[35]

### 1. Proposition 36 Drug Diversion Programs and Penal Code Section 1000

Certain non-violent drug possession felony charges are eligible for probation and diversion in California instead of a jail sentence.[36] After completing a drug treatment program and probation, courts will set aside and dismiss the indictment, complaint, or information against you.[37] You will then be released (with certain exceptions) from all of the conviction's penalties and disabilities.[38]

Some mistakenly believe that if they receive Prop. 36 diversion,[39] their felony conviction will go away and will not affect the rest of their lives. This is incorrect. A Prop. 36 dismissal does *not* eliminate the felony conviction for purposes of triggering firearm restrictions.[40]

---

[32] For a list of state prohibiting charges and situations: *Firearms Prohibiting Categories,* CALIFORNIA DEPT. OF JUSTICE - BUREAU OF FIREARMS, http://oag.ca.gov/sites/all/files/pdfs/firearms/forms/prohibcatmisd.pdf (last visited July 27, 2012). The ATF also lists persons who are federally prohibited from shipping, transporting, receiving, or possessing firearms at: *ATF Online - Firearms - How To - Identify Prohibited Persons,* U.S. DEPT. OF JUSTICE – BUREAU OF ALCOHOL, TOBACCO, FIREARMS AND EXPLOSIVES, http://www.atf. gov/firearms/how-to/identify-prohibited-persons.html (last visited July 27, 2012).

[33] Other countries do not possess the same due process rights as the United States. Thus, under California law you can end up prohibited from possessing firearms and ammunition if you are convicted of a felony in some court in another country that does not provide you with similar due process rights.

[34] *See* P.C. § 29800(a)(1).

[35] P.C. § 29800(c).

[36] P.C. § 1210.1(a).

[37] *People v. Hinkel,* 125 Cal.App.4th 845, 850 (2005); P.C. § 1210.1(e).

[38] P.C. § 1210.1(e).

[39] Prop. 36 is short for California Proposition 36, the "Substance Abuse and Crime Prevention Act of 2000." The Proposition codified section 1210 and allowed for those charged with non-violent drug offenses to receive probation and treatment rather than jail time.

[40] *See* P.C. § 1210.1(e)(2).

For this reason, the alternative drug diversion program under P.C. § 1000 is preferable with respect to preserving firearm rights. As with a disposition of the criminal charges under Prop. 36, under P.C. § 1000 the case is dismissed after you complete the drug program and other court requirements, but instead of receiving a "sentence" and probation like you would with Prop. 36,[41] your sentencing time is waived and your guilty plea[42] does not become a conviction unless you *unsuccessfully perform* the diversion program.[43] If properly completed, however, the case will be considered to have never existed.[44] Moreover, unlike Prop. 36, P.C. § 1000's drug program has no language allowing your offense to still be used as a prohibiting conviction for purposes of firearm prohibitions.[45]

## B. Federal Restrictions for Certain State or Federal Convictions

While California firearm restrictions focus on the *type* of offense for which you were convicted, federal law instead focuses on the type of *sentence* you *could* have received with your conviction.

Specifically, if your conviction under either state or federal law was for a crime *punishable* by imprisonment for more than one year, federal law prohibits you from possessing any firearm or ammunition for life.[46] Whether you have been convicted of a "crime punishable by imprisonment for more than one year" is generally determined according to the jurisdiction where you are being prosecuted,[47] but does not include any:

- "Federal or State offenses pertaining to antitrust violations, unfair trade practices, restraints of trade, or other similar offenses relating to the regulation of business practices, or
- State offense classified by the laws of the State as a misdemeanor and punishable by a term of imprisonment of two years or less[; or]
- [C]onviction [that] has been expunged, or set aside or for which ... [you] ha[ve] been pardoned or ... had [your] civil rights restored ... unless [the] pardon, expungement, or restoration of civil rights [still] expressly provide[d] [for firearm restrictions] ... ."[48]

---

[41] *See* P.C. § 1210.1.

[42] This drug diversion program can also be done before a plea as well. P.C. § 1000.5.

[43] P.C. § 1000.3.

[44] P.C. § 1000.4(a). This is still considered a conviction for those applying to be a peace officer. P.C. § 1000.4(b).

[45] P.C. § 1000 *et seq.*

[46] 18 U.S.C. § 922(g)(1). It is not necessary that you actually receive such a sentence.

[47] *United States v. Marks*, 379 F.3d 1114, 1117 (9th Cir. 2004).

[48] 18 U.S.C. § 921(a)(20).

Because the maximum sentence for any California *felony* conviction always exceeds one year, you are prohibited from owning and possessing firearms under federal law for *any* California felony conviction. But because California *misdemeanor* convictions are only punishable by a year or less in jail, you are not federally prohibited for a California misdemeanor conviction[49] unless – as discussed below – it is for a misdemeanor crime of domestic violence (MCDV).

If you are federally restricted, the firearm prohibition extends to all 50 states.[50]

## C. California Restrictions for Certain "Violent Crimes"

California also restricts firearm possession for certain "violent crime" convictions[51] such as murder, attempted murder, mayhem, rape, and assault with a deadly weapon or force likely to produce great bodily injury.[52] Though most are felonies – convictions which would carry a firearm prohibition anyway – some "violent crimes" can be charged as misdemeanors too.[53] Being convicted of any of these "violent crimes," whether a felony or misdemeanor and whether the conviction was inside or outside of California, will result in a lifetime firearm prohibition.[54]

If you were previously convicted of one of these "violent crimes," you may be prosecuted for a felony if you possess a firearm thereafter.[55] And even "if probation [was] granted, or if the imposition or execution of [your] sentence [was] suspended," you are still likely to be sentenced to a minimum of six months in jail[56] for possessing a firearm.

## D. California Restrictions for Certain Misdemeanor Convictions

If a California misdemeanor conviction has a firearm restriction, it *usually* lasts ten years, but some have lifetime prohibitions.

---

[49] P.C. § 19.2.

[50] *See* 18 U.S.C. § 922(g)(1).

[51] *See* P.C. §§ 29900, 29905.

[52] A full list of "violent crimes" is given in P.C. § 29905.

[53] *People v. Sanchez*, 211 Cal.App.3d 477, 483 (1989) (defendant's conviction for a "violent offense" prohibited him from possessing a firearm without regard to the misdemeanor status of the conviction). Thus, both felonies and misdemeanor convictions can be prohibiting offenses under P.C. § 29900.

[54] *People v. Jaffe*, 19 Cal.Rptr.3d 689, 698-699 (2004), *rev. granted and opinion superseded*, 19 Cal.Rptr.3d 695 (2005).

[55] *See* P.C. § 29900(a)(1).

[56] P.C. § 29900(a)(3).

Convictions for the following misdemeanors result in a lifetime prohibition from possessing firearms:

- P.C. §§ 245(a)(2)-(3) and 245(d) – Assault with a firearm.[57]
- P.C. § 246 – Shooting at an inhabited or occupied dwelling house, building, vehicle, aircraft, housecar, or camper.[58]
- P.C. § 417(c) – Brandishing a firearm in the presence of a peace officer.[59]
- P.C. § 417(a)(2) – Two or more convictions of brandishing a firearm.[60]

Misdemeanor convictions for the following Penal Code sections result in a 10-year prohibition:

- P.C. § 71 – Threatening public officers, employers, and schools officials.
- P.C. § 76 – Threatening certain public officers, appointees, judges, staff, or their families, with the intent and apparent ability to carry out the threat.
- P.C. § 136.1 – Intimidating witnesses or victims.
- P.C. § 136.5 – Possessing a deadly weapon with the intent to intimidate a witness.
- P.C. § 140 – Threatening witnesses, victims, or informants.
- P.C. § 148(d) – Attempting to remove or take a firearm from the person or immediate presence of a public or peace officer.
- P.C. § 171b – Unauthorized possession of a weapon in a courtroom, courthouse, or court building, or at a public meeting.
- P.C. § 171c(a)(1) – Bringing or possessing loaded firearms in the state capitol, legislative offices, etc.
- P.C. § 171d – Bringing or possessing loaded firearms in the Governor's Mansion or residence of other constitutional officers.
- P.C. § 186.28 – Supplying, selling or giving firearm possession to anyone to participate in criminal street gangs.
- P.C. §§ 240, 241 – Assault.

---

[57] P.C. §§ 29800(a)(1) (incorporating portions of section 23515), 23515; *see also Firearms Prohibiting Categories*, CALIFORNIA DEPT. OF JUSTICE - BUREAU OF FIREARMS, http://oag.ca.gov/sites/all/files/pdfs/firearms/forms/prohibcatmisd.pdf (last visited July 27, 2012).

[58] P.C. §§ 29800(a)(1) (incorporating portions of section 23515), 23515; *see also Firearms Prohibiting Categories*, CALIFORNIA DEPT. OF JUSTICE - BUREAU OF FIREARMS, http://oag.ca.gov/sites/all/files/pdfs/firearms/forms/prohibcatmisd.pdf (last visited July 27, 2012).

[59] P.C. §§ 29800(a)(1) (incorporating portions of section 23515), 23515; *see also Firearms Prohibiting Categories*, CALIFORNIA DEPT. OF JUSTICE - BUREAU OF FIREARMS, http://oag.ca.gov/sites/all/files/pdfs/firearms/forms/prohibcatmisd.pdf (last visited July 27, 2012).

[60] P.C. § 29800(a)(2); *see also Firearms Prohibiting Categories*, CALIFORNIA DEPT. OF JUSTICE - BUREAU OF FIREARMS, http://oag.ca.gov/sites/all/files/pdfs/firearms/forms/prohibcatmisd.pdf (last visited July 27, 2012).

- P.C. §§ 242, 243 – Battery.
- P.C. § 243.4 – Sexual battery.
- P.C. § 244.5 – Assault with a stun gun or taser.
- P.C. § 245 – Assault with a deadly weapon other than a firearm, or with force likely to produce great bodily injury.[61]
- P.C. § 245.5 – Assault with a deadly weapon or instrument by any means likely to produce great bodily injury, or with a stun gun or taser on school employee engaged in performing their duties.
- P.C. § 246.3 – Discharging a firearm in a grossly negligent manner.
- P.C. § 247 – Shooting at an unoccupied aircraft, motor vehicle, or uninhabited building or dwelling house.
- P.C. § 273.5 – Inflicting corporal injury on a spouse or significant other.
- P.C. § 273.6 – Wilfully violating a domestic restraining order.
- P.C. § 417 – Drawing, exhibiting, or using a deadly weapon other than a firearm.
- P.C. § 417.6 – Inflicting serious bodily injury as a result of brandishing.
- P.C. § 422 – Threatening to commit a crime that will result in death or great bodily injury to another person.
- P.C. § 626.9 – Bringing or possessing firearms in or upon public schools or grounds.
- P.C. § 646.9 – Stalking.
- P.C. § 830.95 – Wearing of peace officer uniform while picketing or other informational activities.
- P.C. § 17500 – Possessing a deadly weapon to intentionally commit an assault.
- P.C. § 17510 – Carrying firearm or deadly weapon while engaged in labor-related picketing.
- P.C. § 25300 – Criminal possession of a firearm.
- P.C. § 25800 – Armed criminal action.
- P.C. § 26100(b) or (d) – Driver of any vehicle who knowingly allows another person to discharge a firearm from the vehicle, or anyone who willfully and maliciously discharges a firearm from a motor vehicle themselves.
- P.C. § 27510 – Firearms dealer who sells, transfers, or gives firearm possession to a minor or a handgun to anyone under age 21, or person or corporation who sells any concealable firearm to a minor.

---

[61] *See Rash v. Lungren,* 59 Cal.App.4th 1233, 1235-1239 (1997) (indicating conviction for assault with a firearm under P.C. § 245(a)(2) results in a lifetime firearm prohibition because it is specifically listed in former P.C. § 12001.6 (former P.C. § 12021(a); current P.C. § 23515). It is also a lifetime prohibition under former P.C. § 12021.1 (current P.C. §§ 29900-29905)).

- P.C. § 27590(c) – Various violations involving the sale and transfer of firearms.
- P.C. § 30315 – Possessing ammunition designed to penetrate metal or armor.
- P.C. § 32625 – Unauthorized machinegun possession/transportation.
- W.I.C. § 871.5 – Bringing or sending contraband into or possession within juvenile hall. (The contraband must be a firearm for purposes of this restriction).
- W.I.C. § 1001.5 – Bringing or sending contraband into a youth authority institution. (The contraband must be a firearm for purposes of this restriction).
- W.I.C. § 8100 – Purchasing, possessing, or receiving a firearm or deadly weapon while receiving in-patient treatment for a mental disorder, or by someone who has threatened serious physical violence to a licensed psychotherapist against an identifiable victim.
- W.I.C. § 8101 – Providing a firearm or deadly weapon to someone described in W.I.C. § 8100 or 8103.
- W.I.C. § 8103 – Purchasing, possessing, or receiving a firearm or deadly weapon by someone adjudicated a mentally disordered sex offender, or incompetent to stand trial, not guilty by reason of insanity, or placed under conservatorship.[62]

Despite the very specific code sections listed here, one California court ruled that certain related code sections also carry a firearm restriction upon conviction. In one case a juvenile was convicted of P.C. § 243.6 (battery on a school official), and the court decided that because the *definition* of battery (P.C. § 242) and the *offense* of battery (P.C. § 243) were prohibiting offenses, so too should a conviction for P.C. § 243.6, which is not on the list.[63] Therefore, the juvenile was considered prohibited as if convicted of a crime on the list of prohibitions.

---

[62] P.C. § 29805; *Firearms Prohibiting Categories*, CALIFORNIA DEPT. OF JUSTICE - BUREAU OF FIREARMS, http:// oag.ca.gov/sites/all/files/pdfs/firearms/forms/prohibcatmisd.pdf (last visited July 27, 2012).
[63] *In re David S.*, 133 Cal.App.4th 1160, 1163-1168 (2005).

# E. Federal Restrictions for Misdemeanor Crime of Domestic Violence (MCDV)

An MCDV occurs when someone is convicted of an offense that has, as an element,[64] the use or attempted use of physical force or the threatened use of a deadly weapon, and that the accused either:

- is "a current or former spouse, parent, or guardian of the victim[;]"
- "shares a child in common" with the victim; or
- is living, or has lived, "with the victim as a spouse, parent, or guardian, or . . .
- [is] similarly situated to a spouse, parent, or guardian of the victim . . ."[65]

An MCDV is a misdemeanor offense under federal, state, and tribal law,[66] but still triggers a lifetime ban under federal law.[67] You are not considered, however, to have been "convicted" of an MCDV if you: (1) were represented by counsel or waived your right to be represented by counsel and (2) if entitled to a jury trial you either tried the case, waived your right to have the case tried by a jury by entering a guilty plea, or waived your right to a jury trial by some other way.[68] That being said, it is highly unlikely that a California judge would allow your guilty or no contest plea without attorney representation or a jury trial unless you properly waived your rights to both first.

## 1. California Offenses that May Be a Misdemeanor Crime of Domestic Violence (MCDV)

Two California Penal Code sections are typically considered "domestic violence" statutes – P.C. § 273.5 and P.C. § 243(e) – but as further discussed below, other California crimes can be considered "domestic violence" to which the federal MCDV lifetime firearm restriction applies.[69]

---

[64] *See United States v. Hayes*, 555 U.S. 415, 422 (2009) (citing Black's Law Dictionary 559 (8th ed. 2004) that defined an element as "[a] constituent part of a claim that must be proved for the claim to succeed."). For example, one of the elements of speeding is that the prosecutor must prove that the defendant was going faster than the speed limit.

[65] 18 U.S.C. § 921(a)(33)(A)(ii). *See also United States v. Hayes*, 555 U.S. 415 (2009).

[66] 18 U.S.C. § 921(a)(33)(A)(i).

[67] *See* 18 U.S.C. § 922(g)(9).

[68] 18 U.S.C. § 921(a)(33)(B)(i).

[69] 18 U.S.C. § 922(g)(9). Pursuant to P.C. § 29805, a P.C. § 273.5 or P.C. § 243 misdemeanor conviction results in a 10-year California firearm restriction.

### a. Injuring a Spouse or Cohabitant

Injuring a former or current spouse or cohabitant under P.C. § 273.5 is an MCDV under federal law because it includes using or attempting to use physical force or threatening to use a deadly weapon[70] against a spouse or former spouse, cohabitant,[71] or mother or father of one's child[72] and results in a traumatic physical injury.

### b. Battery Against Spouse, Cohabitant, Fiancé(e), Etc.

A conviction under P.C. § 243(e) does not necessarily result in a federal MCDV firearm restriction, but it may. You can be charged under P.C. § 243(e) if you commit a battery[73] and the victim is a spouse, someone you are cohabiting with, someone who is the parent of your child, a former spouse, fiancé(e), or someone you are, or were, dating.[74]

Note that a fiancé(e) or someone you are or were dating or were engaged to does not necessarily meet the definition of a victim under the federal MCDV statute.[75] This means that if you are convicted of a P.C. § 243(e) battery where the victim is one of these people, you may not have a federal lifetime firearm prohibition under 18 U.S.C. § 922(g)(9) because it may not be considered an MCDV. The facts of your relationship need to be further analyzed to determine if the "victim" in the case meets the definition of persons that trigger the restriction.

### 2. Other California Crimes that May Be Considered a Misdemeanor Crime of Domestic Violence (MCDV)

Other California crimes that may be considered an MCDV conviction include assault (P.C. § 240), battery (P.C. § 242), assault with a deadly weapon or force likely to produce great bodily injury (P.C. § 245), and fighting, noise, and offensive words (P.C. § 415).

To determine whether a misdemeanor conviction qualifies as an MCDV under federal law, the California DOJ will first consider the initial charges. Except for being convicted of P.C. § 273.5 (injuring a spouse or cohabitant), whether a conviction has an MCDV restriction requires more investigation. If necessary, the California DOJ will review the court file or plea form for additional facts to determine the nature of the relation-

---

[70] 18 U.S.C. § 921(a)(33)(A)(ii).

[71] *See People v. Holifield,* 205 Cal.App.3d 993, 999-1000 (1999) (providing that for purposes of section 273.5, the term "cohabiting" means "something more than a platonic, rooming-house arrangement . . . [it] means an unrelated man and woman living together in a substantial relationship – one manifested, minimally, by permanence and sexual or amorous intimacy.").

[72] P.C. § 273.5(a).

[73] As discussed below, a "battery" meets the "use of force" requirement for an MCDV.

[74] P.C. § 243(e) (emphasis added).

[75] 18 U.S.C. § 921(a)(33)(A).

ship between the convicted person and the victim. Based on that research, the California DOJ should be able to determine the individual's eligibility based on the conviction and the facts of the case. Sometimes there is confusion in this process that warrants getting an attorney involved to resolve the problem.

Defense attorneys will often try to "plea down" a domestic violence charge to something milder than a P.C. § 273.5 conviction (either a P.C. §§ 242, 243(e), or 415(1)). But beware in doing this because the California DOJ will look at the initial charge of P.C. § 273.5, and if the person has pled to a P.C. § 242 or P.C. § 415, they may still consider the person automatically convicted of an MCDV. This is because the DOJ will assume that if the person was originally charged with a P.C. § 273.5, there are sufficient facts to believe the person was convicted of an MCDV.

If you are facing criminal charges, be sure you discuss all of the possible ramifications of a conviction with your attorney. If your attorney cannot give you answers, or you are concerned that your attorney does not know these answers, you should seek assistance from other counsel.

## F. Juvenile Offenses

California prohibits any person declared "a ward of the juvenile court" from possessing firearms under age 30 per W.I.C. § 602.[76] Prohibitive juvenile offenses include all crimes listed under W.I.C. § 707(b), P.C. § 1203.073(b), P.C. § 29805, and P.C. §§ 25400(a), 25850, and 26100(a).[77]

## G. Persons on Probation or Parole

In some cases, courts may prohibit someone convicted of a crime from owning and possessing firearms or "deadly or dangerous weapons" even if the law itself does not require it. This generally occurs as a probation condition.[78] You will be prohibited as a result of a probation or parole condition for as long as the conditions last. Pursuant to the Full Faith and Credit Clause of the U.S. Constitution, these conditions, like orders issued in restraining orders, travel across state lines.[79]

---

[76] P.C. § 29820(b).

[77] P.C. § 29820(a).

[78] P.C. § 29815.

[79] *Firearms and Full Faith and Credit, Judges Guide to Domestic Violence Cases,* CALIFORNIA COURTS, http://www2.courtinfo.ca.gov/protem/pubs/firearms.pdf (last visited Aug. 6, 2012).

## H. Notice Required

Under California law, if you are convicted of any offenses listed in P.C. §§ 29800 or 29805, courts must notify you at the time of judgment that you are prohibited from owning, purchasing, receiving, possessing, or having custody or control of any firearm. The notice must include a form to facilitate the transfer of any firearms you may have.[80] A court's failure to provide this notice, however, is not a defense to later being prosecuted for possessing firearms while prohibited.[81] Because of this, there are probably hundreds of people in California who possess firearms and are unaware they are prohibited as a result of a criminal conviction.

# VIII. APPLICATION OF EX POST FACTO PROHIBITIONS ON FIREARM POSSESSION

California and federal courts have held that it is constitutional to convict someone for possessing a firearm as a prohibited person even though the conviction for the firearm prohibition resulted from an offense that at the time of conviction had no firearm prohibition attached to it.[82]

This means that it does not matter if you were convicted *before* your offense later included a firearm prohibition. Because you are *now* in a class of persons the legislature has decided to prohibit from possessing firearms, you can be prosecuted for possessing a firearm based on your previous conviction,[83] even though your conviction occurred before the restriction was added to the code.

## A. The Effect of a California Conviction in Other States

Firearm restrictions resulting from certain California convictions generally only apply while you are in California. Once in another state, however, you may lawfully possess firearms while there.[84] Sometimes people living outside California discover that their California conviction prohibits them from owning and possessing firearms in their current state of residence. This is usually a result of a federal restriction or that person's new state of residence treating the California conviction as if it had happened in the

---

[80] P.C. § 29810(a).

[81] P.C. § 29810(b). Courts, historically, failed to give this notice, although they are getting better at providing it.

[82] *People v. Mesce*, 52 Cal.App.4th 618, 622-626 (1997); *Helmer v. Miller*, 19 Cal.App.4th 1565, 1570-1571 (1993); *United States v. Wilhelm*, 65 Fed.Appx. 619, 620 (9th Cir. 2003).

[83] *United States v. Collins*, 61 F.3d 1379, 1382-1383 (9th Cir. 1995).

[84] *People v. Laino*, 32 Cal.4th 878, 889 (2004) (citing *Huntington v. Attrill*, 146 U.S. 657 (1892)); *Williams v. North Carolina*, 317 U.S. 287, 296 (1942).

new home state, thereby subjecting the person to that state's firearm prohibition laws. This means that if you reside in, or visit another state, you must look to that other state's law to determine whether your conviction restricts you in that other state.[85]

Some states also have their own procedures for restoring firearm rights lost because of offenses occurring in a different state, while other states require that the conviction be addressed in the state where it occurred. Contacting an attorney in your new state is best to see if the conviction can be addressed there. If nothing can be done there, you should discuss what can be done to restore your firearm rights with a California attorney. But, as discussed below, California has limited options for vacating convictions or restoring firearm rights under federal law.

To be clear, as mentioned above, California felony convictions prohibit firearm possession in all 50 states under federal law (because a California felony is punishable by more than one year in state prison). This means that California felony convictions prohibit firearm possession under federal law no matter where the person resides.[86] Similarly an MCDV conviction carries a lifetime prohibition under federal law.[87]

# IX. RESTORING FIREARM POSSESSION RIGHTS AFTER A CRIMINAL CONVICTION

If you are restricted from possessing firearms because of a criminal conviction under California law, relief under current law is unlikely. With the exception of reducing your conviction from a felony to a misdemeanor, or waiting until the 10-year misdemeanor restriction expires, chances are the only option available to you is the unlikely granting of a pardon from the governor or, in some cases, the president.[88]

---

[85] Whether you are prohibited from possessing firearms in any state may be unclear from a plain reading of the law. If you have been convicted of a misdemeanor anywhere, it is a good idea to check with an attorney practicing in the state where you plan to travel while possessing a firearm to find out whether your conviction means a firearm restriction in that other state.

[86] 18 U.S.C. § 922(g)(1).

[87] 18 U.S.C. § 922(g)(9).

[88] There are certain situations where a Second Amendment claim to restore your firearm rights may be appropriate, but these claims are very tricky and their merit remains unsettled. An experienced attorney would be crucial to even have a chance at prevailing.

## A. Restoring Firearm Rights for California Felony Convictions

If you have a California felony conviction, with few exceptions, you have two options to restore your firearm rights:

- Request a California court reduce your felony to a misdemeanor; or
- Petition the governor for a pardon.[89]

### 1. Reducing a Felony Conviction to a Misdemeanor

To reduce a felony conviction to a misdemeanor, the offense must first be categorized as a "wobbler." A "wobbler" is any offense that *can be* charged as either a felony or a misdemeanor.[90] Second, you must have received a punishment other than state prison or county jail pursuant to P.C. §1170(h),[91] or been granted probation but without a sentence being imposed.[92]

Reducing a prohibiting felony to a misdemeanor will generally restore your ability to own and possess firearms under both California and federal law because the crime is thereafter considered a misdemeanor "for all purposes."[93] For certain convictions, however, this is not the case. For example, someone convicted of assault with a firearm under P.C. § 245(a)(2) who later reduces his or her conviction from a felony to a misdemeanor is still prohibited because California prohibits those convicted of P.C. § 245(a)(2) *misdemeanors* from possessing firearms.[94]

Under federal law a felony conviction for a "wobbler" that is reduced to a misdemeanor will no longer be considered prohibiting,[95] unless the felony that is reduced meets the definition of an MCDV.

---

[89] P.C. §§ 4852.01, 4852.21.

[90] *Garcia-Lopez v. Ashcroft*, 334 F.3d 840, 844 (9th Cir. 2003); P.C. § 17(b).

[91] Because of state prison overcrowding, the California legislature has revised the Penal Code to allow certain felony offenses to be punishable with county jail sentences while remaining felony convictions. P.C. § 1170 reflects this change.

[92] P.C. § 17(b)(3).

[93] *Gebremicael v. California Comm'n. on Teacher Credentialing*, 118 Cal.App.4th 1477, 1483 (2004); *see also United States v. Marks*, 379 F.3d 1114, 1117 (9th Cir. 2004).

[94] P.C. § 29800(a)(1). P.C. §§ 29805 (criminalizing possession of a handgun while making 29800(a) an exception to the 10-year restriction), 29800(a)(1) (incorporating portions of section 23515), 23515 (incorporating portions of section 245).

[95] *United States v. Marks*, 379 F.3d 1114, 1117 (9th Cir. 2004).

## 2. Obtaining a Pardon

To pardon a felony, a California resident will typically first need to receive a court order, known as a Certification of Rehabilitation.[96] Generally any felons still residing in California may apply to the superior court for this Certificate as long as they show rehabilitation as required by law.[97] The court then forwards this Certificate to the governor's office.[98] Just because the governor receives the Certificate, however, does not at all guarantee a pardon will be granted, and the process can also take up to two years or more.

Additionally, if a "dangerous weapon" was used in the offense leading to your felony conviction, you will still be considered prohibited under both California and federal law from possessing firearms,[99] and it is unlikely you will ever be able to own or possess a firearm again.[100]

But as long as your conviction did not involve a "dangerous weapon," a gubernatorial pardon should restore your firearm rights under California and federal law.

Also, even if you cannot obtain a Certificate of Rehabilitation, you can still try to get a pardon. You can petition the governor directly and apply for a direct pardon[101] even if you have a conviction for a misdemeanor, certain sex offenses, or a felony, and reside outside California, which would otherwise preclude you from obtaining the Certificate of Rehabilitation.

## B. Restoring Rights for Federal Law Restrictions

Those with a federal restriction because of a felony conviction, a misdemeanor conviction punishable by more than two years in prison, or an MCDV conviction are not considered prohibited if the conviction has been expunged, set aside, or pardoned, or if the person has had his or her civil rights restored, unless any of these methods expressly provided that the person may not ship, transport, possess, or receive firearms.[102] Unfortunately, with the limited exception of a pardon, none of these methods, including an expungement or a "set aside," are currently available in Cali-

---

[96] *People v. Parker*, 141 Cal.App.4th 1297, 1303 (2006).

[97] P.C. § 4852.06.

[98] For Certificate of Rehabilitation laws, see P.C. §§ 4852.01-4852.21.

[99] P.C. §§ 4852.17, 4854.

[100] *See Helmer v. Miller*, 19 Cal.App.4th 1565, 1569-1570 (1993) (P.C. "[s]ection 4852.01 et seq. allows a felon to petition for a certificate of rehabilitation and pardon. [P.C.] § 4852.17 specifically restores the right to possess firearms unless the felony resulting in the firearms restriction involved the use of a dangerous weapon.").

[101] *See How to Apply for a Pardon*, CALIFORNIA DEPT. OF CORRECTIONS & REHABILITATION, http://gov.ca.gov/docs/How_To_Apply_for_a_Pardon.pdf (last visited July 27, 2012) on how to apply for a pardon and certificate of rehabilitation.

[102] 18 U.S.C. §§ 921(a)(20)(B), (a)(33)(B)(ii).

fornia to restore firearm rights. This means that in some cases it is more difficult for Californians with lifetime firearm prohibitions resulting from an MCDV conviction to restore firearm rights than it is for felons, because some felons can reduce their conviction to a misdemeanor.

This is because, to restore civil rights, they first must actually be "lost." Civil rights commonly associated with criminal convictions are the rights to vote, hold office, and serve on a jury.[103] Under California law these rights are not "lost" because of a misdemeanor conviction. With nothing "lost," there is nothing to restore.[104] Therefore, you cannot use this federal remedy for a California misdemeanor conviction.[105]

## C. Restoring Rights for Convictions Other Than Those under California Law

There is no remedy to restore your firearm rights under *California law* if they were lost as a result of a *federal* conviction. Accordingly, federal convictions must be addressed in the federal court where the conviction took place or by seeking a pardon from the president.

Felony convictions from other states also need to be addressed in the other state's courts because there is no California law for those convictions to be addressed in a California court.

To be clear, if you have been convicted of a felony[106] anywhere within the United States outside of California, you are still prohibited from possessing firearms under California law, and you cannot address that conviction in a California court.

## D. Exceptions for Federal Law Restrictions

The federal firearm restrictions, except for those from an MCDV conviction, do not apply to possessing any firearm or ammunition imported for the U.S. or any of its departments or agencies, or to any state or any of its departments, agencies, or political subdivisions.[107] This means that if you meet the foregoing exception, you can have a murder conviction and still possess

---

[103] *Logan v. United States*, 552 U.S. 23, 28 (2007).

[104] *Logan v. United States*, 552 U.S. 23, 31 (2007).

[105] Whether losing firearm rights constitutes a loss of civil rights, and whether these rights are restored when the 10-year firearm restriction expires for certain misdemeanor convictions, is currently being litigated. *Enos v. Holder*, No. 2:10–CV–2911–JAM–EFB, 2011 WL 2681249 (E.D. Cal. July 8, 2011). The court in *Enos* granted the defendant's motion to dismiss, and the plaintiffs have appealed to the Ninth Circuit Court of Appeals. *See Enos v. Holder*, 2011 WL 2681249 (E.D. Cal. 2011), *appeal docketed*, No. 12-15498 (9th Cir. Mar. 8, 2012).

[106] Assuming the "felony" is a prohibiting offense under federal law.

[107] 18 U.S.C. § 925(a)(1).

firearms in the military, but someone with a mere MCDV cannot possess firearms in serving the country. This restriction has caused a lot of soldiers to be "Lautenberged"[108] out of the armed forces (*i.e.*, kicked out of the armed forces because they cannot possess a firearm as a result of an MCDV).

## E. Expungements

Contrary to popular belief, a California law expungement has no effect on restoring firearm rights in California,[109] and there is no "expungement" available under federal law. The California law expungement allows you to withdraw a guilty or no contest plea or "set aside" a guilty verdict, but the expungement does not erase the conviction from your record. You are still considered to have been "convicted" if you get in trouble with the law again.[110] You are merely " 'released from all penalties … resulting from the offense.' "[111] And an expungement under this section does not allow you to "own, possess, or have in [your] custody or control any firearm..."[112] So, even after "expunging" a prohibiting offense under California law, you still cannot lawfully possess a firearm under either California or federal law.

Expungement in California does not restore firearm rights for a federal restriction because, as explained above, it specifically keeps any firearm restrictions in place.[113] And, because your conviction can still be used against you in a later prosecution if you violate the law, the California expungement is not considered a true "set aside" or a federally recognized expungement to remove the firearm restriction.[114]

## F. Defunct Federal Law for Firearm Rights Restoration

If you were restricted under federal law "from possessing, shipping, transporting, or receiving firearms or ammunition" you used to be able to apply to the U.S. Attorney General to remove the restriction.[115] Unfortunately this remedy has been unavailable since 1992[116] because Congress has re-

---

[108] A slang term referencing the author of the MCDV restriction, Senator Lautenberg from New Jersey.

[109] P.C. § 1203.4(a).

[110] P.C. § 1203.4(a).

[111] *People v. Frawley*, 82 Cal.App.4th 784, 791 (2000).

[112] P.C. § 1203.4(a)(2).

[113] P.C. § 1203.4(a)(2); *People v. Frawley*, 82 Cal.App.4th 784, 791 (2000).

[114] *See Jennings v. Mukasey*, 511 F.3d 894, 898-899 (9th Cir. 2007) ("This provision [P.C. § 1203.4] alone precludes any notion that the term 'expungement' accurately describes the relief allowed by statute." (quoting *People v. Frawley*, 82 Cal.App.4th 784 , 791-792 (2000)).

[115] 18 U.S.C. § 925(c).

[116] *United States v. Bean*, 537 U.S. 71, 74-75 (2002).

peatedly barred using appropriated funds to investigate or act on relief applications.[117]

## G. Restoring Rights after a California Misdemeanor Conviction

Under California law, if you have a misdemeanor conviction with a firearm restriction, there are only three ways you may be able to restore your firearm rights. First, if your misdemeanor was added to California's list of prohibiting offenses in P.C. § 29805 after your conviction, you can ask the court for relief.[118] Second, if you are a peace officer[119] whose employment or livelihood depends on possessing a firearm, you may be able to lift the restriction for certain offenses by petitioning the court and proving you are likely to use firearms "in a safe and lawful manner."[120]

Unfortunately, if your misdemeanor conviction does not fall within either of those two scenarios, restoring your firearm rights during the restricted period is unlikely without your third option, a gubernatorial pardon. Additionally, even if your firearm rights are restored under California law pursuant to any of the first two scenarios, you may still be prohibited under federal law, if the conviction is prohibiting, because these remedies are not federally recognized as a "set aside," expungement, or a pardon of your conviction.

## H. Modification of Probation or Parole Conditions

Sometimes those subject to firearm restrictions by probation or parole terms may request their terms be modified or terminated early to eliminate the restrictions.[121] If you are faced with such a condition, you or your lawyer may be able to negotiate a shorter restriction or probationary period.

---

[117] *See* S. 3636, 111th Cong. (2010); *S. 3636*, THOMAS (LIBRARY OF CONGRESS), http://thomas.loc.gov/home/gpoxmlc111/s3636_pcs.xml (last visited July. 27, 2012).

[118] P.C. § 29860. Most of these sections were added more than ten years ago; thus, very few people today can use this option, though some may still, or will, be able to in the future.

[119] As described in P.C. §§ 830.1, 830.2, 830.31, 830.32, 830.33, or 830.5.

[120] P.C. § 29855 (offenses eligible for such relief include violations of P.C. §§ 273.5, 273.6, or 646.9). *See also In re Evans*, 49 Cal.App.4th 1263, 1267 (1996).

[121] P.C. § 1203.3.

# X. DRUG ADDICTION FIREARM POSSESSION PROHIBITIONS

If you are considered to be addicted to narcotic drugs, you are also prohibited from possessing firearms under California law.[122] The rationale for this restriction is that those who are addicted to using narcotics "present a clear and present danger to society" because addicts are often forced to purchase drugs through criminal acts or corruption.[123]

Narcotic drugs are specifically defined under California's Health and Safety Code and include opium and cocaine.[124] Marijuana is not included in the California law definition of narcotic drugs. Users, and even marijuana addicts, are thus not per se prohibited from owning or receiving firearms under California law.

The same is not true, however, under federal law. Federal law extends firearm prohibitions to "unlawful users" of any "controlled substance."[125] This includes not just narcotics, but marijuana.[126] The ATF defines "unlawful user" and a "controlled substance" addict as:

A person who uses a controlled substance and has lost the power of self-control with reference to the use of controlled substance; and any person who is a current user of a controlled substance in a manner other than as prescribed by a licensed physician.[127]

Though this definition seems to *exclude* users of medical marijuana if prescribed to them by a licensed physician, the ATF has expressly said that it does *not*.[128]

Though the ATF's letter does not have the force of law, it is a strong indicator of the federal government's position that it will prosecute violations. Several courts have also supported the ATF's view.[129]

Federal regulation 27 C.F.R. § 478.11 also guides the determination of whether someone is an "unlawful user" of a "controlled substance." Some

---

[122] P.C. § 29800(a).

[123] *People v. Washington*, 237 Cal.App.2d 59, 66 (1965).

[124] Cal. Health & Saf. Code § 11019.

[125] The term "controlled substance" is defined in 21 U.S.C. § 802.

[126] 18 U.S.C. § 922(g)(3).

[127] 27 C.F.R. § 478.11.

[128] *Open Letter to All Federal Firearms Licensees*, U.S. Dept. of Justice – Bureau of Alcohol, Tobacco, Firearms and Explosives, http://www.atf.gov/press/releases/2011/09/092611-atf-open-letter-to-all-ffls-marijuana-for-medicinal-purposes.pdf (last visited July 27, 2012).

[129] *See, e.g.*, *United States v. Harvey*, 794 F.Supp.2d 1103, 1105-1106 (S.D. Cal. 2011) (providing that Schedule I drugs like marijuana cannot be lawfully prescribed because other federally defined prescription drug "schedules" intentionally omit Schedule I drugs; and citing several U.S. Supreme Court and California cases purportedly supporting its position).

courts have held that the government must show a defendant's "pattern, and recency, of drug use … or that the … use was 'sufficiently consistent, 'prolonged' and close in time to … possession'" of a firearm.[130] This can be as simple as using drugs while possessing a firearm.[131]

# XI. MENTAL HEALTH FIREARM RESTRICTIONS

Under California law, if you have been found to suffer from certain mental health conditions, you are also prohibited from owning and possessing firearms and deadly weapons.[132] "Deadly weapon," as used here and in W.I.C. §§ 8101, 8102, and 8103, means possessing or carrying any concealed weapon that is prohibited by P.C. § 16590 (i.e., "generally prohibited weapons").[133] Law enforcement often believe "deadly weapon" includes all weapons (bows, BB guns, knives, etc.) and ammunition and therefore incorrectly confiscate or charge the individual for violating the law.

The length of, and availability for relief from, these restrictions depends on the nature of the mental condition. For example, individuals are prohibited from owning and possessing firearms and deadly weapons while they are admitted (either with or without their consent) to a facility to receive inpatient treatment and are deemed by the health professional primarily responsible for the patient's treatment as a danger to themselves or others, as specified in W.I.C. §§ 5150, 5250, or 5300.[134] There is no "inpatient" prohibition once they are discharged from the facility, but they may still be prohibited for any of the reasons below.[135]

## A. Threatening a Psychotherapist

If you communicate "a serious threat of physical violence against a reasonably identifiable victim or victims[]" to a licensed psychotherapist, starting from the date the psychotherapist reports the threat to a local law enforcement agency, you are prohibited from possessing firearms and deadly weapons for a period of six months.[136] The California DOJ is required to mail notice of the restriction to the restricted person who may thereafter

---

[130] *United States v. Williams*, 216 F.Supp.2d 568, 575 (E.D. Va. 2002).

[131] *United States v. Oleson*, 310 F.3d 1085, 1089-1090 (8th Cir. 2002); *United States v. Herrera*, 313 F.3d 882, 885 (5th Cir. 2002).

[132] W.I.C. §§ 8100, 8103.

[133] W.I.C. § 8100(e).

[134] W.I.C. § 8100(a). Danger to self, as used in subdivision (a), means one who has made a serious threat of, or attempted, suicide with the use of a firearm or other deadly weapon. W.I.C. § 8100(f).

[135] W.I.C. § 8100(a).

[136] W.I.C. § 8100(b)(1).

request a hearing to restore his or her firearm rights during the restriction period.[137]

## B. Mental Disorders, Illnesses, or Disordered Sex Offenders

Those who "ha[ve] been adjudicated by a[ny] court … to be a danger to others … [because] of a mental disorder or mental illness, or who ha[ve] been adjudicated to be a mentally disordered sex offender[]" are prohibited from possessing firearms or deadly weapons.[138] Firearm rights may be restored, however, if the same court that adjudicated the mental illness or disorder issues a certificate, either at or after that person's release from treatment, stating the person is now safe to possess a firearm or any other deadly weapon, as long as the person has not been adjudicated again to be a danger to others as a result of a mental disorder or illness before asking for this certificate.[139]

## C. Not Guilty by Reason of Insanity

If you have been found not guilty of any crime by reason of insanity, you cannot purchase or receive, or attempt to purchase or receive, or have under your control any firearm or other deadly weapon.[140] Certain serious offenses have a lifetime firearm restriction without any available relief.[141] For all other less serious convictions where individuals are found not guilty by reason of insanity, firearm rights may be restored if the court finds they have recovered their sanity.[142]

## D. Incompetence to Stand Trial

Someone found to be mentally incompetent to stand trial is likewise prohibited from owning and possessing firearms unless his or her competence to stand trial has been restored by the committing court.[143]

---

[137] W.I.C. §§ 8100(b)(2)-(b)(3).

[138] W.I.C. § 8103(a)(1).

[139] W.I.C. § 8103(a)(1).

[140] W.I.C. §§ 8103(b)-(c); *see also* P.C. § 1026.

[141] W.I.C. § 8103(b)(1). Refer directly to W.I.C. § 8103(b)(1) for a list of offenses.

[142] W.I.C. § 8103(c)(1). *See* P.C. § 1026.2 for recovering sanity.

[143] W.I.C. § 8103(d)(1).

## E. Individuals under Conservatorship

Someone placed under conservatorship who is gravely disabled by a mental disorder or chronic alcoholism cannot possess a firearm or deadly weapon while under the conservatorship if, at the time the conservatorship was ordered, the court found that possession of a firearm or deadly weapon by the individual would present a danger to the individual or others. Here again, courts must notify the person placed under conservatorship of the firearm restriction. Like those committed to a treatment program, the firearm restriction can last the duration of the conservatorship or be lifted by the court if it finds that the individuals no longer present a danger to themselves or others.[144]

## F. Dangerous or Gravely Disabled Persons

Persons in custody under W.I.C. § 5150 because they are a danger to themselves or others and are admitted to a designated facility may not possess a firearm or deadly weapon for five years after they are released from the facility.[145] A 5150 commitment usually occurs after a peace officer or medical health care professional determines the individuals are a danger to themselves or others, or are gravely disabled and have been placed in a mental health treatment facility for 72-hour treatment and evaluation.[146]

Before or at the time of discharge, the facility is required to notify individuals that they are "prohibited from owning, possessing, controlling, receiving, or purchasing any firearm for a period of five years."[147] Individuals shall also be notified of their right to request a hearing to restore their firearm rights.[148] Failure by the facility, however, to provide either notice will not necessarily prevent prosecution of the person for possessing firearms.

## G. Those Committed to Intensive Treatment

If you are to undergo intensive treatment per W.I.C. §§ 5250, 5260, or 5270.15, you also cannot possess any firearm or deadly weapon for five years.[149] Lifting this state restriction is similar to restoring firearm rights for someone with a 5150 commitment, though, unlike a 5150 where the

---

[144] W.I.C. § 8103(e).

[145] W.I.C. § 8103(f)(1).

[146] W.I.C. § 5150.

[147] W.I.C. § 8103(f)(3).

[148] W.I.C. § 8103(f)(3). The procedure for restoring firearm rights after a 5150 commitment is governed by W.I.C. §§ 8103(f)(4)-(9).

[149] W.I.C. § 8103(g)(1). Restoring rights for *state* restrictions is governed by W.I.C. §§ 8103(g)(3)-(4). You are also subject to a federal lifetime ban.

government has the legal burden, these restrictions require *you* to prove that firearms will be used in a safe and lawful manner.[150]

## H. Federal Mental Health Restrictions

Federal law prohibits those "adjudicated as a mental defective or who ha[ve] been committed to a mental institution[]" from owning or possessing firearms for life.[151] No federal statute defines "adjudicated as a mental defective" or "committed to a mental institution." However, this is the Code of Federal Regulations definition:

Adjudicated as a mental defective.

(a) A determination by a court, board, commission, or other lawful authority that a person, as a result of marked subnormal intelligence, or mental illness, incompetency, condition, or disease:

(1) Is a danger to himself or to others; or

(2) Lacks the mental capacity to contract or manage his own affairs.

(b) The term shall include --

(1) A finding of insanity by a court in a criminal case; and

(2) Those persons found incompetent to stand trial or found not guilty by reason of lack of mental responsibility pursuant to articles 50a and 72b of the Uniform Code of Military Justice, 10 U.S.C. 850a, 876b.[152]

. . .

Committed to a mental institution.

A formal commitment of a person to a mental institution by a court, board, commission, or other lawful authority. The term includes a commitment to a mental institution involuntarily. The term includes commitment for mental defectiveness or mental illness. It also includes commitments for other reasons, such as for drug use. The term does not include a person in a mental institution for observation or a voluntary admission to a mental institution.[153]

---

[150] W.I.C. § 8103(g)(4).
[151] 18 U.S.C. § 922(g)(4).
[152] 27 C.F.R. § 478.11.
[153] 27 C.F.R. § 478.11.

## 1.  California Commitments Resulting in Federal Restrictions

Under federal law someone who has been committed to a mental health institution for mental defectiveness, illness, or drug use, is prohibited for life from owning and possessing firearms. Whether someone has been "committed to a mental health institution" is a question of federal law often guided by state law.[154] A commitment pursuant to W.I.C. § 5150 will not result in a federal firearm restriction, but according to DOJ and the FBI, a W.I.C. § 5250 commitment does. While California allows a one-time application with the court to restore firearm rights for an intensive treatment commitment,[155] this has no effect on the *federal* restriction.[156]

## 2.  Restoring Federal Firearm Rights for Mental Health Restrictions

In 2008, the NICS Improvement Act[157] was enacted. In response to the Virginia Tech shootings, Congress outlined a procedure for states to refer mental health records to the NICS program in order to determine a person's eligibility to possess firearms. NICS is supervised by the FBI and is the system that FFLs contact to determine whether would-be purchasers are allowed to lawfully possess firearms.

The NICS Improvement Act not only required mental health information to be transferred to the federal government, but also required states to establish procedures to restore a person's firearm rights for mental health restrictions. In order to receive federal funding, states needed to establish both a medical record transfer program and implement a rights restoration mechanism. Only a few states availed themselves of the funding and implemented these requirements.

When the NICS Improvement Act passed, California already had a state law that satisfied the mental health record referral requirement. So California did not need any additional funds to create the system. However, the problem faced by California residents suffering from a federal mental health firearm restriction is that because California already has the medical record referral system in place, the state has no incentive to pass the firearm rights restoration legislation required by federal law. Consequently California's currently available firearm rights restoration mechanisms do not meet the NICS Improvement Act requirements.

---

[154] *United States v. Whiton*, 48 F.3d 356, 358 (8th Cir. 1995).

[155] W.I.C. § 8103(g)(4).

[156] 18 U.S.C. § 922(g)(4).

[157] NICS Improvement Amendments Act of 2007, Pub. L. No. 110-180, 121 Stat. 2559 (Act effective January 8, 2008); *NICS Improvement Amendments Act of 2007*, U.S. Gov't Printing Office, http://www.gpo.gov/fdsys/pkg/PLAW-110publ180/pdf/PLAW-110publ180.pdf (last visited July 28, 2012).

# XII. RESTRAINING ORDERS AND FIREARM POSSESSION PROHIBITIONS

## A. California Law Restrictions

Under California law, if you are subject to a restraining order, temporary restraining order, or court order under any of the following code sections, you are prohibited from owning, purchasing, receiving, possessing, or attempting to purchase and receive firearms:

- C.C.P. § 527.6 (civil harassment temporary restraining order or injunction).
- C.C.P. § 527.8 (employers seeking a temporary restraining order or an injunction for an employee who has suffered unlawful violence or credible threat of violence).
- C.C.P. § 527.85 (schools seeking temporary restraining orders or injunctions for students who have suffered off-campus credible threats of violence).
- Fam. Code § 6218 (protective orders issued pursuant to Fam. Code §§ 6320, 6321, and 6322).
- P.C. §§ 136.2 and 646.91 (court orders against victim and/or witness intimidation and orders protecting against stalking).
- W.I.C. § 15657.03 (elder or dependent adult abuse).[158]

In instances where a temporary restraining order is issued, and regardless of whether the court issues a permanent restraining order, you are prohibited until the temporary order ends or expires. If you knowingly violate this aspect of the restraining order, you can be held criminally liable for a public offense.[159]

Those served with a restraining order are required to sell their firearms to an FFL or turn the firearms in to law enforcement.[160] These requirements, and the exceptions thereto, are more specifically discussed in Chapter 10.

In certain specific cases the court may grant exemptions from the relinquishment requirement of any of the above mentioned restraining orders[161] for a particular firearm.

---

[158] P.C. §§ 29825(a)-(b). The California Code of Civil Procedure and the California Family Code, Cal. Code Civ. Proc. and Cal. Fam. Code, are respectively herein referred to as C.C.P. and Fam. Code for sake of brevity.

[159] P.C. §§ 29825(a)-(b).

[160] P.C. § 29825(d).

[161] C.C.P. § 527.9(f); Fam. Code § 6389(h).

To do this, the person subject to the order must "show that a particular firearm is necessary ... [for] continued employment and that the[ir] current employer is unable to reassign the [person] to another position where a firearm is unnecessary[,]" or, if the person is a peace officer "who as a condition of employment and whose personal safety depends on the ability to carry a firearm," he or she may be able "to continue ... carry[ing] a firearm, either on duty or off duty, if the court finds ... that the officer does not pose a threat of harm."[162]

California law does not specifically address how those who receive restraining orders per P.C. § 646.91 should dispose of their firearms. P.C. § 29825(d) requires that the firearms be surrendered "to the local law enforcement agency ... [within the court's] jurisdiction or sold to a licensed gun dealer, and ... proof of [the] surrender or sale [must] be filed within a specified time of recei[ving] ... the [restraining] order."

## B. Federal Domestic Violence Restraining Orders

Unlike the broad California firearm restrictions for restraining orders, the federal restrictions are very narrow.

Under federal law, individuals are prohibited from receiving and possessing firearms if they are subject to a court order that:

- "[W]as issued after a hearing ... [where they] received actual notice, and ... had an opportunity to participate;
- [R]estrains ... [them] from harassing, stalking, or threatening an intimate partner ... or child of such intimate partner or person, or engaging in other conduct that would [put] an intimate partner in reasonable fear of bodily injury to the partner or [the] child; and
- [Either] includes a finding that ... [they] represent[] a credible threat to the physical safety of [an] intimate partner or child; or by its terms [specifically] prohibits the use, attempted use, or threatened use of physical force ... [that] would reasonably be expected to cause bodily injury [against the intimate partner or child] ... ."[163]

This means that, unlike California's restraining order restrictions that can take effect without notice of the hearing (*i.e.*, a temporary restraining order), the federal restriction requires notice and an opportunity to participate.[164]

---

[162] C.C.P. § 527.9(f); Fam. Code § 6389(h).

[163] 18 U.S.C. § 922(g)(8).

[164] 18 U.S.C. § 922(g)(8)(A). For example, a protective order signed without either notice of a hearing or appearing before a judge and being allowed to present evidence is not considered one where the defendant received actual notice and accordingly is not within the scope of 18 U.S.C. § 922(g)(8). *United States v. Spruill*, 292 F.3d 207, 215-220 (5th Cir. 2002).

## C. Restoring Firearm Rights from Restraining Order Restrictions

Firearm restrictions last the duration of restraining/protective orders or injunctions. If you are subject to a firearm restriction because of such an order and want to lawfully possess firearms, you should retain an attorney. Certain restraining orders can last up to three years and, if renewed, up to six years. Other restraining orders, especially those issued for domestic violence under the Family Code, can be permanent.

In some cases you may be able to reach a mutual agreement with the other party without involving the court to avoid being prohibited from owning and possessing firearms.

Where a restraining order has been issued after a hearing, you must generally remove or appeal the order to restore your firearm rights. To remove the order, you must show that there "has been a material change in the facts upon which the injunction or temporary restraining order was granted, that the law upon which the … restraining order was granted has changed, or that … justice would be [better] served by … modif[ying] or dissol[ving] … the … restraining order."[165]

# XIII. SELF-DEFENSE EXCEPTION FOR PROHIBITED PERSONS POSSESSING FIREARMS

If you are subject to one of the prohibitions discussed above, there is a *very* limited situation where you may still possess a firearm for self-defense, or to defend others, where:

- You "reasonably believe[]" you or someone else is "in *imminent* danger of suffering great bodily injury;
- [You] … reasonably believe[] … the immediate use of force [is] necessary to defend against that danger;
- A firearm bec[omes] available to … [you] without planning or preparation on [your] part;
- [You] … possess[] the firearm temporarily, … [meaning] no longer than … necessary [or reasonably appeared to … be[] necessary] for self-defense;
- No other means of avoiding the danger of injury [is] available; AND
- [Using a] … firearm was reasonable under the circumstances."[166]

---

[165] C.C.P. § 533.
[166] *See* CALCRIM 2514 (emphasis added).

For example, in *People v. King*, a felon prohibited from possessing firearms was provided a firearm by another person spontaneously when a family gathering he attended was attacked by armed assailants. The California Supreme Court held that the Legislature did not intend to deny prohibited persons the right to use a firearm to defend themselves or others in emergency situations.[167]

This means that when prohibited persons are, or believe themselves or others to be, in immediate danger of great bodily harm, and as long as the firearm was made available to them without their preconceived intent or participation, they may temporarily possess a firearm for no longer than necessary to use it in self-defense without violating P.C. § 29800.

Finally, as in all cases where deadly force is used or threatened in self-defense, using a firearm must be reasonable under the circumstances and may be resorted to only if no other alternative means are available. In the case of felons defending themselves, such alternatives may include having to retreat where other non-prohibited persons would not be required to do so.[168]

# XIV. OTHER FEDERAL LAW FIREARM POSSESSION RESTRICTIONS

## A. Fugitives

Federal law also prohibits fugitives from receiving and possessing firearms.[169] A "fugitive from justice" is anyone "who has fled from any State to avoid prosecution for a felony or a misdemeanor; or any person who leaves the State to avoid giving testimony in any criminal … [case, or] knows that misdemeanor or felony charges are pending against [him or her] … ."[170]

## B. Aliens

Unless they meet an exception, federal law also prohibits "aliens" who are in the U.S. illegally or who have been admitted to the U.S. under a nonimmigrant visa,[171] from receiving and possessing firearms.[172] An "alien" is anyone

---

[167] *People v. King*, 22 Cal.3d 12, 15 (1978).
[168] *People v. King*, 22 Cal.3d 12, 24 (1978).
[169] 18 U.S.C. § 922(g)(2).
[170] 27 C.F.R. § 478.11; *see also United States v. Spillane*, 913 F.2d 1079 (4th Cir. 1990).
[171] As defined in the Immigration and Nationality Act, 8 U.S.C. § 1011(a)(26).
[172] 18 U.S.C. § 922(g)(5).

who is not a U.S. citizen or national,[173] while the phrase "alien[s] illegally or unlawfully in the United States" refers to "[a]liens who are unlawfully in the United States [and] are not in valid immigrant, nonimmigrant or parole status. The term includes any aliens--

- Who unlawfully entered the United States without inspection and authorization by an immigration officer and who ha[ve] not been paroled into the United States under section 212(d)(5) of the Immigration and Nationality Act (INA);
- Who ... [are] nonimmigrant[s] and whose authorized period of stay has expired or who ha[ve] violated the terms of the nonimmigrant category in which ... [they were] admitted;
- Paroled under INA section 212(d)(5) whose authorized parole period has expired or whose parole status has been terminated; or
- Under an order of deportation, exclusion, or removal, or under an order to depart the United States voluntarily, whether or not ... [they] ha[ve] left the United States."[174]

Certain aliens lawfully admitted to the U.S. and who hold a nonimmigrant visa[175] may be exempt from this general federal prohibition if they are:

- "admitted to the United States for lawful hunting or sporting purposes or . . .
- in possession of a hunting license or permit lawfully issued in the United States; [or]
- an official representative of a foreign government who is [either (1)] accredited to the United States Government or the Government's mission to an international organization having its headquarters in the United States or [(2)] en route to or from another country to which that alien is accredited; [or]
- an official of a foreign government or distinguished foreign visitor who has been so designated by the Department of State; or
- a foreign law enforcement officer of a friendly foreign government entering the United States on official law enforcement business."[176]

---

[173] 18 U.S.C. § 922(y)(1)(A); 8 U.S.C. § 1101(a)(3).

[174] 27 C.F.R. § 478.11.

[175] 27 C.F.R. § 478.11 (A nonimmigrant visa is a "visa properly issued to an alien as an eligible nonimmigrant by a competent officer as provided in the Immigration and Nationality Act, 8 U.S.C. 1101 et seq.").

[176] 18 U.S.C. § 922(y)(2). A lawfully issued hunting license or permit includes those issued by a state, local government, or Indian tribe federally recognized by the Bureau of Indian Affairs. See Questions and Answers - Revised ATF F4473 (April 2012 Edition), U.S. DEPT. OF JUSTICE – BUREAU OF ALCOHOL, TOBACCO, FIREARMS AND EXPLOSIVES, http://www.atf.gov/firearms/faq/non-immigrant-aliens.pdf (last visited July 28, 2012).

An exemption is also extended to those aliens admitted to the United States holding a nonimmigrant visa if they have been issued a waiver to possess firearms.[177]

Even if a person has been admitted to the United States *without* a nonimmigrant visa, that person might still be eligible to possess firearms. On July 9, 2012, the ATF enacted a change in the Federal Regulations allowing certain aliens without visas to lawfully possess and acquire firearms.[178] This change occurred because the United States allows citizens of a number of other countries entry into the United States without a visa, and these individuals were considered prohibited from possessing firearms because they did not possess a visa.[179] One common occurrence was with Canadian visitors who entered the United States to hunt. Thus, possession of firearms within the United States by these Canadian visitors prior to this change in the interpretation of the law was illegal.

Now "[n]onimmigrant aliens lawfully admitted to the United States without a visa, pursuant either to the Visa Waiver Program or other exemptions from visa requirements, will not be prohibited from shipping, transporting, receiving, or possessing firearms or ammunition, and the regulations will also no longer proscribe the sale or other disposition of firearms or ammunition to such nonimmigrant aliens."[180]

## C. Dishonorable Discharge from the Armed Forces

Those who have been dishonorably discharged or dismissed by a general court martial from the armed forces are likewise prohibited from possessing and receiving firearms.[181] Those who are merely "separated" from ser-

---

[177] 18 U.S.C. § 922(y)(3).

[178] Firearms Disabilities for Certain Nonimmigrant Aliens, 77 Fed. Reg. 33625-01 (June 7, 2012) (effective July 9, 2012 and to be codified at 27 C.F.R. §§ 478.32, 478.44, 478.45, 478.99, 478.120, and 478.124). The ATF's previous position was that only aliens holding nonimmigrant visas who met an exception to the firearm restriction could possess and acquire firearms. See Implementation of Public Law 105-277, Omnibus Consolidated and Emergency Supplemental Appropriations Act, 1999, Relating to Firearms Disabilities for Nonimmigrant Aliens, and Requirement for Import Permit for Nonimmigrant Aliens Bringing Firearms and Ammunition Into the United States, 67 Fed. Reg. 5422 (Feb. 5, 2002).

[179] Citizens of 36 participating countries may enter the United States under the Visa Waiver Program. *Visa Waiver Program (VWP)*, UNITED STATES DEPT. OF STATE, http://travel.state.gov/visa/temp/without/without_1990.html#countries (last visited July 30, 2012). Certain residents of Canada and Bermuda may also enter the United States without a visa, but under a different exception. *Citizens of Canada and Bermuda*, U.S. DEPT. OF STATE, http://travel.state.gov/visa/temp/without/without_1260.html (last visited July 30, 2012).

[180] Firearms Disabilities for Certain Nonimmigrant Aliens, 77 Fed. Reg. 33625-01, 33627 (June 7, 2012) (effective July 9, 2012 and to be codified at 27 C.F.R. §§ 478.32, 478.44, 478.45, 478.99, 478.120, and 478.124).

[181] 18 U.S.C. § 922(g)(6); *see also* 27 C.F.R. § 478.11.

vice in the armed forces because of any other discharge are not prohibited (*e.g.*, a "bad conduct" discharge does not qualify).[182]

## D. Renouncing United States Citizenship

If you renounce your citizenship, you are also prohibited from receiving and possessing firearms.[183] To be prohibited under this law, you must have renounced your U.S. citizenship before either:

- "[A] diplomatic or consular officer of the [U.S.] in a foreign state ... [per] 8 U.S.C. [§] 1481(a)(5); or
- [A]n officer designated by the Attorney General when the [U.S.] is in a state of war ... [per] 8 U.S.C. [§] 1481(a)(6)."[184]

Your citizenship has not been renounced if the renunciation has been reversed by an administrative or judicial appeal.[185]

## E. Federal Restrictions against Indicted Persons Receiving Firearms

If you are "under indictment for a crime punishable by imprisonment for a term ... [of more than] one year[186] ... [you cannot] ship or transport in interstate or foreign commerce any firearm or ammunition or receive any firearm or ammunition which has been shipped or transported in interstate or foreign commerce."[187] Federal law, however, does not prohibit *possessing* firearms or ammunition during this time; you just cannot acquire new firearms or remove ones you already own from the state.

# XV. HOW TO DETERMINE YOUR ELIGIBILITY TO POSSESS FIREARMS

If you do not know whether you can legally possess or purchase firearms in California, you should submit a Personal Firearms Eligibility Check Application (PFEC) to the California DOJ. This form can be downloaded at http://ag.ca.gov/firearms/forms/pdf/pfecapp.pdf. The DOJ will then tell

---

[182] *See* 27 C.F.R. § 478.11.

[183] 18 U.S.C. § 922(g)(7).

[184] 27 C.F.R. § 478.11.

[185] 27 C.F.R. § 478.11.

[186] This does not include any federal or state offenses regarding antitrust violations, unfair trade practices, restraints of trade, or similar offenses relating to business practices regulation, and any state misdemeanors punishable by imprisonment for two or less years. 18 U.S.C. § 921(a)(20).

[187] 18 U.S.C. § 922(n).

you whether or not you are eligible to possess firearms. If you are ineligible, you can contact them to find out why.

If you think you may be restricted or you find yourself restricted from owning or possessing firearms, you will need to check both California and federal law and obtain copies of specific court and/or medical records relating to your situation to determine the specific nature of your restriction and whether there is a way to restore your rights. For further information on the process of restoring firearm rights, send an email to GunRightsRestoration@michellawyers.com.

## CHAPTER 4:

# HOW TO OBTAIN FIREARMS AND AMMUNITION

The information in this chapter assumes you are eligible to own, possess, and receive firearms under state and federal law. Questions about possessing firearms and ammunition by minors, those between ages 18 and 21, and those with rights restrictions are covered in Chapter 3.

In California *almost all* firearm ownership transfers, whether money is exchanged or not, must be processed through a licensed firearms dealer. A dealer is commonly referred to as an FFL, which stands for Federal Firearms Licensee,[1] as mentioned in Chapter 3. As the name suggests, a federal firearms license is required to be a lawful firearms dealer.

The easiest, and in most cases the *only*, way to lawfully obtain a firearm is through a properly licensed FFL with a California dealer's license. Though most FFLs operate from a retail storefront, it is not unlawful (unless prohibited by local zoning laws) for FFLs to operate in a non-retail setting like their home. These individuals are sometimes called "kitchen-table" FFLs. Though they are legal under federal and state law, make sure when doing "kitchen-table" transactions that the person you are purchasing from is actually an FFL if the transaction requires one, and that all laws are complied with. Except in relatively rare cases involving the transfer of "antique firearms" or long guns that are at least 50 years old,[2] if paperwork is not involved, this is a serious red flag about the legality of the transfer.

The California Penal Code refers to an FFL as a "licensee" or a "dealer." In order to qualify as a licensee or dealer in California, certain additional state-issued (and sometimes even local government) permits and licenses are required.

---

[1] Federal licenses are required for those engaged in business as a firearm dealer, manufacturer, or importer. There is a separate license for "curio or relic" collectors too. For purposes of this book, FFL will mean firearm "dealers" (unless specified otherwise) who possess both a Federal Firearms License to engage in the business of dealing in firearms (a Type 01 license) and possess a California firearm dealer's license.

[2] Discussed later in this chapter.

To legally operate as a firearms dealer under California law, a "dealer" must *minimally* have all of the following:[3]

1. A valid Federal Firearms License;
2. A valid Seller's Permit issued by the State Board of Equalization;
3. A Certificate of Eligibility ("COE") issued by the California DOJ;
4. Any regulatory business license(s) required by local government;
5. If required by the local authority, a local firearms license (or if no such license is required, a letter from the city or county confirming no such license is required);[4] and
6. Be listed in the California DOJ's Centralized List of Firearms Dealers.[5]

# I. PURCHASING FIREARMS FROM A DEALER

## A. Sale Requirements for All Firearms

### 1. Valid Photo ID Showing Your Age

Under both California and federal law an FFL is prohibited from delivering a *handgun* to anyone under age 21 or a non-handgun to anyone under age 18.[6] So you must present clear evidence of your identity and age to the FFL before he or she can release a firearm to you.[7] Under California law clear evidence of your identity and age must be shown with either a valid California driver's license or a valid California identification card issued by the Department of Motor Vehicles.[8] If your license has expired or is suspended, your firearm transaction will be denied.

In most situations a California driver's license or ID will suffice for the identification requirements under federal law.[9] However, it is not unusual for a person to move, and the driver's license reflects the *old* address or does not reflect the person's residential address (*i.e.*, the person uses a P.O.

---

[3] *See* P.C. § 26700.

[4] P.C. § 26705(c)(3).

[5] P.C. § 26700.

[6] You should be aware that even though California law does not prohibit the transfer of any long gun to a person between the ages of 18 and 21, under federal law, a firearm that is neither a "rifle" nor a "shotgun" (*e.g.*, a frame/receiver) *cannot* be sold by a dealer to anyone under age 21. P.C. § 27510; 18 U.S.C. §§ 922(b)(1), (x); *see* Chapter 2 for definitions and examples. It is not unusual for persons reaching the age of 18 to attempt to purchase a receiver to build their own rifle. Under federal law, a dealer is required to deny such a purchase.

[7] 18 U.S.C. §§ 922(t)(1)(C), 1028(d)(3); P.C. §§ 26815(c), 27540(c); 27 C.F.R. § 478.11; 27 C.F.R. § 478.124(c)(3)(i).

[8] P.C. § 16400.

[9] Federal law makes it illegal in most cases for an FFL to transfer a firearm directly to a person who does not reside in the FFL's state of residence. 18 U.S.C. § 922(a)(2).

Box or police station address). In such a case, in addition to a valid California driver's license or valid California identification card,[10] you also present a valid government issued "identification document" that has your name, picture, date of birth, and residence address.[11] According to the ATF, federal law allows a purchaser to use a combination of government-issued documents[12] to satisfy the federal identification requirement.[13] So you could still acquire a firearm if, for example, you have your valid California driver's license (with your P.O. Box listed as your address) and a voter registration card (with your actual address).

## 2. Members of the Military Stationed in California

Despite the fact that California law has limited the accepted forms of identification (*i.e.*, California driver's licenses and DMV identification cards), the California DOJ accepts military identification and permanent duty station orders as proof of identification.[14] These same documents satisfy the ID and proof of residency requirements under federal law as well.

Section 921(b) of the GCA provides that "a member of the Armed Forces on active duty is a resident of the State in which his permanent duty station is located."[15] The purchaser's official orders showing that his or her permanent duty station is within the state where the FFL's premises are located suffice to establish the purchaser's residence for GCA purposes. "In combination with a military identification card, such orders will satisfy the Brady Act's requirement for an identification document, even though the purchaser may actually reside in a home that is not located on the military base."[16]

---

[10] 18 U.S.C. §§ 922(t)(1)(C), 1028(d)(3); 27 C.F.R. § 478.11.

[11] 27 C.F.R. § 478.11.

[12] Documents include those which are "made or issued by or under the authority of the United States Government, a State, political subdivision of a State, a foreign government, political subdivision of a foreign government, an international governmental or an international quasi-governmental organization which, when completed with information concerning a particular individual, is of a type intended or commonly accepted for the purpose of identification of individuals." 27 C.F.R. § 478.11 (definition for "identification document").

[13] Ruling 2001-5 (ATF 2001); *Identification of Transferee*, ATF, http://atf.gov/regulations-rulings/rulings/atf-rulings/atf-ruling-2001-5.html (last visited July 30, 2012) (stating "[e]xamples of documents that may be accepted to supplement information on a driver's license or other identification document include a vehicle registration, a recreation identification card, a fishing or hunting license, a voter identification card, or a tax bill. However, the document in question must be valid and must have been issued by a government agency.").

[14] *Frequently Asked Questions*, CALIFORNIA - DEPT. OF JUSTICE, http://oag.ca.gov/firearms/pubfaqs (last visited July 30, 2012) (The answer to question 3 states, "[a]s part of the DROS process, the buyer must present 'clear evidence of identity and age' which is defined as a valid, non-expired California Driver's License or Identification Card issued by the Department of Motor Vehicles. A military identification accompanied by permanent duty station orders indicating a posting in California is also acceptable.").

[15] 18 U.S.C. § 921(b).

[16] Ruling 2001-5 (ATF 2001); *Identification of Transferee*, ATF, http://atf.gov/regulations-rulings/rulings/atf-rulings/atf-ruling-2001-5.html (last visited July 30, 2012).

## 3. Non-Citizens (Aliens)

As explained in Chapter 3, federal law generally prohibits aliens who are unlawfully in the United States, as well as those who are lawfully in the country via a "nonimmigrant visa" or who are not required to have a visa, from possessing, and of course acquiring, firearms. There are exceptions, however.[17]

For those aliens who may lawfully acquire a firearm in the United States, state and federal laws relating to the acquisition of firearms still apply. The alien must therefore possess a California driver's license or ID[18] to meet the state requirements. In addition, the individual must "reside" in a state to meet the federal requirement because, though there are a few exceptions, federal law generally restricts people from receiving firearms outside of the state in which they reside (this is discussed in much more detail below).[19]

Before the change in law, there was a 90-day residency requirement before aliens could acquire firearms that is no longer in effect. Aliens, when acquiring firearms, must also provide their alien number or admission number on the 4473 form.[20]

## 4. Federal Form 4473

Federal law requires you fill out a federal form, Form 4473, for any firearm (as defined under the GCA) that is *sold* to you by an FFL.[21] Only a single Form 4473 is required regardless of how many firearms are included in the transaction.[22]

On Form 4473 you must provide information such as your name, gender, address, birth date, place of birth, height, weight, ethnicity, state of

---

[17] 18 U.S.C. § 922(g)(5)(A),(B). *See* Chapter 3 for a detailed discussion on who is an "alien" and what firearm restrictions apply to aliens, as well as the exceptions to those restrictions.

[18] P.C. §§ 26815(c), 27540(c).

[19] 18 U.S.C. § 922(a)(3).

[20] 27 C.F.R. § 478.124(c)(1).

[21] 27 C.F.R. § 478.124(a). This does not apply to certain loans from an FFL or the return of firearms after repairs by the FFL.

[22] However, if more than one semiautomatic rifle with a caliber greater than .22 (including .223/5.56) capable of accepting a detachable magazine is transferred to the same person within a five-day period, the FFL must additionally complete Form 3310.4. *See ATF E-Form 3310.12*, U.S. DEPT. OF JUSTICE - BUREAU OF ALCOHOL, TOBACCO, FIREARMS AND EXPLOSIVES, http://www.atf.gov/forms/download/atf-f-3310-12. pdf (last visited July 30, 2012). For firearm transaction reporting purposes, a "detachable magazine" includes a rifle with a bullet button. *See Q&As for the Report of Multiple Sate or Other Disposition of Certain Rifles*, U.S. DEPT. OF JUSTICE - BUREAU OF ALCOHOL, TOBACCO, FIREARMS AND EXPLOSIVES, http:// www.atf.gov/firearms/industry/080911-qa-multiple-rifles.pdf (last visited July 30, 2012). Likewise, if the transaction involves more than one handgun to the same person within a five-day period, the FFL must additionally complete Form 3310.4. 27 C.F.R. § 478.126a. This is generally not a concern for California FFLs unless the customer is exempt from the "one handgun per month" rule or the FFL is facilitating a transfer of multiple handguns between two private parties. As an aside, the District Court for the District of Columbia upheld the ATF's multiple-firearm reporting requirement. *See Nat'l Shooting Sports Found., Inc. v. Jones*, 840 F.Supp.2d 310 (D.D.C. 2012).

residence, and any factors affecting your eligibility to possess firearms.[23] The FFL will fill out information about the specific firearm(s) being purchased and identify the store (if applicable) and their FFL number.[24] FFLs are legally required to maintain all 4473 forms on their premises for 20 years.[25] Those forms must be made available for inspection for law enforcement and legal compliance purposes.[26]

Full-time paid peace officers[27] are not required to fill out Form 4473 if they certify on agency letterhead, with an authorized signature, that they will use the firearm for official duties, and if a record check shows they have no misdemeanor domestic violence convictions.[28]

### 5. California Dealer's Record of Sale (DROS) Form

In addition to the federal form, California requires you to fill out a state DROS form. The DROS information includes firearm type (if the firearm is a pistol or revolver, additional information like the make, model, serial number, etc., is required); transaction type (dealer sale, private party transfer, pawn/consignment, or loan); waiting period requirement exemptions, if any (see below); and your name, address, birth date, etc. Your thumbprint must also be taken unless you qualify for an exception.[29]

Unlike federal law where you can just fill out one 4473 form for more than one firearm purchased at the same time, a separate DROS form and fee is required for each *handgun* transferred.[30] However, you can still buy multiple long guns with a single DROS form.

In a transaction involving both handguns and long guns, a *single* DROS can be used for any number of long guns, but each handgun must still be on its own DROS form. There is no fee discount for processing a handgun and long gun at the same time.[31]

---

[23] *ATF E-Form 3310.4*, U.S. DEPT. OF JUSTICE - BUREAU OF ALCOHOL, TOBACCO, FIREARMS AND EXPLOSIVES, http://www.atf.gov/forms/download/atf-f-3310-4.pdf (last visited Aug. 2, 2012).

[24] *See also* 27 C.F.R. §§ 478.11, 478.124(c) for further details about the transferee and FFL's obligations regarding Form 4473.

[25] 27 C.F.R. § 478.129(b).

[26] 18 U.S.C. § 923(g).

[27] Defined in P.C. § 830 *et seq.*

[28] 27 C.F.R. § 478.134. Because no 4473 is filled out, dealers who conduct this transaction must keep the letter for their records and note in their books how this firearm was transferred. 27 C.F.R. § 478.134(c).

[29] P.C. §§ 28160(b) (handguns), 28165(b) (firearms other than handguns). This will change January 1, 2014, when the requirements for handguns will apply to all firearms.

[30] P.C. § 28170(d).

[31] *Information Bulletin No. 2001 FD-01: Requirement for Dealers to Conduct Private Party Transfers / Allowable Fees*, CALIFORNIA DEPT. OF JUSTICE, FIREARMS DIVISION, http://oag.ca.gov/sites/all/files/pdfs/firearms/infobuls/0101.pdf (last visited July 30, 2012).

The DROS fee for the first handgun, or for one or more rifles or shotguns, is $19. This covers the background checks and, for handguns, the transfer registration. There is also a $1 Firearms Safety Testing fee, and a $5 Safety and Enforcement fee.[32] Assuming you meet an exception which allows you to acquire more than "one handgun per month" (discussed below), the DROS fee for each additional handgun transferred at the same time is $15.[33]

The FFL is required to keep a copy of the DROS on file for at least three years and make it available for any peace officer, DOJ, or ATF inspection.[34]

### a.  Background Checks

The information collected on Federal Form 4473 and the California DROS form is used to check your background and eligibility to possess, own, and receive firearms. Both California and federal law require FFLs to perform background checks for all firearm transfers.[35]

### b.  Registration at Time of Purchase

Currently only *handgun* transfers are registered to the purchaser at the time of purchase.[36] The DOJ takes the information collected by the mandatory DROS form, which includes the purchaser's personal identifying information and the handgun's make, model, serial number, etc., and enters that information into its Automated Firearm System (AFS), thereby registering the handgun in the purchaser's name.[37]

As for non-handgun transfers (rifles, shotguns, etc.), the DROS form does not currently collect any information about the specific firearm, meaning that firearms acquired from an FFL are not registered in the AFS to the recipient.[38]

---

[32] *See generally* P.C. §§ 23690, 28225, 28300(c); 11 Cal. Code Regs. § 4001. As of the date of this book's publication, I filed a lawsuit on behalf of the NRA challenging the constitutionality of these fees, *Bauer v. Harris*, No. 1:11-at-00526 (E.D.Cal. filed on Aug. 25, 2011). *Complaint for Declaratory and Injunctive Relief,* CALGUNLAWS.COM, http://www.calgunlaws.com/images/stories/Docs/DROS/bauer%20et%20al.%20v.%20doj_conformed%20complaint.pdf (last visited July 30, 2012).

[33] 11 Cal. Code Regs. § 4001(a)(2).

[34] P.C. § 28215(c). In comparison, federal law requires FFLs to keep the Federal Form 4473 on file for 20 years. 27 C.F.R. § 478.129(b).

[35] Eligibility requirements and procedures for appealing the DOJ's denial of allowing your firearm transfer to proceed are discussed in Chapter 3.

[36] P.C. § 11106(b).

[37] P.C. §§ 28155, 28160, 28215(d). The handgun registration is not the same registration required for "assault weapons" and ".50 BMG rifles" discussed in Chapter 8. In effect, these firearms are often registered twice.

[38] P.C. §§ 28165, 28215(c)(3). AB 809 will change this beginning January 1, 2014. Like the handgun law now in place, AB 809 requires long guns purchased from or transferred through a dealer to be registered at the time of transfer. Long guns brought into the state by a private individual will also need to be registered with the state. Long guns privately owned and already in the state when AB 809 takes effect on January 1, 2014 will *not* be required to be registered.

Because of the amount of paperwork and the information gathered, it is not unusual for those who went through the DROS process to believe their long gun is registered. But no transaction record on a long gun transfer, other than the documents kept by the dealer and the purchaser, is kept by the government. A disturbingly large number of Californians also mistakenly believe that the DROS process was the same one required to register "assault weapons." But that is also not the case. Unfortunately, because they filled out the long gun purchase paperwork, people are still discovering that firearms they thought were registered as "assault weapons" are not registered as such and, in the case of long guns, are not, in fact, registered at all. As discussed in Chapter 8, there is no way to register your unregistered "assault weapon" today.

You may, however, voluntarily register any lawfully owned firearm by submitting a "Firearm Ownership Record" form to the DOJ. This form is available at the California DOJ Bureau of Firearms website. Though not legally required, having this record on file with the DOJ may help your firearm be returned to you if it is ever seized, lost, or stolen.[39] Registration can also safeguard against a felony if you are ever charged for carrying a handgun illegally concealed or loaded, because a *registered* firearm carried illegally is in most situations only a misdemeanor (discussed in Chapter 5).

## 6. Waiting Period

Under California law you must wait 10 days (ten 24-hour periods) from when your DROS is submitted until you may lawfully receive any firearm transferred through an FFL.[40] If you clear the background check (assuming all other requirements are satisfied), the FFL may transfer the firearm to you after the ten days.[41]

Certain people and transfers are exempt from this 10-day waiting period, including:

- Properly identified full-time paid peace officers authorized by their employer to carry firearms for their confirmed duties.[42]
- Firearm deliveries, sales, or transfers to DOJ-issued special weapons permit holders.[43]

---

[39] *Frequently Asked Questions*, CALIFORNIA DEPT. OF JUSTICE, http://oag.ca.gov/firearms/pubfaqs#26 (last visited July 30, 2012).

[40] P.C. § 26815(a).

[41] P.C. § 26815(a).

[42] P.C. §§ 26950, 27650.

[43] P.C. §§ 26965, 27665. The permits include those issued per P.C. §§ 33300 (short-barreled rifle and shotgun permittees), 32650 (machinegun, "assault weapons," and .50 BMG permits), 32700 (permits to sell machineguns), and 18900 (permits for destructive devices).

- Persons with ATF-issued "curio or relic" collectors licenses who have a valid DOJ-issued COE when purchasing curio and relic firearms.[44]
- FFLs delivering firearms to another FFL, or an FFL transferring a handgun from store inventory to the FFL's personal collection (subject to additional ATF and California requirements).[45]

Additionally you have 30 days from when your DROS is submitted to pick up your firearm from the FFL. Otherwise, federal law voids your background check, and you will be required to go through the entire process again, fees and everything.[46]

## 7. Required Locking Devices and Warnings

California requires all firearms transferred by an FFL, including PPTs, or those manufactured in California be accompanied by a "firearm safety device"[47] and warning language or labels upon delivery.[48] The safety device must be one of those listed on the "Roster of Firearm Safety Devices Certified for Sale" and identified as appropriate for the specific firearm.[49]

This safety device requirement does not apply if:

- You own a gun safe that meets certain standards[50] and you present an original receipt for it or proof of owning the gun safe as authorized by the Attorney General,[51] or
- You purchase an approved safety device no more than 30 days before you take possession of the firearm; you present the approved safety device to the FFL when picking up the firearm; you present an original receipt to the FFL showing the safety device's purchase date, name, and the model number, or[52]

---

[44] P.C. §§ 26970, 27670, 27965, 27820. Acquiring antique and "curio or relic" firearms is discussed later in this chapter.

[45] P.C. §§ 26960, 27660.

[46] See 27 C.F.R. § 478.102(c).

[47] P.C. § 23635(a). A "firearm safety device" means a device other than a gun safe that locks and is designed to prevent children and unauthorized users from firing a firearm. The device may be installed on a firearm, be incorporated into the design of the firearm, or prevent access to the firearm. P.C. § 16540.

[48] P.C. § 23640.

[49] P.C. § 23635. The entire Roster is found on the California Department of Justice's website. *Roster of Approved Firearms Safety Devices - Search by Firearm*, CALIFORNIA DEPT. OF JUSTICE, http://safetydevice.doj.ca.gov/fsearch.asp (last visited July 30, 2012).

[50] P.C. § 23650(a)(3).

[51] P.C. § 23635(b). This safe-affidavit exception is not recognized for *handgun* transfers under federal law however.

[52] P.C. § 23635(c).

- You buy an "antique firearm"[53] or are employed as a salaried full-time peace officer.[54]

Federal law also requires licensed importers, manufacturers, and dealers to provide a "secure gun storage or safety device"[55] when delivering a *handgun* to anyone who is not another FFL or otherwise exempt.[56] This federal requirement is different than California law in both its scope and exceptions because, unlike California law, it only applies to handguns. FFLs should be careful to make sure a locking device meets both state and federal requirements. For the general public, however, the most important distinction is that federal law does not recognize California's gun-safe affidavit exception when the transfer involves *handguns*. Thus, despite California law, a safe affidavit is only valid when the transfer involves a *long gun*.

# B. Additional Handgun Purchase Requirements[57]

## 1. Proof of Residency
In addition to providing proof of your identification and age, to obtain a *handgun* you must also provide documentation that you are a California resident. Under California law this includes a utility bill from the last three months, a residential lease, a property deed, or military permanent duty station orders showing assignment within this state, or other residency evidence allowed by the DOJ.[58] Issues have occurred with people being unable to make this documentary showing; for example, those living at a place where their name is not on any deed, lease, or utility bill. If you find yourself in this situation, contact a lawyer familiar with firearm-related laws.

Also be sure to ask the FFL what its policy is for proving residency *before* you go to buy the firearm because some ask for more than is required by California law. If you are not prepared to comply with that FFL's particular policy, you could be leaving the store on pick-up day empty-handed.

---

[53] Discussed in Chapter 2.

[54] P.C. § 23630.

[55] Defined in 18 U.S.C. § 921(a)(34) as either a device that is designed to prevent the firearm from being operated without first deactivating the device; a device incorporated into the firearm's design to prevent the firearm from being operated by anyone without access to the device; or a safe, gun safe, gun case, lock box, or other device designed to be, or that can be, used to store a firearm and that is designed to only be unlocked with a key, combination, etc.

[56] 18 U.S.C. §§ 922(z)(1)-(2). Exceptions include: transfer to or by the U.S., a state, its departments, agencies, or subdivisions, or law enforcement officers employed by any of these entities; transfer to a rail police officer for law enforcement purposes; transfer of a "curio or relic" to a licensed collector; and transfer whereby the secure gun storage device is unavailable due to theft, casualty, loss, consumer sales, back orders, etc., beyond FFL control, and where the FFL delivers a secure gun storage or safety device within ten days after the transfer.

[57] See Chapter 9 for restrictions on what handguns FFLs can lawfully sell in California.

[58] P.C. § 26845; 11 Cal. Code Regs. § 4045.

## 2. Handgun Safety Certificate (HSC)

### a. "Handgun Safety" Test

Under California law, before submitting the DROS form, most people purchasing a handgun must present a Handgun Safety Certificate (HSC) to the dealer showing they have successfully passed a written "Handgun Safety" test. Certain people and transfers are exempt from this requirement, as explained below. It is a misdemeanor to transfer handgun possession to any non-exempt person who does not have a valid HSC and for that person to *receive* a handgun, with a few exceptions explained below.[59]

The HSC may be obtained by passing a test administered by a DOJ Certified Instructor. Most FFLs are also HSC instructors who can supply the written test in their store, even on the same day as your purchase. The test has 30 multiple choice questions and costs up to $25; $15 goes to the DOJ, and the rest goes to the certified instructor.[60] You must correctly answer at least 75% of the questions to get the HSC. This means you must answer at least 23 questions correctly to pass the HSC test.[61]

After passing the test, the HSC is only good for five years.[62] If your HSC is lost or completely destroyed, you can get a duplicate certificate by asking the issuing instructor for one, proving your identity, and paying up to $15.[63] To be clear, you only need an HSC to *receive* a handgun, not to possess one.

### b. Handgun Safety Certificate Exceptions

The following people are exempt from the HSC requirement:

- Active or honorably retired peace officers.
- Active or honorably retired federal officer or law enforcement agents.
- Reserve peace officers.
- Anyone who has successfully completed the peace officer training course in P.C. § 832.
- California FFLs acting in the scope of their duties as an FFL.
- Handgun owners having their handgun returned to them.

---

[59] P.C. §§ 31615(a)(2)-(b).

[60] P.C. § 31650(b).

[61] P.C. § 31645(a). Do not be concerned about passing this test. It is relatively straightforward, and the FFL has materials you can review before taking it. If English is not your first language, you are entitled to a translator if you need one. P.C. § 31640(b).

[62] *Frequently Asked Questions*, CALIFORNIA DEPT. OF JUSTICE, http://oag.ca.gov/firearms/hscfaqs#a10 (last visited July 30, 2012).

[63] P.C. § 31660.

- Family members of peace officers or deputy sheriffs killed in the line of duty who receive a firearm per Government Code § 50081.
- Anyone with a valid license to carry a firearm per P.C. §§ 26150 and 26155.
- Active or honorably retired members of the U.S. Armed Forces, National Guard, Air National Guard, or the U.S. active reserve.
- Anyone authorized to carry loaded firearms in the scope of their employment pursuant to P.C. §§ 26025 and 26030(a)-(c) such as patrol special police officers, animal control officers, zookeepers, harbor police officers, guards, messengers, private investigators, and private patrol officers.
- DOJ-issued special weapons permit holders.
- Those who take possession of handguns by operation of law in a representative capacity such as the executor or administrator of an estate, a secured creditor or employee who possesses it as collateral, or a bankruptcy trustee.[64]

### 3. Safe-Handling Demonstration

Before receiving a handgun, California requires you to perform a safe-handling demonstration for the DOJ Certified Instructor (*i.e.*, the firearm vendor).[65] For example, if you are receiving a semiautomatic pistol, you must demonstrate basic safety knowledge of how to remove, load, and insert the magazine, lock or pull back the slide, inspect the chamber, and apply the firearm safety device.[66] The dealer may assist you if needed. And, if you have a written letter signed by a physician stating you are physically unable to perform the demonstration, you are exempt from this requirement.[67]

### 4. Only One Handgun Every 30 Days

You are not allowed to purchase, or even *apply* to purchase, more than one handgun within any 30-day period.[68] First-time violators who apply to

---

[64] P.C. § 31700.

[65] P.C. §§ 26850(a)-(b), 26853, 26856, 26859.

[66] P.C. § 26853; *see also Handgun Safety Certificate Study Guide*, STATE OF CALIFORNIA, OFFICE OF THE ATTORNEY GENERAL, http://ag.ca.gov/firearms/forms/pdf/hscsg.pdf (last visited July 30, 2012) (discussing double-action and single-action revolver safety handling tips).

[67] *Frequently Asked Questions*, CALIFORNIA DEPT. OF JUSTICE, http://oag.ca.gov/firearms/hscfaqs#a21 (last visited July 30, 2012). According to the California DOJ, the "HSC program also provides for an exemption when physical disability deprives an individual the necessary agility to execute the demonstration. A signed, written letter from a licensed physician attesting that a physical disability precludes an individual from being able to perform the safe handling demonstration is required for this exemption. This exemption applies to the safe handling demonstration only. There is no exemption from the Handgun Safety Certificate requirement based on physical disability."

[68] P.C. § 27535(a).

purchase more than one handgun within any 30-day period may be fined up to $50. A second violation can be fined up to $100, and a third violation is a misdemeanor.[69]

Specific exceptions to this restriction are allowed for law enforcement agencies, agencies authorized to perform law enforcement duties, California licensed private security companies, full-time paid peace officers, and others.[70] Replacements of stolen or defective firearms are also exempt.[71] Additionally, as explained below, this restriction does *not* apply to PPTs (discussed below).

### 5. Licensed "Curio or Relic" Collector Exceptions

Excepting the residency requirement, those possessing a federal "curios or relics" collector's license along with a DOJ-issued COE[72] are exempt from each of the additional handgun transfer requirements described in this section – the HSC and safe-handling demonstration for handguns and the 10-day waiting period for all "curio and relic" firearms – *as long as* the firearm is a "curio or relic."[73] However, though the Penal Code clearly exempts such individuals from the one handgun per 30 calendar day restriction when acquiring even modern handguns (*i.e.,* non-"curios or relics"),[74] the California DOJ has nevertheless taken the position that they are only exempt when acquiring "curio or relic" handguns.[75] So until this issue is officially resolved, you should not attempt to purchase more than one modern handgun a month, even if you have a collector's license and a DOJ-issued COE.

# II. PRIVATE PARTY FIREARM TRANSFERS (PPT)

A PPT occurs when firearms are transferred between two private parties, neither of whom is a California licensed firearm dealer.[76] The law is different for interstate and *intrastate* PPTs, and for PPTs for handguns versus long guns. With few exceptions PPTs must be processed by an FFL. It is a

---

[69] P.C. § 27590(e).

[70] P.C. § 27535(b).

[71] P.C. §§ 27535(a)(10)-(11).

[72] 27 C.F.R. § 478.41(a); P.C. § 26710.

[73] P.C. §§ 31700(a)(6), 26850, 26970(a).

[74] P.C. § 27535(b)(9).

[75] *Frequently Asked Questions,* CALIFORNIA DEPT. OF JUSTICE, http://oag.ca.gov/firearms/pubfaqs#24 (last visited July 30, 2012).

[76] You should be aware that an FFL that is *not* licensed in California pursuant to P.C. § 26700 is treated like a normal person and not a "dealer" for the purpose of transfers.

misdemeanor to not use an FFL for a PPT, but you can be prosecuted for a felony if the firearm is a handgun.[77] FFLs are *required* to process PPTs upon request unless the FFL does *not* sell, transfer, or keep a handgun inventory.[78] In this case the FFL may choose not to process PPTs involving handguns but must still process non-handgun PPTs.

Most of the same requirements for FFL transfers to an individual buyer also apply to a PPT. A DROS form is still required, but it must include both the transferee's *and* the transferor's information.[79] If the firearm is a handgun, the transferee must have an HSC, perform a safe handling demonstration, and show proof of California residency. The handgun must also have a locking device when the FFL delivers it to the transferee or the transferee must meet one of the exceptions to the locking device requirement (discussed above).

Finally, PPTs are exempt from the "one handgun per month" limitation.[80] This means you can *buy* as many handguns as you want in a month if you do so through a PPT. However, this does *not* mean you can *transfer* as many handguns or firearms as you want in a month. If you are not an FFL, you may only transfer firearms "infrequently" or not "engage in the business" of dealing firearms. (Explained below).

In addition to the DROS and other transfer fees, an FFL may charge a fee to process a PPT, but it cannot be more than $10 per firearm.[81]

If during the 10-day waiting period it is discovered you are prohibited from possessing firearms, the FFL can return the firearm to the transferor before the waiting period expires, unless the FFL determines the transferor is also prohibited. If this happens, the FFL must deliver the firearm to the sheriff or police chief who will dispose of the firearm accordingly.[82]

## III. DEALER LICENSE REQUIREMENTS

### A. California Law

In most cases firearm transfers by anyone without an FFL must be "infrequent," even when the transfers are all processed through an FFL.[83] For handguns, "infrequent" under California law means making no more than six transactions in a "calendar year." A "transaction" in this context means a

[77] P.C. §§ 27545, 27590(c)(5).
[78] P.C. § 28065.
[79] *See* P.C. § 28060(c).
[80] P.C. § 27535(b).
[81] P.C. § 28055.
[82] P.C. § 28050(d).
[83] P.C. §§ 26500, 26520.

single transfer of any number of handguns.[84] This means, under California law, you could sell 100 handguns or more, all at once, without violating the law, as long as you do not do this more than five additional times that same "calendar year." A "calendar year" begins January 1 and ends December 31.[85] By ending in December rather than being *any* twelve-month period, use of the term "calendar year" in this context is significant. It means you can lawfully make six handgun transactions in December and still make up to another six the following January, only a month later, so long as you do not make any other transfers until the following January.

For *non*-handguns "infrequent" means transfers that are "occasional and without regularity."[86] Because this is a vague standard, it is unclear how often you can lawfully transfer non-handguns. Also the term "transaction" is not defined for non-handguns as it is for handguns. Presumably "transaction" means the same thing for both handguns and non-handguns, meaning you can transfer as many non-handguns as you want as long as it is done in a single transaction with the same person.

### 1. Exceptions

- You can transfer as many unloaded "antique firearms" as often as you want without violating the law. Just make sure they are actually "antique firearms" (see Chapter 2).
- A "Gun Show Trader"[87] may transfer up to 75 used[88] non-handguns in a *calendar* year spanning a total of 12 total gun shows (or similar events). And no more than 15 can be transferred during any given event.[89]

## B. Federal Law

Federal law has a different definition of what it means to be a dealer of firearms. Under federal law it is unlawful for any person[90] "except a licensed importer, licensed manufacturer, or licensed *dealer*, to *engage in the business* of importing, manufacturing, or dealing in firearms, or in the course

---

[84] P.C. § 16730.

[85] BLACK'S LAW DICTIONARY 217 (8th ed. 2004).

[86] P.C. § 16730(a)(2).

[87] A non-California FFL with a COE.

[88] "Used" means the firearm has been previously sold at retail and is more than three years old. P.C. § 17310.

[89] P.C. §§ 26500(a), 26525(a).

[90] Under the federal Gun Control Act (GCA) the term "person" includes "any individual, corporation, company, association, firm, partnership, society, or joint stock company." 18 U.S.C. § 921(a)(1).

of such business to ship, transport, or receive any firearm in interstate or foreign commerce."[91]

A "dealer" "means (A) any person *engaged in the business* of selling firearms at wholesale or retail, (B) any person engaged in the business of repairing firearms or of making or fitting special barrels, stocks, or trigger mechanisms to firearms, or (C) any person who is a pawnbroker. The term 'licensed dealer' means any dealer who is licensed under the provisions of [the GCA]."[92]

This definition appears again in the Code of Federal Regulations:

Dealer. Any person *engaged in the business* of selling firearms at *wholesale or retail*; any person engaged in the business of repairing firearms or of making or fitting special barrels, stocks, or trigger mechanisms to firearms; or any person who is a pawnbroker. The term shall include any person who engages in such business or occupation on a part-time basis.[93]

"Engaged in the business" is also a specifically defined term. It means "a person who devotes time, attention, and labor to dealing in firearms as a regular course of trade or business with the principal objective of livelihood and profit through the repetitive purchase and resale of firearms, but such term shall not include a person who makes occasional sales, exchanges, or purchases of firearms for the enhancement of a personal collection or for a hobby, or who sells all or part of his personal collection of firearms."[94]

"The term 'with the principal objective of livelihood and profit' means that the intent underlying the sale or disposition of firearms is predominantly one of obtaining livelihood and pecuniary gain, as opposed to other intents, such as improving or liquidating a personal firearms collection: *Provided*, That proof of profit shall not be required as to a person who engages in the regular and repetitive purchase and disposition of firearms for criminal purposes or terrorism."[95]

It is not unusual for people to believe they are fully complying with the law when they comply only with California's dealer's license requirements. But you must comply with both state and federal laws! Buying and selling

---

[91] 18 U.S.C. § 922(a)(1)(A) (emphasis added). "The term 'interstate or foreign commerce' includes commerce between any place in a State and any place outside of that State, or within any possession of the United States (not including the Canal Zone) or the District of Columbia, but such term does not include commerce between places within the same State but through any place outside of that State. The term 'State' includes the District of Columbia, the Commonwealth of Puerto Rico, and the possessions of the United States (not including the Canal Zone)." 18 U.S.C. § 921(a)(2).

[92] 18 U.S.C. § 921(a)(11) (emphasis added).

[93] 27 C.F.R. § 478.11 (emphasis added).

[94] 18 U.S.C. § 921(a)(21)(C).

[95] 18 U.S.C. § 921(a)(22) (emphasis in original).

*a few* firearms over the course of a year (while complying with both state and federal transfer requirements) might be legal under state and federal law. But conducting multiple transactions, buying and selling a number of firearms, and/or buying and immediately selling a recently purchased firearm may be an indication that you are *dealing* in firearms under federal law. *Dealing* in firearms without the proper licenses has some serious consequences.

# IV. INTERSTATE FIREARM PURCHASES AND TRANSFERS

## A. Transfers from Out-of-State Dealers

A California resident can purchase a firearm from an out-of-state FFL as long as the transfer would be lawful in California (*e.g.*, the firearm cannot be an "assault weapon").[96] There are, however, certain restrictions.

If the firearm is *not* a rifle or shotgun (*i.e.*, a lawful handgun or other non-long gun), under federal law the out-of-state FFL cannot transfer it directly to you, but instead must ship it to a California FFL who will then process the transfer according to California law.[97] This means that once the out-of-state FFL transfers the handgun or other non-long gun to the California FFL for transfer and delivery to you, all pertinent California regulation requirements must be satisfied (*i.e.*, the 10-day wait, DROS, etc.) before it may be finally given to you.

An FFL may transfer California-legal rifles or shotguns over the counter to an out-of-state resident if both states' laws are complied with.[98] However, given California's mandatory 10-day wait on all firearm transactions and the DROS process, it is unlikely an out-of-state dealer will want or be able to abide by California's stringent transfer requirements. Moreover, given California's requirement that all firearm purchasers have a valid California DMV-issued ID (see above), it is also difficult for out-of-state residents to purchase long guns in California, even though such is lawful under federal law.

Your "state of residence" is the state where you are present and where you also intend to make your home.[99] The ATF has explained that:

---

[96] 18 U.S.C. § 922(b)(2); 27 C.F.R. § 478.99(b). Firearms that are illegal to possess in California are discussed in Chapters 8 and 9.

[97] 18 U.S.C. §§ 922(a)(3), 922(b)(3).

[98] 18 U.S.C. § 922(b)(3).

[99] 27 C.F.R. § 478.11.

An individual resides in a State if he or she is present in a State with the intention of making a home in that State. Ownership of a home or land within a given State is not sufficient, by itself, to establish a State of residence. However, ownership of a home or land within a particular State is not required to establish presence and intent to make a home in that State. Furthermore, temporary travel, such as short-term stays, vacations, or other transient acts in a State are not sufficient to establish a State of residence because the individual demonstrates no intention of making a home in that State.[100]

Military members on active duty are residents of the state where their permanent duty station is located.[101] As explained below, a person can be a "resident" of more than one state.

## B. Interstate Private Party Transfers

Federal law requires PPTs between residents of different states to take place through an FFL in the recipient's home state.[102] The private party seller may mail shotguns or rifles through regular U.S.P.S. mail (though registered mail is suggested) to an FFL in the recipient's state.[103] A common or contract carrier must be used to ship handguns.[104] This means that while the Postal Service cannot be used to ship handguns, another carrier such as FedEx or UPS may be used. Ask your FFL ahead of time, however, because many FFLs do not accept firearms shipped to them by anyone other than another FFL.

Federal law also requires that the carrier be told that the shipment has a firearm but prohibits the carrier from requiring that any label on the package indicate that it has a firearm.[105]

Regardless of whether an out-of-state transfer is from an FFL or an individual, the California FFL can charge a service fee for any amount it wants, so determine what your FFL charges ahead of time.

---

[100] Ruling 2010-6 (ATF 2010); Ruling 2010-6, ATF, http://www.atf.gov/regulations-rulings/rulings/atf-rulings/atf-ruling-2010-6.pdf (last visited July 30, 2012).

[101] 18 U.S.C. § 921(b); 27 C.F.R. § 478.11.

[102] 18 U.S.C. §§ 922(a)(3), 922(b)(3).

[103] 18 U.S.C. §§ 922(a)(2)(A), 922(a)(3), 922(a)(5), 922(e); 27 C.F.R. §§ 478.31, 478.30; U.S. Dept. of Justice - Bureau of Alcohol, Tobacco, Firearms and Explosives, *Federal Firearms Regulations Reference Guide* 177 (2005).

[104] 18 U.S.C. §§ 1715, 922 (a)(2)(A), 922(a)(3), 922(a)(5); U.S. Dept. of Justice - Bureau of Alcohol, Tobacco, Firearms and Explosives, *Federal Firearms Regulations Reference Guide* 177 (2005).

[105] 18 U.S.C. § 922(e); U.S. Dept. of Justice - Bureau of Alcohol, Tobacco, Firearms and Explosives, *Federal Firearms Regulations Reference Guide* 177 (2005).

Restrictions (or lack thereof) on interstate ammunition sales are discussed below.

## C. Dual Residency Transfer Issues

Federal law recognizes "dual residency," *i.e.*, when a person maintains a home in two states and resides in one or the other for certain periods of the year.[106] This means that if you are a resident of another state in addition to California, you can purchase firearms in that other state during the time you reside there, presumably even if they would be illegal in California. However, you cannot bring firearms into California that are illegal to possess here, even if you obtained them legally. And if you buy a lawful handgun, it must be registered once you bring it into California.[107]

# V. LOANING FIREARMS TO ADULTS

Under California law, a firearm may be *infrequently*[108] loaned between two people who know each other, as long as the loan does not go over 30 days (with few exceptions). A firearm *other than a handgun* may be loaned to a *licensed hunter* over age 18 as long as the loan period does not exceed the hunting season for which the firearm is to be used, even if it surpasses 30 days.[109] Going beyond 30 days, or the applicable hunting season, makes an otherwise lawful loan an illegal transfer.[110]

If the firearm being loaned is a handgun, the recipient generally must have a valid HSC.[111] Where the recipient does not have an HSC or is not otherwise exempt from the HSC requirement, the person who is loaning the handgun must stay in the presence of the person being loaned the handgun, both people must be at least 18 years old, the individual receiving the handgun cannot be a person who is prohibited from owning or possessing firearms, the loan cannot exceed three days, and the loan must be for a lawful purpose.[112]

---

[106] 27 C.F.R. § 478.11 (see definition of "state of residence"). For example, if you maintain a home in state X and then travel to state Y on a hunting trip, you do not become a state Y resident because of such trip. On the other hand, if you maintain a home in state X and a home in state Y and reside in state X during the week and summer months, and state Y for weekends and the rest of the year, when you are in state X you are a state X resident, and when you are in state Y you are a state Y resident.

[107] P.C. § 27560(a)(1).

[108] P.C. § 16730(a).

[109] P.C. § 27950. It is unclear when the loan period must end if the firearm is loaned for a hunting season that is year-round, such as generally the case with regard to pig hunting.

[110] *See* P.C. § 27545.

[111] P.C. § 27880(d).

[112] P.C. § 27885.

You can also loan any lawful firearm to someone over age 18 for shooting targets at a lawfully licensed target facility as long as the firearm does not leave the premises.[113] In the case of "assault weapons" or .50 BMG Rifles, however, the registered owner must remain present.[114]

Under federal law you may temporarily loan or rent a firearm to an out-of-state resident, as well as to "nonimmigrant aliens,"[115] for lawful sporting purposes if you do not know or have reasonable cause to believe that the person you are loaning to is prohibited from receiving or possessing firearms.[116]

# VI. TRANSFERRING AND LOANING FIREARMS TO YOUNG PEOPLE

## A. Minors under Age 18

With the exception of "assault weapons" and .50 BMG rifles, neither California nor federal law regulates rifle or shotgun *possession* by minors. However, firearm *transfers* to a minor are heavily regulated. This includes loaning firearms without the parent or legal guardian's express permission.

Under California law parents or legal guardians may *loan or transfer* a non-handgun to their minor children. Grandparents may as well, but only with the parent or legal guardian's express permission. All others may *only loan* non-handguns to a minor with the express permission of the minor's parent or guardian for no longer than 30 days and only for a "lawful purpose."[117]

If the firearm is a *handgun* and you are not the minor's parent or legal guardian, you may still *loan* it to the minor if *all* of the following conditions exist:

(1) The minor has written consent from their parent or legal guardian before or at the time of the loan, or is accompanied by their parent or legal guardian at the time the loan is made, and

(2) The loan is for a lawful, recreational sport, including, but not limited to, competitive shooting, or agricultural, ranching, or hunting activities, motion picture, television, video production, entertainment or theatrical event, and

---

[113] P.C. §§ 27910, 31765.

[114] *See* Chapter 8.

[115] As long as they meet one of the exceptions described above.

[116] 18 U.S.C. §§ 922(5), 922(d); 27 C.F.R. §§ 478.29-478.30. The same exceptions allowing transfers of firearms to nonimmigrant aliens apply also to ammunition.

[117] P.C. § 27505(b)(4).

(3) The loan does not last longer than reasonably necessary to engage in those activities in subsection (2) above, and

(4) The loan does not, in any event, exceed 10 days.[118]

If you are the minor's parent or legal guardian, you may *loan* the minor a handgun to engage in the activities listed in subsection (2) above as long as the loan does not last longer than reasonably necessary to engage in those activities.[119]

Under federal law it is unlawful for anyone to knowingly transfer a handgun or "ammunition that is suitable for use only in a handgun"[120] to a minor. But it is legal to *temporarily* transfer a handgun or such ammunition to a minor if:

(1) the handgun and ammunition are possessed and used by the minor in the course of employment, ranching, farming (with consent of the rancher or farmer), target practice, hunting, or in a firearm training course,

(2) the minor's parent, who is not a prohibited person, provides written consent for the minor to possess the handgun or ammunition (subject to transportation and farming exceptions), and

(3) the minor keeps the written consent at all times while possessing the handgun or ammunition.[121]

A minor may also inherit *title* to a handgun or ammunition, but *not* possession.[122]

## B. Those between the Ages of 18 and 21

Once a person reaches 18 years of age, both California and federal law allow the person to purchase long guns from an FFL, but not a handgun or other non-long gun, unless it is an "antique firearm," until the person turns 21.[123] California, however, allows "immediate family" (defined below) to give a handgun to someone between 18 and 21 years of age via an intra-family transfer.[124] Once a person reaches 21 years of age, that person becomes eligible to purchase handguns and other non-long guns.[125]

---

[118] P.C. § 27505(b)(6).

[119] P.C. § 27505(b)(5).

[120] 18 U.S.C. § 922(x)(1). There really is no such thing as ammunition "suitable for use only in a handgun," since some non-handguns can safely discharge virtually any cartridge in existence.

[121] For exact wording of this statute, refer to 18 U.S.C. § 922(x)(3) and/or Chapter 3.

[122] 18 U.S.C. § 922(x)(3)(C).

[123] P.C. §§ 27505(a)-(b)(1).

[124] P.C. § 27875.

[125] P.C. § 27505(a).

# VII. EXCEPTIONS TO TRANSFERRING FIREARMS THROUGH FEDERAL FIREARMS LICENSEE

## A. Intra-Family Transactions

Under California law using an FFL is *not* required for *infrequent*[126] transfers of firearms that are generally lawful to possess in California to an "immediate family" member, whether transferred by gift, bequest, intestate succession or other means.

"Immediate family" is a parent/child and/or grandparent/grandchild relationship.[127] This means that siblings, aunts, cousins, etc. are not allowed to directly transfer firearms to each other without using an FFL.

### 1. Long Guns

For an intra-family transfer involving a long gun that is otherwise legal to transfer in California,[128] the law does not require either party to do anything in the way of paperwork.[129] The only restriction is that the recipient be lawfully eligible to possess firearms. There is no minimum age requirement for the recipient, but if it is a grandparent transferring a gun to a minor, then the minor's parent or guardian must give express permission.[130]

### 2. Handguns

To transfer handguns through an intra-family transaction, the transferring party does not need to do anything, but the receiving party must:

- Give the DOJ a completed "Report of Operation of Law or Intra-Familial Handgun Transaction" form within 30 days of receiving the firearm;
- Get an HSC; and
- Be at least age 18.[131]

---

[126] P.C. § 16730(a).

[127] P.C. § 16720.

[128] If you inherit an "assault weapon" or .50 BMG rifle, you have 90 days for "assault weapons" or 180 days for .50 BMG rifles to make the weapon permanently inoperable, sell it to an approved FFL, get a Dangerous Weapons Permit from the DOJ, or remove the firearm from California. P.C. § 30925 ("assault weapons"); P.C. §§ 30930, 30935 (.50 BMG rifles); P.C. § 27870 (inheritance of firearms). California law is unclear on what you should do if you inherit machine guns, destructive devices, or other highly regulated firearms. It is strongly advised you contact an attorney to assist you.

[129] Per AB 809, starting in 2014, long gun transfers between immediate family members will also need to be registered like handguns. See below.

[130] P.C. §§ 27505(b)(2)-(3).

[131] P.C. § 27875.

## B. Inheriting Firearms from Out of State

Though federal law does not have a general "intra-familial transfer" exception to its requirement (described above) that residents of different states must transfer firearms through an FFL in the recipient's home state, there is an exception for firearms transferred by bequest or intestate succession (*i.e.*, inheritance from someone who passed away without a will).[132] This means that, if you inherit a firearm from a resident of another state (regardless of whether you are a family member of the decedent), you can take delivery of that firearm in the other state and transport it back into California without using an FFL.[133] This exception assumes that the firearm is lawful for you to possess in California in the first place and, if the firearm is a handgun, that you register it with the DOJ upon reentering the state per P.C. § 27875.

## C. Transfers between Spouses or Domestic Partners

Under California law firearm transfers between spouses and domestic partners must go through an FFL unless the transferring spouse "transmutes" his or her interest in the firearm to the recipient spouse. A "transmutation" occurs when, during marriage, a spouse shows an express intent, in a signed writing, to change ownership of his or her property.[134] This means that one spouse's separate property can be transmuted (change classification) into the community property of both spouses or into the separate property of the other spouse.[135]

With a firearm the transferring spouse should create a document stating that he or she wishes to make the firearm transfer or that the transferring spouse is releasing his or her separate or community property interest in the firearm, and that the receiving spouse is taking the property as his or her sole and separate property. Both parties should sign and date the document and keep a copy. Additionally all of the above requirements for "intra-familial transfers" also apply to transmutations of firearms between spouses, meaning the recipient spouse must register any handgun with the DOJ and possess an HSC.

---

[132] 18 U.S.C. § 922(a)(5); 27 C.F.R. § 478.30(a).
[133] 18 U.S.C. § 922(a)(3).
[134] Fam. Code § 852(a).
[135] Fam. Code § 850.

# D. Transfers to Those with an Entertainment Firearm Permit (EFP)

Under California and federal law people who possess an EFP are exempt from several firearm transfer requirements for up to one year from the time they were issued the EFP, including the federal background check and the California DROS.[136] Authorized EFP holders may possess firearms for props in motion picture, television, video, theatrical, or other entertainment productions.[137]

# E. Acquiring Antiques and "Curio or Relic" Firearms

California laws about "antiques" and "curio or relic" firearms are complex. These are two different classes of firearms and accordingly have different state and federal requirements.

## 1. Antique Firearms

As discussed in Chapter 2, "antique firearms" are not generally considered "firearms"[138] for the state and federal laws governing firearm transfers.[139] This means that "antique firearms" can be bought outside of your state of residence, purchased from an FFL or any retailer, without filling out a federal Form 4473 or DROS and transferred between private parties without going through an FFL. But, as discussed in Chapter 3, because someone prohibited from possessing firearms in California is also prohibited from possessing "antique firearms," it is also illegal to give one to someone knowing he or she is prohibited from possessing firearms.[140] Likewise, it is unlawful to transfer an "antique firearm" that is a "handgun" to a minor.[141]

---

[136] P.C. §§ 27960, 29530. The NICS exemption provided by the California EFP is a qualifying alternative to the background check requirements for up to one year from the issue date. To check the status of the EFP as an acceptable alternative to NICS, *see ATF Online - Firearms - Brady Law / NICS - Permit Chart*, U.S. DEPT. OF JUSTICE - BUREAU OF ALCOHOL, TOBACCO, FIREARMS AND EXPLOSIVES, http://www.atf.gov/firearms/brady-law/permit-chart.html (last visited July 31, 2012).

[137] P.C. § 27960(a)(4). For other exemptions provided to EFP holders *see* P.C. §§ 27960(a), 27810(a)(3), 31820(a); *see also Entertainment Firearms Permit, State of California, Dept. of Justice*, STATE OF CALIFORNIA, OFFICE OF THE ATTORNEY GENERAL, http://ag.ca.gov/firearms/epp.php (last visited July 31, 2012).

[138] P.C. § 16170(b); 18 U.S.C. §§ 921(a)(7), (a)(3).

[139] For example, "antique firearms" are not "firearms" for dealer licensing requirements, sales or loans between private parties, firearm safety device requirements, or HSCs. *See* P.C. §§ 16620, 16730(a) and (c), 16960, 17310, 26500-26588 (inclusive), 16130, 16400, 16550, 16810, 17110, 26700-26915 (inclusive), 27510, 27540, 27545, 28100, and 31615.

[140] P.C. § 27500(a).

[141] P.C. §§ 27505(a)-(b)(1).

## 2. "Curio or Relic" Firearms

Since both California and the ATF define a "curio or relic" firearm the same way (see Chapter 2), if the ATF considers a firearm a "curio or relic," then so does California. The regulations of "curio or relic" transfers, however, differ between California and federal law.

"Curio or relic" firearms are associated with a Type 03 FFL license, which is commonly known as a "collector's license."[142] The federal privileges conferred by this license extend *only* to transactions involving weapons classified as "curio or relic" firearms for personal collection purposes. This means a person with a collector's license is still subject to general federal firearm-transfer regulations when purchasing non-"curio or relic" firearms and cannot be "engaged in the business"[143] of selling even "curio or relic" firearms without a separate *dealer's* license (*i.e.*, Type 01 FFL).[144] Additionally Type 03 FFLs must still comply with state laws, meaning they are not exempt from transfer or possession restrictions on certain firearms, even "curio or relic" firearms, if not allowed under state law.[145]

The general advantages of a collector's license are that it exempts you from the federal background check requirement[146] and allows you to purchase "curio or relic" firearms from FFLs from other states.[147] Individuals who do *not* possess a collector's license may acquire "curio or relic" *long guns* in a state where they are not a resident as long as:

1) the rifle/shotgun is acquired from a federally licensed importer, manufacturer, dealer, or collector;

2) the purchaser meets with the licensee at the licensee's premises to accomplish the transfer, sale, and delivery;

3) a background check is conducted and a 4473 is filled out when the firearm is transferred by the importer, manufacturer, or dealer; and

4) the conditions of sale in both parties' states are complied with.[148]

As explained above, the option to acquire "curio or relic" long guns out of state is effectively not available to a California-only resident. This is be-

[142] 18 U.S.C. § 921(a)(13); 27 C.F.R. §§ 478.41(c)-(d).

[143] 18 U.S.C. § 921(a)(21).

[144] 18 U.S.C. §§ 922(a), 923(b), 27 C.F.R. §§ 478.41(c)-(d), 27 C.F.R. § 478.93. To obtain a collector's license, submit ATF Form 7CR, Application for License (Collector of Curios or Relics). 27 C.F.R. § 478.47.

[145] 18 U.S.C. § 922(b)(2); 27 C.F.R. § 478.99(b)(2).

[146] 18 U.S.C. § 922(t)(1). This does not mean that you may possess a "curio or relic" firearm if you are prohibited from possessing firearms in general, just that you do not have to undergo a background check to get one. Likewise, it does not allow you to transfer "curio or relic" firearms to prohibited persons. 27 C.F.R. § 478.32(d).

[147] 18 U.S.C. § 922(a)(2); 27 C.F.R. §§ 478.41(c)-(d).

[148] 27 C.F.R. § 478.96(c)(1).

cause the out-of-state seller likely cannot comply with California's transfer requirements. There is an exception, however, if the out-of-state seller is a collector and *not* a Type 01 FFL. This is because, as explained below, the transfer of some "curio or relic" long guns (those over 50 years old) *from* a collector would not have to go through a Type 01 FFL if transferred in California. Therefore, they would not be subject to California's general transfer requirements (whereas they would be if the seller were a Type 01 FFL). So such a transfer satisfies federal law requirements that both states' laws are complied with (assuming that is also the case for the other state).

There are additional federal requirements and restrictions for those with a collector's license, including record-keeping requirements of their "curio or relic" transactions, which are beyond the scope of this book but which you need to be aware of before you engage in such transactions.[149]

Under California law a California resident can transfer or buy a "curio or relic" *long gun* from another California resident without going through an FFL as long as the rifle or shotgun is 50 years or older.[150] "Curio or relic" handguns, however, must be transferred through an FFL just like modern ones, even if the purchaser is a Type 03 FFL.

An FFL must transfer any "curio or relic" firearm the same way as a non-"curio or relic" modern firearm even if it is being transferred to a Type 03 FFL. There are a few exceptions however.

Specifically a Type 03 FFL who holds a California DOJ COE is exempt from California's 10-day waiting period when buying a "curio or relic" firearm, even if it's *less than* 50 years old.[151] And, as explained above, these FFLs are also exempt from California's general requirements for handgun transfers, such as transferees having an HSC, the need to perform the safe-handling demonstration, and the one handgun per month restriction if the handgun is a "curio or relic."[152] Additionally, firearms listed as "curio or relic" handguns need not pass the safety and functionality tests required

---

[149] For general information on "curio or relic" licenses, related federal laws, and the list of "curio or relic" firearms, *see Firearms Curios or Relics List*, U.S. Dept. of Justice - Bureau of Alcohol, Tobacco, Firearms and Explosives, http://www.atf.gov/publications/download/p/atf-p-5300-11/atf-p-5300-11.pdf (last visited July 31, 2012).

[150] Information Bulletin No. 98-24-BCIA – Curio and Relic Long Guns and 30-day Firearms Delivery Requirements (Cal. Dept. of Justice 1998); *Information Bulletin No. 98-24-BCIA Curio and Relic Long Guns and 30-day Firearms Delivery Requirements*, California Dept. of Justice, http://oag.ca.gov/sites/all/files/pdfs/firearms/infobuls/9824.pdf (last visited July 31, 2012). If you cannot confirm the rifle or shotgun is at least 50 years old, do not purchase it without going through an FFL. As discussed above, you cannot engage in the business of dealing firearms without a license and you must be eligible to possess firearms.

[151] P.C. §§ 26970(a), 27670(a).

[152] P.C. §§ 27535(b)(9), 26970(a), 27670(a). You should be aware that there is a dispute over whether those with a Type 03 FFL and a COE are exempt from the "one handgun a month" restriction for modern handgun transfers too.

to be on the DOJ's Roster of handguns that FFLs can sell in California.[153] And a Type 03 FFL, when obtaining the handgun from out of state,[154] must register it with the DOJ within five days of transporting the firearm into California.[155]

Certain firearms meeting the "curio or relic" definition may still have possession and transfer restrictions (e.g., "machineguns" or destructive devices.) Make sure the firearm is legal to possess federally and in California, and then, no matter what the firearm's age, consult the ATF "Firearms Curio and Relic List." Also consult California's firearm regulations to make sure the firearm does not fall under California's "assault weapons" ban. While that ban does not include certain "antique firearms,"[156] it can include "curio or relic" firearms, even popular ones like some M1A1 carbines. "Curio or relic" firearms are, however, exempt from California's ban on .50 BMG rifles that are not already "assault weapons."[157]

## F. Nonprofit Auction of Non-Handguns

Infrequent[158] PPTs of non-handguns at an auction or similar event by a nonprofit corporation do not need to be processed through an FFL. Likewise, donating a non-handgun through a PPT to a nonprofit for sale at such an auction does not need to go through an FFL if delivered to the nonprofit immediately before or during the auction.[159]

The term "infrequent" does not prohibit different local chapters of the same nonprofit corporation from conducting auctions with such transfers. This means that each *individual* chapter enjoys this exception and can have such transfers at their auctions regardless of the activity of other chapters, as long as each one does so "infrequently"[160] and/or does not "engage in the business" of dealing firearms.

---

[153] P.C. § 32000(b)(3).

[154] Type 03 FFLs from California can obtain a "curio or relic" handgun while outside of the state and bring it back, provided they comply with the California registration requirements for "curio or relic" collectors. 18 U.S.C. § 922(a)(3); P.C. § 27565.

[155] P.C. § 27565(b). Use Form FD 4100A, which is available on the California DOJ website, and pay a $19 processing fee per handgun.

[156] The exception to the "assault weapon" ban for antique firearms only applies to firearms manufactured before January 1, 1899. P.C. § 16170(a).

[157] P.C. § 30530(b).

[158] P.C. §§ 16730(a)-(b).

[159] P.C. § 27900(a).

[160] P.C. § 16730(b).

# VIII. BUILDING YOUR OWN FIREARM

Another way to obtain a firearm is by making one or assembling one from parts. This practice *can be* lawful under both California and federal law. Federal law prohibits "manufacturing" firearms without a license, but only considers those who are "engaged in the business" of making firearms (*i.e.*, those who devote time, attention, and labor to doing so as a regular course of business) to be "manufacturers who need a license."[161] This means that making a firearm for personal use does not require a license under federal or California law as long as you do not build an item that is prohibited to possess or make under California law.[162]

Generally two different processes exist for building a personal firearm, and each has distinct legal implications. First, you can purchase a finished "frame" or "receiver"[163] and then assemble it with additional parts to complete the firearm. Laws generally do not prohibit acquiring "firearm" parts, but because federal law considers a "frame" or a "receiver" to be a "firearm," as does California law governing firearm acquisition,[164] you have to get the frame or receiver through an FFL just like any other firearm (as explained above) or meet one of the exceptions. As mentioned above, you also must be at least age 21 to purchase a receiver.

The second way is to machine a firearm either from completely raw materials or partially finished materials. Making a firearm from partially finished materials is more popular as it takes less skill. Generally you start with an incomplete receiver commonly referred to as an "80% receiver" or "80% side plate."

The "80%" denotes how close the receiver is to being a complete firearm – though this is more of an estimate since it is impossible to say what percentage of work remains for a given firearm, which can vary based on experience, available tools, etc. An "80% receiver" is not considered a "firearm" under either federal or state law for the purposes of transfers. You must machine the remaining "20%" to complete the receiver, at which point it is considered a "firearm." Thereafter, you can either purchase the

---

[161] 18 U.S.C. §§ 921(a)(10), (21); 18 U.S.C. § 923(a)(1).

[162] This does not mean you can *never* sell a firearm you build. It just means you cannot be "engaged in the business" of "manufacturing" firearms to sell them to or through an FFL without a license. What constitutes being "engaged in the business" of "manufacturing" can be a complicated legal question that is beyond the scope of this book. As always, if you question whether your activities require a "manufacturing" license, consult an attorney. Otherwise, the discussion here assumes you are building a single firearm for your own personal use.

[163] A "receiver" is "[t]he basic unit of a firearm which houses the firing mechanism and to which the barrel and stock are assembled. In revolvers, pistols and break-open firearms, it is called the frame." National Shooting Sports Foundation Inc., *The Writer's Guide to Firearms and Ammunition* 40 (2007).

[164] 18 U.S.C. § 921(a)(3)(B); P.C. § 16520(b). *See* Chapter 2.

remaining parts (barrel, stock, etc.) or machine them from raw materials and then attach them to the receiver.

The firearm you build cannot be an item that is generally unlawful to possess or manufacture under either California or federal law (see Chapters 8 and 9).[165]

Excepting licensed manufacturers with government permission and those fixing lawfully acquired firearms,[166] federal law prohibits assembling a semiautomatic rifle or any shotgun using more than ten "imported parts"[167] if the assembled firearm is prohibited from being imported[168] as not "particularly suitable for or readily adaptable to sporting purposes."[169]

Lastly, unless you make a "firearm" as defined under the NFA (see Chapter 9), requiring a tax payment and ATF approval,[170] there is generally no California or federal requirement that you register a firearm assembled for personal use. Although not legally required, it is a good idea to at least identify the firearm with a serial number in case it is ever lost or stolen. Likewise, it should be identified for compliance with 27 C.F.R. § 478.92 if it is ever sold or otherwise lawfully transferred in the future.

# IX. COMING INTO CALIFORNIA WITH FIREARMS

## A. Visiting California

If you are coming into California to visit or establish residency and are bringing firearms, ammunition, or magazines, your first order of business is to determine if these items are legal for you to possess or import into California. You can do this by reviewing Chapters 8 and 9 and the California DOJ's Bureau of Firearms website. If you lawfully possess items out of state that are illegal to possess in California, you will need to get the applicable permits or licenses or meet an exception mentioned in the corresponding chapters *before* bringing them into California.

---

[165] Though there are other prohibited items, the main concern is to avoid inadvertently building an "assault weapon" (Chapter 8) or a "zip gun" (Chapter 9). The receiver must also be unable to accept fire-control components designed to allow full automatic fire, which would make it a machine gun.

[166] 27 C.F.R. § 478.39(b).

[167] 27 C.F.R. § 478.39(a). "Imported parts" are: "(1) Frames, receivers, receiver castings, forgings, or castings (2) Barrels (3) Barrel extensions (4) Mounting blocks (trunnions) (5) Muzzle attachments (6) Bolts (7) Bolt carriers (8) Operating rods (9) Gas pistons (10) Trigger housings (11) Triggers (12) Hammers (13) Sears (14) Disconnectors (15) Buttstocks (16) Pistol grips (17) Forearms, handguards (18) Magazine bodies (19) followers (20) Floor plates." 27 C.F.R. § 478.39(c).

[168] 18 U.S.C. § 925(d)(3); 26 U.S.C. § 5845(a).

[169] 18 U.S.C. §§ 922(r), 925(d)(3); 27 C.F.R. § 478.39(a).

[170] 26 U.S.C. § 5822.

It is legal to bring an "off-Roster" handgun on your visit to California as long as you are not going to sell it.[171]

## B. Moving into California

In addition to the restrictions when just visiting, if you come to California intending to make it your permanent residence and you meet the definition of a "personal handgun importer," you will have to register your handguns[172] with the DOJ or sell or transfer them within 60 days of bringing them into California.[173]

You are considered a "personal handgun importer" if you are over 18 years of age, own a handgun, and meet all of the following:

- You are not licensed pursuant to P.C. §§ 26700 to 26915, inclusive.
- You are not a licensed firearms manufacturer or importer.[174]
- You acquired the handgun outside of California.
- You moved into this state on or after January 1, 1998, as a resident[175] of this state.
- You intend to possess that handgun within this state on or after January 1, 1998.
- The handgun was delivered to you by a person who is not licensed as a California firearm dealer.[176]
- While a California resident, you did not previously report ownership of that handgun to the DOJ with information about you and a description of the firearm.
- The handgun is not prohibited by any of P.C. § 16590's provisions.
- The handgun is not an "assault weapon" or "machine gun."[177]

People are often concerned that they have not properly registered their handguns after the 60-day requirement has lapsed. In the past the DOJ has allowed late handgun registration, but this could change in the future.

---

[171] California law prohibits the importation of an "unsafe handgun" for sales. P.C. § 32000. "Unsafe handguns" and the California DOJ's Roster of Handguns Certified for Sale (Roster) in California is discussed in more detail in Chapter 9.

[172] On January 1, 2014, AB 809 will require those coming to California intending to make it their residence register their long guns in addition to their handguns.

[173] P.C. § 27560.

[174] 18 U.S.C. § 921 et seq.

[175] You are a resident of California if California is your true, fixed, and permanent home and principal residence to which you intend to return whenever you are absent. P.C. § 17000(b)(1); Cal. Veh. Code § 12505. For military members, residency is established when you are discharged from active service in California. P.C. § 17000(b)(2).

[176] The person must be licensed per P.C. §§ 26700 to 26915, inclusive, and must have delivered the firearm as set forth in P.C. § 27540 and P.C. §§ 26700-26915, inclusive.

[177] P.C. § 17000.

Finally it is legal to bring an "off-Roster" handgun that is otherwise legal when moving into California as long as you comply with the above requirements and you are not importing it with the intent of selling it once here.

# X.  FIREARM STORAGE AND CHILDREN

Although both California and federal law require that a "safety device" accompany your firearm purchase, neither set of laws requires that you actually use one. In fact, no state or federal law specifically requires firearms to be stored in any particular manner, although some cities have local firearm-storage requirements.[178]

Despite this you may nonetheless be prosecuted for criminally storing a firearm if you keep a loaded firearm anywhere under your custody or control where you know, or reasonably should know, a child is likely to gain unpermitted access to it, a child does get access to it, and death or great bodily injury occurs as a result.[179]

Though it is a lesser offense, you may also be prosecuted if a child who accesses your firearm either "brandishes" it[180] or carries it to a public place.[181]

Where the person who allegedly stored a firearm in violation of P.C. § 25100 is the parent or guardian of a child injured or killed, California law gives prosecutors express discretion to bring or not bring charges. It suggests charges should only be brought where the parent acted in a grossly negligent manner or where other "egregious circumstances" exist.[182] But it is best to avoid tragedy and relying on a prosecutor's mercy by properly storing your firearms whenever children are present.

You can also be prosecuted for a misdemeanor if you keep a handgun, whether loaded or unloaded, anywhere under your custody or control and know, or reasonably should know, that a child is likely to gain unpermitted access to it, a child does gain access to it, and thereafter carries it off-premises.[183]

It is also a misdemeanor, with a possible steeper maximum fine ($5,000 vs. $1,000) if the child takes any firearm to a preschool, elementary, middle,

---

[178] For example, San Francisco has a firearm storage requirement that I am challenging on behalf of the NRA as a Second Amendment infringement. *Jackson v. City and County of San Francisco*, No. C09-cv-02143 (N.D. Cal. filed May 15, 2009).

[179] P.C. § 25100. Note that a "child" (*i.e.,* "minor") is "a person under 18 years of age." P.C. § 25000.

[180] *See* P.C. § 417, describing crime of "brandishing".

[181] *Compare* P.C. § 25100(b).

[182] P.C. § 25115.

[183] P.C. § 25200(a).

or high school, or to any school-sponsored event, activity, or performance, whether it occurs on school grounds or not.[184]

You should *not*, however, be prosecuted for criminally storing a firearm if:

- The child obtained the firearm as a result of an illegal entry to your premises.
- The firearm is kept in a locked container or place a reasonable person would believe is secure.
- The firearm is carried on you or is so close in proximity to you that you can easily obtain and use it as if it were actually carried on you.
- The firearm has a locking device that has made the firearm inoperable.
- You are a peace officer, National Guard or military member, and the child obtains the firearm during, or incidental to, the performance of your duties.
- The child obtains, or obtains and discharges, the firearm in self-defense or in defense of another person.
- Based on objective facts and circumstances, it would be unreasonable to expect a child to be present on your premises.[185]

# XI. ACQUIRING AMMUNITION

"Armor-piercing," "explosive," and "incendiary" rounds are generally unlawful to acquire,[186] but beyond these very few restrictions exist for law-abiding adults to acquire ammunition or ammunition components. The main restrictions are on certain groups of people who are generally prohibited from receiving ammunition.[187]

Likewise there are no federal or state restrictions on transferring ammunition to non-residents. Someone visiting California from Oklahoma can purchase ammunition without penalty for the person selling it, as long as it is for a lawful purpose. However, as is the case with firearms, the same federal restrictions applicable to transferring firearms to "nonimmigrant aliens" also apply to ammunition.

---

[184] P.C. § 25200(b).

[185] P.C. § 25105.

[186] 18 U.S.C. § 921(a)(3)(B); P.C. § 16520. These are discussed in Chapter 9.

[187] See Chapter 3 for more on individuals restricted from possessing ammunition.

## A. Assembly Bill 962 and Similar Ammunition Regulation Efforts

AB 962 would have imposed burdensome and ill-conceived restrictions on the sale of ammunition within, and into, California. It required "handgun ammunition" be stored out of customers' reach and transferred face to face, thereby making mail-order sales illegal, and also required ammunition vendors to collect sales information that included ammunition purchaser thumbprints.

At the time of printing this book, AB 962's main provisions were found unconstitutionally vague because its "handgun ammunition" is unclear.[188] Legal developments could cause AB 962 to go into effect in the future or be repealed permanently. Subscribe to or check www.calgunlaws.com for AB 962's current status.

Finally, know that several cities and counties currently regulate ammunition transactions similar to AB 962's provisions. But instead of regulating "handgun ammunition" in isolation, they regulate the sale of *all* ammunition. Los Angeles, Sacramento, Inglewood, Santa Ana, Beverly Hills, and Contra Costa County are examples. Consult your local municipal code to confirm whether ordinances like these exist in your city or county.

## B. Shipping Ammunition

Assuming AB 962's provisions are not in effect and it is legal to mail ammunition, certain regulations still apply. If within the continental U.S., the ammunition must be less than .50 caliber (except for shotgun shells), weigh less than 60 lbs., be in a box marked on at least one side with "ORM-D" in writing or have such a sticker, and be packaged per 49 C.F.R. § 173.63(b)(2). The laws relating to shipping ammunition are expected to change in the near future.

---

[188] *See Parker v. State of California*, No. 10CECG02116 (Super. Ct. Fresno Jan. 31, 2011), *appeal docketed*, No. F062490 (Cal. App. May 20, 2011); *see also Firearms Cases*, MICHEL & ASSOCIATES, P.C., http://michel-lawyers.com/significant-cases/firearms-cases/ (last visited July 31, 2012). I litigated this case on behalf of the CRPA Foundation.

## CHAPTER 5

# CARRYING FIREARMS OPENLY, CONCEALED, AND/OR LOADED

alifornia generally makes it illegal to carry "handguns"[1] or "any rocket, rocket propelled projectile launcher, or similar device containing
any explosive or incendiary material"[2] in a "concealed" manner anywhere, regardless of whether it is loaded.[3] It likewise generally prohibits
carrying in most "public places" any "loaded" *firearm*[4] or unloaded *handgun*, even if the handgun is not concealed but carried "openly."[5]

As discussed next in Chapter 6, these general prohibitions have multiple exceptions. Together, the laws that prohibit carrying firearms openly,
concealed, and/or loaded, and their exceptions, create the general frame-
work of California's regulation of firearms outside the home.

To understand when the prohibitions apply, and when they do not, you
first need to know how the terms used in the statutes are interpreted and
defined. That is the focus of this chapter.[6]

---

[1] "Handgun" means "any pistol, revolver, or firearm capable of being concealed upon the person." P.C.
§16640(a). "Firearm capable of being concealed upon the person," "pistol," and "revolver" include "any
device designed to be used as a weapon, from which is expelled a projectile by the force of any explosion, or other form of combustion, and that has a barrel less than 16 inches in length" or that "has
a barrel 16 inches or more in length which is designed to be interchanged with a barrel less than 16
inches in length." P.C. § 16530(a). When the term "handgun" is used in this book, it will mean firearms
to which the open and concealed carry laws apply (including "rockets," etc.).

[2] P.C. § 16520(c). It is irrelevant whether the device is designed for emergency signaling purposes. This
means you can be charged for carrying a signal flare launcher that is concealed or loaded, unless an
exception applies (as discussed in Chapter 6).

[3] P.C. § 25400.

[4] P.C. § 25850(a).

[5] P.C. § 26350. At the time of this book's publication, there was a bill pending in the California Legislature to extend the restriction on carrying unloaded handguns "openly" in most "public places" to
generally include non-handguns, *i.e.*, rifles, shotguns, etc.

[6] Note that this chapter assumes that the person possessing the firearm may legally do so and the firearm itself is legal in California. For exceptions to carrying firearms openly, concealed, or loaded, refer
to Chapter 6. For firearms that may be generally prohibited, refer to Chapters 8 and 9.

# I. CONCEALED CARRY LAW

## A. Carrying "Concealed"

Unless an exception applies, you can be found guilty of carrying a concealed handgun if you knowingly do any of the following:

- Carry any concealed handgun in any vehicle under your control or direction.
- Carry any concealed handgun on your person.
- Cause a handgun to be carried concealed in a vehicle where you are an occupant.[7]

Note that the concealed carry law only applies to handguns and it does not matter whether the handgun is loaded or unloaded. The concealed carry law applies anytime a handgun is hidden from view, possibly even if partially so.

Carrying concealed is generally a misdemeanor[8] unless you are not in "lawful possession" of the handgun[9] or are generally prohibited from possessing firearms (discussed in Chapter 3),[10] have been convicted of certain firearm-related crimes,[11] the handgun is stolen and you knew or had reason to believe it was stolen,[12] you participate in a criminal street gang,[13] or you have been convicted of certain crimes against person or property or of a narcotic or dangerous drug violation.[14] In those cases the charge is either a "wobbler" (can be charged as a misdemeanor or felony) or a straight felony offense.[15]

Also, if you are carrying a handgun that is not registered to you and that handgun is either loaded (definition explained below) or its unexpended ammunition is in your immediate possession or readily accessible, you can be charged with a felony.[16] If you did not obtain the handgun through an

---

[7] P.C. § 25400(a).

[8] P.C. § 25400(c)(7).

[9] "Lawful possession" means the person possessing the firearm either lawfully owns it or has permission from the lawful owner or a person who otherwise has apparent authority to possess it. P.C. § 16750(a).

[10] P.C. § 25400(c)(4).

[11] P.C. §§ 25400(c)(1), 16580.

[12] P.C. § 25400(c)(2).

[13] P.C. § 25400(c)(3).

[14] P.C. § 25400(c)(5).

[15] P.C. § 25400(c).

[16] P.C. § 25400(c)(6).

FFL or register it with the DOJ yourself, it is probably not registered to you, and may be registered to someone else.[17]

## B. What Does "Concealed" Mean?

The Penal Code does not define "concealed," other than to say a firearm carried in a belt-holster is *not* "concealed."[18] Case law provides a little additional guidance as to its definition.

At least one court has suggested that a semiautomatic handgun is considered legally "concealed" just by ejecting its magazine and placing the magazine in a nearby location where it is not visible, even though the firearm itself is.[19] In that case, *People v. Hale*, the defendant's handgun was on the passenger seat of his car in plain view. The handgun's magazine, full of ammunition, was underneath the ashtray in the center console. The court said concealing a vital part of a visible weapon threatens public order just like concealing the entire firearm would, if it would "make the weapon *readily available for use as a firearm ...*"[20]

It is unclear what other "necessary components" of a visible firearm – beyond a magazine containing ammunition – would render, if concealed, the entire firearm "concealed" for purposes of the concealed restriction. It is also unclear whether a concealed magazine must have ammunition in it to make a visible handgun "readily available for use as a firearm," and thus be considered "concealed" under *Hale*. Unless you want to be a test case, you should assume concealing even an *empty* magazine is prohibited if you are also "carrying" the handgun that uses it. To be safe, you should assume concealing any part of a handgun is prohibited.

The exact definition of "concealed" is thus not entirely clear. Beyond a few gray areas, like where one's shirt or jacket covers part of a holstered handgun, it is generally obvious whether a firearm is "concealed" as that term is commonly understood – kept secret, hidden, or kept out of sight.[21]

---

[17] If you want to find out what firearms are registered in your name, you can submit to the California DOJ an Automated Firearms System [AFS] Request for Firearm Records, *available at* http://oag.ca.gov/sites/all/files/pdfs/firearms/forms/AFSPrivateCitizen.pdf. *See* Chapter 4.

[18] P.C. § 25400(b).

[19] *People v. Hale*, 43 Cal.App.3d 353, 356 (1974).

[20] *People v. Hale*, 43 Cal.App.3d 353, 356 (1974) (emphasis added). It should be noted that this case does not specifically deal with California's concealed carry laws but provides an analysis of them that a court may find persuasive.

[21] A concealed weapon is "[a] weapon that is carried by a person but that is not visible by ordinary observation." BLACK'S LAW DICTIONARY 775 (9th ed. 2009).

## C. What Does "Carry" Mean?

The term "carry" has been construed as not requiring actual locomotion (*i.e.*, movement from one place to another). Rather, to be considered "carried" according to the law, a handgun need only be so connected with the person (or a vehicle) in a way that the body (or vehicle) *would* carry the firearm with it as concealed if in locomotion.[22] Therefore, a firearm within a vehicle[23] (even if not in a person's exclusive possession),[24] despite not being in contact with the person, is still legally considered as being "carried."

Obviously, if a firearm is in your hand or attached to your person, it is being "carried." Some courts, however, have held that firearms are "carried" even when they are not physically attached to the body, such as a firearm kept inside a suitcase.[25]

Likewise, a handgun in a vehicle does not need to be on your person to be "carried" by you. Rather, if you are controlling the vehicle and know the handgun is in it, you are "carrying" the handgun.[26]

How to lawfully transport firearms is discussed in Chapter 6.

# II. LOADED CARRY LAW

## A. Loaded Firearm Restrictions

California also generally prohibits carrying a "loaded" firearm in most public places. You are guilty of carrying a loaded firearm if you carry it on your person or in your "vehicle while in any public place or on any public street in an incorporated city or in any public place or on any public street in a prohibited area of unincorporated territory."[27]

Even *inoperable* firearms may violate loaded carry laws.[28]

---

[22] *See People v. Smith*, 72 Cal.App.2d Supp. 875 (1946).

[23] *People v. Smith*, 72 Cal.App.2d Supp. 875 (1946).

[24] *People v. Davis*, 157 Cal.App.2d 33, 35-36 (1958) (defendant found to be "carrying" a concealed revolver under the driver's seat; exclusive possession was not required because the vehicle was under the control and/or direction of the defendant).

[25] *People v. Dunn*, 61 Cal.App.3d Supp. 12, 14 (1976) (defendant found to be "carrying" a concealed handgun in his locked suitcase when the locked suitcase passed through an airport x-ray machine).

[26] *People v. Davis*, 157 Cal.App.2d 33, 35-36 (1958) (defendant found to be "carrying" a concealed revolver under the driver's seat; exclusive possession was not required because the vehicle was under the control and/or direction of the defendant).

[27] P.C. § 25850(a). This includes "rockets" and related devices. P.C. § 16520(c)(4). Pay particular attention to this "prohibited area of an unincorporated territory" language. Even if the area is unincorporated and is not a place where you may lawfully discharge a firearm, do not assume that carrying a loaded firearm there is not a crime.

[28] *See People v. Taylor*, 151 Cal.App.3d 432, 437 (1984) (holding that "operability is not an element of possession of a loaded firearm in a public place.") *See also* Chapter 2 (defining "firearm").

You can be prosecuted for carrying a loaded firearm even if you did not know that the firearm was loaded. The prosecuting attorney does not have to prove that you knew the firearm was loaded, just that you knew you were carrying a firearm.[29] In the case of *People v. Dillard,* Mr. Dillard was stopped while riding his bicycle and carrying a rifle in its case. The officer examined the rifle and found a round in the chamber and six more in the "cylinder." Mr. Dillard testified that the firearm was his, that he just picked the firearm up from his stepfather's house, and he did not examine the firearm. The court determined that, in light of the "legislative concern for public safety as against the presence of armed individuals in public places," the restriction against possessing a loaded firearm in public is a "quintessential public welfare statute" and no actual knowledge that the firearm was loaded must be proven.[30]

California law authorizes peace officers to examine any firearm carried in any "public place" where the loaded restriction applies to determine whether it is loaded. Refusing such an inspection is grounds for arrest.[31]

Like carrying a concealed handgun unlawfully, possessing a loaded firearm in a restricted public place unlawfully is also generally a misdemeanor[32] unless you are not in "lawful possession" of the firearm,[33] you are generally prohibited from possessing firearms (discussed in Chapter 3), you have been convicted of certain firearm-related crimes,[34] the firearm is stolen and you knew or had reason to believe it was stolen,[35] you participate in a criminal street gang,[36] or you have been convicted of certain crimes against person or property or of a narcotic or dangerous drug violation.[37] In those cases the charge is either a "wobbler" or a straight felony.[38] Also, if it is a "loaded" *handgun,* carrying it "concealed" can be charged as a separate offense, and can warrant a felony charge.[39]

---

[29] CALCRIM 2530.

[30] *People v. Dillard,* 154 Cal.App.3d 261, 266 (1984).

[31] *See* P.C. § 25850(b) and Chapter 10.

[32] P.C. § 25850(c)(7).

[33] As defined in P.C. § 16750(a).

[34] P.C. § 25850(c)(1).

[35] P.C. § 25850(c)(2).

[36] P.C. § 25850(c)(3).

[37] P.C. § 25850(c)(5).

[38] P.C. § 25850(c).

[39] *See* P.C. §§ 25400, 25850.

## B. What Does "Loaded" Mean?

There are different definitions of "loaded" in the Penal Code. Even the Fish and Game Code has its own definition of "loaded" that applies to shotguns and rifles while hunting. So it is not surprising that people, even law enforcement, get confused about whether a firearm is legally considered "loaded."

### 1. General Definition of "Loaded"

Generally a firearm is "loaded" when it has "an unexpended cartridge or shell consisting of a case that holds a charge of powder and a bullet or shot, in, or attached to, the firearm, including, but not limited to, in the firing chamber, magazine, or clip attached in any manner to the firearm."[40] This general definition of "loaded" also applies to "any rocket, rocket propelled projectile launcher, or similar device containing any explosive or incendiary material ..."[41] A muzzle-loader firearm is considered "loaded" "when it is capped or primed and has a powder charge and ball or shot in the barrel or cylinder."[42]

Under the general definition a firearm must have ammunition in a position from where it can be fired or be "ready for firing." For example, if ammunition is placed in the chamber or cylinder, the ammunition would be "attached" and the firearm would be considered "loaded."[43]

In *Clark* the police seized the defendant's shotgun, which did not have a shell in the firing chamber. Three shells, however, were located in a covered compartment at the rear of the shotgun's stock. The shells could not be fired from their position but would have to be manually inserted into the shotgun's chamber. The defendant was convicted, but the appellate court reversed the decision, holding that the shotgun was not "loaded." The appellate court reasoned that "attached to the firearm" applies where "the [ammunition] is placed in a position from which it can be fired" or if it is "ready for firing." Additionally the court interpreted the statute's legislative intent to *not* "indicate a clear intent to deem a gun 'loaded' when the ammunition... is in a storage compartment which is not equivalent to either a magazine or clip and from which the ammunition cannot be fired."[44]

The *Clark* court's reasoning for why the shotgun was not "loaded" is not necessarily applicable to determining whether a handgun is "loaded"

---

[40] P.C. § 16840(b)(1).

[41] P.C. § 16520(c).

[42] P.C. § 16840(b)(2). A muzzle-loading firearm is typically a firearm that uses black powder as a propellant, which along with the bullet (ball or shot) is inserted through the muzzle.

[43] *People v. Clark*, 45 Cal.App.4th 1147, 1154 (1996).

[44] *People v. Clark*, 45 Cal.App.4th 1147, 1154 (1996).

when its uninserted magazine or clip (or speed loader) contains ammunition. The court distinguishes a permissible separate storage compartment "from which ammunition cannot be fired" from "a magazine or clip" (which likely includes a speed loader).[45] Of course this language was intended to explain what does *not* constitute "loaded," and it is possible, and even likely, that such language does *not* mean having ammunition in a magazine or clip that is ejected from the firearm makes that firearm "loaded." And the fact that a shotgun with ammunition inside its stock, as was the case in *Clark*, is not considered "loaded" further supports the view that a handgun with a full magazine nearby should not be considered "loaded" since both scenarios allow the firearm to accept and discharge a round with similar speed. But it remains unclear.

A semiautomatic firearm without a round in the chamber but having a magazine containing ammunition inserted in the magazine well may be (and in practice usually is) considered "loaded" even though the firearm is not completely "ready for firing" until a round is cycled into the chamber. But if a semiautomatic firearm does not have a round in the chamber and the magazine is not inserted into the magazine well, it is probably not considered "loaded" under this general definition. This likely remains true even if you have a magazine full of ammunition near the firearm, such as in the same locked container. Of course, because it is not clear, law enforcement could see it another way.

Because of the different definitions of "loaded," ammunition should be transported in a way that it cannot contact the firearm to avoid problems with law enforcement, even though it may not be required.

## 2.  "Loaded" While Committing a Felony or in Sensitive Places

The general definition of "loaded" described above does not apply when someone is charged with "armed criminal action." "Armed criminal action" occurs when someone "carries" a "loaded" firearm and intends to commit a felony.[46] Here, a firearm is considered "loaded" if the person immediately possesses *both* the firearm and the ammunition to fire it.[47] The ammunition does not need to be physically touching the firearm.

An almost identical definition of "loaded" applies to carrying firearms in certain sensitive places like those listed in P.C. §§ 171c and 171d, including places like the State Capitol building and legislative offices.[48]

---

[45] *People v. Clark*, 45 Cal.App.4th 1147, 1154 (1996).

[46] P.C. § 25800(a).

[47] P.C. § 16840(a).

[48] *See, e.g.*, P.C. § 171e and Chapter 7.

### 3. Fish and Game's Definition of "Loaded"

Under Fish and Game Code § 2006, a *rifle* or *shotgun*[49] is loaded if it has a live round (or unexpended cartridge or shell) *in the firing chamber.*[50] This means that even if the firearm has ammunition in it, like in a magazine, it is still not "loaded" unless it has a round in the chamber.

This definition applies while "in any vehicle or conveyance or its attachments, which is standing on, along, or is being driven on or along any public highway *or other way open to the public.*"[51] Typically individuals will be charged under this section while hunting, though they can be charged under the general loaded restriction instead, which does not require that a round be chambered to be in violation.

## III. OPEN (UNCONCEALED) UNLOADED CARRY OF HANDGUNS[52]

You may be guilty of a misdemeanor if you openly[53] carry an unloaded[54] *handgun*[55] on you or inside or on a vehicle while in or on any of the following:

- "A public place or public street in an incorporated city or city and county;"
- "A public street in a prohibited area of an unincorporated area of a county or city and county;" or
- "A public place in a prohibited area of a county or city and county."[56]

Violating these restrictions is a misdemeanor generally punishable by up to six months in county jail and/or a maximum $1,000 fine.[57] But you

---

[49] *See* Chapters 2 and 9 for definitions of "rifle" and "shotgun."

[50] *See* Cal. Fish & Game § 2006(b).

[51] *See* Cal. Fish & Game § 2006(a) (emphasis added).

[52] In response to people protesting California's restrictive firearm laws by publicly carrying unloaded handguns in holsters, the California legislature passed AB 144 amending the Penal Code to make that practice a crime. Prior to January 1, 2012, it was generally legal to publicly carry an unloaded handgun if it was not concealed.

[53] The Penal Code provides that a handgun is carried "openly" when it is not being "carried concealed within the meaning of section 25400." P.C. § 16950. But, as explained above, section 25400 itself does not define "concealed," other than to say a firearm carried in a belt-holster is *not* "concealed" under that section. P.C. § 25400(b). So what "openly" means, just as with the definition of "concealed," is not entirely clear.

[54] A handgun is "unloaded" if it is not "loaded" within the meaning of P.C. § 16840(b). P.C. § 17295. See discussion above for determining whether a firearm is "loaded."

[55] For this restriction, "rockets" and related devices are *not* covered.

[56] P.C. § 26350(a).

[57] P.C. § 26350(b)(1).

can be sentenced with up to one year in county jail or a maximum $1,000 fine, or both, if you openly carry an unloaded handgun:

1) outside of a vehicle;
2) in a public place or public street in an incorporated city or city and county;
3) have ammunition that can be used with the handgun in your immediate possession; *and*
4) you are not in lawful possession[58] of the handgun.[59]

Note that like the prohibition on concealed carry – the charge for which can be enhanced to a felony if ammunition for the concealed handgun is readily accessible *and* the handgun is not registered[60] – the penalty for violating the prohibition on openly carrying an unloaded handgun can also be enhanced (though the charge remains a misdemeanor) if ammunition for it is readily accessible, but only if the person is not in "lawful possession" of the handgun. This distinction means that while a person who *lawfully* acquired and owns an unregistered handgun may be charged with a felony for carrying it concealed with ammunition accessible, a person who *unlawfully* acquired an unregistered handgun may be charged at most with a misdemeanor for carrying it openly, even with ammunition accessible.

Each handgun carried in violation of P.C. § 26350(a) is chargeable as a separate offense. For example, if you are openly carrying two unloaded handguns unlawfully at the same time, you can be charged with two separate misdemeanors.

If you are the driver or owner of a motor vehicle and knowingly allow another person "to carry into or bring into" your vehicle (or the vehicle you are driving) a handgun openly carried in violation of section 26350(a), you are guilty of a misdemeanor.[61] Since the possible punishments for a violation are not specified, the Penal Code limits the possible punishment to "imprisonment in the county jail not exceeding six months, or by fine not exceeding one thousand dollars ($1,000), or by both."[62]

---

[58] "Lawful possession" means that the person who has possession of the firearm either lawfully acquired and lawfully owns the firearm or has the permission of the lawful owner. P.C. § 16750(b). In other words, if you are prohibited by law from possessing firearms based on a criminal conviction, mental illness, restraining order, etc., or acquired the firearm by stealing it, borrowing it without permission, exceeding California's time limits for a lawful loan, or without going through an FFL (unless acquired prior to that requirement becoming law or you meet an exception thereto), you are *not* in "lawful possession" of the firearm per section 26350(b)(2).

[59] P.C. § 26350(b)(2).

[60] *See* P.C. § 25400(c)(6).

[61] P.C. § 17512.

[62] P.C. § 19.

Note that the question of whether a firearm being openly carried in a "public place" as described in section 26350(a)(1)(A)-(C) is "loaded" or not is generally only important with respect to what Penal Code statute is being violated. If it is "loaded," you will be charged with violating section 25850(a), and if not "loaded," you will be charged with violating P.C. § 26350(a). Either activity is generally a criminal act. However, as explained in detail above, the penalties for unlawfully carrying a "loaded" firearm are potentially much more severe than those for unlawfully carrying an unloaded firearm.

## IV. WHAT DOES "PUBLIC PLACE" MEAN?

California's general prohibitions on carrying a loaded firearm or an unloaded handgun openly apply when a person is "in any public place or on any public street in an incorporated city or in any public place or on any public street in a prohibited area of unincorporated territory."[63] A "prohibited area" is "any place where it is unlawful to discharge a weapon."[64]

This means that an unincorporated territory where discharging a firearm is lawful is *not* a "public place" for purposes of the general carry restrictions. But this leaves unanswered what else *is* such a "public place."

Unfortunately this has been unclear throughout the Penal Code, especially regarding firearm possession. Many sources and laws define "public place" differently. For example, *Black's Law Dictionary*, a dictionary lawyers use, defines "public place" as "[a]ny location that the local, state, or national government maintains for the use of the public, such as a highway, park, or public building."[65] A California Government Code section governing litter receptacles defines "public place" as "any area that is used or held out for the use of the public," whether publicly or privately owned or operated, not including indoor areas (enclosed areas covered with a roof and protected from weather).[66]

Other examples are P.C. § 653.20 (governing prostitution loitering), defining a "public place" as an area "open to the public, or an alley, plaza, park, driveway, or parking lot, or an automobile, whether moving or not, or a building open to the general public, including one which serves food or drink, or provides entertainment, or the doorways and entrances to a building or dwelling, or the grounds enclosing a building or dwelling,"[67]

---

[63] *See* P.C. 25850(a) and 26350(a).
[64] P.C. § 17030.
[65] BLACK'S LAW DICTIONARY 1267 (8th ed. 2004).
[66] Cal. Gov't Code § 68055.1.
[67] *See also* Cal. Health & Saf. Code § 11530 (governing drug activity loitering).

and P.C. § 647(f) (prohibiting public intoxication), including an "area outside a home in which a stranger is able to walk without challenge" in its definition of a "public place."[68]

The closest thing to a definition for "public place" with respect to firearms is the one given for "*imitation* firearms," which is any "area open to the public" including streets, sidewalks, bridges, alleys, plazas, parks, driveways, front yards, parking lots, automobiles – whether moving or not – and buildings open to the general public, including those that serve food or drink, or provide entertainment, and the doorways and entrances to buildings or dwellings, including public schools and colleges or universities.[69] However, because this definition was provided for "imitation firearms" but not for real firearms, it is not very helpful.

Numerous courts have also attempted to define the term with mixed results. Ultimately "[w]hether a particular location is a 'public place' depends upon the facts of the individual case."[70] For example, supermarkets,[71] hospital parking lots,[72] barbershops,[73] and apartment complex driveways[74] can be "public places" due to their open access to the public.

But an area is *not* a "public place" just because it is exposed to public view. This means that your front yard is not necessarily a public place if it is not "open to common use"[75] or if you exclude the public. However, this would not be the case with a privately-owned sidewalk where the public has an easement or with walkways and driveways without fences, gates,

---

[68] *People v. Cruz*, 44 Cal. 4th 636, 674 (2008); *see also People v. Olson*, 18 Cal.App.3d 592, 598 (1971) (finding that public refers to areas that are "[c]ommon to all or many; general; open to common use" and "[o]pen to common, or general use, participation, [and] enjoyment.").

[69] P.C. § 20170(b).

[70] *See People v. White*, 227 Cal.App.3d 886, 890-892 (1991) (in determining whether the defendant was in a "public place," the court took into account the fact that he was in his own front yard, that the yard was surrounded by a three-and-a-half-foot-tall fence with a gate that could be locked, and that the defendant had released his three dogs into the yard).

[71] *See People v. Vega*, 18 Cal.App.3d 954, 958 (1971) (defendant unlawfully carried a loaded firearm in a "public place" by having a firearm in his vehicle, which was in the parking lot of a market. A "parking lot of a market, being accessible to members of the public having business with the market, is a public place …").

[72] *See People v. Green*, 15 Cal.App.3d 766, 771 (1971) (providing that "[t]he [hospital] parking lot, being accessible to members of the public having business with the hospital, was a public place.").

[73] *In re Zorn*, 59 Cal.2d 650, 652 (1963) (defendant found to be in public while in a barbershop because "'public' has been defined as '[c]ommon to all or many; general; open to common use,' and '[o]pen to common, or general use, participation, enjoyment, etc.; as, a *public* place, tax, or meeting.'") (Emphasis in original).

[74] *See generally People v. Overturf*, 64 Cal.App.3d Supp. 1 (1976) (apartment complex manager was properly subject to criminal conviction for "carrying" a firearm onto his driveway).

[75] *See People v. White*, 227 Cal.App.3d 886, 891-892 (1991) (appellant was *not* in a "public place" when found in his own front yard surrounded by a three-and-a-half-foot-tall fence with a closed but unlocked gate with three dogs in the yard; fence, closed gate, and dogs all provided challenge to public access, and the area was thus not "open to common use").

etc.,[76] making them easily accessible to anyone, or if the public can access them "without challenge."[77]

In other words, even though your front yard, for instance, might be private property, it is likely a "public place" if the general public can walk across it to gain access to your front door.[78] It would be *unlikely*, however, for that same front yard to be a "public place" if it were blocked off by a 3½ foot fence with three dogs in the yard (or some other similar deterrent), as this would then be a "challenge to public access," even if the gate were unlocked.[79]

In sum the foregoing demonstrates that case law provides some guidance as to what a "public place" is, but gray areas remain. A general rule in determining whether an area is a "public place" is, if the public can lawfully enter an area with little challenge, then the area is likely a "public place" where the general carry restrictions apply. However, if you are at a public place where you are lawfully permitted to shoot, (*i.e.*, a shooting range), then the carry restrictions should not apply.

[76] *People v. Tapia*, 129 Cal.App.4th 1153, 1160 (2005) (defendant was in a "public place" by standing on a sidewalk in front of his house, though defendant argued his father owned the property in front of his house up to the curb including the sidewalk. Court held that "a sidewalk on an easement of way which has been granted to a public entity is not private property ...").

[77] *People v. Krohn*, 149 Cal.App.4th 1294, 1298-1299 (2007) (defendant was *not* in a "public place" in the courtyard of his apartment complex because the complex was guarded by a fence and an automatically locked gate; the complex's rear parking lot was also guarded by an electric gate, thereby impeding public access to that area).

[78] *See, e.g., People v. Yarbrough*, 169 Cal.App.4th 303, 318-319 (2008) (upholding a conviction for carrying a loaded firearm in the driveway of a private residence because it was "reasonably accessible to the public without a barrier.").

[79] *See, e.g., People v. White*, 227 Cal.App.3d 886, 892 (1991).

CHAPTER 6:
# FIREARM CARRY RESTRICTION EXCEPTIONS AND TRANSPORTING FIREARMS

A s discussed in Chapter 5, P.C. § 25400 generally prohibits carrying a concealed *handgun*, whether or not it is loaded, anywhere; P.C. § 26350 prohibits openly carrying *unloaded handguns* in most public places; and P.C. § 25850(a) generally prohibits carrying a loaded *firearm* in most public places.[1] This chapter explains each of the exceptions to those general prohibitions.

## I. EXCEPTIONS TO THE GENERAL CARRY RESTRICTIONS IN NON-PUBLIC PLACES

If you are age 18 or older, a lawful United States citizen or resident, and are not prohibited by law from possessing firearms,[2] you may carry a handgun openly or concealed within your residence, place of business, or on other private property you own or lawfully possess.[3] To enjoy this exception to the general carry restrictions, you must have "a *proprietary, possessory*, or substantial ownership interest in the place."[4] To have a "possessory interest" in real property, you must have the right to (1) exclude others from using it, and (2) control activities occurring on it.[5]

---

[1] As explained in Chapter 5, the restrictions on carrying "concealed" handguns or "loaded" firearms also apply to "rockets" and related devices, including signal flares. Though the "loaded" carry exceptions discussed in this chapter generally apply to such devices, the "concealed" exceptions do not. It is unlawful to carry a concealed "rocket" or related device, even though such devices are not "firearms." But, if a rocket-launching device is unloaded, you can carry it openly.

[2] *See* Chapter 3 for prohibited persons.

[3] P.C. § 25605(a).

[4] *People v. Barela*, 234 Cal.App.3d Supp. 15, 20 (1991) (citing "Stats. 1989, ch. 958, § 2, No. 8 West's Cal. Legis. Service, pp. 2988-2989 [No. 5 Deering's Adv. Legis. Service, p. 3340]") (emphasis in original).

[5] *People v. Barela*, 234 Cal.App.3d Supp. 15, 20 (1991) (citing "Stats. 1989, ch. 958, § 2, No. 8 West's Cal. Legis. Service, pp. 2988-2989 [No. 5 Deering's Adv. Legis. Service, p. 3340]").

119

Because California law only prohibits the carrying of loaded firearms in certain *public* places,[6] any firearm you carry within your residence may be loaded. Likewise, if your place of business or other private property is not a "public place" where the loaded restriction applies, then you can carry your loaded firearm in those locations (see below for the applicable law when they *are* in such "public places").

# II. EXCEPTIONS TO THE GENERAL CARRY RESTRICTIONS IN PUBLIC PLACES

## A. Temporary Residences and Campsites

California law provides that you may *have* a loaded firearm, if otherwise lawful, while in a "temporary residence" or campsite.[7] Neither term is defined, but, presumably, this provision is meant to exempt people from the loaded restriction when lawfully residing in non-permanent shelters that are in a "public place" where the loaded restriction applies, since you can generally have a loaded firearm anywhere that restriction does not apply.

It is unclear whether you can *carry* a loaded firearm in a "temporary residence" or campsite without a Carry License (discussed below), since case law distinguishes the two terms, "carry" and "have."[8] And if it is legal to carry, it is unclear whether you can carry a concealed firearm, whether loaded or not, in either such place, since the exception to the concealed carry restriction for one's residence does not expressly mention "temporary residences" or campsites.[9] Of course, as explained below, if the "temporary residence" is on private property that you own or lawfully possess, you can carry the firearm however you want.

Note, however, that the agency or department governing the land you are camping on may have its own rules concerning firearms, so check with them before bringing your firearms camping.[10]

---

[6] *See* P.C. § 25850; *see also* Chapter 5.

[7] P.C. § 26055.

[8] *See People v. Overturf,* 64 Cal.App.3d Supp. 1, 6 (1976) (holding that where a statute only says it is lawful to "have" without mentioning "carry," then the statute does not allow "carrying" a loaded firearm). It is unlikely this distinction, to the extent it prohibits carrying a firearm in any manner within a "temporary residence," will be upheld as constitutional in the wake of *Heller* and *McDonald,* though it remains legally unsettled. *See* Chapter 1.

[9] *See* P.C. § 25605(a).

[10] P.C. § 25550(b).

## B. Within One's Business or Other Privately Owned or Possessed Property

Persons engaged in a lawful business (or nonprofit organization) operating from a "public place" where the loaded restriction applies (see Chapter 5 for examples) may nevertheless *have* a loaded firearm in their business if it is for lawful purposes connected with that business, as may their authorized agents or employees.[11]

For the reasons discussed above concerning carrying at a "temporary residence" or campsite, this means you can lawfully *have* a loaded firearm at your business, but you cannot necessarily *carry* a loaded firearm there. The distinction between "having" a firearm and "carrying" one is blurred if you conduct your business, or reside in, a moving vehicle, as discussed below.

As explained above, you may certainly *carry* a concealed handgun – if you are age 18 or older, a lawful United States citizen or resident, and you are not prohibited from possessing firearms – while within your business if it is *unloaded*.[12] But it is unclear whether you can carry a loaded handgun while it is concealed. This is because the exception that allows for concealed carry at one's business does not mention the loaded restriction, which still applies in "public places."

The same exceptions that apply to a firearm lawfully possessed within your place of business generally apply to firearms on your other privately owned or possessed property[13] (*e.g.*, farmland). Moreover, there is arguably stronger Second Amendment protection on private property, depending on the circumstances, but this remains uncharted territory.

## C. Being in "Grave Danger"

### 1. Protected by a Restraining Order

You may lawfully carry a *loaded* firearm *openly* or *concealed* if you reasonably believe you are "in grave danger because of circumstances forming the basis of a current restraining order" issued against someone who has been found to pose a threat to your safety.[14]

---

[11] P.C. § 26035.

[12] P.C. § 25605(a).

[13] P.C. §§ 25605(a), 26035.

[14] P.C. §§ 25600, 26045(b), 26362. It should be noted that this is only an affirmative defense to those crimes and may not apply if there is a mutual restraining order in place that applies to the person carrying the firearm.

## 2. Not Protected by a Restraining Order

If no restraining order exists, but you still reasonably believe you or someone else is in "immediate"[15] "grave danger" of being attacked, you are allowed to carry a firearm *openly*, but *not concealed*, whether loaded or not.[16]

# D. Other Exceptions, Including Personal Exceptions to Carrying Concealed, Open, or Loaded Firearms in Public

In addition to the persons, places, and activities exempt from the general laws against carrying firearms openly, concealed, and/or loaded in public that have been mentioned, there are still others:

## 1. Exceptions for Carrying Concealed Handguns

The following persons and activities are exempt from the general law against carrying a concealed firearm, but *not* the laws against carrying firearms loaded or unloaded and openly in public:

- Organization members whose purpose is lawfully collecting or displaying firearms, while at organization meetings with the handgun in a locked container (P.C. § 25515);
- Transporting a handgun by someone who recently brought it into the state to lawfully transfer, sell, or turn it over to an individual, FFL, or law enforcement per P.C. § 27560 (P.C. § 25575);
- Transporting a handgun from the place a person lawfully received it to the person's residence, business, or private property (P.C. § 25525(b));
- Military or civil organization members transporting a handgun when going to and from their organization's meetings (P.C. § 25625);
- Licensed fishermen while fishing[17] or transporting an unloaded handgun to or from a fishing expedition (P.C. § 25640).

In all the above situations involving transporting a handgun, the handgun must be kept unloaded and in a locked container (except for a licensed

---

[15] "Immediate" means "the brief interval before and after the local law enforcement agency, when reasonably possible, has been notified of the danger and before the arrival of its assistance." In other words, the brief interval between law enforcement being notified of the danger and their arrival. P.C. § 26045(c).

[16] P.C. §§ 26045(a), 26362.

[17] Unlike hunting areas, you cannot lawfully discharge a firearm in all of the same places where you can lawfully fish. This means that some fishing areas are "public places" where loaded firearms are illegal. Though you may carry it concealed while fishing, unless you are somewhere firearms can be lawfully discharged, or are otherwise exempt from the loaded prohibition (*e.g.*, you have a Carry License), the firearm must be unloaded.

fishermen going to or from fishing expeditions), and travel shall only include deviations between authorized locations as are reasonably necessary when your handgun is outside the vehicle.[18]

## 2. Exceptions for Carrying Concealed and Open, but Not Loaded Handguns

The following activities and/or persons are exempt from the general law against carrying concealed handguns, even if the handgun is *not* in a locked container, as well as the ban on carrying handguns openly in public, as long as they are not loaded:

- Authorized participants in a motion picture, television, video production, or entertainment event when they lawfully use firearms as part of that production or event (P.C. §§ 25510(a), 26375);
- Transporting unloaded firearms by licensed common carriers or their authorized agent or employee, when transported according to federal law (P.C. §§ 25645, 26367);
- Possessing or transporting handguns by those who are licensed to manufacture, import, wholesale, repair, or deal in firearms (or their agents) while lawfully engaged in their business (P.C. §§ 25615, 26363);
- Transporting unloaded firearms when going to or from a hunting expedition (P.C. §§ 25640, 26366);
- Military or civil organization possessing a handgun while parading or, if gun is openly carried, while rehearsing or practicing parading at the organization's meeting place (P.C. §§ 25625, 26364).

## 3. Exceptions for Carrying a Loaded Firearm Only

The following persons, places, and activities are exempt from the general law against carrying a loaded firearm, but *not* the general law against carrying a concealed handgun:

- Certain guards, private investigators and their employees, uniformed patrol operators, uniformed security guards, and alarm company operators, listed in P.C. § 26030(a)(1)-(10), who have a certificate from the Department of Consumer Affairs per P.C. § 26030(d);
- Armored vehicle guards,[19] while acting in the course and scope of their employment
  - If hired before January 1, 1977, or
  - If hired on or after January 1, 1977, if they have received a firearms qualification card from the Department of Consumer Affairs (P.C. § 26030).

---

[18] P.C. § 25505.
[19] As defined by the Cal. Bus. & Prof. Code § 7582.1(d).

- Those making or attempting to make a lawful arrest (P.C. § 26050);
- Members of shooting clubs while hunting on the club's premises (P.C. § 26005);
- Storing a rocket, rocket-propelled projectile launcher, or similar device designed primarily for emergency signaling purposes on any vessel or aircraft, or carrying one in a permitted hunting area or while traveling to or from a hunting area with a valid California hunting license (P.C. § 26060).

## 4. Exceptions for Concealed and Loaded Carry, but Not Open Carry

The following persons, places, and activities are exempt from *both* the general loaded and concealed restrictions:[20]

- Current or honorably retired law enforcement members listed in P.C. §§ 25450 and 25900;[21]
- State or U.S. military members as part of their duties (P.C. §§ 25620, 26000);
- Guards or messengers of common carriers, banks, and other financial institutions while carrying valuable items for work and who have a certificate from the Department of Consumer Affairs for successfully completing a course[22] in carrying and using firearms and the powers of arrest (P.C. §§ 25630, 26030(a)(1) and (d)).

## 5. Exceptions for Concealed and Open Carry and Loaded Prohibitions

The following persons, places, and activities are exempt from *all* the general prohibitions discussed in Chapter 5:

- Licensed hunters while lawfully hunting (P.C. §§ 25640, 26366);[23]
- Members of organizations whose purpose is to practice shooting targets with handguns at established ranges (P.C. §§ 25635, 26005).[24]

---

[20] This does not apply to the ban on carrying handguns openly in public.

[21] Full-time salaried federal law enforcement officers who are Department of Defense police officers at the Los Angeles Air Force Base may be "exempt from the state law prohibition against carrying concealed, loaded firearms even when they are not on duty." *See* Op. Att'y Gen. No. 01-1005 (2002).

[22] The course must meet the Department of Consumer Affairs standards per California Business and Professions Code § 7583.5.

[23] There is no specific law exempting hunters from the general law against carrying a *loaded* firearm in public, but since areas where hunting is allowed are not considered restricted "public places" because discharging firearms is necessarily allowed there, the ban on loaded firearms does not apply there in the first place. If you are lawfully hunting in city limits, even if in a place where loaded firearms are otherwise not allowed, you are exempt from that prohibition while hunting. *See* P.C. § 26040.

[24] Technically, only shooting club "members" are exempt from the general law against carrying *concealed* firearms on the club's range, while both members and non-members are allowed to carry *loaded* firearms at the range. *See* P.C. §§ 25635.

## 6. Further Exceptions for Openly Carrying Unloaded Handguns

The ban on openly carrying an unloaded handgun has many exceptions. Recall from Chapter 5 that unloaded long guns that do not technically meet the "assault weapon" definition may be openly carried[25] because the ban only applies to *handguns*.[26] The ban against open carry is also inapplicable to antique firearms.[27] So technically you could carry an antique handgun around just like you can a long gun, but due to law enforcement confusion this practice is not recommended.

Starting with P.C. § 26361, there are many exceptions to the open carry restriction. Some exceptions are to the entire restriction, *i.e.*, carrying both on your person and in/on a vehicle, while others are exceptions that relate only to carrying handguns on your person. The general exceptions include:

- Those who meet the exceptions to carrying *loaded* handguns in P.C. §§ 26000-26060 (P.C. § 26362).
- Members of organizations chartered by the U.S. Congress or nonprofit mutual or public benefit corporations meeting the nonprofit tax-exempt organization requirements while on official parade duty, during ceremonial occasions or while rehearsing or practicing for these events (P.C. § 26368).
- Those in school zones as defined in P.C. § 626.9 with the superintendent's written permission or other equivalent authority (P.C. § 26370).
- Acting in accordance with P.C. § 171b's exceptions concerning possessing weapons in state or local public buildings/meetings (P.C. § 26371).
- Making or attempting to make a lawful arrest (P.C. § 26372).
- When a handgun is being loaned, sold, or transferred under California law (P.C. § 27500 *et seq.*) on private property with the property owner's permission (P.C. § 26373).
- Those engaged in firearm-related activities, while on business premises licensed to conduct activities related to firearm sales, manufacturing, repairs, transfers, pawning, or use/training (P.C. § 26374).
- Those summoned and actually assisting a peace officer in making an arrest or preserving the peace (P.C. § 26378).
- Incident to and during sworn peace officer training as part of a Peace Officer Standards and Training (POST) course (P.C. § 26380).

---

[25] Subject to restrictions applying to *all* firearms in certain areas. *See* Chapter 7.

[26] Although, at the time of this book's publication, a bill pending in the legislature seeks to extend this restriction to long guns, so check the law in 2013.

[27] P.C. § 16520(d). According to P.C. § 16170(b), "antique firearm" has the same meaning as in 18. U.S.C. § 921(a)(16). *See* Chapter 2.

- Incident to and during the training course required to obtain a Carry License (P.C. § 26150 *et seq.*) with permission from the person authorized to issue it (P.C. § 26381).
- Incident to and at the request of a sheriff, police chief, or other municipal police department head (P.C. § 26382).
- Persons with permission from the Chief Sergeants at Arms of the State Assembly *and* the State Senate (pursuant to P.C. §§ 171c(b)(3)), (P.C. § 26385).
- Those exempt from the restrictions against possessing firearms in state legislative members' and governor's homes mentioned in P.C. § 171d (P.C. § 26386).
- Those exempt from the restriction against carrying firearms in sterile areas of public transportation facilities in P.C. § 171.7(c)(1)(F) (P.C. § 26387).
- Those lawfully carrying and possessing handguns on publicly owned land if specifically allowed by the land's managing agency (P.C. § 26388).

The following exceptions only apply to openly carrying *unloaded* handguns *on your person*:

- Carrying a handgun at a gun show conducted according to P.C. §§ 27200 *et seq.* and 27300 *et seq.* (P.C. § 26369).
- Incident to obtaining a DOJ identification number or mark for the handgun according to P.C. § 23910 (P.C. § 26376).
- Carrying a handgun at any established range while using the handgun at the target range (P.C. § 26377).
- Incident to any of the following as outlined in P.C. § 26379:
  - The requirements for registering or transferring a handgun as a personal handgun importer (P.C. § 27560) or registering "curio or relic" handguns by a collector who is bringing them into the state (P.C. § 27565).
  - Reporting handgun acquisition by those exempt from P.C. § 27545's private party transfer requirements or otherwise not required to report handgun acquisition, ownership, or disposition (P.C. § 28000).
  - Firearm transfers to authorized governmental representatives for voluntary gun buy-back programs (P.C. §§ 27850, 31725).
  - Handgun transfers between immediate family members (P.C. §§ 27870, 27875).
  - Operation of law transfers (P.C. §§ 27915, 27920, 27925).

- Carrying a handgun in a business, residence, or private property with the permission of someone allowed to openly carry a firearm in that same place under P.C. § 25605(a) (P.C. § 26383).
- Carrying a handgun if all of the following apply:
  - You are at an auction or similar event of a nonprofit public benefit or mutual benefit corporation, at which firearms are auctioned or otherwise sold to fund the corporation or its local chapters;
  - The handgun is to be auctioned or otherwise sold to benefit that corporation; and
  - The handgun is to be delivered by an FFL (P.C. § 26384).

# III. LICENSES TO CARRY A LOADED HANDGUN

To be generally exempt from the loaded and concealed (and in some cases open) carry restrictions in public, the average person must obtain a Carry License.[28] These licenses may only be issued to you by the police chief or the sheriff in your city or county of residence, although a *sheriff* may issue a temporary Carry License to non-residents if their principal place of employment or business is in that county and they spend a substantial amount of time there.

   If you live in an unincorporated county territory, you can only apply for a Carry License with the Sheriff of your county. If you live in an incorporated city, you can apply with either your local police department or with your county sheriff. Issuing authorities are required to accept and process all Carry License applications.[29] However, chiefs of police have the option to cede their issuing authority to the sheriff of the county, in which case they *must* reject *all* Carry License applications.[30] If that is the case with your city police department, you will have to apply with the sheriff of your county.[31]

   The most common type of Carry License (excluding those for law enforcement) only allows you to carry a *concealed* handgun and is valid statewide. In counties of less than 200,000 residents, however, the sheriff or police chief may issue you a license to *openly* carry a handgun, but *only*

---

[28] A Carry License is also widely known as a "CCW" (carry concealed weapon). *See* P.C. § 16360. However, the trend is to move away from that term because of the negative connotation associated with the phrase "concealed weapon," and because not all licenses are for carrying "concealed" firearms – some are for *open* carry.

[29] *Salute v. Pitchess,* 61 Cal.App.3d 557 (1976).

[30] P.C. §§ 26150, 26155.

[31] Some issuing authorities have adopted the policy of requiring applicants to first apply with the other issuing authority. This is likely an unlawful practice and is currently being litigated.

while within that county.[32] A Carry License is typically valid for two years.[33] Temporary Carry Licenses issued to non-residents based on their employment or business in that county are valid for 90 days and only within the county where issued.[34]

## A. Criteria for Issuance

An issuing authority may only issue you a Carry License if you demonstrate:

- "Good cause" exists for issuance of the license;
- You are of "good moral character;"
- You are a "resident" of that city or county (or your principal place of business is in the county and you spend substantial time there); and
- You have completed a course of training that the issuing authority required.[35]

The law does not specify what age a Carry License applicant must be, but presumably the minimum age is 18 years since a minor cannot generally possess a handgun. However, many if not most issuing authorities will only issue to persons 21 years of age and over.

Even if you meet all these requirements, an issuing authority may still refuse to issue you a Carry License because the law is currently understood as granting the issuing authorities broad discretion in deciding whether to issue one.[36] Though what is more common is that the issuing authority will set its standards to meet the criteria so high that most people cannot meet them. Either way, the end result is the same: they refuse to issue the Carry License.

### 1. "Good Cause"

The ability to obtain a Carry License in any given jurisdiction generally depends on the respective issuing authority's interpretation of what constitutes "good cause." Different jurisdictional interpretations of what con-

---

[32] P.C. §§ 26150(b)(2), 26155(b)(2). Sheriffs or police chiefs may also issue a Carry License to anyone they deputize or appoint as a peace officer. P.C. § 26170. These types of Carry Licenses are generally exempt from the training and fee requirements for such licenses.

[33] P.C. § 26220(a). Certain Carry Licenses for judges, commissioners, and magistrates are valid for up to three years. P.C. § 26220(c). Carry Licenses for custodial officers working for a sheriff or peace officers per P.C. § 830.6 can be valid for up to four years. P.C. § 26220(d)-(e).

[34] P.C. § 26220(b).

[35] P.C. §§ 26150(a), 26155(a).

[36] See *Gifford v. City of Los Angeles*, 88 Cal.App.4th 801, 805 (2001). Note that this case was before *Heller*, where the U.S. Supreme Court recognized an individual Second Amendment right. The constitutionality of this standard is thus dubious and is still being litigated. See Chapter 1.

stitutes "good cause" have led to wide disparity in whether Carry Licenses are issued in any given jurisdiction. Some issuing agencies simply require the assertion of a need for self-defense to establish "good cause," while others refuse to issue any licenses at all, essentially no matter what evidence of "good cause" an applicant provides. For policy reasons they simply do not want civilians to have Carry Licenses.

## 2. "Good Moral Character"

While issuing authorities conceivably have the same authority to determine whether an applicant is of "good moral character" as they do to determine one's "good cause," this standard has, practically speaking, generally been of little consequence. This is likely because those issuing authorities that do not want to issue many licenses will simply rely on the "good cause" standard to bar an applicant, never reaching this standard. And those issuing authorities with a more liberal "good cause" standard are likely much less prone to rejecting an applicant based on lack of "good moral character" unless there is a legitimate concern.

## 3. Residency

What constitutes "residency" for the purposes of qualifying for a Carry License is not very clear. You are obviously a resident of the city and county in which you own or rent a residence that is your exclusive dwelling, meaning you do not spend substantial amounts of time elsewhere. However, some issuing authorities reject applicants for lack of residency who are "part-time" residents or who have only resided in the area for a short time. The legality of such restrictive residency definitions is unclear and will likely need to be litigated eventually. If you are denied for lack of residency, you may want to contact an attorney to determine what your options are.

## 4. Training Course

First-time Carry License applicants are required to complete a training course chosen by the sheriff or police chief. The course cannot last more than 16 hours and must include instruction on firearm safety and the laws about permissible firearm uses.[37] Renewal applicants are also required to complete a minimum four-hour training course. Renewal applicants may also become certified trainers, in which case they would be exempt from the training requirement altogether.[38]

Alternatively sheriffs or police chiefs may require first-time Carry License applicants to pass a community college course of up to 24 hours

---

[37] P.C. § 26165(a).
[38] P.C. § 26165(c).

that is certified by the Commission on POST, but only if this is required of *all* initial applicants.[39] Requiring this type of course for renewal applicants does not appear to be allowed.

## B. Issuing Authorities' Mandatory Written Policy

Effective January 1, 2012, issuing authorities *must* publish an official written policy explaining the circumstances under which they consider an applicant to:

a) have "good cause" for a Carry License;
b) be of "good moral character;" and
c) be a "resident" of the respective county or city (or, for sheriffs only, to qualify for a non-resident license based on business activity in the county).

Additionally this official written policy must explain exactly what firearm training is required by the issuing authority per P.C. § 26165.[40]

A copy of your issuing authority's official written policy should be available online or upon request to that agency.

## C. Application Process and Fees

Carry License applications must be on a form prescribed by the Attorney General and be the same throughout the state. You cannot be required to provide any additional information beyond what is required on the standard California DOJ form, except to clarify any information you provided on the application.[41] Any false statement on the application is at least a misdemeanor and may be a felony if the false statement is about any of the following:

- The denial or revocation of a license, or the denial of an amendment to a license;
- A criminal conviction;
- A finding of not guilty by reason of insanity;
- The use of a controlled substance;
- A dishonorable discharge from military service;
- A commitment to a mental institution;
- A renunciation of United States citizenship.[42]

---

[39] P.C. § 26165(b).
[40] P.C. § 26160 (formerly P.C. § 12050.2). This requirement was the result of an NRA and CRPA sponsored bill, Senate Bill SB 610 (2011).
[41] P.C. § 26175.
[42] P.C. § 26180.

Generally, along with the standard application, you must also provide two copies of your fingerprints and the DOJ's requisite fee ($95), all of which is forwarded to the DOJ to conduct your background check.[43]

In addition to the background check fee, you may also be charged a fee for the sheriff or police chief's costs to process the Carry License application. This additional fee cannot exceed $100. The first 20% (maximum of $20) may be collected up front. For a renewal application, you may be charged up to $25 total.[44]

Unless a fee relating to the application process is expressly authorized by P.C. § 26190, it is against the law, as are any conditions requiring the applicant to pay additional money.[45] And requiring liability insurance for a Carry License is specifically prohibited.[46]

Once an initial or renewal Carry License application is completed and submitted, you must be given written notice whether your application is granted or not. This should occur within 90 days of your application being received, or 30 days after the sheriff or police chief receives your background check from the DOJ, whichever is later.[47]

As of January 1, 2012, P.C. § 26202 requires issuing authorities to provide Carry License applicants with *written* notice that either:

- "Good cause" exists and the applicant should continue with any training required pursuant to P.C. § 26165; or
- The Carry License is denied for lack of "good cause," stating the specific reason why the applicant lacks "good cause" under the issuing authority's written policy (as required by section 26160).[48]

You cannot be required to pay for any required training course until you have received this written notice.[49] If you are denied a Carry License for something *other than* "good cause," the issuing authority must explain in writing what requirement you did not satisfy but need not explain the specific reason(s) you may have failed to meet that requirement, though nothing precludes it from explaining.

---

[43] P.C. § 26185.

[44] P.C. § 26190(f)(2) (an additional fee not to exceed $150 may be collected by the issuing authority if psychological testing is required).

[45] P.C. § 26190(g).

[46] P.C. § 26190. This was also created by SB 610.

[47] P.C. § 26205.

[48] The specific reason should come from the issuing authority's published policy required under P.C. § 26160. This notice requirement was also part of SB 610.

[49] P.C. § 26165.

## D. License Revocation

The circumstances allowing sheriffs or police chiefs to revoke currently valid Carry Licenses are unclear. But it is clear that they can revoke it if you become a prohibited person.[50] Many will have their revocation policies in writing.

## E. License Restrictions

Any type of Carry License may have "reasonable restrictions or conditions" placed on it by the sheriff or police chief including, but not limited to, time, place, manner, and circumstance restrictions. Any such restriction(s) must be indicated on the license itself.[51]

If you change addresses, you must notify the sheriff or police chief of this within 10 days. An address change cannot be the basis for *revoking* the Carry License, even if you move outside of the county it was issued in. However, if your residence was the basis for the issuance of the license, it will *expire* 90 days after you move from the county of issuance. And if your license is for loaded and exposed carry, it will expire immediately upon the change of your residence to another county.[52]

State law generally allows Carry License holders to take a handgun into normally prohibited places such as state courts, schools, and the state Capitol. There are still places, though, where it is unlawful to possess a firearm even with a Carry License. You are responsible for knowing what restrictions exist where you travel. And the sheriff or police chief who issued your Carry License may restrict you from entering additional places as well.

Check with the authorities who have jurisdiction over the place(s) you want to go with your firearm. Its presence, even if legal, could be a sensitive matter – especially on federal property where it generally will *not* be legal. State court judges, for example, regularly prohibit Carry License holders from possessing firearms in their courtrooms even though state law allows it.

## F. Form of Physical License

California law requires that any Carry License issued shall be laminated and have the license holder's name, occupation, residence and business address, age, height, weight, color of eyes and hair, the reason for desiring the license (*i.e.*, "good cause"), and a description of any handgun carried

---

[50] P.C. § 26195. *See* Chapter 4.

[51] P.C. § 26200.

[52] P.C. § 26210.

pursuant to the license with the manufacturer's name, the serial number, and the caliber.[53]

## G. License Amendments

Carry License holders may request the agency that issued their license to amend it by doing any of the following:

- Add or delete a handgun that is allowed to be carried pursuant to the license;
- Change permission to carry the handgun from openly to concealed, or from concealed to openly (if allowed in the particular county);
- Change any restrictions or conditions placed on the license by the issuing authority.[54]

If the issuing authority amends the license, a new physical license reflecting the amendment(s) will be issued to the license holder.[55] The original license's expiration date does not change however, meaning the license will still need to be renewed upon expiration as it would if no amendment had been made.[56]

A final note: Some states honor Carry Licenses issued in another state, but this varies between states. California, for example, does *not* recognize Carry Licenses issued in *any* other state, even though some states recognize California licenses. However, as discussed below, federal law requires California to recognize Carry Licenses issued in another state to certain law enforcement officers, even retired ones.

For more information on Carry License issues, visit www.calgunlaws.com.

## H. Retired California Peace Officer Carry Licenses

Any honorably retired peace officer listed in P.C. § 25450 who was authorized to, and did, carry a firearm on the job is generally entitled to be issued a certificate by the agency from which the officer retired that is equivalent to a regular Carry License.[57] Certain officers who honorably retired prior to January 1, 1981 need not, and cannot be required to, obtain one of these Carry License certificates to lawfully carry a concealed firearm.[58]

---

[53] P.C. § 26175(i).
[54] P.C. § 26215(a).
[55] P.C. § 26215(b).
[56] P.C. § 26215(c).
[57] P.C. § 25455. The required format of the certificate is provided in P.C. § 25460. *See also* P.C. § 26300.
[58] P.C. § 25455(d).

An "honorably retired" peace officer includes any peace officer who has qualified for, and has accepted, "a service or disability retirement," but does not include "an officer who has agreed to a service retirement in lieu of termination."[59]

Generally honorably retired peace officers must petition to renew their Carry License certificate every five years with the agency they retired from.[60] Those listed in P.C. § 830.5(c), however, must qualify every year to maintain a valid Carry License certificate.[61]

The agency the officer retired from may only deny or revoke a Carry License certificate for "good cause."[62] Though it is unspecified, the following appear to be "good cause" for denial or revocation:

- Psychological disability;
- "[V]iolating any departmental rule, or state or federal law that, if violated by an officer on active duty, would result in that officer's arrest, suspension, or removal from the agency;" or
- Conduct that compromises public safety.[63]

An officer whose Carry License certificate is denied or revoked has 15 days after receiving proper notice of this to request a hearing.[64] Failing to request a hearing in that time forfeits the officer's right to one.[65]

## I. Honorably Retired Federal Law Enforcement Officer License

Certain honorably retired federal officers or agents are exempt from the laws against carrying handguns openly or concealed and loaded in public. The sheriff of the county that the officer resides in *must* issue a permit allowing such open or concealed loaded carry, to an officer or agent who:

- was authorized to carry weapons while on duty,
- was assigned to duty within California for a period of not less than one year, or
- retired from active service in California.[66]

---

[59] P.C. § 16690.
[60] P.C. § 25465.
[61] P.C. § 25475(a).
[62] P.C. §§ 25470(a), 26305(d).
[63] P.C. § 26305(a)-(c).
[64] P.C. § 26312. This notice must be personally served. The hearing is governed by P.C. § 26320.
[65] P.C. §§ 26310, 26312, and 26315.
[66] P.C. § 26020(a).

These officers and agents must give the sheriff a certification from the agency from which they retired certifying their service in the state, stating the nature of their retirement, and indicating the agency's agreement that they should be allowed to carry a loaded firearm.[67]

This permit is valid for a period not exceeding five years, and must be carried by the retired federal officer or agent at all times while carrying a loaded firearm. The permit may be revoked for "good cause."[68]

## J. Other Officer Exceptions to Loaded Carry Prohibitions

Any of the following individuals are also exempt from the general laws against carrying loaded firearms in public, as long as they complete a regular firearms training course approved by the POST Commission; this does *not* mean they are exempt from prohibitions on *concealed* carry, however:

- "Patrol special police officers" appointed by the city or county police who meet P.C. § 26025(a)(1)-(4)'s criteria;
- Authorized animal control officers and zookeepers compensated by the government in the scope of their duty (P.C. § 26025(b));
- Persons authorized to carry the weapons listed in Corporations Code § 14502 while actually engaged in their duties per that section (P.C. § 26025(c));
- Harbor police officers (P.C. § 26025(d)).

## K. Law Enforcement Officers Safety Act (LEOSA/H.R. 218)

The Law Enforcement Officers Safety Act (LEOSA)[69] amended the federal GCA to exempt qualified law enforcement officers (QLEO) and qualified retired law enforcement officers (QRLEO) who meet LEOSA's requirements from most state and local laws prohibiting the carrying of concealed firearms.[70] LEOSA generally allows those qualified people to carry a concealed firearm in all states, regardless of whether the respective state laws allow it, as long as they meet the statute's requirements and have the proper photo ID from the law enforcement agency they separated from.

Though they are exempt from *general* prohibitions on concealed carry, QLEOs and QRLEOs are still subject to local and state laws restricting firearm possession on government property including schools, government

---

[67] P.C. § 26020(b).

[68] P.C. § 26020(c).

[69] Also known as "H.R. 218" found at 18 U.S.C. §§ 926B, 926C.

[70] Machine guns, silencers, and destructive devices are not firearms under LEOSA. 18 U.S.C. §§ 926B(e), 926C(e). Beyond those limitations, however, "firearm" is not defined.

buildings, and parks, as well as federal laws restricting firearm possession in airports, courts, and federal buildings. You should therefore be familiar with the local laws of places you intend to travel with a concealed firearm if you are carrying pursuant to LEOSA.

A more detailed LEOSA memorandum addressing who is a QLEO and QRLEO, the specific photo identification requirements, and other Frequently Asked Questions are available at www.calgunlaws.com.

# IV. TRANSPORTATION OF FIREARMS

## A. Transporting Non-Handguns[71]

Since no general prohibition exists on publicly carrying unloaded non-handguns, like rifles and shotguns, you can transport them openly or concealed, as long as they are *unloaded*. Unlike handguns, long guns do not need to be kept in a "locked container" when being transported unless they enter a Gun Free School Zone (see Chapter 7).

## B. Transporting Handguns

P.C. § 25610(a) allows you to carry an *unloaded*, concealed handgun in a "public place" when it is in an appropriate "locked container" and in a motor vehicle, or while being carried *directly* to or from a motor vehicle "for any lawful purpose."

As used in P.C. § 25610, " 'locked container' means a secure container that is fully enclosed and locked by a padlock, key lock, combination lock, or similar locking device."[72] The DOJ provides a list of "locked containers" it has tested and approved (see Chapter 4). Though not legally required, it is recommended you use one of these listed "locked containers" to avoid any problems with the law.

### 1. Transporting Handguns to and from Certain Places
It is unclear what all is considered a "lawful purpose" for which a handgun may be carried in a locked container without violating P.C. § 25400's general prohibition on carrying a concealed handgun in public. But transporting a handgun while going directly to or from your vehicle and to and from the following activities or places is certainly allowed by California law, assuming the handgun is transported in a locked container and the

---

[71] Non-handguns that are considered "assault weapons" and .50 BMG caliber rifles, as discussed in Chapter 8, have additional requirements for their transportation, also discussed below. *See* P.C. § 30945.

[72] P.C. § 16850.

course of travel between the above listed places/activities and your vehicle only includes those deviations as are reasonably necessary under the circumstances:[73]

- Motion picture, television, video productions, or entertainment events where a firearm is used lawfully, if by an authorized participant or firearm supplier (or the supplier's agent) (P.C. § 25510(a)-(b));
- Meetings for clubs or organizations whose purpose is to lawfully collect and display pistols, revolvers, or other firearms (P.C. § 25515);
- Recognized safety or hunter safety classes, or sporting events involving the handgun (P.C. § 25520);
- Your residence, business, or other private property you lawfully possess (P.C. § 25525(a));
- Any place you lawfully received the handgun, but only if going *to* your residence, business, or other private property you lawfully possess (P.C. § 25525(a));
- A fixed place of business or residence for lawful handgun repairs, transfers, sales, or loans (P.C. § 25530);
- Gun shows, swap meets, or similar public events, to lawfully display handguns (P.C. § 25535(a));
- Gun shows or similar events, as defined under federal law, to lawfully transfer, sell, or loan a handgun to a private party using an FFL (P.C. § 25535(b));
- A licensed target range for practicing handgun shooting (P.C. § 25540);
- Offices of law enforcement agencies authorized to issue handgun Carry Licenses to carry a handgun when the agency requests you bring in the handgun (P.C. § 25545);
- Lawful camping activities (P.C. § 25550(a));
- Lawful handgun transfers to immediate family members by gift, bequest, intestate succession, other means, or by operation of law (P.C. § 25555);
- Transportation of a handgun by a person exempt from the requirements to use an FFL for firearm transfers and register firearm transfers, or who moves out of state with a handgun, to report the handgun's status to the DOJ per P.C. § 28000 (P.C. § 25560);
- Gun buy-back event to transfer handguns to a government agency (P.C. § 25565);
- A law enforcement agency for lawful disposition of a handgun that you found after giving notice to the agency (P.C. § 25570);

---

[73] P.C. § 25505.

- Transporting a handgun to comply with the personal handgun importer requirements of 27560 (P.C. § 25575);
- Transporting a lawfully obtained "curio or relic"[74] handgun into the state by a federally licensed "curio or relic" collector[75] whose licensed premises are in California (P.C. §§ 25580, 27565);
- A place for obtaining a DOJ assigned number or mark for the handgun (P.C. § 25585);
- Any of the following:
  - A place where you can carry a firearm concealed pursuant to an exemption to the carry concealed restriction.
  - A place where you may carry a firearm loaded either pursuant to an exemption to the loaded carry restriction or where that restriction does not apply.
  - A place where you may openly carry a firearm pursuant to an exemption to the open carry ban or where that restriction does not apply (P.C. § 25590).

Lastly, the law states that these transportation provisions do "not prohibit or limit the otherwise lawful carrying or transportation of any handgun in accordance with the provisions listed in Section 16580."[76] As mentioned in Chapter 1, most of the Penal Code sections concerning firearms have been recently renumbered. P.C. § 16580 explains which newly renumbered sections are continuations of statutes under the previous numbering system. So the statute here stating that lawful transportation under any provision listed in P.C. § 16580 is not affected is just a clarification that the legislature did not intend to go beyond its express limitations on transporting firearms in place at that time.

## 2. Transporting Handguns in Vehicles

### a. Vehicle as the "Locked Container"

Firearm owners most often get into trouble while unknowingly transporting firearms in their vehicles in an unlawful manner. The most common mistake is not having a proper "locked container."

The term "locked container" includes a lockable trunk of a vehicle, but *does not* include a vehicle's "utility or glove compartment," even if it is locked.[77]

---

[74] As defined in 27 C.F.R. § 478.11.

[75] 18 U.S.C. § 921 and related regulations.

[76] P.C. § 25595.

[77] P.C. §§ 16850, 25610.

Because the law does not define "utility compartment," handguns should never be transported in a vehicle's center console or in the storage area behind the rear seat in most "hatchback" type automobiles because these areas may be considered a "utility compartment."

It is also inadvisable to use the various storage compartments found in today's popular sport utility vehicles. Further, while most of us would consider a cross-bed tool box in a pickup truck as functionally equivalent to a vehicle's trunk, it too may be considered an off-limits "utility compartment." But this is a "gray area."

Even if your vehicle has a trunk, you should still additionally use an appropriate "locked container" (*i.e.*, fully enclosed and locked by a padlock, key lock, combination lock, or similar locking device) that is *solely* for transporting your handgun. This is because, if you need to open the trunk or unlock the container with the firearm to get a separate item from it, the container could then be considered "unlocked" at that point – arguably violating the concealed and/or open carry restrictions.[78]

Hard cases that can be locked are reasonably priced and, when used correctly (*i.e.*, handgun is unloaded and case is locked), are the best way to comply with California law.

### b.   No Destination Restrictions While in Vehicle

To qualify for the exception to the concealed carry restriction for having a concealed handgun in your vehicle, it has been debated whether you must be directly transporting it to, or from, one of P.C. §§ 25510 - 25595's expressly listed locations or activities (discussed above) like you would when transporting the handgun to and from a vehicle.

But that exception's plain language supports the interpretation that you *can* keep an *unloaded* handgun in a locked container in a vehicle *at all times*, regardless of your destination.[79] This means you do not need to be on the way to the shooting range, hunting, or any other firearm-related "lawful purpose" to enjoy this exemption; you may leave your *unloaded* handgun in a "locked container" in your vehicle at all times as long as you are not in a prohibited area.[80]

---

[78] P.C. §§ 25400, 26350.

[79] P.C. § 25610(a). **WARNING:** This is subject to a few limitations including school grounds (*see* P.C. § 626.9), playgrounds and youth centers (*see* P.C. § 626.95), and others (*see* Chapter 7). This is not an exhaustive list of limitations, however, and you should always be sure to consult local county and city laws.

[80] **WARNING:** Although this interpretation appears accurate, this practice is risky since law enforcement officers may be unaware that it is legal or have a differing view.

### c. Transporting in a Motorcycle's Box

The law is unclear about how motorcyclists may transport their handguns. When an unloaded handgun is transported in a locked box affixed to a motorcycle, this arguably is lawful because the firearm is in a "locked container" – not a "utility or glove compartment." However, it could be considered one because it is easily accessible and within the driver's reach.

Until the law is clearly interpreted, motorcyclists should be particularly careful when transporting their firearms in locked boxes attached to the motorcycle. A better suggestion would be to have the unloaded handgun in a separate "locked container" inside the motorcycle's box or a rider's backpack.

### d. Vehicle or Boat as Residence

While being driven, motor homes are generally treated like a "motor vehicle," meaning you must keep your firearm like you would in a car. While "camping" in a motor home, however, it *may* be treated like a residence. As mentioned, you can have a loaded firearm at a temporary residence or campsite.[81] Unfortunately, since "temporary residence" and "campsite" are undefined terms, this is another legal "gray area" and may depend on how you are using the motor home at the time.[82]

If you are in an established campground with your motor home "hooked up," it should qualify as a "temporary residence" or "campsite," and you may keep your firearms like you would in your home (except, as discussed above, it is unclear whether you can carry them, especially concealed). However, pulling into a rest stop to sleep for a few hours may not qualify for this exception. If you are prosecuted for having a loaded firearm in your motor home, the issue will likely be whether you were at a "temporary residence" or "campsite." Public campgrounds may have other firearms restrictions, so check the rules beforehand.

The law is unclear with respect to boats, but it is reasonable to assume that if the boat is designed to be lived on, like a house boat, it should be treated similarly to a motor home. This means, if it is moored, the same firearm laws that apply to one's residence should apply to the boat. But, if the boat is motoring through "internal waters" like a marina (see Chapter 7), the firearm should be kept as if it were being transported in a vehicle – meaning unloaded and in a "locked container" (although,

---

[81] P.C. § 26055.

[82] *See Garber v. Superior Court*, 184 Cal.App.4th 724 (2010) *modified by Garber v. Superior Court*, No. 045632, 2010 Cal.App.LEXIS 740 (Cal. App. 2d Dist. May 25, 2010) (holding that at the time of violating the concealed and loaded restrictions, appellant was not using his mobile home for residential purposes, though it was parked, and thus was not entitled to a "place of residence" defense).

as explained above, licensed fishermen are exempt from the concealed carry restriction).

Keep in mind that though the concealed and loaded restrictions also apply to rockets and related devices, including signal flares, storing a rocket, rocket-propelled projectile launcher, or similar device designed primarily for emergency signaling purposes on any vessel is lawful.[83]

### e. Vehicle or Boat as Place of Business

If your vehicle is also your place of business, and depending on the type of business it is, you may have a loaded and concealed firearm in your vehicle. In one case, a defendant possessed a loaded pistol on the floorboard of his leased taxicab. Although he kept it in the vehicle for self-defense, he did not have a Carry License. The court said he possessed the firearm in his place of business and therefore met one of the exceptions to the concealed and loaded restrictions.[84]

On the other hand a bounty hunter carrying a loaded and concealed firearm in his glove compartment did *not* meet this exception because, though he was often in a car for his work, it was not his "place of business."[85]

The same rules about vehicles operating as your place of business also presumably apply to boats generally.

### 3. Transporting Ammunition

Despite the popular belief that ammunition must be a certain distance away or carried in a separate container from the firearm, if the ammunition itself is legal, there are no state or federal laws against having ammunition in the same motor vehicle or same compartment as the firearm, as long as the firearm is unloaded.[86] In fact, other than the rules about transporting ammunition on an airplane, no regulations exist on how to transport ammunition. Because law enforcement is often unaware that ammunition and firearms may be transported in the same container, it is strongly advised you keep ammunition separate from the firearm, however.

## C. Transporting Registered "Assault Weapons"

Firearms meeting the definition of an "assault weapon" must be transported like handguns, even if they are non-handguns. As explained in Chapter 8, only the registered owner of the "assault weapon" may lawfully transport it, and only between the following places or activities:

---

[83] P.C. § 26060.
[84] *People v. Marotta*, 128 Cal.App.3d Supp. 1 (1981).
[85] *People v. Wooten*, 168 Cal.App.3d 168 (1985).
[86] *See* P.C. §§ 25400, 25605, 25850. The definition of "loaded" is explained in Chapter 5.

- The owner's residence, business, or other property, or that of other persons with their permission;
- A lawfully licensed target range;
- A shooting club licensed pursuant to the Fish and Game Code;
- A law enforcement or other state or national entity exhibition, display, or educational project about firearms;
- Publicly owned land, if specifically allowed by that land's agency;
- An FFL for service or repair.[87]

## D. Transporting Firearms on Airplanes

If you plan to transport firearms on an airplane, you must use the ticket counter check-in process and tell the airline you are transporting a firearm or ammunition. The firearm must be unloaded and transported as *checked* baggage in a locked, hard-sided container that only you have the key or combination to; not even law enforcement should have it. You can and should open the container for them if they request it.[88] The hard-sided, locked container may either be separate from your suitcase or inside it unless the airline tells you otherwise.

These requirements apply equally to disassembled firearms. If you have a frame or receiver, you have a firearm.

Ammunition[89] must also be transported as *checked* baggage, securely packed in boxes[90] or other packaging specifically designed to carry small amounts of ammunition (*e.g.,* the manufacturer's packaging). You are limited to 11 pounds of ammunition, so if you have a significant amount, weigh it before arriving at the airport. Magazines and clips must also be securely boxed.[91] TSA requires ammunition, magazines, and clips be transported in a hard-sided, locked case, even if together with an unloaded firearm, as long as properly packaged. To be allowed on an airplane, the ammunition cannot be designed to shoot from firearms of caliber larger than 19.1 mm (.75 inches) unless they are shotgun cartridges, *any* caliber of which is

---

[87] P.C. § 30945.

[88] 49 C.F.R. § 1540.111(c). *See also* TSA, TRAVELING WITH SPECIAL ITEMS: FIREARMS & AMMUNITION, *available at* http://www.tsa.gov/travelers/airtravel/assistant/editorial_1666.shtm (last visited Feb. 22, 2012); and NRA-ILA, GUIDE TO THE INTERSTATE TRANSPORTATION OF FIREARMS, *available at* http://www.nraila.org/gun-laws/articles/2010/guide-to-the-interstate-transportation.aspx (last visited Feb. 22, 2012).

[89] For transporting by plane, "ammunition" means: "Ammunition consisting of a cartridge case fitted with a center or rim fire primer and containing both a propelling charge and solid projectile(s)." 49 C.F.R. § 173.59.

[90] The TSA recommends the box be made of a fiber (such as cardboard), wood, or metal. *See Traveling with Special Items,* TRANSPORTATION SECURITY ADMINISTRATION, http://www.tsa.gov/travelers/airtravel/assistant/editorial_1666.shtm (last visited Aug. 9, 2012).

[91] 49 C.F.R. § 175.10(a)(8).

permitted.[92] Additionally black powder is not considered ammunition but rather an explosive[93] and thus cannot be transported on a plane.

This means firearms and ammunition must be checked in and out of your possession before you go through the airport's metal detectors (and into a "sterile area" as explained in Chapter 7). All firearms and ammunition are subject to law enforcement inspection within the airport.

It is best to call the airline in advance to ask about its policy for transporting firearms and ammunition. Airline policies may differ as to what containers or locks (or number of locks) are acceptable, or the maximum number of firearms you may transport at once, since the law does not specify. The fees airlines may charge for transporting firearms also vary. It is also a good idea to print out the airline's written policy from its website, confirm your compliance with it, and bring it with you to the airport in case your compliance is questioned. The TSA warns that failing to follow the proper transport regulations will preclude you from traveling with firearms, ammunition, or firearm parts.

If you are flying to another state, and especially other countries, know that other state and/or country's laws about transporting firearms and ammunition, as well as whether your particular firearm or ammunition is legal there. That way you can comply with their law as soon as you leave the airport.

Though federal law generally protects you from being prosecuted under state laws when transporting an unloaded firearm between places where it is legal for you to have the firearm, as long as neither the firearm nor any ammunition is "readily accessible" (*e.g.*, in a locked case),[94] people have nevertheless still been arrested and prosecuted while doing so. One famous case is that of a man who was traveling by plane from Utah to Pennsylvania. He had a layover in New Jersey, a state that requires a state-issued permit to possess a firearm and prohibits possessing hollow-point ammunition. A missed connecting flight caused him to have to take a bus in lieu of a flight, but he missed the bus when he realized his luggage was not on it. The next day, after finding his luggage with his firearm, pursuant to federal law he told the airlines that he had a firearm and that it was unloaded and locked. He was then arrested for possessing a firearm without a New Jersey permit and for possessing hollow-point ammunition.

Though criminal charges were eventually dropped, he spent four days in jail and did not get his firearm or related items back until over two years

---

[92] 49 C.F.R. § 173.59.

[93] 49 C.F.R. § 173.59. *See also* 27 C.F.R. § 555.11, excluding black powder from the definition of "ammunition."

[94] 18 U.S.C. § 926A.

later. He sued the New Jersey officials over the incident but lost. The court held that the general federal immunity for transporting firearms ended once he took possession of his luggage in New Jersey because the firearm was then "readily accessible."[95] The moral of the story is that transporting firearms by plane can be risky, and you should protect yourself by knowing whether a situation like this could potentially arise in your connecting or destination state(s).

The gentleman in New Jersey would not have violated the law had he not taken possession of his luggage, but it is unclear what he should have done instead. The court suggested people in this situation request law enforcement or airport personnel keep their luggage overnight but failed to provide further guidance if they refuse to do so.

Along with Newark, La Guardia Airport also reportedly arrests and prosecutes unwitting and blameless "violators" of firearm transport laws, some of whom are not technically committing crimes.

## E.  Transporting Firearms by Boat

Though the law is unclear, as explained above, it is reasonable to assume boats are treated like motor homes while in local waters. This means they will probably be treated either like a residence or a vehicle, depending on how the boat is being used at the time.[96]

## F.  Transporting via Bus or Other Public Transportation

Assuming there is no restriction on having firearms on the specific type of public transportation, the same laws that apply when going directly to or from your vehicle "for any lawful purpose" likely apply. California law does not otherwise expressly address how to lawfully transport firearms on public transportation.

## G.  Transporting Firearms across State Lines

Despite state or local laws to the contrary, you can transport firearms "for any lawful purpose" by motor vehicle between any states where you may legally possess a firearm. The firearm must be unloaded, and neither the firearm nor any ammunition can be easily or directly accessible from within the vehicle's passenger compartment. If your vehicle does not have a

---

[95] *Revell v. Port Auth. of New York, New Jersey*, 598 F.3d 128 (3d Cir. 2010), *cert. denied*, 131 S. Ct. 995 (2011).

[96] *See* Chapter 7 for more on firearm possession and use on boats. As previously explained, signal flares, though considered firearms, are exempt on boats. P.C. § 26060.

compartment separate from the passenger compartment, the firearm or ammunition must be in a separate locked container other than a "utility or glove compartment."[97]

The NRA's "Guide to the Interstate Transportation of Firearms"[98] lists numerous places with special rules about transporting firearms. Be careful because, like California, some states prohibit possessing firearms considered to be "assault weapons."[99]

---

[97] 18 U.S.C. § 926A (part of the Firearm Owners' Protection Act (FOPA)).

[98] *See* GUIDE TO THE INTERSTATE TRANSPORTATION OF FIREARMS, NRA-ILA (2012) *available at* http://www.nraila.org/gun-laws/articles/2010/guide-to-the-interstate-transportation.aspx (last visited Feb. 23, 2012).

[99] Discussed further in Chapter 8.

## CHAPTER 7

# PLACES WHERE FIREARM POSSESSION IS PROHIBITED AND FIREARM USE IS RESTRICTED

As explained in previous chapters, the regulation of firearm possession in California is primarily based on whether the firearm is in a private or a "public" place, "carried" or "possessed," "loaded" or "unloaded," and "concealed" or in plain view.

In addition to these categorical restrictions, however, both California and federal law prohibit firearms in certain places completely or, if allowed at all, restrict who may possess them and/or in what manner. Sometimes the scope of these restrictions is not as clear as it should be. California and federal law impose different, sometimes overlapping restrictions. You need to know where and what these areas are so you do not violate the law.

The following sections discuss when and where you can, or more appropriately when and where you *cannot*, possess a firearm.

Also, while this book covers mostly federal and state laws, keep in mind that cities and counties can pass certain laws about where and how you may possess firearms. For example, Los Angeles Municipal Code regulates the possession of firearm parts (*i.e.*, frame, receiver, or firearm barrel) and any ammunition at Los Angeles International Airport.[1]

Many local municipal codes and county ordinances also prohibit discharging firearms.[2] Los Angeles County, for example, has a large number of "districts" where discharging a firearm is prohibited.[3] The most common

---

[1] L.A., Cal., Mun. Code § 55.17 (2002). "Ammunition" is defined in P.C. § 16150.

[2] The California state legislature has provided in Cal. Gov't Code § 25840 that a county "board of supervisors may prohibit and prevent the unnecessary firing and discharge of firearms on or into the highways and other public places and may pass all necessary ordinances regulating or forbidding such acts."

[3] Descriptions of these districts can be very specific and in some cases border on the absurd. *See* L.A. Cnty. Code § 13.66.130 *et seq.* L.A. Cnty. Code also prohibits the discharge of firearms in §§ 17.04.620 and 19.12.1420(o).

local restrictions prohibit or regulate firearm possession in city or county public parks.[4]

If you are going to possess a firearm in public, familiarize yourself with your city and county's applicable local regulations, in addition to the state and federal restrictions discussed below. Though local governments are somewhat limited in the type of firearm restrictions they can have, knowing these additional local rules may save hours of your life and thousands of dollars in attorneys' fees if you must prove you were acting lawfully.

# I. FIREARM POSSESSION IN GOVERNMENT BUILDINGS

## A. California Law

It is illegal to bring a loaded firearm onto or in "the State Capitol, any legislative office, any office of the Governor or other constitutional officer, or any hearing room in which any committee of the Senate or Assembly is conducting a hearing, or upon the grounds of the State Capitol, which is bounded by 10th, L, 15th, and N Streets in the City of Sacramento . . . ."[5]

It is also illegal to possess or bring a loaded firearm onto the grounds of or within the Governor's Mansion or any other residence of the Governor, a constitutional officer, or any member of the Legislature.[6] These offenses are "wobblers," punishable as either felonies or misdemeanors.[7]

California peace officers may examine any firearm in any place where possessing a loaded firearm is prohibited by P.C. §§ 171c or 171d. And refusing to allow a peace officer to inspect a firearm in such a place or, as explained in Chapter 5, while in most "public places" is grounds for arrest.[8]

Both the prohibition on loaded firearms in the State Capitol and related offices and that on loaded firearms in the Governor's mansion and on its grounds have exceptions for certain authorized peace officers, those summoned by law enforcement to assist in making an arrest or preserv-

---

[4] As of this book's publication, litigation challenging the lawfulness of such local ordinances was pending, arguing that they are preempted by state laws, *Calguns Found. v. Cnty of San Mateo*, No. CIV509185 (Super. Ct. San Mateo, filed October 20, 2011).

[5] P.C. § 171c.

[6] P.C. § 171d.

[7] P.C. §§ 171c, 171d. Although the definition of "loaded" is discussed thoroughly in Chapter 5, for purposes of P.C. §§171c and 171d, "loaded" means whenever both the firearm and unexpended ammunition are immediately possessed by the same person. *See* P.C. § 171e. This means the ammunition does *not* have to be in the firearm to be "loaded."

[8] P.C. §171e.

ing the peace, and holders of a valid Carry License (see Chapter 6).[9] The prohibition on loaded firearms in the State Capitol and related offices also has an exception for those with permission from the Chief Sergeants at Arms of the State Assembly and Senate. And the prohibition on loaded firearms at the Governor's mansion and its grounds, any other residence of the governor, other constitutional officer, or member of the legislature also has exceptions for military members performing their duties and other persons authorized by the occupants of the specified residences.[10]

Anyone who possesses firearms, knives with a blade longer than four inches that is either fixed or capable of being fixed in an unguarded position, switchblade knives,[11] generally prohibited weapons,[12] tasers, stun guns, or anything that expels a metallic projectile such as a BB or pellet, through air or CO2 pressure, spring action, or any spot marker or paint gun in any state or local public building or public meeting, violates California law.[13]

This prohibition does not apply to:

- Those possessing or transporting weapons into court for evidence as long as they are not a party to the action;[14]
- Authorized peace officers or those summoned by a peace officer to assist with an arrest or preserving the peace;
- Those with valid Carry Licenses;[15]
- Those with written permission from an authorized official in charge of state or local government building security;
- Those who lawfully reside in, own, or possess those portions of the building that are not owned or leased by the state or local government;
- Those hired[16] by the building's owner or manager who have permission to possess firearms in those areas they lawfully reside in, own, or lawfully possess that the state or local government does not own or lease;

---

[9] P.C. § 171c(b). Notably absent from those exempt are military personnel while performing their duties.

[10] P.C. § 171d.

[11] As described in P.C. § 17235.

[12] Listed in P.C. § 16590; *see also* Chapter 9.

[13] *See* P.C. § 171b for "state or local public building" definition, which includes any buildings, or part of a building, the state or local government owns or leases where government employees regularly go to perform their official duties. It includes courthouses, but not government employees' residences. *See also* Cal. Gov't Code §§ 11120, 54950 for places intended for public business.

[14] P.C. § 171b(b)(2)(B).

[15] P.C. § 171b. Although no law prohibits carrying firearms into a state courthouse with a valid Carry License, most state court policies prohibit it by anyone other than law enforcement.

[16] This exemption only applies to those who are "licensed or registered in accordance with, and acting within the course and scope of" their duties as private investigators (*see* Bus. & Prof. Code § 7512, *et seq.*) and/or alarm company operators (*see* Bus. & Prof. Code § 7590, *et seq.*).

- Those who lawfully bring a weapon to a gun show for sale or trade.[17]

## B. Federal Law

Under federal law it is generally illegal to knowingly possess or bring a firearm or other dangerous weapon[18] into any federal facility. A "federal facility" is a building or part thereof owned or leased by the federal government where federal employees regularly report for work.[19] Exceptions to this rule exist for officers, agents, and state or U.S. employees performing their official law enforcement duties; federal officials and military members, if authorized by law to possess a firearm; or those carrying firearms for hunting or other lawful purposes.[20]

Anyone who "knowingly possesses or causes to be present a firearm or other dangerous weapon in a 'Federal facility' (other than a Federal court facility), or attempts to do so, shall be fined . . . or imprisoned not more than 1 year, or both."[21] If you knowingly have a firearm or other dangerous weapon in a federal *court* facility, or even attempt to do so, you can be fined and/or imprisoned for up to two years.[22] If you use, or attempt to use, a firearm to commit a crime in a federal facility, you can be fined and/or imprisoned for up to five years.[23] You cannot, however, be convicted of bringing a firearm into a federal facility unless the facility is clearly labeled or you had actual notice of this rule.[24]

## II. FIREARM POSSESSION IN "SCHOOL ZONES"

Though exceptions exist, it is generally unlawful under both California and federal law to possess a firearm – whether loaded or unloaded – in an area you know, or reasonably should know, is a "school zone."[25]

---

[17] P.C. § 171b(b).

[18] A " 'dangerous weapon' means a weapon, device, instrument, material, or substance, animate or inanimate, that is used for, or is readily capable of, causing death or serious bodily injury . . . ." It does not include pocket knives with a blade less than 2 ½ inches long. 18 U.S.C. § 930(g)(2).

[19] 18 U.S.C. § 930(g)(1).

[20] 18 U.S.C. § 930(d). This "other lawful purpose" exception does not apply to federal courts (18 U.S.C. § 930(e)(2)) and is unclear as to what activities it does apply.

[21] 18 U.S.C. § 930(a).

[22] 18 U.S.C. § 930(e).

[23] 18 U.S.C. § 930(b).

[24] 18 U.S.C. § 930(h).

[25] P.C. § 626.9(b); *see* 18 U.S.C. § 922(q)(2)(A).

## A. California Law

California's Gun-Free School Zone Act defines "school zone" as "an area in, or on the grounds of, a public or private school providing instruction in kindergarten or grades 1 to 12, inclusive, or within a distance of 1,000 feet from the grounds of the public or private school." Though this law is somewhat unclear, to be on the safe side you should measure the 1,000 feet starting from the school's *perimeter*, not its center-point. This advice is especially warranted since violating a "school zone" law may be a felony with mandatory jail time.

Curiously California does not require "school zones" be marked,[26] so the 1,000-foot "school zone" border is often difficult to determine. Whether you know, or reasonably should know, you are in a "school zone" will be a question of fact for a jury to decide in case you are prosecuted – which is an expensive process, so be careful around schools!

The California Gun-Free School Zone Act (but not federal law) also generally prohibits possessing firearms – whether loaded or unloaded – at university or college campuses and their buildings for student housing, teaching, research, or administration.[27] Either offense is a felony, but possessing a "loaded"[28] firearm on university or college property where possession is prohibited has a steeper sentence.[29]

Exceptions to the "school zone" and California university/college campus firearm prohibitions are:

- when the person has written permission from the school superintendent or the university or college president, respectively, or their equivalent authority;[30]
- while on an existing shooting range at a school, university, or college campus;[31]
- when the person holds a valid Carry License;[32]

---

[26] P.C. § 626.9(k).

[27] Unlike "school zones," which need not be marked as such, universities and colleges must "post a prominent notice at primary entrances on noncontiguous property [*i.e.*, property not connected to the campus] stating that firearms are prohibited on that property . . ." P.C. §§ 626.9(h)-(i).

[28] The term "loaded" in this context is defined in P.C. § 626.9(j).

[29] This general prohibition is notwithstanding the general exception to firearm restriction in one's residence (P.C. § 25605). *People v. Anaim*, 47 Cal.App.4th 401 (1996) (defendant violated the Gun-Free School Zone Act because he possessed a loaded firearm on university property even though the university-owned apartment complex was his residence). P.C. § 626.9(h)-(i). Post-*Heller* this may change, however. But until it does, you cannot lawfully have a firearm in your residence if your residence is part of university property and marked as such.

[30] P.C. § 626.9(b), (h), and (i). Good luck getting this permission since at least one court has ruled they do not have to give it. *See Hall v. Garcia*, No. 10-03799, 2011 WL 995933 (N.D. Cal. Mar. 17, 2011).

[31] P.C. § 626.9(n).

[32] Per P.C. § 26150. *See* Chapter 6.

- when the person is a duly appointed California peace officer,[33] either a federal officer or one from another state carrying out official duties, an individual summoned by any of those officers to make an arrest or keep the peace, or any military members performing their duties;[34]
- an armored vehicle guard performing their duties;[35]
- a security guard authorized to carry loaded firearms;[36] or
- an honorably retired peace officer authorized to carry concealed or loaded firearms.[37]

Under California law "school zones" have additional exceptions including:

- when the firearm is lawfully possessed in a residence, place of business, or on private property *as long as* such places are not part of the school *grounds*;[38]
- any handgun being lawfully transported (meaning handguns that are unloaded and *either* in a "locked container"[39] or in the locked trunk of a car);[40]
- when you reasonably believe you are in "grave danger because of circumstances forming the basis of a current restraining order issued by a court against another person or persons who has or have been found to pose a threat to ... [your] life or safety;"[41] or
- when the firearm is possessed by persons exempt from the general concealed firearm prohibition (see Chapter 5) per specific Penal Code provisions.[42]

---

[33] As defined in P.C. § 830.

[34] P.C. § 626.9(l).

[35] As defined in Bus. & Prof. Code § 7521(e); P.C. § 626.9(l).

[36] Per P.C. § 26000; P.C. § 626.9(m).

[37] Per P.C. § 25450; P.C. §§ 25650, 25900-25910, 26020; P.C. § 626.9(o).

[38] P.C. § 626.9(c)(1). A "school zone" is not the same as the actual "school grounds."

[39] *See* Chapter 6 for a definition of "locked container" and how to lawfully transport firearms.

[40] P.C. § 626.9(c)(2).

[41] P.C. § 626.9(c)(3). This exception may not include mutual restraining order circumstances.

[42] Per P.C. § 626.9(c)(4). The P.C. sections listing these exemptions are: P.C. § 25615 (transporting unloaded handguns by a licensed person who manufactures, imports, wholesales, repairs, or deals with firearms in their business); P.C § 25625 (authorized military or civil organizations carrying firearms while parading or going to and from their organization); P.C § 25630 (guards, financial institution employees, or common carriers while working); and P.C § 25645 (operating a licensed common carrier to transport unloaded firearms per federal law). *See also* Chapter 6.

## B. Federal Law

The federal definition of "school zone" is effectively the same as that of California.[43]

Federal law also has exceptions similar to California law concerning firearm possession in a "school zone."[44] The following people and situations are exempt from the federal firearm restriction in a "school zone:"

- when on private property not part of school grounds;
- certain state-licensed individuals;[45]
- when the firearm is unloaded and in a locked container or locked firearm rack on a motor vehicle;
- someone in a school-approved program;
- someone who has contracted with a school to possess a firearm;
- law enforcement officers acting in their official capacity; or
- someone carrying unloaded while going over school premises to gain access to lawful hunting lands if the school authorizes the entry.[46]

Note that while California's exception only requires *handguns* be in a locked container when in a "school zone," federal law additionally requires that long guns also be in locked containers.[47] The California Gun-Free School Zone Act does not prohibit or limit transporting long guns if done according to California law.

## C. California and Federal Discharge Restrictions

Both California and federal "school zone" laws also prohibit knowingly or recklessly *discharging*, or attempting to discharge, a firearm in a "school zone."[48] They both, however, exempt discharging a firearm on private property.[49] Federal law further exempts discharging a firearm if the activity is

---

[43] P.C. § 626.9(e)(1); *see* 18 U.S.C. § 921(a)(25) and (26) for the federal definition.

[44] 18 U.S.C. § 922(q)(2)(A). The federal "school zone" restriction, however, only applies to a firearm that "has moved in or otherwise affects interstate or foreign commerce." Conceivably the restriction still applies to nearly all firearms, since even "homemade" firearms contain parts that have "moved in" or "affect" interstate commerce.

[45] For this exception to apply, federal law requires "the individual possessing the firearm [be] licensed to do so by the State in which the school zone is located or a political subdivision of the State, and the law of the State or political subdivision requires that, before an individual obtains such a license, the law enforcement authorities of the State or political subdivision verify that the individual is qualified under law to receive the license." 18 U.S.C. § 922(q)(2)(B)(ii).

[46] 18 U.S.C. § 922(q)(2)(B).

[47] *See* 18 U.S.C. § 922(q)(2)(A).

[48] P.C. § 626.9(d); 18 U.S.C. § 922(q)(3)(A). As with the possession restriction, for the federal discharge prohibition to apply, the firearm must have moved in, or affected, interstate or foreign commerce, *and* the person must have *known* it was a "school zone."

[49] P.C. § 626.9(d); 18 U.S.C. § 922(q)(3)(B)(i). However, beware of local discharge restrictions.

part of a school-approved program, in accordance with a school contract, or by law enforcement officers acting in their official capacity.[50]

Be careful differentiating between California and federal "school zone" exceptions. You can be prosecuted for violating *either* federal or California law. An exception to one will not necessarily exempt you from prosecution under the other.

## III. FIREARM POSSESSION IN AIRPORTS, ON AIRPLANES, AND ON COMMON CARRIERS

### A. Possession in Airport "Sterile Areas"

Under California law it is generally illegal to knowingly possess firearms, frames, receivers, barrels, firearm magazines, BB devices, imitation firearms, tasers or stun guns,[51] or ammunition, in a "sterile area"[52] of an airport or passenger vessel terminal.[53] A "passenger vessel terminal" is "a harbor or port facility . . . regularly serv[ing] scheduled commuter or passenger operations."[54] Exceptions to this include:

- Authorized peace officers and those summoned to assist them;
- Retired peace officers with Carry Licenses issued pursuant to P.C. § 25450;
- Persons with written authorization from an airport security coordinator; and
- Those responsible for passenger vessel terminal security who have written authorization pursuant to an approved U.S. Coast Guard facility security plan.[55]

Under federal law you can be imprisoned up to 10 years if you have a concealed "dangerous weapon" that would be accessible to you while on, or trying to get on, a plane.[56] This restriction does not apply to government law enforcement officers authorized to carry arms in their official capacity, those authorized by the Federal Aviation Administration (FAA) or the Secretary of Transportation, or those transporting "unloaded" firearms in

---

[50] 18 U.S.C. § 922(q)(3)(B)(ii)-(iv).
[51] As defined in P.C. § 244.5.
[52] "Sterile area" is defined in P.C. § 171.5(a)(3).
[53] P.C. § 171.5(b).
[54] P.C. § 171.5(a)(2).
[55] P.C. § 171.5(d).
[56] 49 U.S.C. § 46505(b)(1).

baggage not accessible to them during flight as long as the air carrier is told about the firearm.[57]

Note there is *no* exception to these restrictions for valid holders of a Carry License. These licensees can be charged just like anyone else for possessing firearms in a "sterile area" of an airport or for attempting to bring a firearm onto a plane.

The federal Transportation Safety Authority (TSA) can also separately fine you up to $3,000 ($7,500 if loaded).[58] If this happens, TSA will normally send you a letter informing you of the violation and your options, which include paying a civil fine, submitting evidence that the violation did not occur, submitting information to reduce the fine, or requesting an informal conference or a formal hearing. If you get a letter like this, hiring an attorney is strongly advised.

Laws regulating firearms or ammunition in airports are most commonly violated by people who simply forget they have a firearm or ammunition in their carry-on bags. This may seem unbelievable to those who do not shoot often, but in fact people sometimes use the same bags to carry other personal items as they use to carry firearms. Depending on the weight of the firearm and the type of bag, this is a common mistake.

Although California laws prohibiting possession at airports generally have a "knowing" requirement – meaning you may not be found guilty of the offense if you legitimately forgot the firearm was in your bag – prosecutors are typically skeptical. Adding to the difficulty, people usually see their bag being removed from the x-ray conveyor belt and wonder why. At that point they usually remember the firearm in their bag and say something along the lines of: "That's my bag. There's a gun in there." This "admission" becomes very difficult to disprove or explain.

Don't let this mistake happen to you. Take your firearm(s) out of the bag when you get home from the range or other lawful activity if you also use the bag for other purposes like traveling!

## B. Possession on Commercial Airplanes

Federal law generally prohibits having firearms and ammunition accessible on commercial or charter aircraft and private aircraft over a certain passenger or payload capacity.[59] Law enforcement officers authorized to carry firearms on duty who have completed the "Law Enforcement Officers Flying Armed" training program and whose employer has determined a

---

[57] 49 U.S.C. § 46505(d).

[58] *See* TSA, ENFORCEMENT SANCTION GUIDANCE POLICY, *available at* http://www.tsa.gov/assets/pdf/enforcement_sanction_guidance_policy.pdf (last visited Aug. 6, 2012).

[59] *See* 49 C.F.R. §§ 1544.201(d), 1544.1(a)(1); *see also* 14 C.F.R. § 119.1(a); 14 C.F.R. § 135.119.

need exists to carry the firearm while on the aircraft are allowed to carry firearms on airplanes as long as they declare the firearm to the aircraft operator, keep it concealed – but never in the overhead compartment – and on their person if in uniform, and notify the pilot and crew members of its location. If the flight does *not* require screening, those officers are not required to have special approval from their agency as long as they comply with all other requirements.[60]

This law enforcement exception does not apply to any officer who has been drinking alcohol, nor may officers drink alcohol while on the aircraft if carrying a firearm.[61]

To be clear, barring any local ordinance to the contrary, you may lawfully possess firearms and ammunition in places outside airport "sterile areas" as long as you are complying with other applicable laws like those that apply in public generally. You can also lawfully transport unloaded firearms in *checked* luggage on planes.[62]

## C. Possession on Amtrak Trains

As of December 15, 2010, stations that accept checked baggage allow passengers to transport unloaded firearms in checked baggage under specific conditions. Among the requirements are: 1) the passengers must declare to Amtrak their intent to transport a firearm at the time the reservation is made (online reservations for checking firearms are not accepted), or at least 24 hours before departure, 2) the firearm must be unloaded and in their checked baggage, and 3) transportation of the firearm must comply with other carriage regulations (i.e., unloaded, hard-sided, locked container, etc).[63] Check www.Amtrak.com for further information about taking firearms on Amtrak trains.

## D. Possession on Greyhound Buses

Greyhound prohibits transporting firearms and ammunition on their buses.[64] Though this is their rule, not a law, you could still be prosecuted for trespassing or for a similar violation if you break this rule.

---

[60] *See* 49 C.F.R. §§ 1544.201(d), 1544.219, 1544.221. Air marshals are covered by a different set of laws. *See* 49 C.F.R. § 1544.223.

[61] *See* 49 C.F.R. § 1544.219(c).

[62] P.C. § 171.5(g). *See* Chapter 6 for how to lawfully transport unloaded firearms in checked luggage and for problems that may arise in airports like New Jersey or New York City.

[63] *See* AMTRAK, CHECKED FIREARMS PROGRAM (2010), *available at* http://www.amtrak.com/servlet/Content Server?c=Page&pagename=am%2FLayout&cid=1248542758975 (last visited Aug. 6, 2012).

[64] TSA, PROHIBITED ITEMS FOR CHECKED BAGGAGE, *available at* http://www.greyhound.com/en/ticket-sandtravel/baggageinformation.aspx (last visited Aug. 6, 2012).

## E. Possession on All Other Common Carriers

If you cross state lines with a common carrier, even if the carrier allows firearm possession, federal law requires you to declare and surrender it to the carrier operator for the trip.[65]

Also, federal law only protects you from state prosecution for violating a state's firearm laws if your firearm is not immediately accessible.[66] This means, if you enter a state on a carrier where it is illegal to possess a firearm without a permit (e.g., New Jersey) and you do not have that permit, federal law does *not* protect you from prosecution under that state's law if a firearm is in your carry-on bag and not stored away where you cannot access it.[67]

# IV. FIREARM POSSESSION IN PARKS, FORESTS, AND REFUGES

## A. California State Lands

Firearms are generally prohibited in the state park system[68] and are only permitted in areas (including state marine recreational management areas) that are developed for their use.[69] The exceptions to the general restriction are:

- Designated archery ranges;
- Lands open to lawful hunting; and
- Unloaded firearms within either a temporary lodging or a mechanical mode of conveyance (e.g., car, bike, RV, boat, etc., but not a horse) if inoperable or stored to prevent their ready use.[70]

The restrictions listed above are separate from those in "state wildlife areas." "No person, except authorized personnel, shall possess or discharge a firearm" in the following state wildlife areas: "Battle Creek, Crescent City Marsh, Elk Creek Wetlands, Eureka Slough, and Hill Slough wildlife areas;

---

[65] 18 U.S.C. § 922(e).

[66] 18 U.S.C. § 926A (part of FOPA).

[67] *See* Chapter 6 for properly transporting firearms across state lines and consequences for not doing so properly.

[68] The Department of Parks and Recreation controls the state park system (*i.e.*, California state parks, park property, recreation areas, natural reserves, etc.). 14 Cal. Code Regs. §§ 4300 and 4313. This restriction includes "any weapon, firearm, spear, bow and arrow, trap, net, or device capable of injuring, or killing any person or animal, or capturing any animal, or damaging any public or private property . . ." 14 Cal. Code Regs. § 4313(a).

[69] *See* 14 Cal. Code Regs. § 4501 (allowing hunting in specific state park lands).

[70] 14 Cal. Code Regs. § 4313.

Cordelia Slough and Montezuma Slough management units of Grizzly Island Wildlife Area; White Slough Unit of Napa-Sonoma Marshes Wildlife Area; and Bahia, Day Island, Green Point, Novato Creek, Point Sonoma, and Rush Creek units of the Petaluma Marsh Wildlife Area."[71] In other state wildlife areas the use and discharge of firearms can be limited (as to the type/quantity of ammunition, type of firearm, and when the firearm may be used) and in some cases outright banned.[72]

California also has designated "State Game Refuges." Unless you have a permit or specific authorization, it is illegal to possess or discharge a firearm (or BB device or bow and arrow) in a game refuge, with few exceptions.[73] They *can* be transported through a game refuge, however, if they are taken apart or encased and unloaded.[74] Also, when traveling on something other than a public highway, public thoroughfare, or right of way, you have to give notice to the Department of Fish and Game at least 24 hours beforehand that you will be transporting a firearm. You have to give your name and address, the name of the refuge, the approximate route, and the approximate time when you intend to travel through the refuge.[75]

The state has also created "ecological reserves"[76] where possessing and discharging firearms is generally prohibited except for by law enforcement and in areas that allow hunting.[77]

## B. Federal Lands

### 1. National Parks and Wildlife Refuges

Federal law allows firearm possession on National Park land and within National Wildlife Refuge Systems as long as you are not otherwise prohibited from possession,[78] and you comply with the state law where the National Park System or National Wildlife Refuge System is located.[79]

---

[71] 14 Cal. Code Regs. § 550(b)(19).
[72] 14 Cal. Code Regs. §§ 551, 552.
[73] Fish & Game Code § 10500.
[74] Fish & Game Code § 10506.
[75] Fish & Game Code § 10506.
[76] These areas are outlined in 14 Cal. Code Regs. § 630.
[77] 14 Cal. Code Regs. § 630.
[78] 16 U.S.C. § 1a-7b. *See* Chapter 3 for who is prohibited from possessing firearms.
[79] H.R. 627, § 512(b) (2009). Prior to this law changing, *United States v. Masciandaro*, 638 F.3d 458 (4th Cir. 2011) was decided. In this case, which went to the U.S. Supreme Court on a petition for writ of certiorari but was rejected, the petitioner fell asleep in his car on National Park property. A federal park ranger woke him and found a loaded handgun in a backpack in his trunk. Unfortunately this incident occurred before firearms were allowed in national parks. The Fourth Circuit upheld Masciandaro's conviction. Additionally it noted that Second Amendment rights outside the home, and the appropriate standards for if and how those rights can be regulated by the government, is still uncertain. So make sure you comply with state laws in National Parks.

This means while federal law allows for firearm possession in National Parks and Wildlife Refuges, California's loaded, concealed, or open carry restrictions still apply, as do their exceptions, which include lawfully transporting a firearm to an activity where carrying a firearm is permitted, such as hunting, camping, target shooting, etc., or if discharging firearms is allowed in that area.[80]

Though federal law allows *possessing* firearms in National Park land and within National Wildlife Refuge Systems as long as you comply with the state law where the park or refuge is located, *discharging* firearms is a different story. Discharging firearms on National Wildlife Refuges is federally prohibited unless specifically authorized.[81] National Parks and Refuges, or specified areas within those parks and refuges, in California may be open for hunting as outlined in 36 C.F.R. Part 7 and 50 C.F.R. § 32.24 but are still subject to California laws and requirements.

## 2. National Forests

National Forests are not to be confused with National Parks. These are two separate types of lands regulated by different portions of the federal code and government (Department of Agriculture and the Department of the Interior, respectively). Within the National Forest System it is unlawful to discharge "a firearm or any other implement capable of taking human life, causing injury, or damaging property as follows:

- In or within 150 yards of a residence, building, campsite, developed recreation site or occupied area, or
- Across or on a National Forest System road or a body of water adjacent thereto, or in any manner or place whereby any person or property is exposed to injury or damage as a result of such discharge.
- Into or within any cave."[82]

The use of tracer bullets and incendiary ammunition is also prohibited in the National Forest System.[83] The Department of Agriculture Forest Service may also close or restrict those areas where discharging firearms is lawful.[84]

---

[80] *See* Chapter 6 for the specific restrictions and exceptions.
[81] 50 C.F.R. § 27.41.
[82] 36 C.F.R. § 261.10(d).
[83] 36 C.F.R. § 261.5(b). Tracers are also illegal "destructive devices" under California law. *See* Chapter 9.
[84] 36 C.F.R. § 261.58(m).

### 3. Bureau of Land Management (BLM) and Other Federally Protected Areas

The Bureau of Land Management's (BLM) "California policy is to allow the use of firearms on public lands,[85] as provided for in state law, and to co-operate with state authorities in the enforcement of firearms regulations."[86] It is still unlawful, however, to discharge or use firearms on developed recreation sites and areas[87] unless authorized.[88] BLM can also limit hunting and discharging firearms to protect certain locations.[89] Before you head to BLM land to use your firearms, contact the local BLM office for information on where they think you can lawfully shoot.[90]

### 4. Other Parks

Be aware that city, county, state, and national parks may be run by different government agencies that have different rules and regulations. As discussed at the beginning of this chapter, local ordinances also often restrict possessing firearms in city or county public parks. If you plan on visiting one of these parks, call ahead, check the park's website, and familiarize yourself with the rules regarding firearms *before* you go.

## V. FIREARM POSSESSION IN UNITED STATES AND INTERNATIONAL WATERS

Federal, state, local and/or another country's laws may apply depending on where your boat is in the water.

Federal, state, and local firearm laws apply in waters within California's baseline boundary (coastline),[91] called its "internal waters."[92] As explained

---

[85] Maps of BLM land are available at http://www.blm.gov/ca/st/en/info/iac/maps_pubroom.html.

[86] *See Hunting and Target Shooting information*, U.S. DEPT. OF INTERIOR, *available at* http://www.blm.gov/ca/st/en/prog/recreation/hunting.html (last visited Aug. 6, 2012).

[87] "Developed recreation sites and areas means sites and areas that contain structures or capital improvements primarily used by the public for recreation purposes. Such sites or areas may include such features as: Delineated spaces for parking, camping or boat launching; sanitary facilities; potable water; grills or fire rings; tables; or controlled access." 43 C.F.R. § 8360.0-5.

[88] 43 C.F.R. § 8365.2-5.

[89] 43 U.S.C. § 1733 and 43 C.F.R. § 8364.1.

[90] Recently BLM has taken a strong position against shooters on BLM property and inspects all firearms at certain locations and pulls over shooters leaving BLM land.

[91] Except where otherwise provided, the baseline boundary is the low-water line along the coast. *See* UNITED NATIONS CONVENTION ON THE LAW OF THE SEA, (hereinafter, "UNCLOS") 27, art. 5, *available at* http://www.un.org/depts/los/convention_agreements/texts/unclos/unclos_e.pdf. Note that the U.S. has never ratified UNCLOS in its entirety but has selected a few sections for adoption via presidential proclamation. It is therefore not controlling law, but its descriptions of the various maritime zones are generally accurate.

[92] "Internal waters" includes rivers, bays, and harbors. *See* SCOTT JASPER, SECURING FREEDOM IN THE GLOBAL COMMONS 52 (2010).

in Chapter 6, whether your boat is treated like a residence, vehicle, or place of business likely depends on the boat's particular design, your use of it, and/or its location. To lawfully possess firearms on your boat while in "internal waters," you need to know how your boat is classified because "internal waters" are likely "public places" where general firearm restrictions apply.[93]

Three nautical miles[94] from the state's coastline is the state's "seaward boundary." All waters within this three mile stretch are subject to federal and California firearm laws. Local laws do not apply.[95] You may therefore possess firearms in these waters as long as you comply with state and federal law. But this is no easy task as knowing *how* you are supposed to lawfully possess a firearm depends on whether you are in a restricted "public place." If you are not, then there are generally no restrictions on possessing firearms. But if you are in such a place, then how you possess firearms depends on whether your boat is considered a residence, vehicle, or place of business. You may also be a licensed fisherman who is exempt from the concealed carry laws.[96]

Since there are no express California restrictions on discharging firearms in this area, whether it is lawful depends on whether it is a restricted "public place," which is sometimes unclear. Whether it is such a "public place" may depend on how close you are to land and other vessels at the time. What is clear, however, is that California does ban discharge in certain other areas. For example, the discharge ban also includes the "sea otter translocation zone" surrounding San Nicolas Island (except for government employees performing their duties).[97] Possessing and discharging firearms in certain marine areas and ecological reserves is also prohibited.[98]

From the "seaward boundary" to the 12-mile mark is the U.S.'s "territorial waters," in which only federal firearm laws apply.[99] Since federal law does not generally regulate where and how a non-prohibited person can *possess* firearms, there are no real restrictions on possessing a regular firearm within this twelve mile zone.[100]

---

[93] *See* Chapters 5 and 6.

[94] All "miles" in this section refer to nautical miles unless otherwise specified (1 "nautical mile" is approximately 1.15 statute miles).

[95] *See People v. Weeren*, 26 Cal.3d 654, 661-663, 665 (1980); *see also* 43 U.S.C. §§ 1301(b), 1312.

[96] P.C. § 25640; *see also* Chapter 6.

[97] Fish & Game Code § 8664.2. See this section for the coordinates of the areas around San Nicolas Island.

[98] *See* 14 Cal. Code Regs. §§ 630, 632 for a list of areas and specific restrictions.

[99] *See* UNCLOS 27, arts. 3-4, *available at* http://www.un.org/depts/los/convention_agreements/texts/unclos/unclos_e.pdf. The U.S. accepted this portion of UNCLOS via Presidential Proclamation in 1988. *See* Proclamation No. 5928, 54 Fed. Reg. 777 (Dec. 27, 1988).

[100] Unless it is an NFA firearm as discussed in Chapters 2 and 9.

From the baseline out to 200 miles from the coastline is the "exclusive economic zone" (EEZ).[101] From the end of the EEZ to 350 miles from the coastline (or to the end of subsurface land, whichever is shorter) is the "continental shelf."[102] The U.S. has generally asserted authority over natural resources in the continental shelf region beyond the EEZ. Because firearms are not natural resources, the federal government likely does not assert jurisdiction over them in this region.

Past the "continental shelf" you will either be in international waters or waters belonging to another country. It appears U.S. firearm laws generally do not apply in the EEZ or on the "continental shelf." However, the first twelve miles of the EEZ is called the "contiguous zone."[103] In this zone federal pollution, taxation, customs, and immigration laws, and possibly international laws, may apply.[104] Though it is unclear what, if any, firearm or ammunition possession restrictions apply, if you are boating in the "contiguous zone," be sure to check the laws concerning pollution, as expended bullets, shot, and casings may bring you under the purview of pollution laws.

Again, even if federal firearm laws apply beyond U.S. "territorial waters" (i.e., past the 12-mile mark) – perhaps under a "flag of the state" theory, where the law of the state (country) a boat originally embarks from is controlling – federal law has very few restrictions on firearm possession, aside from being prohibited from possessing firearms under the GCA and possessing NFA firearms.

Finally, if you will be boating in Canadian, Mexican, or another country's waters, you should learn that country's firearm laws and act accordingly. Also, check with the ATF and Customs and Border Protection, as you may have to get a permit and/or fulfill other requirements in order to enter another country's waters or re-enter U.S. waters with firearms.

This is a simplified overview of the laws concerning firearms on boats. Specific questions concerning your boating activities with firearms should be directed to a maritime attorney.

---

[101] See UNCLOS 43-44, arts. 55-57, available at http://www.un.org/depts/los/convention_agreements/texts/unclos/unclos_e.pdf.

[102] See UNCLOS 53-54, art. 76, available at http://www.un.org/depts/los/convention_agreements/texts/unclos/unclos_e.pdf.

[103] See UNCLOS 35, art. 33, available at http://www.un.org/depts/los/convention_agreements/texts/unclos/unclos_e.pdf. To be clear, the first 24 miles past the "seaward boundary" is considered the contiguous zone. The U.S. accepted this portion of UNCLOS via Presidential Proclamation in 1999. See Proclamation No. 7219, 64 F.R. 48, 701 (Aug. 2, 1999).

[104] See UNCLOS 35, art. 33, available at http://www.un.org/depts/los/convention_agreements/texts/unclos/unclos_e.pdf.

# VI. FIREARM POSSESSION AT PROTEST EVENTS

California law prohibits carrying concealed, loaded, or deadly weapons while picketing or engaging in other informational activities in public that relate to refusing to work. Violating this is a misdemeanor, and there is *no exception* for those with a valid Carry License.[105]

Under federal law Congress has directed and authorized the U.S. Secret Service to protect the President of the United States, as well as other presidential personnel and their family members, where it is warranted. So although federal possession laws do not expressly mention the president, the Secret Service can protect the president from private party firearm possession if it threatens the president.[106]

Law enforcement personnel are thus not obligated to arrest or charge peaceful demonstrators who do not pose a threat to the president and who are not violating any laws. But whether the Secret Service considers someone a threat is left to its discretion.

# VII. OTHER RESTRICTED PLACES UNDER CALIFORNIA LAW

## A. Gun Shows

You must be at least age 18 to go to gun shows or events, unless you are accompanied by a parent, grandparent, or legal guardian.[107] Except for sworn peace officers, show/event security, and vendors, any firearm you bring to the gun show or event must be checked, cleared of any ammunition, and secured to prevent it from being operated. An identification tag or sticker must also be attached to it identifying the owner[108] and explaining that sales must go through an FFL before you will be allowed into the show.[109] Except for sworn peace officers, security, and vendors, you cannot possess a firearm with ammunition designed to be fired in that firearm at the same time as you are attending a gun show.[110]

---

[105] P.C. § 17510.
[106] 18 U.S.C. § 3056.
[107] P.C. § 27335.
[108] Including the owner's signature, printed name, and government-issued ID.
[109] P.C. § 27340.
[110] P.C. § 27330.

## B. Playgrounds and Youth Centers

If you draw a firearm in an unlawful, rude, angry, or threatening manner while you are knowingly on, or within, the grounds of certain child care facilities or carry a concealed and/or loaded firearm in public while on or around a playground or youth center when it is open for business, classes, or school-related programs, or whenever minors are using it, you can be prosecuted with a felony or misdemeanor.[111]

A "playground" is "any park or recreational area specifically designed to be used by children that has play equipment installed, including public grounds designed for athletic activities such as baseball, football, soccer, or basketball, or any similar facility located on public or private school grounds, or on city or county parks."[112] A "youth center" is "any public or private facility that is used to host recreational or social activities for minors while minors are present."[113]

## C. Polling Places

Any person possessing a firearm at a polling place without city or county written authorization can be prosecuted with a felony or a misdemeanor.[114] This restriction does not apply to:

- A peace officer conducting official business or who is at the polling place to cast a vote.
- A private guard or security personnel hired or arranged for by an elections official or by the owner or manager of the polling place, as long as not hired solely for election day.[115]

Note that, just like sterile areas in airports, there is *no* exception to these restrictions for valid Carry License holders. They can be charged just like anyone else for possessing firearms at a polling place.

---

[111] P.C. §§ 417(a)-(b), 25400, 25850, 626.95(a).
[112] P.C. § 626.95(c)(1).
[113] P.C. § 626.95(c)(2).
[114] Cal. Elections Code § 18544(a).
[115] Cal. Elections Code § 18544(b).

# VIII. GENERAL FIREARM DISCHARGE RESTRICTIONS

Outside of specific areas like state parks and refuges generally owned by the state, California does not generally regulate non-negligent[116] or non-felonious discharge of firearms, leaving it to local entities or those that manage public lands to regulate instead. You should therefore generally look to them to determine where it is lawful to discharge firearms.

That being said, California makes it unlawful for you to discharge a firearm at an *unoccupied* motor vehicle or *uninhabited* building or dwelling house *without the owner's permission.*[117]

California also makes it unlawful to discharge "any firearm or other deadly weapon within 150 yards of any occupied dwelling house, residence, or other building or any barn or other outbuilding" related to it, without being the owner or person possessing the premises, or without having the owner or lawful possessor's permission.[118] It is also illegal to shoot a firearm from or onto a public road or highway[119] or to "intentionally discharge any firearm or release any arrow or crossbow bolt over or across any public road or other established way open to the public, in an unsafe and reckless manner."[120] It is also unlawful to "willfully and maliciously" shoot a firearm at an *unoccupied* aircraft.[121] You cannot "discharge any firearm within 500 feet of any magazine or any explosive manufacturing plant."[122]

The discharge of firearms in California state forests (of which there are five) is prohibited in the vicinity of camps or within 150 yards of designated camping areas, "residence sites, recreation grounds and areas, and over lakes or other bodies of water adjacent to or within such areas, whereby any person is exposed to injury as a result of such discharge."[123] The Fish and Game Code also prohibits *discharging* firearms in certain specified refuges.[124]

If you enter private lands, be wary of trespassing. "It is unlawful to enter any lands under cultivation or enclosed by a fence, belonging to, or

---

[116] *See* P.C. § 246.3(a) and (b) making a willful discharge of a firearm in such a *grossly negligent* manner a possible felony, and a misdemeanor if done so with a BB device.

[117] P.C. § 247(b).

[118] Fish & Game Code § 3004(a).

[119] P.C. § 374c.

[120] Fish & Game Code § 3004(b).

[121] P.C. § 247(a).

[122] Cal. Health & Saf. Code § 12084.

[123] 14 Cal. Code Regs. § 1413.

[124] Fish & Game § 10662. For example, certain areas of California Fish and Game District 4D in Riverside County are outlined in Fish & Game § 10837.

occupied by, another, or to enter any uncultivated or unenclosed lands …
where signs forbidding trespass or hunting, or both, are displayed at inter-
vals not less than three to the mile along all exterior boundaries and at all
roads and trails entering those lands, for the purpose of discharging any
firearm or taking or destroying any mammal or bird, including any waterfowl, on those lands without having first obtained written permission
from the owner, or his or her agent, or the person in lawful possession of,
those lands."[125]

Also, except for lawful self-defense, aiming or pointing a laser scope[126]
or laser pointer[127] at anyone in a threatening manner to cause them fear of
bodily harm is a misdemeanor.[128]

"[W]illfully and maliciously discharg[ing] a laser at an aircraft,"[129]
whether it is moving or not, is also a crime.[130] This rule does not apply to
laser development activity by or on behalf of the U.S. Armed Forces.

# IX.  SHOOTING RANGE USE RESTRICTIONS

A well-established range can provide an environment where you can discharge your firearm without fear of criminal prosecution.[131] For the first-
time shooter going to the range, make sure you contact the range ahead
of time and get information on what kinds of firearms they allow (some
ranges are handguns or rifles or shotguns only). If you are bringing ammunition to the range, inquire into what kinds of ammunition you can bring
(some ranges do not allow you to shoot steel-jacketed, steel-core, or semi-
jacketed ammunition, etc.), what kind of eye/ear wear they require, and if
they provide such protection. If you plan on renting firearms, ask whether
the range has firearms for rent and, if so, what the requirements are to rent
(I.D., age restrictions, number of persons, etc.).

---

[125] Fish & Game Code § 2016. *See also* P.C. § 602(l).

[126] A "laser scope" is "a portable battery-powered device capable of being attached to a firearm and capable of projecting a laser light on objects at a distance." The "laser scope" does not need to be attached
to a firearm to be a crime. P.C. § 417.25(a) and (b).

[127] A "laser pointer" is "any hand held laser beam device or demonstration laser product that emits a
single point of light amplified by the stimulated emission of radiation that is visible to the human eye."
P.C. § 417.25(c).

[128] P.C. § 417.25(a).

[129] "Aircraft" means any contrivance intended for and capable of transporting persons through the
airspace.

[130] P.C. § 247.5.

[131] Keep in mind that law enforcement members frequent firearm ranges for firearm qualification and
training. Make certain the firearms you possess and your activities are lawful.

# X. SUGGESTIONS FOR SHOOTING IN PUBLIC

If you have found a place where you may lawfully shoot, here are some tips:

- Since areas where you can discharge your firearm may be closed or restricted, contact state and/or national authorities in these areas *before* shooting. They will be your best authority as to where you can lawfully shoot in these areas.
- Know your surroundings. Even if you find a place to lawfully shoot, you may be near an area where the sound of firearms being fired is not appreciated. Contact law enforcement to let them know where you plan to shoot and ask for suggestions to avoid complaints.
- Watch the area behind your intended target. Make certain no one can enter into the area where you are shooting without you seeing them first.
- Leave the area as you found it. Pick up your trash, spent casings, targets, etc. If you are using clays or any other launch targets, do not launch them into areas where you cannot go and retrieve pieces later, such as cliffs, steep hillsides, or water.
- Discharging firearms into the air on the Fourth of July, New Year's Eve, or really *anytime* is illegal.

For more information on where to shoot and how to shoot safely, visit the websites of the NRA, CRPA, and the National Shooting Sports Foundation (NSSF).

## CHAPTER 8:

# REGULATION OF "ASSAULT WEAPONS" AND .50 BMG RIFLES

Technically the term "assault weapon" is a meaningless description. In fire-arm language, an "assault *rifle*" is military jargon believed to have original-ly been coined by the Nazis for a rifle that could fire a sub- or mid-caliber round, and allowed choosing either a semiautomatic or fully-automatic (*i.e.*, a "machinegun") fire mode – something unique at that time.[1]

The term fell out of use until it was revived by anti-gun publicists and expanded to cover common semiautomatic rifles with the intention of casting them in a negative light based on their threatening assault-rifle-like appearance.[2] The firearms California considers "assault weapons," how-ever, are civilian semiautomatics that are incapable of fully-automatic fire despite their military appearance. They have been legally defined as "as-sault weapons" for political reasons, based on appearance, name, or cos-metic characteristics, and *not* because they function differently from other popular semiautomatic firearms. In fact, various firearms legally available in California are practically identical to some that are "assault weapons," having only minor modifications and different names. Why some civilian semiautomatics are defined as "assault weapons" while others are not is beyond the scope of this book and in most cases defies logic.

For a while federal law prohibited creating new firearms with certain characteristics, classifying them as "assault weapons." That federal restric-tion ended in 2004 and is no longer enforceable. Confusion still exists, however, about the differences and overlap between California and federal "assault weapon" restrictions, and it is common for people to think that certain federal "assault weapon" provisions apply under California law too.

---

[1] The assault rifle first appeared as "the Sturmgewehr 44, a lighter, rapid fire military small arm [that] fired a projectile smaller (and logistically lighter and cheaper) than … the standard battle rifle." JOSEPH P. TARTARO, THE GREAT ASSAULT WEAPON HOAX 3 (The Second Amendment Foundation, 1993).

[2] Bruce H. Kobayashi & Joseph E. Olson, *In Re 101 California Street: A Legal and Economic Analysis of Strict Liability for the Manufacture and Sale of "Assault Weapons"* 8 STAN. L. & POL'Y REV. 41, 43 (1997) (citing *The Assault Rifle Smokescreen*, NEW YORK POST, July 18, 1991, at 30).

For example, one of the federally prohibited features was a bayonet mount. Bayonet mounts are legal under California law.

# I.   "ASSAULT WEAPON" DEFINED

"Assault weapons" now fall under one (and potentially two) of three categories: Categories 1, 2, and/or 3.

## A.  Category 1 "Assault Weapons"

Firearms listed in the 1989 Assault Weapons Control Act (AWCA) and those added in 1991, which included: "Made in China AK, AKM, AKS, AK47, AK47S, 56, 56S, 84S, and 86S," are commonly known as Category 1 "assault weapons."[3] They are the same firearms specifically named by make and model in P.C. § 30510.[4] They had to be registered with the DOJ on or before March 31, 1992.[5]

For a while, the DOJ allowed "late" firearm registration but later invalidated those registrations to settle litigation brought by the gun-control lobby. That move invalidated 16,000 registrations – making those firearms illegal "assault weapons" overnight. Notices then went out that those late-registered firearms had to be surrendered, *i.e.*, registration led to confiscation. Fortunately NRA attorneys stopped this process.[6]

*Kasler v. Lockyer*[7] and 1999's SB 23 triggered the next two major changes in California "assault weapon" law.

## B.  Category 2 "Assault Weapons"

The AWCA previously contained a provision authorizing the DOJ to petition certain courts to declare firearms as "assault weapons" where they were essentially similar to those already listed in P.C. § 30510 (former P.C. § 12276). Then, by regulation, they were added to the list of firearms already restricted under the AWCA (*i.e.*, Category 1 "assault weapons").[8] It was commonly referred to as the "add-on" provision.

---

[3] P.C. § 30510 (former P.C. § 12276). See Appendix A for the "Assault Weapon" list.

[4] Formerly P.C. §§ 12276(a)-(c). *See also* 11 Cal. Code Regs. § 5495 and Appendix A.

[5] *Assault Weapons Identification Guide*, STATE OF CALIFORNIA, OFFICE ATTORNEY GENERAL, http://oag.ca.gov/sites/all/files/pdfs/firearms/forms/awguide.pdf (last visited July 26, 2012).

[6] *HCI v. Lungren*, No. A083872 (Cal.App. 1 Dist. filed Dec. 15, 1997).

[7] *Kasler v. Lockyer*, 23 Cal.4th 472 (2000).

[8] P.C. § 30520 (former P.C. § 12276.5).

In 2000 the California Supreme Court upheld the AWCA as valid, including the "add-on" provision, in the face of a lawsuit challenging its constitutionality.[9]

Perhaps emboldened by the *Kasler* decision, the DOJ subsequently utilized a different "add-on" provision to put more firearms on the "assault weapon" list. For example, former P.C. § 12276(a) includes in its list of restricted "assault weapons" all Colt AR-15 and AK-47 "series" firearms. "Series" in this context "includes all other models that are only variations, with minor differences, of those models listed in [P.C. § 30510] subdivision (a), regardless of the manufacturer."[10] It thus essentially acted as another "add-on" provision, allowing the DOJ to simply declare a firearm an "assault weapon" based on its determination that the firearm has "minor differences" from already listed "assault weapons."

The DOJ added over sixty AR-15 and AK "series" firearms to the list of restricted "assault weapons," making those firearms illegal to possess in California if not registered by the applicable deadline. These new additions are referred to as Category 2 "assault weapons," and the deadline to register them was January 23, 2001. These added Category 2 "assault weapons" are listed at 11 Cal. Code Regs. § 5499.

Those possessing these newly listed firearms had less than six months to register them to be in compliance with the AWCA. Accordingly, because no real "public education" or "notification program" was ever provided announcing these newly added "assault weapons," many firearm owners never heard about this change to the law. Those who failed to register their firearms became criminal possessors of "assault weapons" overnight, often unknowingly.

However, the California Supreme Court weighed in again on the validity of this other "add-on" provision, and, unlike in *Kasler*, this time it ruled somewhat favorably to firearm owners. In *Harrot v. County of Kings*, the Court held that for the DOJ to add any firearm as a "series" "assault weapon" under P.C. § 12276, the AG must use P.C. § 12276.5's "add-on" procedure[11] or else could only add AR-15 and AK firearms to the list, but in either event, in order for an "assault weapon" to be illegal by make and

---

[9] *Kasler v. Lockyer*, 23 Cal.4th 472 (2000). The DOJ has been unable to use this provision to add to the prohibited "assault weapons" list since January 1, 2007, because it was statutorily "sunsetted" – meaning it expired – by passage of AB 2728, and the list has remained fixed ever since.

[10] P.C. § 30510(f).

[11] *Harrott v. County of Kings*, 25 Cal.4th 1138, 1155 (2001).

model it must be listed in the California Code of Regulations or the Attorney General's Assault Weapon Identification Guide (AWIG).¹²

In short, today this means that if a firearm is not currently listed as an "assault weapon" in the California Penal Code, California Code of Regulations, or the AG's AWIG, it is not a Category 1 or 2 "assault weapon."

The DOJ has argued, somewhat inconsistently, that Category 1 and 2 "assault weapons" are "assault weapons" at the bare receiver/frame level – regardless of any other particular characteristic. This is debatable, because frames and receivers are considered firearms according to certain Penal Code sections,¹³ but *not* for the AWCA. Under the AWCA, therefore, a frame should not be considered a "firearm." And before a frame can be an "assault weapon," it must first not only be a "firearm" that is either a rifle, pistol, or shotgun, but must also be a semiautomatic one.¹⁴

Since a bare frame or receiver alone cannot function as a firearm at all because it does not have the characteristics of a rifle, pistol, or shotgun, and particularly not in a manner to justify designating it "semiautomatic," a fully functioning "make and model" firearm must be present to be a "firearm" under the AWCA, not just a frame or a receiver.

However, since the DOJ disagrees, it is not recommended that you possess even bare firearm receivers listed as "assault weapons" unless registered.

## C. Category 3 "Assault Weapons"

In 1999 the AWCA was again amended to define "assault weapons" a third way, generically by a firearm's characteristics.¹⁵ SB 23 created a new category of "assault weapons," Category 3, that are generically based on a firearm's characteristics, not by name or make and model.¹⁶ These Category 3 "assault weapons" are rifles, pistols, and shotguns with certain external characteristics that do not alter their rate of fire. Today, these characteristics are

---

¹² *Harrott v. County of Kings*, 25 Cal.4th 1138, 1153-1154 (2001). The Assault Weapons Identification Guide, *see Assault Weapons Identification Guide*, STATE OF CALIFORNIA, OFFICE ATTORNEY GENERAL, http://oag.ca.gov/sites/all/files/pdfs/firearms/forms/awguide.pdf (last visited July 26, 2012), classifies "assault weapons" into three categories:
• Category 1 "assault weapon" – P.C. §§ 12276(a)-(c) (original make and model list);
• Category 2 "assault weapon" – P.C. §§ 12276(e)-(f) (regulatory make and model additions to the original make and model list) (partially repealed in 2006); and
• Category 3 "assault weapon" – P.C. § 12276.1 (SB 23 - generic characteristics/features based "assault weapons").
¹³ P.C. § 16520.
¹⁴ P.C. § 30510 (former P.C. § 12276).
¹⁵ P.C. § 30515 (former § 12276.1(a)).
¹⁶ P.C. § 30515 (former § 12276.1(a)).

listed in P.C. § 30515, and if present on a firearm in certain combinations, they can convert a firearm into a Category 3 "assault weapon."[17]

## 1. Category 3 – Rifles

Rifles are Category 3 "assault weapons" if they are:

- semiautomatic; *and*
- centerfire; *and*
- capable of accepting a detachable magazine; *and*
- have any one, or a combination, of the following:
  - "A pistol grip that protrudes conspicuously beneath the action of the weapon.
  - A thumbhole stock.
  - A folding or telescoping stock.
  - A grenade launcher or flare launcher.
  - A flash suppressor.
  - A forward pistol grip."[18]

Semiautomatic centerfire rifles with *fixed* magazines capable of accepting more than 10 rounds and semiautomatic centerfire rifles with overall lengths of less than 30 inches are also Category 3 "assault weapons."[19]

## 2. Category 3 – Pistols

Semiautomatic pistols capable of accepting a detachable magazine are "assault weapons" if they have any of the following:

- "A threaded barrel, capable of accepting a flash suppressor, forward handgrip, or silencer.
- A second handgrip.
- A shroud that is attached to, or partially or completely encircles, the barrel that allows the bearer to fire the weapon without burning the bearer's hand, except a slide that encloses the barrel.
- The capacity to accept a detachable magazine at some location outside of the pistol grip."[20]

Semiautomatic pistols with *fixed* magazines capable of accepting more than 10 rounds are also considered Category 3 "assault weapons."[21]

---

[17] *See* P.C. § 30515 and Appendix A.
[18] P.C. § 30515(a)(1).
[19] P.C. §§ 30515(a)(2)-(3).
[20] P.C. § 30515(a)(4).
[21] P.C. § 30515(a)(5).

## 3. Category 3 – Shotguns

Finally, shotguns are considered "assault weapons" if they are semiautomatic and have *both* of the following:

- "A folding or telescoping stock[; *and*]
- A pistol grip that protrudes conspicuously beneath the action of the weapon, thumbhole stock, or vertical handgrip."[22]

Additionally, shotguns can be "assault weapons" if they are semiautomatic and can accept detachable magazines or have a revolving cylinder.[23]

## 4. Category 3 – Definitions

The California Code of Regulations provides definitions for the various characteristics listed above that, when featured on a firearm in certain configurations, create a Category 3 "assault weapon."

- " 'Detachable magazine' … [is] any ammunition feeding device that can be removed readily from the firearm with neither disassembly of the firearm action nor use of a tool being required. A bullet or ammunition cartridge is considered a tool. Ammunition feeding device includes any belted or linked ammunition, but does not include clips, en bloc clips, or stripper clips that load cartridges into the magazine."[24]
- " 'Pistol grip that protrudes conspicuously beneath the action of the weapon' [is] a grip that allows for a pistol style grasp in which the web of the trigger hand (between the thumb and index finger) can be placed below the top of the exposed portion of the trigger while firing."[25]
- " 'Thumbhole stock' [is] a stock with a hole that allows the thumb of the trigger hand to penetrate into or through the stock while firing."[26]
- " 'Flash suppressor' [is] any device designed, intended, or that functions to [clearly] reduce or redirect muzzle flash from the shooter's field of vision."[27]
- " 'Forward pistol grip' [is] a grip that allows for a pistol style grasp forward of the trigger."[28]

---

[22] P.C. § 30515(a)(6).
[23] P.C. §§ 30515(a)(7)-(8).
[24] 11 Cal. Code Regs. § 5469(a) (emphasis added).
[25] 11 Cal. Code Regs. § 5469(d) (emphasis added).
[26] 11 Cal. Code Regs. § 5469(e) (emphasis added).
[27] 11 Cal. Code Regs. § 5469(b) (emphasis added).
[28] 11 Cal. Code Regs. § 5469(c) (emphasis added).

■ "Fixed magazine" is a magazine that stays attached to the firearm while loading. Often fixed magazines are charged or loaded "from a clip (en bloc or stripper) of cartridges inserted through the open breech into the magazine."[29]

## D. Making Category 3 "Assault Weapons" Comply with California Law

Some firearm owners and manufacturers comply with California law by removing one of the three prerequisite characteristics (semiautomatic, centerfire, or accepting a "detachable magazine") from their firearms so they are no longer legally considered "assault weapons." Some convert their semiautomatic rifles or pistols to manual-cycled, convert their centerfire rifles to rimfire, or try to make "detachable magazines" legally "non-detachable" so the firearm (rifle, pistol, or shotgun) cannot accept a "detachable magazine." As explained below, however, this does not work for all firearms.

In making the firearm unable to accept a "detachable magazine," these individuals typically retrofit their firearms with an aftermarket product generally called a "magazine lock." The most common kind is known as a "Bullet Button." The standard magazine release for a "detachable magazine" can usually operate with the push of a finger, so no "tool" is required to release the magazine. The typical "magazine lock," however, replaces the standard one-piece magazine release button with a two-piece assembly that cannot be operated with just the push of a finger.

The new two-piece magazine release typically has an inner and outer button. The outer button directly replaces the standard magazine release button in shape and size but without actuating the spring that allows magazine removal. The much smaller inner button sits recessed within the outer button and becomes the firearm's true magazine removal mechanism. Since the inner button is too small and recessed to be pushed by a finger, a tool is needed to push the inner button in to release the magazine so it can be removed. The most common "tool" used to push the recessed button and remove the magazine is the tip of a bullet, hence the common term "Bullet Button." Because a tool is needed to release the magazine, the firearm can no longer be said to have the capacity to accept a "detachable magazine."

The Sacramento Police and the Orange County Sheriff have advised their officers about the legal effect of magazine locks consistent with our

---

[29] *Assault Weapons Identification Guide*, STATE OF CALIFORNIA, OFFICE ATTORNEY GENERAL, http://oag. ca.gov/sites/all/files/pdfs/firearms/forms/awguide.pdf (last visited July 26, 2012).

analysis.[30] However, confusion still exists among other law enforcement agencies. Nevertheless, thousands of magazine locks are currently being manufactured and used in California, generally without any legal consequences (though there have been isolated incidents of improper arrests).

Again, attaching a magazine lock like a "Bullet Button" to a firearm renders the magazine "non-detachable." Doing this removes one of the features some rifles, pistols, and shotguns must have to be legally considered a Category 3 "assault weapon."[31] This means that if a "magazine lock" is attached to a semiautomatic, centerfire rifle that is not already a Category 1 or 2 "assault weapon," even with any of the other characteristics listed in P.C. § 30515(a)(1)(A)-(F), the rifle should not be legally classified as an "assault weapon" based on the 30515(a)(1) definition, nor should someone with such a firearm be considered "in possession" of an unregistered "assault weapon."[32]

As mentioned, however, some firearms are not capable of accepting a "detachable magazine" but are still Category 3 "assault weapons." Semiautomatic, centerfire rifles, semiautomatic pistols with "fixed magazines" that can accept more than 10 rounds, and semiautomatic, centerfire rifles with an overall length of less than 30 inches still classify as Category 3 "assault weapons," despite not having "detachable magazines."[33] Shotguns can be Category 3 "assault weapons" if they are semiautomatic, have a folding or telescoping stock, and a pistol grip, thumbhole stock or vertical handgrip[34] or if the shotgun has a revolving cylinder,[35] regardless of whether it has a "magazine lock." And a "magazine lock" may actually convert an otherwise legal rifle or pistol *into* a Category 3 "assault weapon." This is based on the DOJ's apparent opinion that attaching a "magazine lock" to a firearm renders the magazine "fixed," and thus an "assault weapon" if a magazine capable of accepting more than 10 rounds is used.[36]

The AWIG defines a "fixed magazine" as "[a] magazine which remains affixed to the firearm during loading. Frequently a fixed magazine is charged (loaded) from a clip (en bloc or stripper) of cartridges inserted

---

[30] Copies of these opinions are available at http://michellawyers.com.

[31] Pistols and shotguns with "magazine locks" are also considered incapable of accepting "detachable magazines."

[32] *See* P.C. § 30605.

[33] P.C. §§ 30515(a)(2)-(3).

[34] P.C. § 30515(a)(6).

[35] P.C. § 30515(a)(8).

[36] P.C. § 30515(a)(2). For example, a standard Ruger Mini 14 rifle (*i.e.*, without a pistol grip or "flash suppressor") is not an "assault weapon" under any category. You can lawfully use magazines capable of accepting more than 10 rounds in the rifle. But if you were to put a "magazine lock" on that same rifle, using magazines that hold over 10 rounds could convert it into an "assault weapon" according to the DOJ. So making a rifle *more* difficult to reload could actually convert it into an "assault weapon."

through the open breech into the magazine."[37] As discussed above, semiautomatic, centerfire rifles, and semiautomatic pistols with "fixed magazines" that can accept more than 10 rounds are "assault weapons." But firearms with magazine locks are usually not reloaded with the magazine remaining affixed to the firearm. Shooters tend to use the magazine release tool to eject the magazine and insert a fresh magazine. Rarely do they go through the tedious process of manually reloading their firearm through the breech (by using a clip) when the "magazine lock" is attached. Because shooters do not have to manually reload their firearms through the breech or by using a clip, it is inaccurate to say that firearms with "magazine locks" have a "fixed magazine." They also cannot be said to have "detachable magazines" either because a tool is needed to remove the magazine. Firearms with "magazine locks" thus fall into a legal "gray area." This is why the term "non-detachable" is used above to describe firearms with magazine locks.

Because distinguishing "non-detachable" and "fixed magazines" still causes confusion and the DOJ considers firearms with "magazine locks" to have a "fixed magazine," magazines capable of accepting more than 10 rounds should not be used in firearms with a "magazine lock."

Since the birth of the "magazine lock," companies have altered its design and created other devices to use with it. While some of these improvements and devices make it easier to use, they also present new problems.

Some "magazine lock" versions now have different settings. One version allows the firearm owner to use the "magazine lock" regularly on one setting, and then by a simple twist of a screw or Allen wrench, the "magazine lock" functions as a standard magazine *release*. Manufacturers advertise these devices for use in and outside of California, with the standard "magazine lock" setting intended for use in California and the magazine release button setting for use outside of California.

Because this device's settings can be easily changed from one to the other and because of possibilities like forgetting to reset the device to the standard setting upon returning to California, device failure, and possible felony prosecution, it is risky to use devices that allow you to switch between the "magazine lock" style release and the standard magazine release.

Another common device is the "Wonder Wrench," which is designed to remain inserted in the "magazine lock" while the firearm is being used. When inserted it functions like a standard magazine release. Like the magazine lock with different settings, the "Wonder Wrench" is designed to be used *outside* of California. Never leave any device or item inserted in the "magazine lock" while in California. If the device left in allows it to func-

---

[37] *Assault Weapons Identification Guide*, STATE OF CALIFORNIA, OFFICE ATTORNEY GENERAL, http://oag.ca.gov/sites/all/files/pdfs/firearms/forms/awguide.pdf (last visited July 26, 2012).

tion like a standard magazine release, the firearm can presumably still accept a "detachable magazine" and thus may constitute an illegal "assault weapon."

Instead of using "magazine locks" to render a magazine non-detachable in an effort to avoid making their firearm an "assault weapon," some people remove restricted features or use modified after-market features. For example, they remove the "pistol grip" from an AR-15 rifle. Or some shooters add stocks or attachments that modify the shooter's grip like the "U-15" stock[38] and the "Monsterman Grip."[39] These attach to AR-15 and AK-47 type receivers, replacing the pistol grip, which takes them out of Category 3 "assault weapon" status – assuming they have no other prohibited characteristics.

Removing or altering the pistol grip only works for rifles with "off-list lowers" that are otherwise lawful in California. Adding these items to rifles that are considered Category 1 or 2 "assault weapons," however, does *not* make those rifles lawful.

## E. "Constructive Possession" of "Assault Weapons"

If you merely possess parts that, if assembled, would make a "machinegun," you can be prosecuted for possessing a "machinegun."[40] The same is usually true if you possess parts that, if assembled, would make a "short-barreled shotgun" or "short-barreled rifle."[41] However, the same is not true for "assault weapons." Possessing unassembled parts that, if assembled, would make a firearm an "assault weapon" is *not* considered "constructive possession" of an "assault weapon."

The Penal Code defines "assault weapons" as "rifles," "pistols," or "shotguns" listed by make and model, or that have certain features, not mere *parts* of a firearm.[42] Nothing prohibits having mere "assault weapon" *parts*, even if those parts can be assembled into a complete "assault weapon." In other words a firearm, as assembled, is either an "assault weapon" or it

---

[38] The U-15 stock is a complete stock and is curved to allow a "rifle-style grasp" while still allowing you to rest the stock against your shoulder. Because the U-15's stock does not have a hole, it cannot classify as a "thumbhole stock." And it is not a pistol grip because the webbing of the shooter's trigger hand between the thumb and index finger is placed above the top of the exposed portion of the trigger while firing.

[39] The "Monsterman Grip" also allows a "rifle-style grasp" but is designed to function *with* the rifle's stock, not replace it. The "Monsterman Grip" extends below and parallel to the rifle's stock and away from its action. The shooter holds the "Monsterman Grip" just like a normal rifle stock, but it has a fin that extends from the "Grip" that runs next to the stock. This fin prevents the shooter from holding the "Grip" in a pistol-style grasp by keeping the thumb in line with the fingers.

[40] P.C. § 16880.

[41] P.C. §§ 17180, 17170.

[42] P.C. §§ 30510, 30515.

is not. Having parts around that might turn a firearm into one does not change the analysis. But continuing to possess an unregistered receiver for a firearm listed by make and model as a California "assault weapon" is still playing with fire given law enforcement's interpretation of the law.

## II.  .50 BMG RIFLES

A .50 BMG rifle is a centerfire rifle that is not already an "assault weapon" or a "machinegun"[43] and can fire a .50 BMG cartridge. It does not include any "antique firearm" or "curio or relics."[44]

A .50 BMG cartridge is a cartridge for firing from a centerfire rifle that has the following criteria:

- An overall length of 5.54 inches from the base to the tip of the bullet.
- The bullet diameter for the cartridge is from .510 to, and including, .511 inch.
- The case base diameter for the cartridge is from .800 inch to, and including, .804 inch.
- The cartridge case length is 3.91 inches.[45]

To be clear, just because a firearm is chambered in .50 BMG does not necessarily mean it is a .50 BMG rifle; the firearm must be a "rifle." In order to be a "rifle," the firearm should be "intended to be fired from the shoulder[.]"[46] For example, a firearm chambered in .50 BMG, without a stock, that is fired from a mount using spade grips is not a .50 BMG rifle and thus need not be registered to lawfully possess in California. Since many law enforcement officers are unaware of this distinction, know that even a legal firearm chambered in .50 BMG may still cause law enforcement issues.

## III.  "ASSAULT WEAPON" AND .50 BMG RIFLE USE RESTRICTIONS

With few exceptions, anyone in California who manufactures, distributes, transports, imports, sells, gives, or lends any "assault weapon" or .50 BMG

---

[43] P.C. § 30530(a). *See also* P.C. § 16880(a) (defining a "machinegun" as "any weapon that shoots, is designed to shoot, or can readily be restored to … automatically [shoot] more than one shot, without manual reloading, by … [one] function of the trigger.").

[44] P.C. § 30530(b). *See* Chapters 2 and 4 for "antique firearm" and "curio and relics" definitions.

[45] P.C. § 30525.

[46] P.C. § 17090 (defining "rifle" generally for purposes of defining "short-barreled rifle").

rifle is guilty of a felony. And if you transfer, loan, sell, or give an "assault weapon" or .50 BMG rifle to a minor, an additional one year penalty could be added to your sentence.[47]

Mere possession of an "assault weapon" or .50 BMG rifle that is not properly registered to you may also result in a felony or misdemeanor conviction for "assault weapons" and a misdemeanor for .50 BMG rifles.[48] And transporting one improperly can result in a separate felony charge (or a misdemeanor) *even if registered to you.*[49] You can be prosecuted for any of these violations even if you lawfully obtained the "assault weapon" or .50 BMG rifle before the law requiring their registration took effect if you did not properly register it.

For the first year after these "assault weapon" and .50 BMG rifle restrictions took effect, violations were charged as infractions. For some reason, however, the same conduct that was an infraction several years ago is now a felony or misdemeanor with possible jail time and a possible lifetime ban on your right to possess a firearm.

In 1991 P.C. § 12289 was added to the Penal Code allowing for "assault weapon" registration education and notification programs.[50] Despite the legislature's mandate that the DOJ create an education and notification program, California's confusing "assault weapon" laws have not become any clearer in the 20 years since the AWCA was passed. Law-abiding citizens with no criminal history are *still* being prosecuted today for possessing firearms they were unaware met the "assault weapon" definition even though they may have lawfully purchased them years ago.

## A. Civil Compromise for Illegally Possessing an "Assault Weapon" or .50 BMG Rifle

Penal Code section 30800 allows government attorneys to settle criminal cases involving "assault weapon" and/or .50 BMG rifle *possession* with a civil compromise instead of criminal charges. This rule allows those charged with possession of these firearms a way to resolve their case without the consequences of a criminal conviction.[51] In this instance, you will not be convicted of a criminal offense, but you will almost certainly have to surrender the firearm to law enforcement permanently and pay a fine. However, the availability of this option is subject to the sole discretion of the prosecuting agency.

---

[47] P.C. §§ 30600(a)-(b).
[48] P.C. §§ 30605, 30610.
[49] P.C. §§ 30600(a), 30945.
[50] P.C. § 12289 (current version at P.C. § 31115).
[51] P.C. § 30800.

# IV. EXCEPTIONS TO "ASSAULT WEAPON" AND .50 BMG RIFLE LAWS

## A. Law Enforcement and Other Government Agencies

The general "assault weapon" and .50 BMG rifle possession restrictions do not apply to their sale, purchase, import, or possession "by the … [DOJ], police departments, sheriffs' offices, marshals' offices, the Department of Corrections and Rehabilitation, the Department of the California Highway Patrol, district attorneys' offices, the Department of Fish and Game, the Department of Parks and Recreation, or the military or naval forces of this state or of the United States, or any federal law enforcement agency for use in the discharge of their official duties."[52]

Sworn peace officers who are members of the aforementioned agencies may also possess and use "assault weapons or … .50 BMG rifle[s] … for law enforcement purposes, *whether on or off duty.*"[53]

## B. Peace Officers and Federal Law Enforcement

Sworn peace officers may also acquire, register, and possess "assault weapons" or .50 BMG rifles if authorized in writing by the head of their agency.[54] They must also register their "assault weapon" with the DOJ within 90 days of receiving it (or one year for .50 BMG rifles) and include a copy of the required authorization with their registration.[55] This is the only exception that allows *registering* a newly acquired "assault weapon" and/or .50 BMG rifle.

Unlike the "law enforcement purposes" exception for *agency*-owned "assault weapons," this exception does *not* limit an officer's "assault weapon" or .50 BMG rifle use. This means that an officer obtaining an "assault

---

[52] P.C. § 30625.
[53] P.C. § 30630(a) (emphasis added).
[54] P.C. § 30630(b)(1).
[55] P.C. § 30630(b)(1)-(3).

weapon" or .50 BMG rifle under this exception is not limited to only using it for "law enforcement purposes."[56]

Federal law enforcement members may also purchase, receive, and possess "assault weapons" or .50 BMG rifles as long as they are authorized by their employer to possess the firearm.[57]

## C. Estate Executor and Inheritance

An executor or administrator of an estate cannot be prosecuted for possessing or transporting an "assault weapon" or .50 BMG rifle properly registered (or lawfully possessed by a sworn peace officer pursuant to P.C. § 30630(a)) if it is being lawfully disposed of as authorized by a probate court.[58]

If you inherit title to a properly registered "assault weapon," you must make it permanently inoperable, sell it to an FFL with an "assault weapon" permit, obtain a Dangerous Weapons Permit from the DOJ, or remove it from California within 90 days (180 days for .50 BMG rifles) of receiving it.[59]

## D. Loaning and Returning an "Assault Weapon" or .50 BMG Rifle

If you lawfully possess an "assault weapon" or .50 BMG rifle, you may lend it to someone else as long as the person you lend it to is at least age 18[60] and is not otherwise prohibited from possessing, receiving, owning, or purchasing a firearm, *the registered owner remains in the "assault weapon" or .50 BMG rifle's presence,* and the "assault weapon" or .50 BMG rifle is possessed at any of the following:

- A target range holding a regulatory or business license for practicing shooting at that target range.
- The target range premises of a club or organization organized for practicing shooting at targets.

---

[56] A recent AG Opinion states that any peace officer who legally purchased and registered an "assault weapon" or .50 BMG rifle under this exception cannot continue to possess it after retiring. Opinion No. 09-901, 93 Ops. Cal. Atty. Gen. 130 (2010); http://ag.ca.gov/cms_attachments/opinions/pdfs/0564_09-901.pdf. This Opinion is still disputed and not binding law, but may be persuasive to courts interpreting the law.

[57] P.C. § 30630(c).

[58] P.C. § 30655.

[59] P.C. §§ 30915, 30935.

[60] Anyone under age 18 cannot even *touch* an "assault weapon." No exceptions. *See* P.C. § 30660.

- Any exhibition, display, or educational project about firearms that is sponsored or approved by a law enforcement agency or national or state recognized entity that fosters firearm education.[61]

## E. Nonresident Possession at Match or Competition

Subject to the transportation requirements,[62] California non-residents over age 18 who are not otherwise prohibited from possessing firearms may possess and import "assault weapons" or .50 BMG rifles in California if they are "going directly to or coming directly from an organized competitive match or league competition that involves the use of an assault weapon or a .50 BMG rifle."[63] For this exception to apply, the competition or match must take place at: "[a] target range that holds a regulatory or business license for the purpose of practicing shooting at that target range[, or a] … target range of a public or private club or organization that is organized for the purpose of practicing shooting at targets."[64] In addition, "[t]he match or competition … [must be] sponsored by, conducted under the auspices of, or approved by, a law enforcement agency or a nationally or state recognized entity that fosters proficiency in, or promotes education about, firearms."[65] Because the law says you must be going directly to or from the approved locations, detours are risky.

## F. Department of Justice Permits

Today anyone other than certain peace officers can, *in theory*, acquire an "assault weapon" or .50 BMG rifle in California if they first obtain a Dangerous Weapons Permit.[66] The permit process involves filling out a six-page form with references, fingerprints, and a statement of "good cause," and it is the same process used to acquire a "machinegun" license and a "destructive device" permit in California.[67]

For "good cause" you must give "clear and convincing evidence that there is a bona fide market or public necessity for the issuance of a dan-

---

[61] P.C. § 30660.

[62] "Assault weapons" and .50 BMG rifles must be transported according to P.C. §§ 25610 or 25505.

[63] P.C. § 30665(a).

[64] P.C. § 30665(b).

[65] P.C. § 30665(c).

[66] P.C. §§ 31000, 32650; 11 Cal. Code Regs. § 4128; *see also Dangerous Weapons License/Permit(s) Application*, CALIFORNIA DEPT. OF JUSTICE, http://ag.ca.gov/firearms/forms/pdf/FD030DWApp.pdf (last visited Aug. 2, 2012).

[67] Out-of-state residents who have lawfully acquired an "assault weapon" or a .50 BMG rifle before moving to California cannot simply register their firearms; they have to get a Dangerous Weapons Permit first. P.C. §§ 30925, 30940 (formerly P.C. § 12285(b)(2), (4)).

gerous weapons license or permit and that … [you will not] endanger[] public safety."[68] "Good cause" includes the following scenarios:

- Designing, demonstrating, selling, and/or manufacturing it to law enforcement, military and/or other Dangerous Weapon Permit holders.
- "Training, research and development; and/or manufacturing pursuant to government contract.
- Use and/or manufacture of dangerous weapons as props in commercial motion picture, television production, or other commercial entertainment events.
- Possession for the purpose of maintaining a collection of destructive devices as defined in Penal Code section 16460 but such possession shall not be allowed for short-barreled shotguns, short-barreled rifles, machineguns or *assault weapons*.
- Repair and maintenance of dangerous weapons lawfully possessed by others.
- Use of dangerous weapons in activities sanctioned by government military agencies by members of those agencies.
- The sale of assault weapons and/or the manufacture of assault weapons for the sale to, purchase by, or possession of assault weapons by: the agencies listed in Penal Code section 30625 and the officers described in Penal Code section 30630; entities and persons who have been issued assault weapon permits; entities outside the state who have, in effect, a federal firearms dealer's license solely for the purpose of distribution to an entity listed herein; federal law enforcement and military agencies; law enforcement and military agencies of other states; and foreign governments and agencies approved by the United States State Department."[69]

In the highly unlikely event that the DOJ gives you a Dangerous Weapons Permit, you are required to *annually* renew it along with paying a renewal and inspection fee of up to $1,500, keep an inventory of all "dangerous weapons," and store them in a safe place.[70] If you have less than five devices that require the permit, then you will only have to have an inspection once every five years.[71]

---

[68] 11 Cal. Code Regs. § 4128(c).

[69] 11 Cal. Code Regs. § 4128. *See also* P.C. § 31005 (giving the DOJ authority to issue "assault weapons" permits upon a finding of "good cause").

[70] 11 Cal. Code Regs. §§ 4129, 4130, 4145.

[71] 11 Cal. Code Regs. § 4145(b).

## G. Federal Firearms Licensee (FFL) Exceptions

For purposes of "assault weapons" and .50 BMG rifles, FFLs are not those with only a standard license to sell firearms (as discussed in Chapter 4), but are those who *also* possess a Dangerous Weapons Permit for "assault weapons" and/or .50 BMG rifles.

### 1. Service or Repair

These FFLs can take possession of "assault weapons" or .50 BMG rifles to service or repair them from a lawfully registered owner or Dangerous Weapons Permit holder. The FFL may also give possession of them to a gunsmith to help with the service or repair as long as the gunsmith is employed by, or has a contract with, the dealer for gunsmithing[72] services.[73]

### 2. Other Special Allowances

These FFLs may also transport an "assault weapon" or .50 BMG rifle between dealers or to out-of-state dealers per the NFA,[74] display firearms at licensed state or local government gun shows, sell them to out-of-state residents, or sell them to someone with a Dangerous Weapons Permit.[75]

# V. ACQUIRING NEW "ASSAULT WEAPONS" OR .50 BMG RIFLES

## A. Registration

As mentioned above, "assault weapon" and .50 BMG rifle registration periods have long expired.[76] With the exception of peace officers, the DOJ no longer accepts registration applications. To have properly registered an "assault weapon" or .50 BMG rifle, you must have paid a $20 fee for an "assault weapon," or a $25 fee for a .50 BMG rifle, and submitted an application to the DOJ that included the firearm's description and all unique

---

[72] For this exception the gunsmith must have an FFL of his or her own and a business license required by a state or local governmental agency. P.C. § 31050(c).

[73] P.C. § 31050.

[74] NFA firearms are discussed in Chapter 2. Almost all "assault weapons" and .50 BMG rifles are not "firearms" under the NFA, showing that the legislature did not know what it was doing when writing these laws. Also remember that transporting "assault weapons" has specific requirements discussed in Chapter 6.

[75] P.C. § 31055.

[76] All of the deadlines for registering Category 1, Category 2, and Category 3 "assault weapons" have passed. April 30, 2006 was the deadline for applying to register .50 BMG rifles. P.C. § 30905.

identification marks, the applicant's full name and address, date of birth, owner's thumbprint, and any other required information.[77]

If you properly sent in your registration within the specified time period and all of the information was accurately provided, the registration should have been entered into the DOJ's Automated Firearm System (AFS) database, and you would have received a confirmation notice. If you have a firearm that should have been registered as an "assault weapon" but was not, there will be no record in the AFS. In other words, if your "assault weapon" is not registered to you as an "assault weapon" in the AFS, you may be possessing it illegally.

There have been reports of the DOJ inadvertently omitting "assault weapon" registrations from the AFS, and recently an ex-DOJ official testified to the unreliability of the AFS system for keeping accurate firearm disposition records. It is therefore wise to keep the confirmation notice of your "assault weapon" registration in a safe place, along with copies saved in paper and electronic format. Some "assault weapon" owners keep a copy of the registration in the hollow of their "assault weapon's" pistol grip or buttstock in case law enforcement asks them about it.

## B. Moving into California with an "Assault Weapon" or .50 BMG Rifle

If you plan on moving to California and bringing an "assault weapon" or .50 BMG rifle, you must get a Dangerous Weapons Permit from the DOJ *before* you can bring your firearm into California. Alternatively you can have the firearm sent to an FFL in California, and once you get a Dangerous Weapons Permit, *then* the FFL will redeliver the firearm to you.[78] If the FFL is prohibited from delivering the firearm to you, either because you did not obtain the DOJ permit or because you are prohibited from owning firearms in general (see Chapter 3), the FFL will keep possession or lawfully dispose of it according to California law.[79]

# VI. LAWFULLY USING "ASSAULT WEAPONS" AND .50 BMG RIFLES

Unless the DOJ issues you a permit for additional uses, you may only possess an "assault weapon" or .50 BMG rifle *registered to you*:

---

[77] P.C. §§ 30900(c)-(d) ("assault weapons"), 30905(b)-(c) (.50 BMG rifles).

[78] P.C. §§ 30925, 30940.

[79] *See* P.C. §§ 30925 ("assault weapons"), 30940 (.50 BMG rifles).

- "At ... [your] residence, place of business, or other property [you] own[] ... or on [the] property ... [of] another with the[ir] ... express permission.

- While on the premises of a target range of a public or private club or organization organized for the purpose of practicing shooting at targets.

- While on a target range that holds a regulatory or business license for the purpose of practicing shooting at that target range.

- While on the premises of a shooting club ... licensed pursuant to the Fish and Game Code.

- While attending any exhibition, display, or educational project that is about firearms and that is sponsored by, conducted under the auspices of, or approved by a law enforcement agency or a nationally or state recognized entity that fosters proficiency in, or promotes education about, firearms.

- While on publicly owned land, if the possession and use of a[n "assault weapon"]... is specifically permitted by the managing agency of the land.

- While transporting the assault weapon or .50 BMG rifle between any of the places [mentioned here, or to any FFL (who also has a dangerous weapons permit)] for servic[e] or repair[.]"[80]

If you want to use an "assault weapon" or .50 BMG rifle for something other than the things above, you have to get a Dangerous Weapons Permit from the DOJ first.[81]

# VII. WHAT TO DO IF YOU THINK YOU HAVE AN "ASSAULT WEAPON" OR .50 BMG RIFLE

## A. Determine if It *Is* an "Assault Weapon" or .50 BMG Rifle

Using the above information, determine if your firearm meets the definition of an "assault weapon" or .50 BMG rifle. As discussed above, some of the laws prohibiting "assault weapons" were passed with little fanfare. No doubt thousands of California residents are unknowingly "in possession" of unregistered "assault weapons." If you have any doubts about your firearm, ask an attorney familiar with California firearm laws.

---

[80] P.C. § 30945.
[81] P.C. § 31000(a).

## B. Determine if Your "Assault Weapon" or .50 BMG Rifle Was Registered

If you do not know or *think* that you registered your "assault weapon" or .50 BMG rifle, you may request a list of all firearms of which you are the registered owner by submitting an Automated Firearms System Record Request to the DOJ. This form can be found at http://ag.ca.gov/firearms/forms/pdf/AFSPrivateCitizen.pdf.

If you know or believe you registered your "assault weapon" or .50 BMG rifle but no registration record appears in the DOJ's system, you should contact an attorney immediately for possible options.

## C. If Your "Assault Weapon" or .50 BMG Rifle Is Unregistered

If you possess an unregistered "assault weapon" or .50 BMG rifle and do not meet any of the above exceptions, you are violating California law. Unfortunately, there is no way for you to register it as an "assault weapon" or .50 BMG rifle now. You should contact an attorney familiar with California firearm laws immediately to determine what to do with it.

## CHAPTER 9

# OTHER HEAVILY REGULATED FIREARMS AND DEVICES

As discussed throughout this book, California and federal laws often differ and overlap. To comply with laws about heavily regulated firearms and devices, you must comply with both state and federal requirements.

Unlike California, federal law does not have many restrictions on what types of firearms a person may possess. There is one notable exception however: the National Firearms Act (NFA). Items meeting the NFA's unusual definition of "firearm"[1] have a separate set of federal requirements you must meet before you can lawfully possess them. These requirements are discussed briefly at the end of this chapter.

If you want to possess any of the items described below, believe you already do, and/or have questions on whether your possession of them is legal, you should contact an attorney familiar with firearms law.

## I.  "MACHINEGUNS"

Under both California and federal law, a "machinegun" is "any weapon which shoots, is designed to shoot, or can be [easily] restored to ... automatically [shoot,] more than one shot, without manual reloading, by a single function of the trigger." A "machinegun" "also include[s] the frame or receiver[,] ... any part designed solely and exclusively, or combination of parts designed and intended, for use in converting a weapon into a machinegun, ... [any weapon the ATF considers easily convertible to a "machinegun,"[2] or] any combination of parts from which a machinegun

---

[1] *See* Chapter 2 for "firearm" definitions.

[2] 26 U.S.C. § 5845(b); P.C. § 16880.

can be assembled if" they were under the same person's possession or control.[3]

These parts vary in size and description. For some firearms you only need a specially shaped metal piece that will allow a firearm to fire fully-automatic (a.k.a. an auto or conversion sear). So this one single part could be considered a "machinegun." For other firearms, small mechanisms that attach to the firearm or replace internal parts are all you need. These metal parts and pieces can be considered "machineguns" by themselves even if you do not possess the actual firearm they are designed to be used with.

Also firearm parts wearing out over time can lead to two shots being fired per trigger pull, and law enforcement might believe you have created or modified you firearm into a "machinegun." Take it apart and to a gunsmith as soon as possible if this happens.

The term "automatic" firearm is used and abused a lot. An "automatic" firearm is simply one that "automatically" loads another round into the chamber after a round is discharged. The term can include "semiautomatic," meaning one shot per trigger pull, and "fully-automatic," meaning rounds will continue to fire as long as the trigger is pressed down or until the firearm runs out of ammunition. The media often uses the phrases "automatic weapon" or "automatic firearms." Because the term "automatic" can include many firearm types – ranging from semiautomatic pistols to tank-mounted "machineguns" – pay attention to how the word is used. The next time you come across "automatic" firearm in a news story, consider whether the word is being used incorrectly, or whether it is being used to elicit a certain public reaction.

People often think of Gatling guns as "machineguns" because of their relatively rapid fire potential. But, because they have no trigger and instead are crank-operated, they cannot meet the "machinegun" definition. Their ammunition feeding devices, however, likely constitute "large-capacity magazines" and are thus regulated as such, as discussed below.

## A. Prohibitions

It is generally illegal for anyone to knowingly possess, transport, manufacture, sell, or convert an existing firearm into a "machinegun" under both California and federal law.[4] Severe penalties exist for violating this prohi-

---

[3] 26 U.S.C. § 5845(b); P.C. § 16880. The ATF's position is that a shoestring attached to a semiautomatic rifle that causes the firearm to fire more than one round per trigger pull is, when attached to the firearm, a "machinegun." *ATF Opinion Letter of June 25 2007*, EVERYDAY NO DAYS OFF, http://www.everydaynodaysoff.com/2010/01/25/shoestring-machine-gun (last visited Aug. 6, 2012). This position is a modification of a previous ATF opinion which stated a shoestring, by itself, could be a "machinegun."

[4] P.C. § 32625; 18 U.S.C. § 922(o); 26 U.S.C. § 5861.

bition including potentially years in prison following a California felony conviction[5] and up to 10 years and/or not more than a $10,000 fine for federal violations.[6]

Under federal law, however, it can be legal to acquire a "machinegun" that was lawfully possessed before May 19, 1986, *as long as* you comply with the strict requirements for transferring and possessing NFA firearms discussed at the end of this chapter.

But even if you meet the federal NFA requirements to lawfully possess a "machinegun," you must also meet one of the exceptions to California's general ban on possessing them. Otherwise the ATF is required to deny the transfer.[7]

# B. California Exceptions to "Machinegun" Restrictions

## 1. Law Enforcement and Military

Certain law enforcement agencies and military forces may receive and possess "machineguns," including ones made after 1986.[8] Though such agencies and military forces are exempt from the NFA's tax[9] (discussed below), they still must register the "machineguns."[10]

## 2. Permits to Possess, Manufacture, and Transport

Upon satisfactorily showing that "good cause" exists, the California DOJ may issue you a permit to possess, manufacture, or transport "machineguns."[11] These permits must be renewed annually.[12] Unless you are involved with law enforcement, the military, or the entertainment industry or have a business that supports, advises, trains, or supervises these organizations, it

---

[5] P.C. § 32625.

[6] 26 U.S.C. § 5871.

[7] 26 U.S.C. § 5812(a). "Applications [for NFA firearms] shall be denied if the transfer, receipt, or possession of the firearm would place the transferee in violation of law."

[8] The federal exception to the ban on "machineguns" made after 1986 includes "a transfer to or by, or possession by or under the authority of, the United States or any department or agency thereof or a State, or a department, agency, or political subdivision thereof." 18 U.S.C. § 922(o)(2)(A). Under California law these entities' personnel may possess "machineguns" too, but only while acting within the scope of their duties. P.C. § 32610(a).

[9] 26 U.S.C. §§ 5852, 5853; 27 C.F.R. §§ 479.89-479.90.

[10] Unless the firearms are possessed or under the control of the U.S., the "machineguns" must be registered in the National Firearms Registration and Transfer Record. 26 U.S.C. § 5841. Federal law also allows certain government entities to acquire and register NFA firearms (including "machineguns") for official use when the firearm has been abandoned or forfeited. 27 C.F.R. § 479.104

[11] P.C. § 32650.

[12] P.C. § 32655(d).

is unlikely you will be able to establish the "good cause" required to obtain this permit.[13]

If granted, however, the permit must be kept on you or with the "machinegun" and must be made available for law enforcement inspection.[14] The DOJ will also annually inspect the license holder for proper security and safe storage of any "machinegun" and to confirm the "machinegun" inventory.[15]

If at any time the DOJ determines your need for the "machinegun" ceases, the "machinegun" was used for an unauthorized purpose, or you failed to exercise great care in retaining custody of any firearm possessed under the permit, the DOJ may revoke the permit.[16]

Federal law does not require a separate permit to lawfully *possess* "machineguns"[17] but does require that you get California's "machinegun" permit or be otherwise exempt from the "machinegun" restriction. Without a permit or exemption the ATF will deny the transfer. And since it is almost impossible for common people to obtain such a permit from the California DOJ (and most people do not fall under an exemption), the fact that you can theoretically own a "machinegun" in California under federal law is practically irrelevant.

## C. Licenses to Sell Machineguns

The ATF may grant licenses to engage in the business of selling "machineguns."[18] But, for the license to be valid in California, you must get a separate license from the California DOJ, renew it annually, and comply with numerous regulations.[19]

# II. "DESTRUCTIVE DEVICES"

Under California law a "destructive device" is any of the following:

- Any projectile containing any explosive or incendiary material or any other chemical substance, including, but not limited to, that which is commonly known as tracer or incendiary ammunition, except tracer ammunition manufactured for use in shotguns.

---

[13] *See* 11 Cal. Code Regs. §§ 4128(c)(1)-(7) and/or Chapter 8 for examples.
[14] P.C. § 32660.
[15] P.C. § 32670. However, if a permittee has fewer than five "machineguns," the inspection is only once every five years, unless the DOJ determines additional inspections are necessary. P.C. § 32670(b).
[16] P.C. § 32665.
[17] Remember, federal law still requires registration and importer, dealer, and manufacturing licenses.
[18] 18 U.S.C. § 923(a); 26 U.S.C. § 5802; 27 C.F.R. § 478.44.
[19] P.C. § 32700 *et seq.*

- Any bomb, grenade, explosive missile, or similar device or any launching device therefor.
- Any weapon of a caliber greater than 0.60 caliber which fires fixed ammunition, or any ammunition therefor, other than:
  - a shotgun (smooth or rifled bore) conforming to the definition of a 'destructive device' found in subsection (b) of Section 479.11 of Title 27 of the Code of Federal Regulations,
  - shotgun ammunition (single projectile or shot),
  - antique rifle,[20] or
  - an antique cannon.[21]
- Any rocket, rocket-propelled projectile, or similar device of a diameter greater than 0.60 inch, or any launching device therefor, and any rocket, rocket-propelled projectile, or similar device containing any explosive or incendiary material or any other chemical substance, other than the propellant for that device, except those devices as are designed primarily for emergency or distress signaling purposes.
- Any breakable container that contains a flammable liquid with a flashpoint of 150 degrees Fahrenheit or less and has a wick or similar device capable of being ignited [*i.e.,* devices like a Molotov cocktail], other than a device which is commercially manufactured primarily for the purpose of illumination [*i.e.,* Tiki torches].
- Any sealed device [with] dry ice (CO2) [*i.e.,* a dry ice bomb] or other chemically reactive substances assembled for the purpose of causing an explosion by a chemical reaction.[22]

"Destructive device" definitions vary between California and federal law. Under federal law a "destructive device" is:

(1) Any explosive, incendiary, or poison gas

(A) bomb,

(B) grenade,

(C) rocket having a propellent charge of more than four ounces,

(D) missile having an explosive or incendiary charge of more than one-quarter ounce,

---

[20] The term "antique rifle" means a firearm conforming to the definition of an "antique firearm" in 27 C.F.R. § 479.11. P.C. § 16180.

[21] For this section, the term "antique cannon" "means any cannon manufactured before January 1, 1899, which has been [made] incapable of firing or for which ammunition is no longer manufactured in the [U.S.] and is not readily available in the ordinary channels of commercial trade." P.C. § 16160. With the internet, what "ordinary channels of commercial trade" means may change in coming years. Please see www.calgunlaws.com for a more detailed discussion on this topic.

[22] P.C. § 16460(a)(1)-(6). "A bullet containing or carrying an explosive agent is not a destructive device ... ." P.C. § 16460(b). But it may be considered ammunition "containing ... an explosive agent[]" as discussed in P.C. § 30210(b).

(E) mine, or

(F) similar device;

(2) any type of weapon by whatever name known which will, or which may be readily converted to, expel a projectile by the action of an explosive or other propellant, the barrel or barrels of which have a bore of more than one-half inch in diameter, except a shotgun or shotgun shell which the Secretary [of the Treasury][23] finds is generally recognized as particularly suitable for sporting purposes; and

(3) any combination of parts either designed or intended for use in converting any device into a destructive device as defined in subparagraphs (1) and (2) and from which a destructive device may be readily assembled.[24]

Under federal law "[t]he term 'destructive device' [does] *not* include any device which is neither designed nor redesigned for use as a weapon; any device, although originally designed for use as a weapon, which is re-designed for use as a signaling, pyrotechnic, line throwing, safety, or similar device; surplus ordnance sold, loaned, or given by the Secretary of the Army pursuant to … [federal codes;] or any other device which the Secretary finds is not likely to be used as a weapon, or is an antique or is a rifle which the owner intends to use solely for sporting purposes."[25] Much like "machineguns," the ATF strictly regulates transferring these devices.

A "destructive device" is an NFA "firearm" and *can be* lawfully acquired and possessed if, in addition to meeting the strict federal requirements discussed at the end of this chapter, you also meet California's exceptions if the device is regulated under California law.

Under California law it is generally illegal for any person or entity to possess,[26] sell, offer for sale, knowingly transport,[27] make or intend to make,[28] import, export, manufacture, or use in business any "destructive device" in the state without a valid permit.[29] Federal law likewise restricts

---

[23] The NFA is part of the Internal Revenue Code, which is typically under the Secretary of the Treasury. After the events of September 11, 2001, the ATF was placed under the supervision of the U.S. Attorney General. So, while the NFA refers to the Secretary of the Treasury, these references now actually mean the U.S. Attorney General.

[24] 26 U.S.C. § 5845(f). The definition of "destructive device" under the GCA (18 U.S.C. § 921(a)(4)) is phrased slightly different than the NFA definition.

[25] 26 U.S.C. § 5845(f) (emphasis added).

[26] P.C. § 18710.

[27] P.C. § 18730.

[28] P.C. § 18720.

[29] P.C. § 18900.

activities like importing, manufacturing, dealing, transporting, and possessing "destructive devices."[30]

Under California law possessing a "destructive device" unlawfully can be punished as a misdemeanor or a felony.[31] If the possession is reckless or malicious and "[o]n a public street or highway[,] [i]n or near any theater, hall, school, college, church, hotel, … private habitation[,] [i]n, on, or near any aircraft, railway passenger train, car, cable road, cable car, … [vessel engaged in carrying passengers for hire[, or] … other public place ordinarily passed by human beings[,]" it is a felony.[32]

The unlawful sale, offer for sale, or knowing transportation of a "destructive device" is a felony punishable by up to four years in prison.[33] It is also a felony to "possess[] any substance, material, or … combination of substances or materials … inten[ding] to make a[] destructive device" without the proper permit.[34] If, however, the "destructive device" that is unlawfully possessed, sold, offered for sale, or transported is fixed ammunition greater than .60 caliber, the first offense is only a misdemeanor. Any offenses committed after that can be a misdemeanor or a felony.[35]

Regardless of whether it is a misdemeanor or a felony offense, under California law any conviction involving a "destructive device" is ineligible for probation or a suspended sentence, meaning jail or prison time will almost certainly be imposed.[36]

## A. Permits

If you are a dealer, manufacturer, importer, or exporter of "destructive devices" or use a "destructive device" in a motion picture or television studio, you must first get a special permit from the DOJ and renew it annually.[37] Likewise, if you, your firm or corporation is not listed in the preceding sentence and you wish to possess or transport a "destructive device," you must obtain a permit from the DOJ and meet specific criteria.[38] Similar to "machinegun" inspections, the DOJ may inspect places where "destructive devices" are kept.[39] Such inspections are held annually. If the permit holder

---

[30] 18 U.S.C. § 923; 26 U.S.C. § 5871. The federal definition of "destructive device" is slightly different from California's. See 26 U.S.C. § 5845 (defining "destructive device").
[31] P.C. § 18710.
[32] P.C. § 18715.
[33] P.C. § 18730.
[34] P.C. § 18720.
[35] P.C. § 18735.
[36] P.C. § 18780.
[37] P.C. §§ 18900(a), 18905(b).
[38] P.C. § 19800(b).
[39] P.C. § 18910.

has less than five "destructive devices," the DOJ will only inspect every five years, unless they determine additional inspections are necessary.[40]

## B. Exceptions for Peace Officers, Firefighters, and Military

Certain peace officers,[41] including those in the California DOJ authorized by the California AG, military personnel, and national guardsmen, may purchase, possess, transport, store, or use a "destructive device" "while on duty and acting within the scope and course of employment."[42]

Exceptions also apply to "any person who is a regularly employed and paid officer, employee, or member of a fire department or fire protection or firefighting agency of the … state, [local or federal government,] while on duty and acting within the scope and course of employment, of any equipment used by that department or agency in the course of fire suppression."[43]

## C. 37mm Flare Launchers v. 40mm Grenade Launchers

Some firearm enthusiasts possess 37mm *flare* launchers. These devices are typically stand-alone launchers or attach under the barrel of a rifle.[44] Because flare launchers closely resemble 40mm *grenade* launchers, law enforcement often mistake them for "destructive devices." But they are not. You should make sure that any launcher you have is the 37mm variety, not the 40mm version.

Also, even though 37mm launchers are available nationwide, some California law enforcement agencies still classify them as "destructive devices," claiming that a 37mm grenade exists *somewhere* that can launch from the device. You should therefore carefully consider whether you want to possess one and what your local law enforcement agency's position is.

## D. "Fireworks" and "Explosives"

"Fireworks" and "explosives" are wide and varying topics with special state and federal laws regulating their transportation, importation, sale, and pos-

---

[40] P.C. § 18910(b).
[41] Those listed in P.C. §§ 830.1 and 830.2.
[42] P.C. §§ 18800(a)-(b).
[43] P.C. § 18800(b).
[44] Note that when a flare or grenade launcher is attached to a semiautomatic centerfire rifle with the capacity to accept a detachable magazine, the rifle meets the restricted "assault weapon" definition in California (see Chapter 8).

session.[45] "Explosives" are especially a concern for firearm enthusiasts who enjoy reloading their own ammunition. Chapter 2 discusses how much black and smokeless powder you can legally possess.

## III. "GENERALLY PROHIBITED WEAPONS"

Former P.C. §12020 was an extremely long statutory provision that generally prohibited the manufacturing, importing, selling, gifting, loaning, or possessing of an odd array of weapons and related equipment. That provision had numerous exceptions, some of which related to all the listed weapons, while others only related to one specific type. This means that people interested in a particular weapon's legality had to read a lot of irrelevant material before finding the portion of former P.C. § 12020 relevant to them.[46]

To ease confusion and eliminate having to sort through irrelevant material, the revised Penal Code, effective January 1, 2012, separated former P.C. § 12020 and its subdivisions and now lists them in new separate sections according to the specific firearm, equipment, or device to which they pertain. Some of these items are "firearms" and some are not. For example, all information about "cane guns" can now be found in new separate sections specifically concerning "cane guns."

Former California P.C. § 12020 also discussed all sorts of exotic items, including but not limited to: wallet guns, undetectable firearms, firearms not immediately recognizable as firearms, camouflaging firearm containers, ammunition containing or consisting of flechette darts, bullets containing or carrying an explosive agent, ballistic knives, multi-burst trigger activators, nunchakus, short-barreled shotguns, short-barreled rifles, metal knuckles, belt buckle knives, leaded canes, zip guns, shurikens, unconventional pistols, lipstick case knives, cane swords, shobi-zues, air gauge knives, writing pen knives, metal military practice handgrenades, metal replica handgrenades, instruments/weapons of the kind commonly known as a blackjack, slungshot, billy, sandclub, sap, or sandbag, "large-capacity magazines," carrying concealed explosive substances other than fixed ammunition, dirks, and daggers.[47] For most of these items manufacturing, importing, keeping for sale, offering or exposing for sale, giving, lending,

---

[45] *See, e.g.,* Cal. Health & Saf. Code §§ 12500-12759. *See also* 19 Cal. Code Regs. §§ 979-1039; 27 C.F.R. §§ 555.221-555.224. There may also be other relevant statutes, regulations, or local municipal codes that address fireworks and pyrotechnics. However, those are beyond the scope of this book, so if you have specific questions, you should consult an attorney who specializes in that area of law.

[46] *Nonsubstantive Reorganization of Deadly Weapon Statutes Recommendation,* 38 Cal. L. Revision Comm'n Reports 217, 245 (2009).

[47] *See* former P.C. § 12020(a).

and possessing are illegal.[48] Certain items like "large-capacity magazines," dirks, and daggers may be legal to possess, but other restrictions on them exist and are discussed below.

All of these weapons are now listed as "generally prohibited weapons" under P.C. § 16590, and each is defined in its own additional code section.

If you are concerned that you possess any of the above-listed non-firearm items or if you have questions about them, you should refer directly to the California Penal Code and the sections defining these items. And, as always, when in doubt consult an attorney knowledgeable in California weapon laws.

## A. "Cane Gun"

"Cane guns" are "any firearm mounted or enclosed in a stick, staff, rod, crutch, or similar device, designed to be, or capable of being used as, an aid in walking, if the firearm may be fired while mounted or enclosed therein."[49] "Cane guns" were popular in the mid-1850s and served not only as a walking accessory, but also for self-defense.[50]

## B. "Wallet Gun"

" '[W]allet gun' means any firearm mounted or enclosed in a case, resembling a wallet, designed to be or capable of being carried in a pocket or purse, if the firearm may be fired while mounted or enclosed in the case."[51] Because of its shape and size, a "wallet gun" can look and feel like an actual wallet. These devices are also problematic under federal law's "any other weapon" definition.[52]

Interestingly enough, the "wallet" is not illegal under California law by itself, nor is the "gun" necessarily illegal by itself. Once the "gun" is mounted or enclosed in the "wallet," however, it becomes illegal. This means you could lawfully possess either the "wallet" or the "gun" by themselves or both, as long as the "gun" is not "mounted or enclosed" in the "wallet."

The device also may not need to be a conventional wallet. Certain holsters come dangerously close to a "wallet gun" by allowing you to shoot them while they are mounted or enclosed in them, and could fall under the definition.

---

[48] *See* P.C. § 16590 for a list of the "generally prohibited weapons" and the code sections restricting them.

[49] P.C. § 16330.

[50] *Gun Canes*, GADGETCANES.COM, http://www.gadgetcanes.com/gun-canes.php (last visited July 26, 2012).

[51] P.C. § 17330.

[52] 26 U.S.C. § 5845(e).

## C. "Undetectable Firearm"

An "undetectable firearm" is any weapon that satisfies either of the following:

> "(a) After removal of grips, stocks, and magazines, the weapon is not as detectable as the Security Exemplar, by a walk-through metal detector calibrated and operated to detect the Security Exemplar[; or]
>
> (b) Any major component of the weapon ... defined [by federal law] when ... inspect[ed] by ... X-ray machines commonly used at airports, does not generate an image that accurately depicts the shape of the component. Barium sulfate or other compounds may be used [to make the] component."[53]

In the past lawmakers were concerned that firearms made out of composite materials or polymers would not show up in metal detectors or x-ray machines. These concerns proved baseless. These firearms, such as most Glock models (high-tech polymer based, corrosion resistant, 86% lighter,[54] and tougher than steel), still have enough metal to be easily detected by metal detectors and x-ray machines, especially when loaded.

## D. Firearms Not "Immediately Recognizable"

The Penal Code does not specifically define "immediately recognizable" or a "firearm" that is not "immediately recognizable." So exactly what is prohibited by this California statute is unclear. Obvious examples are firearms disguised as cell phones and the "Braverman Stinger."[55] The "Palm Pistol"[56] is also arguably covered.

Painting a firearm to resemble a BB device or an imitation firearm by adding a fluorescent orange tip or other painting is highly risky. It is also likely illegal because it might be considered disguising a real firearm as an imitation firearm and thus not "immediately recognizable" as a firearm.

---

[53] P.C. § 17280. *See* 18 U.S.C. § 922(p) for a comparison to federal law.

[54] *See Glock "Safe Action,"* GLOCK.COM, http://www.glock.com/english/index_pistols.htm (last visited July 26, 2012).

[55] *See Stinger Penguns,* PENGUN.COM, http://pengun.com (last visited July 26, 2012).

[56] *See Strange Guns: Palm Pistol,* OUTDOORLIFE.COM, http://www.outdoorlife.com/blogs/gun-shots/2011/04/strange-guns-palm-pistol (last visited July 19, 2012).

# E. "Camouflaging Firearm Container"

A "camouflaging firearm container" is a container with all of the following:

"(1) It is designed and intended to enclose a firearm;

(2) It is designed and intended to allow the firing of the enclosed firearm by external controls while the firearm is in the container; [and]

(3) It is not readily recognizable as containing a firearm."[57]

A common "camouflaging firearm container" is the briefcase for a "briefcase gun" where the firearm is mounted inside of a normal-looking briefcase. The case has an internal mechanism that allows the operator to discharge the firearm by either pulling a trigger on the briefcase handle or by pushing a secret button somewhere on the case.

# F. "Multiburst Trigger Activator"

A "multiburst trigger activator" means one of the following:

- "A device designed or redesigned to be attached to a semiautomatic firearm, which allows the firearm to discharge two or more shots in a burst by activating the device; [or]
- A manual or power-driven trigger-activating device constructed and designed so that when attached to a semiautomatic firearm it increases the rate of fire of that firearm."[58]

Examples of these devices are the "Hell-Fire" or "Hellstorm 2000." While these devices differ in design, they function using the same principle. When a shooter attaches the device to a semiautomatic rifle and the rifle is fired from the shoulder, the shooter holds the firearm to allow the rifle to move forward and backward against the shooter's shoulder, causing the trigger to be rapidly pulled by the shooter's finger – a shooting technique commonly referred to as "bump fire." These devices reset the trigger quickly with some resistance and, combined with the "bump firing," allow the operator to fire rapidly.

Another design of a "multiburst trigger activator" may be attached to the trigger guard and has a crank-like device that sticks out of the side of the firearm. The operator holds the firearm with his or her non-trigger hand like normal. The shooter's trigger hand is then used to turn the crank.

---

[57] P.C. § 16320(a). " 'Camouflaging firearm container' does not include any camouflaging covering used while … lawful[ly] hunting or while going to or returning from a lawful hunting expedition." P.C. § 16320(b).

[58] P.C. § 16930.

When the crank is turned, the device pulls the trigger. The rate at which the trigger is pulled coincides with the speed the crank is turned. Some devices can pull the trigger four times per rotation. By this method, 20- or 30-round magazines and 50-round drums can be emptied in seconds. These devices likely meet the "multiburst trigger activator" definition.

There are no published opinions, and the DOJ has refused to opine on what is or is not a "multiburst trigger activator." If you possess any device that allows you to fire your firearm at an increased rate of speed, know that you can be subject to the subjective interpretation of this law by law enforcement, a prosecuting attorney, and/or the court. You should be mindful of this if you decide to own one in California.

If you are out in public or at a range shooting ammunition at high rates of speed, you may alert law enforcement to investigate whether you are firing a fully-automatic firearm.

## G. "Short-Barreled Shotguns" and "Short-Barreled Rifles"

Both California and federal law restrict possessing and transferring shotguns and rifles if they are under a certain length.

### 1. "Short-Barreled Shotguns"

Under California law a "short-barreled shotgun" means any of the following:

"(a) A firearm that is designed or redesigned to fire a fixed shotgun shell and has a barrel or barrels of less than 18 inches in length[;]

(b) A firearm that has an overall length less than 26 inches and that is designed or redesigned to fire a fixed shotgun shell[;]

(c) Any weapon made from a shotgun (whether by alteration, modification, or otherwise) if that weapon, as modified, has an overall length of less than 26 inches or a barrel or barrels of less than 18 inches in length[;]

(d) Any device that may be readily restored to fire a fixed shotgun shell, when so restored, is a device defined in subdivisions (a) to (c), inclusive[; or]

(e) Any part, or combination of parts, designed and intended to convert a device into a device defined in subdivisions (a) to (c), inclusive, or any combination of parts from which a device defined in subdivisions (a) to (c), inclusive, can be readily assembled if those parts are in the possession or under the control of the same person."[59]

Know that the California "short-barreled shotgun" definition above does not require the firearm to actually *be* a "shotgun."[60] Any *firearm* "designed or redesigned" to shoot fixed shotgun ammunition can be a "short-barreled shotgun" if it meets the length requirements. In fact, even a handgun can be considered one.[61] As explained below, California's "short-barreled shotgun" definition is different from the federal definitions for "shotguns" that are restricted based on their length.

"Short-barreled shotguns" are generally restricted under California law the same way as all "generally prohibited weapons" listed in P.C. § 16590.

Two separate definitions exist under federal law for restricted shotguns of certain lengths. The GCA has one, and the NFA does too.

Under the GCA, "[t]he term 'short-barreled shotgun' means a shotgun having one or more barrels less than eighteen inches in length and any weapon made from a shotgun (whether by alteration, modification or otherwise) if such a weapon as modified has an overall length of less than twenty-six inches."[62] The GCA defines "shotgun" as "a weapon designed or redesigned, made or remade, and intended to be fired from the shoulder and designed or redesigned and made or remade to use the energy of an explosive to fire through a smooth bore either a number of ball shot or a single projectile for each single pull of the trigger."[63]

The GCA restricts transferring and transporting firearms meeting this definition but does not generally restrict possessing them.[64] The GCA does, however, add additional penalties if these firearms are possessed while committing a crime.[65]

In contrast to the GCA, the NFA does *not* refer to shotguns of prohibited lengths as "short-barreled shotguns," but instead describes them by their physical dimensions. The NFA specifically restricts "shotguns" with one or more barrels less than 18 inches long and weapons made from "shotguns" with overall lengths of less than 26 inches or that have one or more barrels

---

[59] P.C. § 17180.

[60] *See* P.C. § 17190 (defining "shotgun" for purposes of defining "short-barreled shotgun" under California law). *See also* Chapter 2.

[61] P.C. §§ 16530(b), 16640(b).

[62] 18 U.S.C. § 921(a)(6).

[63] 18 U.S.C. § 921(a)(5).

[64] 18 U.S.C. §§ 922(a)(4), (b)(4).

[65] 18 U.S.C. § 924(c)(1)(B).

that are less than 18 inches long.[66] The NFA defines the term "shotgun" the same way as the GCA but additionally includes "any such weapon which may be readily restored to fire a *fixed shotgun shell*."[67]

Like all NFA firearms, "shotguns" restricted based on length can be lawfully acquired, possessed, and transferred under federal law *as long as* you meet all of the NFA requirements discussed at the end of this chapter. As noted below, however, the possession of most NFA firearms is strictly prohibited under California law, even if they can be lawfully possessed under federal law.

Under both the GCA and the NFA, a firearm has to actually be a "shotgun" – meaning it must be "intended to be fired from the shoulder" – or made from a "shotgun" to be federally restricted as a "short-barreled shotgun." This may sound obvious based on the name, but as mentioned above, California law considers any "firearm" with certain dimensions that fires fixed shotgun shells, even handguns, to be "short-barreled shotguns." Because this is not the case under federal law, firearms like the Taurus Judge and Smith & Wesson Governor (handguns designed to shoot .410 shotgun shells) are legal under federal law but not California law.[68]

## 2.   "Short-Barreled Rifles"

Under California law, a "short-barreled rifle" is any of the following:

"(a) A rifle[69] having a barrel or barrels of less than 16 inches in length[;]

(b) A rifle with an overall length of less than 26 inches[;]

(c) Any weapon made from a rifle (whether by alteration, modification, or otherwise) if that weapon, as modified, has an overall length of less than 26 inches or a barrel or barrels of less than 16 inches in length[;]

(d) Any device which may be readily restored to fire a fixed cartridge which, when so restored, is a device defined in subdivisions (a) to (c), inclusive[; or]

---

[66] Note that the NFA has an additional category of restricted short-barreled shotguns that the GCA does not, *i.e.*, weapons made from a "shotgun" that have one or more barrels less than 18 inches long. This means that a firearm no longer meeting the "shotgun" definition (*e.g.*, one not intended to be fired from the shoulder) but made from a "shotgun" is restricted under the NFA but not necessarily under the GCA. The NFA also restricts "weapons with combination shotgun and rifle barrels 12 inches or more, less than 18 inches in length, from which only a single discharge can be made from either barrel without manual reloading, and shall include any such weapon which may be readily restored to fire." Those are discussed in the "any other weapon" section. 27 C.F.R. § 479.11.

[67] 26 U.S.C. § 5845(d) (emphasis added).

[68] *Judging the Judges – Illegal Firearms in California?*, CALGUNLAWS.COM, http://www.calgunlaws.com/wp-content/uploads/2012/09/Judging-the-Judges-Illegal-Firearms-in-California.pdf (last visited Sept. 19, 2012).

[69] *See* P.C. § 17090 for the California definition of "rifle." *See also* Chapter 2.

(e) Any part, or combination of parts, designed and intended to convert a device into a device defined in subdivisions (a) to (c), inclusive, or any combination of parts from which a device defined in subdivisions (a) to (c), inclusive, may be readily assembled if those parts are in the possession or under the control of the same person."[70]

As with "short-barreled shotguns," even a handgun can meet the definition of a "short-barreled rifle."[71] "Short-barreled rifles" are generally subject to the same restrictions under California law as all "generally prohibited weapons" listed in P.C. § 16590.

As with shotguns, two separate federal definitions exist under the GCA and the NFA for restricted "rifles" of certain lengths.

Under the GCA, a "short-barreled rifle" "means a rifle having one or more barrels less than sixteen inches in length and any weapon made from a rifle (whether by alteration, modification, or otherwise) if such weapon, as modified, has an overall length of less than twenty-six inches."[72] The GCA defines the term "rifle" as "a weapon designed or redesigned, made or remade, and intended to be fired from the shoulder and designed or redesigned and made or remade to use the energy of an explosive to fire only a single projectile through a rifled bore for each single pull of the trigger."[73]

The GCA restricts these rifles the same way it does "short" shotguns as described above.

As with shotguns, the NFA also does *not* refer to rifles with prohibited lengths as "short-barreled," but instead describes them by their physical dimensions. It specifically restricts "rifles" with one or more barrels less than 16 inches long and weapons made from a "rifle" with an overall length of less than 26 inches or that have one or more barrels that are less than 16 inches long.[74] The NFA also defines "rifle" the same way the GCA does, but additionally includes "any such weapon which may be readily restored to fire a fixed cartridge."[75]

---

[70] P.C. § 17170.

[71] P.C. §§ 16530(b), 16640(b).

[72] 18 U.S.C. § 921(a)(8).

[73] 18 U.S.C. § 921(a)(7).

[74] 26 U.S.C. § 5845(a)(3)-(4). Note that, as with shotguns, the NFA has an additional restricted short rifle category not found in the GCA, *i.e.*, weapons made from a "rifle" that have one or more barrels less than 16 inches long. 26 U.S.C. § 5845(a)(3). The same implications apply as for shotguns discussed above.

[75] 26 U.S.C. § 5845(c). Note that under both California law and the federal NFA, a firearm must fire a "fixed cartridge" to be a "rifle," but to be a restricted "short" rifle it only needs to be *readily able to be restored to* fire a "fixed cartridge," so be careful. Interestingly, if the firearm does not meet either of these definitions (*i.e.*, it does not and cannot be readily made to fire a "fixed cartridge"), it *cannot* be a "short-barreled rifle" under California law or the federal NFA. This means that you could lawfully possess a muzzle-loading firearm that would otherwise be considered a restricted "short" rifle based on its length without violating California law or the federal NFA. Such a firearm *would*, however, still be subject to the federal GCA limitations on transfers explained above.

Under the NFA, "short" rifles are restricted the same way shotguns are restricted as described above.

"Short-barreled rifles are illegal simply because they are short, which makes them 'suitable for unlawful purposes because of their concealability and ease of handling.' "[76] This is also the case with "short-barreled shotguns." This can be a problem for a defendant who was not required to know the firearm's actual dimensions because the prosecution can use circumstantial evidence to show the defendant knew a firearm was unusually short and could be classified as a "short-barreled shotgun/rifle."[77]

While the California Penal Code does not specify how a rifle's or shotgun's "overall length" is determined, law enforcement will measure any "short-barreled shotgun/rifle" with the firearm in its shortest configuration (e.g., with its stock folded).[78] Unlike California law, to determine whether the firearm is either a "short" shotgun or rifle, federal law measures firearms in their lengthiest configuration (e.g., with a folding stock extended).[79]

Though not expressly adopted by California, the ATF has explained that the proper way to measure barrel length is by inserting a rod down the barrel from the muzzle through the chamber to the back of the breach.[80] This should be standard practice but is often overlooked by California law enforcement who incorrectly exclude the chamber in measuring overall barrel length.

### 3. Possession of Parts Constituting "Short-Barreled Shotguns/Rifles"

Note that under both California and federal law, mere parts can be considered a "short-barreled shotgun/rifle" if, when combined, they could readily be made into one.[81] In *United States v. Thompson/Center Arms Co.*, the U.S. Supreme Court explained that pistol parts and carbine kits – parts that can

---

[76] *People v. King*, 38 Cal.4th 617, 643 (2006) (citing *People v. Rooney*, 17 Cal.App.4th 1207, 1211 (1993)); see also *People v. Stinson*, 8 Cal.App.3d 497, 500 (1970).

[77] *People v. King*, 38 Cal.4th 617, 627-628 (2006).

[78] *People v. Rooney*, 17 Cal.App.4th 1207, 1211-1213 (1993).

[79] 27 C.F.R. § 479.11 (stating in pertinent part: "The overall length of a weapon made from a shotgun or rifle is the distance between the extreme ends of the weapon measured along a line parallel to the center line of the bore.").

[80] *See* U.S. DEPT. OF JUSTICE, BUREAUS OF ALCOHOL, TOBACCO, FIREARMS, AND EXPLOSIVES, ATF NATIONAL FIREARMS ACT HANDBOOK 6 (2009) ("The ATF procedure for measuring barrel length is to measure from the closed bolt (or breech-face) to the furthermost end of the barrel or permanently attached muzzle device. Permanent methods of attachment include full-fusion gas or electric steel-seam welding, high-temperature (1100°F) silver soldering, or blind pinning with the pin head welded over. Barrels are measured by inserting a dowel rod into the barrel until the rod stops against the bolt or breech-face. The rod is then marked at the furthermost end of the barrel or permanently attached muzzle device, withdrawn from the barrel, and measured.").

[81] P.C. §§ 17170(d)-(e)(rifles), 17180(d)-(e) (shotguns).

be assembled to create either a handgun or a rifle – are not necessarily a "short" rifle under federal law if the parts could possibly be assembled in a way that would *not* constitute a "short" rifle. The court clarified, however, that if the parts, when assembled, could *only* create a "short" rifle, or are so assembled, then the parts would themselves be considered a restricted "short" rifle.[82] The Ninth Circuit Court of Appeals (the controlling Court of Appeals for California) further explained that "an aggregation of weapons parts may not constitute [an NFA] firearm if the parts have an apparent legal purpose other than the creation of such a firearm" (*e.g.*, a "short" rifle under federal law).[83]

Although there is no California case law on this subject, presumably this same analysis would apply in determining whether parts would constitute a "short-barreled shotgun" or "short-barreled rifle" under California law.

Parts kits that are used to make firearms into pistols or rifles like those considered by the U.S. Supreme Court in the *Thompson* case – with a receiver that you can attach the parts for a pistol (a short-barrel and pistol grip) and the parts for a rifle (a long barrel and shoulder stock) to – have caused a lot of confusion. Because of *Thompson* and its progeny, case law has explained that such kits are legal unless the parts can *only* be, or *are*, configured in a way to create a "short" rifle (this is not such a problem with shotguns). But people run into problems when they attach their pistol barrel and shoulder stock to the receiver. This kind of firearm is one designed to be fired from the shoulder with a rifled barrel, but the barrel (and usually the overall length of the firearm) is too short under both California and federal law, thereby creating a "short-barreled rifle." Having the wrong parts attached at the wrong time can subject you to serious criminal charges.

## H. "Zip Gun"

Under California law, a "zip gun" is any weapon that meets all of the following:

"(a) It was not imported as a firearm by a[] ... licensed [importer] ... .[84]

---

[82] *United States v. Thompson/Center Arms Co.*, 504 U.S. 505, 511-512 (1992) (plurality opinion).

[83] *United States v. Kwan*, 300 Fed.Appx. 485 (9th Cir. 2008) (citing *United States v. Thompson/Center Arms Co.*, 504 U.S. 505, 512-513 (1992)); *see also United States v. Kent*, 175 F.3d 870 (11th Cir. 1999). For more in-depth analysis of this and other federal firearm law related topics, see Stephen Halbrook's *Firearms Law Deskbook*.

[84] Licensed pursuant to 18 U.S.C. §§ 921 *et seq.*

(b) It was not originally designed to be a firearm by a ... licensed [manufacturer] ... .[85]

(c) No tax was paid on the weapon or device nor was [it] exempt[] from ... [a] tax [and] ... .[86]

(d) It is made or altered to expel a projectile by the force of an explosion or other form of combustion."[87]

"Zip guns" are typically small homemade firearms. Thus they are usually destroyed once fired. This does not mean however, that a larger, sturdier item could not be considered a "zip gun."

In the past, some law enforcement agencies have claimed that *all* firearms made from raw materials are "zip guns."[88] But that is incorrect. It is not necessarily illegal for people to assemble or build firearms for their own personal use (see Chapter 2).

Firearms made to expel projectiles by combustive force but that have been made from raw materials have clearly not been imported as a firearm, nor would tax be paid on them.[89] The issue, then, is about the firearm's *design*. If you make a brand new firearm from an original design (*i.e.*, not based on an existing firearm design), you have arguably created a "zip gun" unless you are a licensed firearm manufacturer (see Chapter 4). This means that, if you create a firearm based on a licensed firearm manufacturer's design, it should *not* be considered a "zip gun" under the above criteria.

## I. "Unconventional Pistol"

Under California law an "unconventional pistol" is a firearm: 1) without a rifled bore, and 2) that "has a barrel or barrels of less than 18 inches in length or has an overall length of less than 26 inches."[90]

---

[85] Licensed pursuant to 18 U.S.C. §§ 921 *et seq.*

[86] This exemption is granted under 26 U.S.C. §§ 4181, 4216-4227 and the regulations issued pursuant thereto.

[87] P.C. § 17360.

[88] If the "zip gun" is created from a receiver acquired from an FFL, a tax would have been paid.

[89] There is an argument to be made that, if the "zip gun" was manufactured for personal use, no tax was due, and therefore the gun was exempt from the tax requirement. But the ins and outs of federal tax law far exceed the scope of this book.

[90] P.C. § 17270.

## J. "Large-Capacity Magazine"

### 1. Definition

Under California law a "large-capacity magazine" is "any ammunition feeding device with the capacity to accept more than 10 rounds ... ." It does *not* include:

(a) A feeding device that has been permanently altered so that it cannot accommodate more than 10 rounds.

(b) A .22 caliber tube ammunition feeding device.

(c) A tubular magazine that is contained in a lever-action firearm.[91]

California law does not explain further what a "large-capacity magazine" is, but in the definition of "detachable magazine," an "ammunition feeding device" includes "any belted or linked ammunition"[92] but not "clips, en bloc clips, or stripper clips that load cartridges into the magazine."[93] This means that "clips" should not be considered "large-capacity magazines."

Ammunition feeding devices of any size and capacity may be permanently[94] altered to make them unable to accept more than ten rounds. If this happens, they lose their "large-capacity magazine" status and are thus not restricted.

Some law enforcement agencies have tried to cram an eleventh round into magazines designed, sold, and used as ones with a ten-round maximum capacity. Some magazines' springs will allow this and still function, even though they are not designed to accept that eleventh round. Though this scenario is unlikely and uncommon, it is worth trying to force an eleventh round into a magazine before you transfer it in a way that would be unlawful were it a "large-capacity magazine" (explained below).

### 2. Restricted Activity for "Large-Capacity Magazines"

Like most of the items discussed in this chapter, under California law it is generally illegal to manufacture or cause to be manufactured, to import, keep for sale, offer or expose for sale, give, or lend a "large-capacity

---

[91] P.C. § 16740.

[92] "A large-capacity magazine also includes linked ammunition with more than 10 rounds linked together or an ammunition belt with the capacity to accept more than 10 rounds." *Assault Weapons Identification Guide*, STATE OF CALIFORNIA, OFFICE ATTORNEY GENERAL, http://oag.ca.gov/sites/all/files/pdfs/firearms/forms/awguide.pdf (last visited July 26, 2012).

[93] 11 Cal. Code Regs. § 5469(a).

[94] Whether an alteration is "permanent" can affect the magazine's legal status and is not always clear. In fact, the California DOJ attempted to define "permanently altered" in the Code of Regulations but deleted the definition. *See Notice of Modification to Text of Proposed Regulations*, CALIFORNIA DEPT. OF JUSTICE, http://oag.ca.gov/sites/all/files/pdfs/firearms/regs/sb23rev.pdf (last visited July 28, 2012).

magazine."[95] But, unlike the other items, it is *not* illegal to merely possess one. This means that those who possessed a "large-capacity magazine" prior to P.C. § 32310 taking effect on January 1, 2000, may continue to possess them. Be careful, however. This does not mean law enforcement agencies cannot prosecute you for a "large-capacity magazine" found in your possession if they can prove you imported, manufactured, or sold it unlawfully, *i.e.*, after January 1, 2000.

If you possess a lawfully obtained "large-capacity magazine" and need to replace the magazine's parts, no law prohibits doing so. Transferring or importing "large-capacity magazine" parts is lawful. In fact, it appears perfectly legal to transfer or import disassembled "large-capacity magazine" parts kits. These kits typically have all the magazine parts, which, if reassembled, would meet the definition of a "large-capacity magazine." But because the magazine is disassembled, it cannot "accept more than 10 rounds of ammunition," or *any* rounds for that matter, and thus is not a "large-capacity magazine."[96]

You may use these kits to replace your existing lawfully-obtained "large-capacity magazine" parts or to create magazines that hold 10 rounds or less. You may not, however, assemble the kit parts into a *new* magazine because that could be considered "manufacturing" a "large-capacity magazine." Since Californians are still being incorrectly prosecuted for merely *possessing* "large-capacity magazines," if you want to sell or import parts kits, you should know that, even though the practice appears legal, you could possibly face felony prosecution for this.[97]

# IV. EXCEPTIONS TO CALIFORNIA LAW FOR "GENERALLY PROHIBITED WEAPONS"

Former P.C. §12020(b) combined all 32 exceptions to the "generally prohibited weapons" restrictions into one large list. Those exceptions are now laid out as one exception per section number. Unless otherwise indicated, the following exceptions apply to each of the above firearms, weapons, devices, and ammunition that are considered "generally prohibited weapons" and listed in P.C. § 16590.

---

[95] P.C. § 32310.

[96] *Clarification of California Law Regarding Large-Capacity Magazines*, CALGUNLAWS.COM, http://www.calgunlaws.com/wp-content/uploads/2012/09/Clarification-on-California-Law-Regarding-Large-Capacity-Magazines.pdf (last visitedSept. 19,, 2012).

[97] Note that while this appears sound under California law, since this issue has never been litigated, it could be open to different judicial interpretation.

## A. "Antique Firearms"

An item is not considered a "generally prohibited weapon" if it is an "antique firearm."[98] See Chapter 2 for the definition of "antique firearm" applicable to "generally prohibited weapons."[99]

## B. "Curios or Relics"

Certain firearms and ammunition are not prohibited if they are lawfully possessed "curios or relics" under federal law.[100] "Curios or relics" are of special interest to collectors for "some quality other than [those] associated with firearms intended for sporting use or as offensive or defensive weapons."[101] See Chapter 2 for the definition of "curios or relics."

## C. "Any Other Weapons"

Under federal law, "any other weapons" are regulated firearms. The NFA defines "any other weapon" as "any weapon or device capable of being concealed on the person from which a shot can be discharged through the energy of an explosive, a pistol or [a] revolver having a barrel with a smooth bore designed or redesigned to fire a fixed shotgun shell, weapons" less than 18 inches in total length with combined shotgun and rifle barrels of 12 inches or more "from which only a single discharge can be made from either barrel without manualreloading" it; or "any such weapon which may be readily restored to fire."[102] "Any other weapon" does not include pistols or revolvers[103] with rifled bores or weapons for firing from the shoulder "and not capable of firing fixed ammunition" (e.g., a blunderbuss or musket).[104] This means these firearms cannot be considered and regulated as "any other weapons."

Be careful, however. Certain pistols with forward pistol grips may meet the definition of "any other weapon" (in addition to possibly meeting the

---

[98] P.C. § 17700.

[99] P.C. § 16170(c).

[100] P.C. § 17705. For example, someone not prohibited from possessing firearms under 18 U.S.C § 922.

[101] 27 C.F.R. § 478.11.

[102] 26 U.S.C. § 5845(e).

[103] According to 27 C.F.R. § 479.11, a "pistol" is "[a] weapon originally designed, made, and intended to fire a projectile (bullet) from one or more barrels when held in one hand, and having (a) a chamber(s) as an integral part(s) of, or permanently aligned with, the bore(s); and (b) a short stock designed to be gripped by one hand and at an angle to and extending below the line of the bore(s)." A "revolver" is "[a] projectile weapon, of the pistol type, having a breechloading chambered cylinder so arranged that the cocking of the hammer or movement of the trigger rotates it and brings the next cartridge in line with the barrel for firing." 27 C.F.R. § 479.11.

[104] 26 U.S.C. § 5845(e).

"assault weapon" definition). Despite the fact that these handguns meet the general "pistol" definition under California law (see Chapter 2), they likely are not "pistols" under the federal definition because they are no longer designed, made, or intended to fire a projectile when "held in one hand," which is a precondition to being "any other weapon." But they still fall under the definition of "any other weapon" since, though not "pistols," they *are* firearms with rifled bores that are "capable of being concealed on the person."

A "generally prohibited weapon" meeting the definition of "any other weapon" is legal to possess if you are not otherwise generally prohibited from possessing these firearms under the GCA.[105] Unlike other NFA firearms ("machineguns," "silencers," "short-barreled shotguns/ rifles"), most items meeting the "any other weapon" definition *can be* possessed, imported, or transferred (to persons age 21 or older) in California as long as they satisfy the respective NFA requirements.

## D. Historical Society, Museum, or Institutional Collection

The "generally prohibited weapons" restrictions "do not apply to any instrument or device that is possessed by a federal, state, or local historical society, museum, or institutional collection that is open to the public" as long as they are "properly housed," "secured from unauthorized handling," and, if firearms, are unloaded.[106]

## E. Media or Entertainment Events

The "generally prohibited weapons" restrictions (other than those for "short-barreled shotguns/rifles"), do not apply when they are "possessed or used during the course of a motion picture, television, or video production or entertainment event by an authorized participant therein in the course of making that production or event or by an authorized employee or agent of the entity producing that production or event."[107]

---

[105] P.C. § 17710. Oddly, it is the NFA, not the GCA, that strictly regulates "any other weapons." It is unclear why the California legislature said GCA instead of NFA or if it was a mistake. While the GCA regulates who may lawfully possess firearms under federal law, "any other weapons," like other NFA firearms, are highly regulated.

[106] P.C. § 17715.

[107] P.C. § 17720.

## F. People Who Sell Items to Historical Societies, Museums, Institutional Collections, or Entertainment

The "generally prohibited weapons" restrictions (other than those for "short-barreled shotguns/rifles") do not apply when they are "sold by, manufactured by, exposed or kept for sale by, possessed by, imported by, or lent by" those whose business it is to sell instruments or devices to historical societies, museums, or institutional collections for entertainment events, while "engaging in transactions with those entities."[108]

## G. Law Enforcement Firearm Purchases and Those Who Sell Firearms to Law Enforcement

The "generally prohibited weapons" restrictions (other than those for "short-barreled shotguns/rifles") do not apply to selling, possessing, or purchasing "any weapon, device, or ammunition" (other than short-barreled shotguns and rifles) that is used by any law enforcement agency in discharging their official duties. Nor does it restrict their possession by any federal, state, or local peace officers when on duty and authorized by the agency and when the possession is "within the course and scope of the[ir] ... duties."[109] The "generally prohibited weapons" restrictions also do not apply (other than those for short-barreled shotguns and rifles) when "sold by, manufactured by, exposed or kept for sale by, possessed by, imported by, or lent by," anyone whose business it is to sell these items to law enforcement agencies "when engaging in transactions with those entities."[110]

## H. Transporting Non-Firearms and Most Other "Firearms" to Law Enforcement

The "generally prohibited weapons" restrictions do not apply to the non-firearm devices listed therein when possessed by someone who is allowed to possess firearms or ammunition (see Chapter 3) if possessed no longer than necessary to transport it to a law enforcement agency to turn it in.[111]

The "generally prohibited weapons" restrictions (other than those for "short-barreled shotguns/rifles") do not apply to firearms when possessed by someone allowed to possess firearms or ammunition, as long as they are possessed no longer than necessary to transport them, in a locked

---

[108] P.C. § 17725.
[109] P.C. §§ 17730(a)-(b).
[110] P.C. § 17730(c).
[111] P.C. § 17735.

container,[112] to a law enforcement agency. Such persons must also give prior notice that they are transporting the firearms for disposition.[113]

## I. Forensic Laboratory

The "generally prohibited weapons" restrictions (other than those for "short-barreled shotguns/rifles") do not apply to a forensic laboratory's possession of "any weapon, device, or ammunition," including its authorized agents or employees, as long as in the course of authorized activities.[114]

# V. ADDITIONAL CALIFORNIA LAW EXCEPTIONS FOR "LARGE-CAPACITY MAGAZINE" RESTRICTIONS

Recall that after January 1, 2000, it is generally illegal for anyone to manufacture, import, sell, or give any "large-capacity magazine" and is punishable as a felony or a misdemeanor.[115] Exceptions to this are:

## A. Law Enforcement Agencies

The general "large-capacity magazine" restrictions do not apply to selling, giving, lending, importing, or purchasing any "large-capacity magazine" to or by any government agency charged with enforcing any law for use in "discharg[ing] … their official duties, whether on or off duty, and where the use is authorized by the agency and is within the course and scope of their duties."[116]

## B. Peace Officers

The general "large-capacity magazine" restrictions do not apply to selling to, lending to, transferring to, purchasing, receiving, or importing into this state a "large-capacity magazine" "by a sworn peace officer[117] … authorized to carry a firearm in the course and scope of that officer's duties."[118]

---

[112] As defined at P.C. § 16850.
[113] P.C. § 17740(d).
[114] P.C. § 17745.
[115] P.C. § 32310.
[116] P.C. § 32400.
[117] As defined in P.C. § 830 *et seq.*
[118] P.C. § 32405.

## C. Dealer Acquisition

The general "large-capacity magazine" restrictions do "not apply to the sale or purchase of any large-capacity magazine to or by a … licensed [firearm dealer] …"[119]

## D. Loans between Individuals

The general "large-capacity magazine" restrictions do not apply to loaning a lawfully possessed "large-capacity magazine" to any individual who is not otherwise prohibited from possessing firearms (see Chapter 3), as long as the exchange occurs at a location where "large-capacity magazines" are lawful. The lender must also stay in the recipient's "accessible vicinity."[120]

## E. Returned to the State

The general "large-capacity magazine" restrictions do not apply to someone who lawfully possessed a "large-capacity magazine" within California prior to January 1, 2000, then lawfully took it out-of-state, and now has returned with it.[121]

But bringing a "large-capacity magazine" back into California, even if it was previously owned in the state lawfully, is risky since it can be difficult to prove prior ownership or possession on a certain date. On the other hand, unless someone makes a statement to law enforcement admitting when or how the person obtained a "large-capacity magazine," it is very difficult for law enforcement to meet the burden of proof and *prove* someone did *not* previously own the magazine in the state lawfully. Remember though, even if you are not convicted, it still may cost you a lot in legal costs, time, and anguish to avoid conviction.

## F. Dealer or Gunsmith Loan for Maintenance/Repair

The general "large-capacity magazine" restrictions do not apply to lending or giving a "large-capacity magazine" to an FFL[122] or gunsmith for maintenance, repair, or modification. It also does not apply to an FFL or gunsmith returning it to the lawful possessor.[123]

---

[119] Pursuant to P.C. §§ 26700-26915, 32410.
[120] P.C. § 32415.
[121] P.C. § 32420.
[122] P.C. §§ 26700-26915.
[123] P.C. § 32425.

# G. Importing or Selling with a Permit

The general "large-capacity magazine" restrictions do not apply to those FFLs issued a permit to import, transport, or sell "large-capacity magazines"[124] between themselves and out-of-state clients.[125] The terms and conditions for these permits can be found on the permit application at the DOJ website.[126]

# H. Armored Vehicle Business Entities

The general "large-capacity magazine" restrictions do not apply to the selling, giving, lending, importing, or purchasing of "large-capacity magazines" to or by entities lawfully operating armored vehicle businesses.[127]

The general "large-capacity magazine" restrictions do not apply to those entities lending "large-capacity magazines" to their "authorized employees, while in the course and scope of employment for purposes that pertain to the entity's armored vehicle business[,]" or those employees returning them to the business.[128]

# I. Manufacturing "Large-Capacity Magazines" by Law Enforcement

The general "large-capacity magazine" restrictions do not apply to manufacturing "large-capacity magazines:"

- By any law enforcement agency for use by their employees in the discharge of their official "duties, whether on or off duty, and where the use is authorized by the agency and is within the course and scope of their duties[;]"
- For use by sworn officers[129] "authorized to carry a firearm in the course and scope of th[eir] … duties[;]" or
- "[F]or export or for sale to government agencies or the military … [per] federal regulations."[130]

---

[124] P.C. § 32315.

[125] P.C. § 32430.

[126] *Application for Large-Capacity Magazine Permit*, CALIFORNIA DEPT. OF JUSTICE, http://ag.ca.gov/firearms/forms/pdf/CLlcmpapp.pdf (last visited July 28, 2012).

[127] P.C. § 32435(a).

[128] P.C. §§ 32435(b)-(c).

[129] Defined in P.C. § 830 *et seq.*

[130] P.C. § 32440.

## J. Media Props

The general "large-capacity magazine" restrictions do not apply when a "large-capacity magazine" is loaned "solely as a prop for a motion picture, television, or video production."[131]

## K. Purchase by Special Weapons Permit Holder

The general "large-capacity magazine" restrictions do not apply when a special weapons permit[132] holder purchases a "large-capacity magazine" to:

- Use solely as a prop for a motion picture, television, or video production;
- Export pursuant to federal regulations; or
- Resell it "to law enforcement agencies, government agencies, or the military, pursuant to applicable federal regulations."[133]

# VI. ADDITIONAL EXCEPTIONS TO CALIFORNIA LAW FOR RESTRICTIONS ON "SHORT-BARRELED SHOTGUNS/RIFLES"

There are two additional exceptions to the general ban on possessing "short-barreled shotguns/rifles." Both exceptions, however, are conditioned on you also meeting the requirements to lawfully possess or make an NFA firearm.

## A. Law Enforcement Agencies

The "short-barreled rifle" and "short-barreled shotgun" restrictions do not apply to sales to, purchases, or possession by a "police department, sheriff's office, marshal's office, the California Highway Patrol, the Department of Justice, the Department of Corrections and Rehabilitation, or the military or naval forces … for use in the discharge of their official duties."[134] Peace officers who are "members of a police department, sheriff's office, marshal's office, the California Highway Patrol, the Department of Justice, or the Department of Corrections and Rehabilitation" may also possess a "short-barreled rifle" and/or "short-barreled shotgun" "when on duty and

---

[131] P.C. § 32445.
[132] Special weapons permits are issued per P.C. §§ 31000, 32650, 33300,18900 *et seq.*, 32700 *et seq.*
[133] P.C. § 32450.
[134] P.C. § 33220.

the use is authorized by the agency and is within the course and scope of their duties, and the officers have completed a training course in the use of these weapons certified by the Commission on Peace Officer Standards and Training."[135] Though law enforcement agencies are exempt from the NFA tax, they must comply with the other requirements, including registration.

## B. Permit Authorization

P.C. § 33215 does not apply when the DOJ authorizes the manufacture, possession, transportation, or sale of "short-barreled shotguns" or "short-barreled rifles" by issuing a permit.[136]

A Dangerous Weapons Permit can be obtained from the DOJ by submitting an application to the DOJ's Bureau of Firearms.[137]

One must have "good cause" for this permit, including showing the DOJ that issuing the permit does not endanger public safety. "Good cause" for obtaining a permit relating to "short-barreled shotguns" or "short-barreled rifles" exists only when:

"(1) The permit is sought for the manufacture, possession, or use with blank cartridges, of a short-barreled rifle or short-barreled shotgun, solely as a prop for a motion picture, television, or video production or entertainment event[;]" or

(2) The permit is sought for the manufacture of, exposing for sale, keeping for sale, sale of, importation or lending of short-barreled rifles or short-barreled shotguns to [certain law enforcement entities] by persons who are licensed as dealers or manufacturers" under the NFA.[138]

# VII. "SILENCERS"/"SOUND SUPPRESSORS"

"Silencers" are also generally prohibited. A "silencer" is a:

device or attachment of any kind designed, used, or intended for use in silencing, diminishing, or muffling the report of a firearm. The term 'silencer' also includes any combination of parts, designed or redesigned, and intended for use in assembling or fab-

---

[135] P.C. § 33220.

[136] P.C. § 33225 (issued per P.C. § 33300 *et seq.* and in compliance with federal law).

[137] *Dangerous Weapons License/Permit(s) Application,* CALIFORNIA DEPT. OF JUSTICE, http://ag.ca.gov/firearms/forms/pdf/FD030DWApp.pdf (last visited July 28, 2012).

[138] P.C. § 33300. *See also* P.C. § 33220 (providing the approved law enforcement entities for whom "short-barreled shotguns" and "short-barreled rifles" may be manufactured).

ricating a silencer [including] any part intended only for use in assembly or fabrication of a silencer.[139]

Unlawfully possessing a "silencer" is a felony.[140]

The practice of attaching homemade devices to the end of a firearm to make it look "cooler" is risky because the device could be considered a "silencer" if it diminishes or muffles the firearm's sound.

"The sale to, purchase by, or possession of silencers by" certain law enforcement agencies[141] or state or U.S. military forces for "use in the discharge of their official duties" is lawful.[142] Members of these law enforcement agencies (provided they are regular, salaried, full-time peace officers) and members of the military may possess "silencers" "when [they are] on duty and when the use of silencers is authorized by the agency and is within the course and scope of their duties."[143]

Also, FFLs and manufacturers (who are also licensed under the NFA) may manufacture, possess, transport, sell or transfer "silencers" to any of the entities listed above.[144]

The NFA also regulates "silencers" (they are considered "firearms" under the NFA), but without defining the term "silencer." Instead, the NFA refers to the GCA's definition.[145] Under the GCA, a "firearm silencer" and "firearm muffler" "mean any device for silencing, muffling, or diminishing the report of a portable firearm, including any combination of parts, designed or redesigned, and intended for use in assembling or fabricating a firearm silencer or firearm muffler, and any part intended only for use in such assembly or fabrication."[146]

The ATF has reportedly considered simple homemade items to be "silencers" – and thus subject to NFA "firearm" requirements – including even copper pot scrubbers used with fiberglass insulation.

## VIII. OBLITERATED OR COVERED SERIAL NUMBERS

Under California law it is a felony to change, alter, remove, or obliterate either the name of a firearm maker, its model, the manufacturer's number,

---

[139] P.C. § 17210.
[140] P.C. § 33410.
[141] These law enforcement agencies are specified in P.C. § 830.1.
[142] P.C. § 33415(a).
[143] P.C. § 33415(b).
[144] P.C. § 33415.
[145] 26 U.S.C. § 5845(a) (defining a "silencer" as that in 18 U.S.C. § 921).
[146] 18 U.S.C. § 921(a)(24).

or other identification mark on any firearm without first receiving written permission from the California DOJ.[147] There are no exceptions.

Contrary to the federal restriction on obliterating *serial numbers*,[148] California's rule is much more restricting. This means that if you enjoy modifying and refurbishing firearms, you have to be very careful not to remove the manufacturer's or model's name, and certainly not the serial number.

Even if you are not the one who actually altered the firearm's *identifying marks*, it is a misdemeanor under California law to possess, receive, transfer, or offer for sale any firearm, knowing that the name of the maker, model, or manufacturer's number, or other identification mark has been changed, altered, removed, or obliterated.[149] This restriction does not apply to such a firearm being acquired or possessed by any:

- State or U.S. military members while on duty and acting within their employment scope;
- Peace officers while on duty acting within their employment scope;[150] or
- Forensic laboratory employees while on duty and acting within their employment scope.[151]

Nor do they apply to firearm possession and disposition by someone who:

- Is not prohibited by state or federal law from possessing, receiving, or owning a firearm (see Chapter 3); and
- Possessed the firearm no longer than necessary to deliver it to law enforcement for lawful disposition; and
- Gave prior notice to law enforcement, then transported the firearm in a locked container (as defined in P.C. § 16850) and in accordance with the law to law enforcement for its lawful disposition.[152]

---

[147] P.C. § 23900.

[148] 18 U.S.C. § 922(k). ("It shall be unlawful for any person knowingly to transport, ship, or receive, in interstate or foreign commerce, any firearm which has had the importer's or manufacturer's serial number removed, obliterated, or altered or to possess or receive any firearm which has had the importer's or manufacturer's serial number removed, obliterated, or altered and has, at any time, been shipped or transported in interstate or foreign commerce.").

[149] P.C. § 23920. At least one court has upheld a conviction for possessing a firearm with an obliterated serial number over a Second Amendment challenge. *United States v. Marzzarella*, 614 F.3d 85 (3d Cir. 2010). Though not a California case, the result here would almost certainly be the same (California's prohibition and your conviction will probably be upheld).

[150] These officers are described in the Penal Code commencing with section 830.

[151] P.C. §§ 23925(a)-(c).

[152] P.C. § 23925(d).

It is generally lawful to possess a firearm *without* identifying marks because, as explained in Chapter 4, not all firearms must have identifying marks in the first place, *e.g.*, lawfully home-built firearms.[153] The problem arises when already existing identifying marks are altered.

Possessing a firearm with its serial number or identification number covered from view seems clearly illegal under P.C. § 537e. However, since P.C. § 23920 says it is only unlawful if the marks are "changed, altered, removed, or obliterated," it is unclear whether it is legal to *temporarily* cover a firearm's otherwise valid and intact identification marks (*e.g.*, with tape). P.C. § 537e provides:

> Any person who knowingly ... has in his or her possession any personal property from which the manufacturer's serial number, identification number, electronic serial number, or any other distinguishing number or identification mark has been removed, defaced, *covered*, altered, or destroyed, is guilty of a public offense ... .

P.C. §§ 23920 and 537e seem to conflict because P.C. § 537e covers almost all of the prohibited activity in P.C. § 23920, making P.C. § 23920 somewhat redundant.

When statutes are inconsistent with each other, or when a specific statute covers almost the same things as a more general law does, the more specific law usually applies.[154] This means that since P.C. § 23920 is more specific, it should be followed with respect to firearm identifying marks.

# IX. "UNSAFE" HANDGUNS

The California DOJ maintains the Roster of Handguns Certified for Sale (Roster) in California.[155] With certain exceptions, California residents cannot buy handguns not appearing on the Roster *from* FFLs. Those not listed on the Roster are legally referred to as "unsafe" handguns, though this description is not factually accurate.

It is illegal for "any person in this state who manufactures or causes to be manufactured, imports into the state for sale, keeps for sale, offers or ex-

---

[153] If requested, the California DOJ "may assign a distinguishing number or identification mark to any firearm" if it lacks one or if the previous one was destroyed or obliterated. P.C. § 23910.

[154] *People v. Vessell*, 36 Cal.App.4th 285, 289 (1995); *People v. Jenkins*, 28 Cal.3d 494, 505 (1980); *People v. Gilbert*, 1 Cal.3d 475, 481 (1969).

[155] The DOJ's Roster can be searched by a handgun's make, model, type, barrel length, or caliber, or when the handgun is scheduled to be removed from the Roster. *See Roster of Handguns Certified for Sale*, CALIFORNIA DEPT. OF JUSTICE, http://certguns.doj.ca.gov (last visited Aug. 2, 2012).

poses for sale, gives, or lends"[156] an unsafe handgun, subject to the limited exceptions discussed below. One exception is if the "unsafe" handgun is being imported for sale to law enforcement.[157] Depending on the handgun type (whether a revolver or a pistol), handguns must meet certain "safety" criteria before they can be placed on the Roster.[158] Firearm manufacturers must have their handguns tested and pay a fee before their handguns can be put on the Roster, but must also pay another annual fee.[159]

Typically, if a handgun is not on the Roster, the manufacturer has not submitted it for DOJ testing or has allowed it to drop off the list by not paying the annual fee.

The restriction on "unsafe" handgun transfers does not apply to PPTs (as further discussed below), pawn or consignment sales, intra-family transfers, operation of law transfers, and other specifically described transfers.[160] These transfers must still, however, go through an FFL (when an FFL is required).

## A. Exceptions to "Unsafe" Handgun Roster Requirement

Certain handguns are exempt from the Roster requirement. All listed "curio or relics" as defined in 27 C.F.R. § 478.11 are exempt.[161] Single-action revolvers with at least a 5-cartridge capacity and barrel lengths of at least three inches are also exempt if the firearm meets *any* of the following specifications:

- "Was originally manufactured prior to 1900 and is a curio or relic, as defined in" 27 C.F.R. § 478.11.
- "Has an overall length measured parallel to the barrel of at least … [7 ½] inches when the handle, frame or receiver, and barrel are assembled."
- "Has an overall length measured parallel to the barrel of at least … [7 ½] inches when the handle, frame or receiver, and barrel are assembled and that is currently" lawful to import into the U.S. per 18 U.S.C. § 925(d)(3).[162]

The Roster requirement also does not apply to single-shot pistols with a barrel length of six inches or more and "an overall length of at least 10½

---

[156] P.C. § 32000.

[157] P.C. § 32000(b)(4).

[158] P.C.§ 31910; *see also* P.C. §§ 31905, 31900, 32010 for the requirements.

[159] P.C. § 32015.

[160] P.C. § 32110.

[161] P.C. § 32000(b)(3).

[162] P.C. § 32100(a).

inches when the handle, frame or receiver, and barrel are assembled."[163] Certain pistols designed expressly for Olympic target shooting events are also exempt.[164]

Some Californians wishing to buy certain pistols not on the approved Roster have discovered a way to import them into California through an FFL, although the legalities of this route have not been confirmed. Typically the purchaser will buy the pistol from an out-of-state FFL. That FFL (if it has a manufacturer's license) or another FFL (with a manufacturer's license) installs a longer barrel so that the pistol meets the length requirements for the exception to apply and then inserts a mechanism to make the handgun a single-shot.[165] This modified single-shot pistol is then sent to an FFL in California. The transfer is then conducted like any other handgun transaction. The California FFL should note in the DROS form that the handgun is exempt from these Roster requirements because it is single-shot and note the appropriate dimensions.

Importing "off-Roster" handguns this way is a relatively new process. There is no case law concerning its legality yet. Though it appears lawful, importing handguns this way is risky and may subject you, the FFL, and the out-of-state FFL to criminal prosecution.[166] If asked about it by law enforcement, you may wish to exercise your right to remain silent and to consult a lawyer.

As a practical matter, the DOJ's Roster has greatly limited the number of handguns available for purchase in California. To get people to buy their newer (*i.e.*, more expensive) handguns, manufacturers often let their older models "fall off" the Roster, replacing them only with newer versions and models. The DOJ does not always notify manufacturers that their handguns are close to falling off the Roster, and, once off, the manufacturer is less likely to try to get the handgun re-listed.

## B. "Microstamping"

The concept of "microstamping" ammunition gained recognition a few years back. "Microstamping" is the process of laser-engraving a pistol's make, model, and serial number on parts of a firearm, typically including its firing pin, so the information is stamped on the cartridge casing upon discharging the pistol. This means that when the casing is ejected from the

---

[163] P.C. § 32100(b).

[164] *See* P.C. § 32105 and 11 Cal. Code Regs. § 5455 for a list of exempt Olympic pistols.

[165] Most handguns imported this way are pistols, *i.e.*, not revolvers.

[166] At the time of publishing, the Roster Requirement was still being challenged on Second Amendment grounds. *See Peña v. Cid*, No. 2:09-cv-01185 (E.D.Cal. filed Apr. 30, 2009).

pistol after being shot, you can examine it under a microscope and theoretically know what pistol it was shot from.

As of January 1, 2010, all semiautomatic pistols not already listed on the DOJ's Roster must be "designed and equipped" with "microstamping" technology that the DOJ certifies is *not* encumbered by a patent and is thus available to more than one manufacturer.[167]

As of publishing, there is still *no* DOJ-certified microstamping technology, or any such technology that is not patented. So, even though this requirement was supposed to go into effect in 2010, it still has not. However, if a "microstamping" process becomes available that is not subject to a patent or the patents on current technology expire, new pistols may have to be "microstamped" to be sold by FFLs in California.

# X. AMMUNITION RESTRICTIONS

There are several different types of prohibited ammunition under California and federal law.

## A. Ammunition with "Flechette Darts" and "Explosive Agents"

Under California law it is illegal to manufacture, cause to be manufactured, import into the state, offer or expose for sale, give, lend, or possess ammunition with a "flechette dart" or "[a]ny bullet containing or carrying an explosive agent."[168]

A "flechette dart" is a dart that can be "fired from a firearm, that measures approximately one inch in length, with tail fins that take up approximately … [5/16] of an inch of the body."[169]

The Penal Code does not say what constitutes a "bullet containing or carrying an explosive agent," only that tracer ammunition manufactured for shotguns does not qualify.[170] One case, however, found a defendant guilty of possessing ammunition with an explosive agent when he pos-

---

[167] P.C. §§ 31910(b)(7)(A)-(B).
[168] P.C. § 30210.
[169] P.C. § 16570.
[170] P.C. § 30215.

sessed a hollow-point bullet[171] with a primer[172] wedged into the hollow portion of the bullet and held in place by paraffin wax.[173]

Thus, although undefined in the Penal Code, any ammunition with an additional explosive agent designed to explode after being fired, or once the bullet strikes its target, may violate California law.

Both ammunition with flechette darts and ammunition with an explosive agent are listed among the "generally prohibited weapons." The exceptions for those weapons and devices would therefore apply to these two kinds of ammunition, where applicable, as well.

## B. Armor Piercing Ammunition

It is also illegal under California law for a person or entity to knowingly possess, manufacture, import, sell, or transport "handgun ammunition" primarily designed to penetrate metal or armor.[174] This includes "any ammunition, except a shotgun shell or ammunition primarily designed for use in a rifle, that is designed primarily to penetrate a body vest or body shield, and has either of the following characteristics:

(a) Has projectile or projectile core constructed entirely, excluding the presence of traces of other substances, from one or a combination of tungsten alloys, steel, iron, brass, beryllium copper, or depleted uranium, or any equivalent material of similar density or hardness[, or]

(b) Is primarily manufactured or designed, by virtue of its shape, cross-sectional density, or any coating applied thereto, including but not limited to, ammunition commonly known as 'KTW ammunition,' to breach or penetrate a body vest or body shield when fired from a [handgun] ... ."[175]

---

[171] A "hollow point bullet" is a "bullet with a cavity in the nose, exposing the lead core, to facilitate expansion upon impact. Hollow point cartridges are used for hunting, self-defense, police use and other situations to avoid over-penetration." National Shooting Sports Foundation Inc., *The Writer's Guide to Firearms and Ammunition* 35 (2007).

[172] "Primer" is defined as an "ignition component consisting of a brass or gilding metal cup, priming mixture, anvil and foiling disc. It creates a spark when hit by a firing pin, igniting the propellant powder." National Shooting Sports Foundation Inc., *The Writer's Guide to Firearms and Ammunition* 35 (2007).

[173] *People v. Lanham*, 230 Cal.App.3d 1396 (1991).

[174] P.C. §§ 30315, 30320.

[175] P.C. § 16660.

Military personnel, police agencies, persons with permits, and other persons listed in P.C. §§ 30325 and 30330 are exempt from this prohibition.

Like California, federal law also restricts "armor piercing ammunition." Under the GCA, "armor piercing ammunition" is:

- "[A] projectile or projectile core which may be used in a handgun and which is constructed entirely (excluding the presence of traces of other substances) from one or a combination of tungsten alloys, steel, iron, brass, bronze, beryllium copper, or depleted uranium; or

- [A] full jacketed projectile larger than .22 caliber designed and intended for use in a handgun and whose jacket has a weight of more than 25 percent of the total weight of the projectile."[176]

The phrase " 'armor piercing ammunition' does not include shotgun shot required by Federal or State environmental or game regulations for hunting purposes, a frangible projectile designed for target shooting, a projectile which the Attorney General finds is primarily intended to be used for sporting purposes, or any other projectile or projectile core which the Attorney General finds is intended to be used for industrial purposes, including a charge used in an oil and gas well perforating device."[177]

Federal law restricts manufacturing and importing armor piercing ammunition, unless it is manufactured for:

- The use of the United States, any department or agency of the United States, any State, or any department, agency, or political subdivision of a State;

- The purpose of exportation; or

- Attorney General–authorized testing or experimentation. This exception also applies to importation.[178]

Further, those who manufacture or import "armor piercing ammunition" may not sell or deliver it unless the sale or delivery is also for: the use by the United States, any department or agency of the United States, any State, or any department, agency, or political subdivision of a State; exportation; or AG-authorized testing or experimentation.[179] It is also illegal for any federally licensed firearm importer, manufacturer, dealer, or collector

---

[176] 18 U.S.C. § 921(a)(17)(B).
[177] 18 U.S.C. § 921(a)(17)(C).
[178] 18 U.S.C. § 922(a)(7).
[179] 18 U.S.C. § 922(a)(8).

to sell or deliver "armor-piercing ammunition" to another person without recording that person's information[180] into the FFL's records.[181]

## C. Tracer Ammunition

As mentioned above, any projectile with an explosive or incendiary material or other chemical substance like tracer ammunition (except tracer ammunition made for shotgun use) is illegal to possess in California without proper permits and/or licensing, as it meets one of the state's definitions of a "destructive device."[182] Specific military members, peace officers, firefighters, permit holders, and other groups listed in P.C. §§ 18800 and 18900 may possess and use "destructive devices," including tracer ammunition.

For some reason tracer ammunition is lumped in with "destructive devices" and consequently carries that stigma in California. In fact, tracer ammunition is generally available in all states and can be purchased over the internet. Firearm enthusiasts, often with no criminal record, unknowingly violate California's law when they are discovered with tracer ammunition they lawfully purchased in another state. Because this ammunition is readily available in other states, it is common for people to be unaware that they cannot possess it in California.

## D. Lead Ammunition Bans and Hunting

California prohibits using or even possessing projectiles with more than 1% lead when hunting big game (deer, black bear, wild pig, elk, pronghorn antelope, and bighorn sheep) or coyotes[183] and other non-game birds or mammals[184] in designated California condor range areas.[185]

Federal law limits the type of ammunition that can be used to hunt certain animals. Specifically federal law prohibits using lead shot when hunting waterfowl.[186] When hunting migratory birds, any method not listed in 50 C.F.R. § 20.21 and not otherwise restricted by state or local laws is lawful. Some of the restricted methods of hunting a migratory bird include

---

[180] 18 U.S.C. § 922(b)(5) ("[N]ame, age, and place of residence of such person if the person is an individual, or the identity and principal and local places of business of such person if the person is a corporation or other business entity.").

[181] The records are those required to be kept pursuant to 18 U.S.C. § 923. 18 U.S.C. § 922(b)(5).

[182] P.C. § 16460(a) (defining "destructive device"); P.C. §§ 18720, 18900 (permit requirement).

[183] Fish & Game Code § 3004.5; 14 Cal. Code Regs. §§ 353(h), 350.

[184] 14 Cal. Code Regs. § 475(f).

[185] Fish & Game Code § 3004.5(a). For the California Condor range, *see Ridley-Tree Condor Preservation Act*, CALIFORNIA DEPT. OF FISH AND GAME, http://www.dfg.ca.gov/wildlife/hunting/condor/docs/Ridley-TreeCondorPreservationAct.pdf (last visited Aug. 2, 2012).

[186] 50 C.F.R. § 20.21(j).

taking by "a trap, snare, net, rifle, pistol, swivel gun, shotgun larger than 10 gauge, punt gun, battery gun, machine gun, fish hook, poison, drug, explosive, or stupefying substance[.]"[187] Although federal law places several different restrictions on hunters and sportsmen when it comes to using lead ammunition in hunting and for recreation, groups like the Center for Biological Diversity are pushing for stricter laws.

As of the date of this book's publication, a *New York Times* article stated that "roughly 100 environmental groups formally asked the federal Environmental Protection Agency" to impose some type of ban or limit on the amount of lead that goes into "bullets and shotgun pellets for hunting or recreation."[188] This request was rejected.[189] Jeff Miller, an advocate for the Center for Biological Diversity, alleges that 20 million birds each year die from lead poisoning. Mr. Miller further claims that the meat eaten from animals shot with lead bullets leads to "unacceptable levels" of metals in people's diets. The Environmental Protection Agency (EPA) was faced with a similar proposal in August of 2010, which it denied.

On the other side of this battle are groups like the National Shooting Sports Foundation (NSSF). Lawrence Keane, the Senior Vice President of NSSF, has countered arguments from the Center for Biological Diversity, arguing that a ban would likely result in ammunition prices skyrocketing because roughly 95% of ammunition used for hunting and recreation includes some portion of lead. The NSSF and other hunters' rights activists are seeking to safeguard the rights of hunters and sportsmen through a bill known as the Hunting, Fishing, and Recreational Shooting Protection Act. According to the *New York Times* article, the bill "would specify that the Toxic Substances Control Act's exemption on regulating ammunition also prevents the E.P.A. from regulating the components of bullets and pellets."[190] This essentially would tie the EPA's hands. This hot button issue will continue to find its way into the national media for some time.

There are also other relevant California and federal statutes and regulations not mentioned herein that address hunting with lead ammunition. However, those are beyond the scope of this book, so if you have specific questions, you should consult an attorney who specializes in that area of law.

---

[187] 50 C.F.R. § 20.21(a).

[188] *Zeroing In on Lead in Hunters' Bullets*, N.Y. TIMES, http://green.blogs.nytimes.com/2012/03/15/zeroing-in-on-lead-in-hunters-bullets/ (last visited July 28, 2012).

[189] *See EPA Again Rejects Petition to Ban Lead Ammo*, NRAHUNTERSRIGHTS.ORG, http://www.nrahuntersrights.org/Article.aspx?id=6400 (last visited Aug. 2, 2012).

[190] *Zeroing In on Lead in Hunters' Bullets*, N.Y. TIMES, http://green.blogs.nytimes.com/2012/03/15/zeroing-in-on-lead-in-hunters-bullets/ (last visited Aug. 2, 2012).

# XI. OTHER REGULATED DEVICES

## A. "BB Guns"

California law does not use the term "BB gun" but rather "BB device." A "BB device" is anything "that expels a projectile, such as a BB or a pellet, ... [under] 6mm caliber, through ... air pressure, gas pressure, or spring action, or any spot marker gun."[191] Devices that meet this definition are *not* "firearms."[192]

It's illegal to sell "BB devices" to minors, and no one may loan or give a "BB device" to a minor without permission from that minor's parent or legal guardian.[193]

Despite generally being considered a non-lethal weapon, a BB gun used by a juvenile while committing a robbery was considered a "dangerous weapon."[194] Under California law a person who uses a deadly or dangerous weapon in the commission of a felony can receive an additional jail sentence on top of the jail sentence they receive for a conviction for the felony. These are referred to as enhancements.[195] Despite the usual non-lethal nature of a BB gun, cases have historically recognized BB guns or pellet guns as "dangerous weapons."[196] So do not think you cannot face serious charges just because you misuse a BB gun and not a real firearm.

## B. Toy Guns a.k.a. "Imitation Firearms"

When discussing "imitation firearms" it is best to start with federal law and work back to California law.

Under federal law it is illegal for anyone "to manufacture, enter into commerce, ship, transport, or receive any toy, look-alike, or imitation firearm unless such firearm contains, or has affixed to it, a marking approved by the Secretary of Commerce ..."[197]

Unless there is an exception or the Secretary of Commerce has provided for an alternate marking or device,[198] "each toy, look-alike, or imitation firearm shall have as an integral part, permanently affixed, a blaze orange

---

[191] P.C. § 16250.

[192] "Firearms" are discussed and defined in Chapter 2.

[193] P.C. §§ 19910, 19915.

[194] *In re Bartholomew D.*, 131 Cal.App.4th 317, 322-326 (2005).

[195] P.C. § 12022(b).

[196] *In re Bartholomew D.*, 131 Cal.App.4th 317, 322 (2005).

[197] 15 U.S.C. § 5001(a).

[198] The Secretary of Commerce has promulgated a number of regulations concerning alternate markings and identifies how to request a waiver from the marking requirement if you seek to use an imitation firearm in the entertainment industry. *See* 15 U.S.C. § 50001(b)(2) and 15 C.F.R. § 1150.1 *et seq.*

plug inserted in the barrel of such toy, look-alike, or imitation firearm. Such plug shall be recessed no more than 6 millimeters from the muzzle end of the barrel of such firearm."[199]

A " 'look-alike firearm' means any imitation of any original firearm which was manufactured, designed, and produced since 1898, including and limited to toy guns, water guns, replica nonguns, and air-soft guns firing nonmetallic projectiles."[200] A "look-alike firearm" does *not include* "any look-alike, nonfiring, collector replica of an antique firearm developed prior to 1898, or traditional B-B, paint-ball, or pellet-firing air guns that expel a projectile through the force of air pressure."[201] That is why certain air-soft guns need the orange tips while BB guns that fire metallic pellets do not, despite looking in all other respects identical.

Going back to California law, an "imitation firearm" is "any BB device, toy gun, replica of a firearm, or other device that is so substantially similar" in color and overall appearance to an existing firearm that a reasonable person would think it is a firearm.[202]

Anyone who modifies an "imitation firearm" to look more like a firearm is guilty of a misdemeanor.[203] This does not apply to manufacturers, importers, or imitation firearm distributors or those who lawfully use imitation firearms for theatrical, film, or television productions.[204] Manufacturers, importers, or distributors of imitation firearms who fail to comply with federal law or regulations relating to the markings of "a toy, look-alike, or imitation firearm, as defined by federal law or regulation" (discussed above) can be prosecuted criminally under California law.[205]

California puts additional burdens on those who purchase, sell, manufacture, ship, transport, distribute, or receive (by mail order or in any other manner) "imitation firearms" for commercial purposes, unless it is:

(1) only for "export" (interstate or internationally) in commerce;
(2) only "for lawful use in theatrical productions, including motion picture, television, and stage productions[;]"
(3) for "a certified or regulated sporting event or competition[;]"
(4) for "military or civil defense activities, or ceremonial activities[;]" or
(5) "[f]or public displays authorized by public or private schools."[206]

---

[199] 15 U.S.C. § 5001(b)(1).
[200] 15 U.S.C. § 5001(c).
[201] 15 U.S.C. § 5001(c).
[202] P.C. § 16700(a).
[203] P.C. § 20150(a).
[204] P.C. §§ 20150(b)-(c).
[205] P.C. § 20155.
[206] P.C. § 20165.

*However*, these restrictions do not include: non-firing collector's replicas that are "historically significant and offered for sale in conjunction with a wall plaque or presentation case; a "*BB device*," or a "device where the entire exterior surface of the device is white, bright red, bright orange, bright yellow, bright green, bright blue, bright pink, or bright purple, either" by itself or predominantly "with other colors in any pattern, as provided by federal regulations governing imitation firearms or where the entire device is constructed of transparent or translucent materials which permits unmistakable observation of the device's complete contents, as provided by federal regulations governing imitation firearms."[207]

Finally, a person cannot openly display or expose an "imitation firearm" in a "public place,"[208] unless it is:

- Packaged or concealed so it is not subject to public viewing;
- Displayed or exposed for commerce, including commercial film or video productions, or for service, repair, or restoration;
- Used for a theatrical, movie, video, television, or stage production;
- Used in conjunction with a certified or regulated sporting event or competition;
- Used in conjunction with lawful hunting or pest control activities;
- Used or possessed at a certified or regulated shooting range;
- Used at a fair, exhibition, exposition, or other similar activity for which the proper permits have been obtained;
- Used in military, civil defense, or civic activities, including flag ceremonies, color guards, parades, award presentations, historical re-enactments, and memorials;
- Used for public displays authorized by any school or museum;
- Used in a parade, ceremony, or other similar activity for which proper permits have been obtained;
- Displayed on a wall plaque or in a presentation case;
- Used where discharging a firearm is lawful; or
- "The entire exterior surface of the imitation firearm is white, bright red, bright orange, bright yellow, bright green, bright blue, bright pink, or bright purple," either by itself or mainly with other colors, or "the entire device is constructed of transparent or translucent material that permits unmistakable observation of the device's com-

---

[207] P.C. § 16700(b).

[208] A "public place" is any "area open to the public" including streets, sidewalks, bridges, alleys, plazas, parks, driveways, front yards, parking lots, automobiles, whether moving or not, and buildings open to the general public, including those that serve food or drink, or provide entertainment, and the doorways and entrances to buildings or dwellings, including public schools and colleges or universities. P.C. § 20170(b).

plete contents." Merely having an orange tip is not enough. "The entire surface must be colored or transparent or translucent."[209]

Also, even if you meet one of the above "displaying" exceptions, you may still be prosecuted for possessing the device[210] at a state or local public building or meeting,[211] in an airport,[212] or on school grounds.[213]

# C. "Tear Gas," "Less Lethal Weapons," and "Stun Guns"

## 1. "Tear Gas," Pepper Spray, and Mace

"Tear gas" is a catch-all term in California that "includes any liquid, gaseous or solid substance intended to produce temporary physical discomfort or permanent injury through being vaporized or otherwise dispersed in the air."[214] Obviously "tear gas" includes items like mace and pepper spray.

A "tear gas weapon" is:

- "Any shell, cartridge, or bomb capable of being discharged or exploded, when the discharge or explosion will cause or permit the release or emission of tear gas[; or]
- "Any revolver, pistol, fountain pen gun, billy, or other form of device, portable or fixed, intended for the projection or release of tear gas, except those regularly manufactured and sold for use with firearm ammunition."[215]

Most people may purchase and use tear gas and tear gas weapons (the devices must only expel the tear gas by aerosol spray and have no more than 2.5 ounces net weight of aerosol spray)[216] if they use them for self-defense purposes. Using tear gas or a tear gas weapon for a purpose other than self-defense is a crime.[217] The following people, however, are prohibited from purchasing, possessing, or using tear gas or tear gas weapons:

---

[209] P.C. § 20175.

[210] *See* P.C. § 20180(c) ("Nothing in Section 20170, 20175, or this section shall be construed to preclude prosecution for a violation of Section 171b, 171.5, or 626.10.").

[211] P.C. § 171b.

[212] P.C. § 171.5.

[213] P.C. § 626.10.

[214] P.C. § 17240(a). However, "tear gas" does not include substances such as an "economic poison," as listed in the Food and Agricultural Code at section 12751 *et seq.*, "provided that the substance is not intended to be used to produce discomfort or injury to human beings." P.C. § 17240(b).

[215] P.C. § 17250.

[216] P.C. § 22810(e)(1).

[217] P.C. § 22810(g).

- Persons convicted of a felony or any crime involving an assault;
- Those convicted of misusing tear gas; and
- Persons addicted to any narcotic drug.[218]

It is further unlawful for minors to possess a tear gas weapon and for people to sell or give tear gas or a tear gas weapon to a minor unless the minor is at least age 16 and is accompanied by, or has written consent from, a parent or guardian.[219] Parents or legal guardians who allow their minor over age 16 to possess tear gas may, however, be civilly liable if the minor misuses it.[220]

Many tear gas devices on the market store their contents in a form other than aerosol spray. It is questionable whether these devices are legal for ordinary citizens to possess in California.

Specified peace officers, custodial officers, military personnel, and private investigators/patrol guards are exempt from tear gas and tear gas weapon restrictions.[221]

For additional laws about permissible tear gas amounts that may be possessed, warning label and instruction requirements, and permits for using tear gas for anything other than self-defense, see §§ 22810 through 23025.

## 2. "Less Lethal Weapons"

A "less lethal weapon" is any device "designed to or that has been converted to expel or propel less lethal ammunition[222] by any action, mechanism, or process for the purpose of incapacitating, immobilizing, or stunning a human being through the infliction of any less than lethal impairment of physical condition, function, or senses, including physical pain or discomfort." It is unnecessary for the weapon to "leave any lasting or permanent incapacitation, discomfort, pain, or other injury or disability to be a less lethal weapon."[223]

A "less lethal weapon" includes the weapon's frame or receiver "but does not include any of the following unless the part or weapon has been converted" as described in the previous paragraph:

---

[218] P.C. §§ 22810(a)-(b).

[219] P.C. §§ 22810(c)-(d), 22815(a)-(b).

[220] P.C. § 22815(c).

[221] P.C. §§ 22820, 22825, 22830, 22835.

[222] "Less lethal ammunition" is any ammunition "designed to be used in any less than lethal weapon or any other kind of weapon (including ... any firearm, pistol, revolver, shotgun, rifle, or spring, compressed air, or compressed gas weapon)" and, "[w]hen used in ... [any] ... weapon, it is designed to immobilize, incapacitate, or stun a human being through the infliction of any less than lethal impairment of physical condition, function, or senses, including physical pain or discomfort." P.C. § 16770.

[223] P.C. § 16780(a).

- "Pistol, revolver, or firearm.
- Machinegun.
- Rifle or shotgun using fixed ammunition consisting of standard primer and powder and not capable of being concealed upon the person.
- A pistol, rifle, or shotgun that is a firearm having a barrel less than 0.18 inches in diameter and that is designed to expel a projectile by any mechanical means or by compressed air or gas.
- When used as designed or intended by the manufacturer, any weapon that is commonly regarded as a toy gun, and that as a toy gun is incapable of inflicting any impairment of physical condition, function, or senses.
- A destructive device.
- A tear gas weapon.
- A bow or crossbow designed to shoot arrows.
- A device commonly known as a slingshot.
- A device designed for the firing of stud cartridges, explosive rivets, or similar industrial ammunition.
- A device designed for signaling, illumination, or safety.
- An assault weapon."[224]

Selling a "less lethal weapon" to anyone under the age of 18 years is a misdemeanor.[225]

## 3. "Stun Guns"

A "stun gun" is "any item except a less lethal weapon used or intended to be used as either an offensive or defensive weapon that is capable of temporarily immobilizing a person by the infliction of an electrical charge."[226] A "stun gun" is not a "less lethal weapon."

As with tear gas weapons, most people may purchase, possess, and use a "stun gun." The following people cannot:

- Those convicted of a felony, misusing a stun gun, or any crime involving an assault;
- Those addicted to narcotic drugs; and
- Minors (it is illegal for you to sell or furnish a stun gun to a minor and it is illegal for a minor to possess a stun gun unless the minor is age 16 or older and has written parental or legal guardian consent).[227]

---

[224] P.C. § 16780(b).

[225] P.C. § 19405.

[226] P.C. § 17230.

[227] P.C. § 22610 (referencing P.C. § 244.5 governing stun gun misuse).

## D. "Blowguns"

A "blowgun" is a hollow tube through which a dart is propelled by force of breath.[228] "Blowgun ammunition" is the "dart designed and intended for use in [the] blowgun."[229]

Unless an individual falls under an exception,[230] manufacturing, selling, offering for sale, possessing, or using a "blowgun" or "blowgun ammunition" is unlawful in California.[231]

# XII. NATIONAL FIREARMS ACT – FIREARM POSSESSION

Unlike California, federal law allows those who can lawfully possess firearms to possess certain "machineguns," "any other weapons," "destructive devices," "short-barreled shotguns/rifles," and "silencers" – also known as "NFA firearms." Transferors of NFA firearms must be the registered owners, file the proper ATF forms, and make sure the applicable transfer tax is paid.[232] The ATF must also approve the transfer[233] and the transferee generally must obtain certification (*i.e.*, permission) from the local chief of police, sheriff of the county, head of the state police, state or local district attorney or prosecutor, or such other authority where the transferee resides.[234] It is otherwise illegal to possess unregistered NFA firearms.[235] If you want to *build* one of these types of firearms, you must have the proper permission from the federal government and, if you are in the business of making NFA firearms, a federal license and tax stamp.[236]

Though federal law makes it much easier to lawfully obtain and own those items constituting NFA firearms, if you are a California resident, this will not help you much. As mentioned above, California requires an additional permit (or exception) to possess most of these items, which is nearly impossible to obtain for "normal" people. And the ATF will not approve

---

[228] P.C. § 16270.

[229] P.C. § 16280.

[230] This includes zookeepers, animal control officers, Fish and Game personnel, certain humane officers, and veterinarians "in the course and scope of their business in order to administer medicine to animals." P.C. § 20015.

[231] P.C. § 20010.

[232] The tax is $200 generally or $5 for "any other weapons." 26 U.S.C. § 5811(a).

[233] 26 U.S.C. § 5812(b); 27 C.F.R. § 479.86.

[234] 27 C.F.R. § 479.85.

[235] *United States v. Freed*, 401 U.S. 601, 607 (1971).

[236] 26 U.S.C. §§ 5822, 5801, 5802; 18 U.S.C. § 922(a)(1)(A).

the transfer of an NFA firearm where state or local law would be violated by doing so.[237]

Nevertheless people have recently found a way to avoid some federal restrictions and procedures associated with getting an NFA firearm by creating a legal document known as an NFA Trust. This trust avoids several hassles associated with obtaining NFA firearm transfers, including the requirement that the head of local law enforcement from your area must approve the transfer first.[238] It does *not*, however, avoid California's licensing requirements for certain NFA firearms. This is a complex area of law, so keep in mind that while possession is lawful under federal law, those who possess an NFA firearm in California will still need to comply with California's applicable permitting requirements for such firearms or devices. Moreover, some people have been prosecuted for violating the NFA because their NFA Trust was not properly created or executed.

# XIII. IGNORANCE OF THE LAW IS NO EXCUSE

Despite California's massive amount of confusing laws about which firearms and devices are and are not legal, ignorance of the law is no excuse. You essentially violate California and federal law if you knowingly possess an item and it is something California prohibits you from possessing.[239] It does not matter if you did not know it was illegal.[240]

In some rare instances, however, you may be able to use the "entrapment by estoppel" defense. "Entrapment by estoppel" means that a government representative has informed you that a certain act is lawful, then prosecutes you for that same act.[241] For example, California law enforcement informs you that a certain firearm is legal in California and then you

---

[237] 26 U.S.C. § 5812(a). 27 C.F.R. § 479.85.

[238] 27 C.F.R. § 479.85. Law enforcement policy in certain jurisdictions is to deny or never to sign NFA transfer requests.

[239] *See, e.g., In re Jorge M.*, 23 Cal.4th 866, 869-870 (2000) (state must prove defendant knew that he possessed it and knew or reasonably should have known the firearm was prohibited by make and model or its features, but need not prove defendant knew of the law banning unregistered "assault weapon" possession or that the make, model, or features caused the firearm to be classified as an "assault weapon").

[240] *People v. King*, 38 Cal.4th 617, 643 (2006) ("[T]he prosecution must prove that the item had the necessary characteristic to fall within the statutory description. It must also prove that the defendant knew of the characteristic. That is, it must prove that a defendant charged with possession of a short-barreled rifle knew the rifle was unusually short, but the defendant need not know the rifle's actual dimensions. Similarly, a defendant charged with illegally possessing a cane sword must know that the cane contained a sword, and a defendant charged with possessing a writing pen knife must know that the pen contained a stabbing instrument. Knowledge can, of course, be proved circumstantially. Further, the prosecution need not prove that the defendant knew there was a law against possessing the item, nor that the defendant intended to break or violate the law.").

[241] *United States v. Batterjee*, 361 F.3d 1210, 1216-1217 (2004).

are arrested because the firearm is actually *illegal* under California law. You might be able to claim "entrapment by estoppel" to defend yourself since law enforcement previously informed you that the firearm was legal.

In general, however, the law expects you as a firearm owner to be familiar with all of the laws discussed above, and those that might not be mentioned as well.

## CHAPTER 10

# LOSING YOUR FIREARMS AND GETTING THEM BACK

S everal circumstances exist where law enforcement may lawfully seize your firearms. Both constitutional principles and California law, however, limit this authority. Whether the government can keep the firearm or must give it back involves additional legal issues.

## I. FIREARMS ARE PROTECTED "PROPERTY" UNDER THE UNITED STATES AND CALIFORNIA CONSTITUTIONS

Both the U.S. Supreme Court and California courts recognize that even *temporarily* depriving you of your property without a hearing may violate your constitutional right to "due process."[1] This means that the government must provide you with some form of legal process for even temporarily seizing your firearms, and strict compliance with these laws is required.[2]

Even if the initial seizure was lawful, failing to return the firearm after it was legally seized may violate the constitutional due process doctrine if there is no other legal justification for not returning it.[3] Moreover, if your property is harmed while you are temporarily but wrongfully deprived of your property, you may be compensated.[4]

---

[1] *Connecticut v. Doehr*, 501 U.S. 1, 12 (1991); *Sniadach v. Family Finance Corp.*, 395 U.S. 337, 338-339 (1969); *Connolly Development, Inc. v. Superior Court*, 17 Cal.3d 803, 812 (1976); *Carrera v. Bertaini*, 63 Cal.App.3d 721, 727 (1976).

[2] *City of San Diego v. Kevin B.*, 118 Cal.App.4th 933, 941 (2004).

[3] *Spinelli v. City of New York*, 579 F.3d 160, 171-175 (2nd Cir. 2009).

[4] *Sandrini Bros. v. Voss*, 7 Cal.App.4th 1398, 1404 (1992).

The California Supreme Court has said that the government is like a bailee when it seizes property that is not contraband (see below for an explanation of "contraband").[5]

California has a comprehensive set of statutes governing the seizure and return of firearms. Since firearms are property, they are usually governed by the same laws that apply to the seizure and return of personal property. For example, firearms can be seized pursuant to a properly executed search warrant[6] or if law enforcement has "probable cause" to believe they were used to commit a crime.[7] Sometimes, however, California law allows firearms to be seized where other property could not necessarily be seized, including:

- At a domestic violence incident involving a threat to human life or a physical assault (P.C. § 18250);
- When someone is detained for a mental examination or is described in W.I.C. §§ 8100 or 8103, and is found to own or possess any firearm or any other deadly weapon (W.I.C. § 8102);
- When a firearm is owned or possessed by a "criminal street gang" member to commit a crime listed in P.C. §186.22(e) (P.C. § 186.22a(f));
- When law enforcement needs to determine if the firearm is loaded (P.C. § 25850(b)).

While California allows firearms to be seized in these instances, such seizures by law enforcement may still be challenged as a Fourth Amendment violation.[8] You should *never* consent to law enforcement taking your property.

## II.  TYPES OF FIREARM SEIZURES

### A.  Firearms Seized Pursuant to a Search Warrant

The complex laws about search warrants are beyond the scope of this book. But one common issue that regularly comes up when law enforcement seeks to seize firearms is that their warrant is too broad. Too often law enforcement will request a search warrant to seize every firearm, piece of

---

[5] *Minsky v. City of Los Angeles*, 11 Cal.3d 113, 121 (1974). As a bailee, the government receives possession of the firearm, but not title or ownership to it.

[6] U.S. CONST. amend. IV; CAL. CONST. art. I, § 13; P.C. § 1525. If law enforcement finds a firearm while executing a valid search warrant, it may only be seized if the warrant specifically says it may be seized or if the firearm is readily apparent as contraband. *See Marron v. United States*, 275 U.S. 192, 197-199 (1927); *People v. Gallegos*, 96 Cal.App.4th 612, 622 (2002).

[7] *Payton v. New York*, 445 U.S. 573, 587 (1980).

[8] *See Terry v. Ohio*, 392 U.S. 1 (1968), and its progeny.

ammunition, firearm-related paperwork (*e.g.*, receipts, registration documents, even firearm reading materials), firearm parts, clips, and magazines, no matter what the underlying alleged offense is or whether each individual item has some connection to the alleged offense.

If probable cause exists to believe the person whose residence or business being searched is a firearm smuggler or unlawful firearm dealer, a warrant may be justified to seize all firearms located therein.[9] In most other cases, however, this type of "general" warrant is illegal.[10]

For example, if someone is accused of robbing a liquor store and there is video of the robber holding a pistol, law enforcement may lawfully seize all pistols from the accused matching the one in the video's description, but not otherwise legally possessed shotguns or rifles.

Despite this whenever firearms are part of a criminal investigation, law enforcement often uses the presence of *one* firearm to seize *all* firearms and any other property, even if only remotely related. The constitutionality of this practice is doubtful; however, legal challenges have been rejected in certain specific contexts.[11]

## B. Domestic Violence Firearm Seizures

At a "domestic violence" incident[12] involving "a threat to human life or a physical assault," law enforcement *must*, at least temporarily, take custody of any firearm or other deadly weapon in plain sight, with consent from the firearm's possessor or pursuant to an otherwise lawful search conducted for the protection of an officer or other persons present.[13]

---

[9] See *United States v. Biswell*, 406 U.S. 311 (1972) (Affirming legality of a search and seizure even without a warrant, based upon the GCA of 1968, 18 U.S.C. § 921 *et seq.*, which authorizes official entry into the premises of any firearms or ammunition dealer to inspect or examine required records or documents and firearms or ammunition kept or stored by such a dealer on the premises).

[10] *Payton v. New York*, 445 U.S. 573, 583 (1980) ("indiscriminate searches and seizures conducted under the authority of 'general warrants' were the immediate evils that motivated the framing and adoption of the Fourth Amendment.").

[11] *Messerschmidt v. Millender*, 132 S. Ct. 1235, 1245 (2012) (ruling that an officer is entitled to immunity from civil liability for an unconstitutional search and seizure undertaken pursuant to a warrant so long as the affidavits were not "so lacking in indicia of probable cause as to render official belief in its existence entirely unreasonable") (internal quotes omitted).

[12] A "domestic violence" incident is defined in P.C. § 16490 as an abuse against any of the following:
    (a) A spouse or former spouse.
    (b) A cohabitant or former cohabitant (defined in Fam. Code § 6209).
    (c) Someone with whom the respondent is or had a dating or engagement relationship.
    (d) Someone with whom the respondent has had a child, where it is presumed the male parent is the father of the child (Fam. Code § 7600).
    (e) A child who is the subject of a Uniform Parentage Act action, where it is presumed the male parent is the father of that child.
    (f) Any other person related by blood or marriage within the second degree.

[13] P.C. § 18250.

Law enforcement officers who fill out domestic violence reports must include whether they thought it necessary to inquire if a firearm or other deadly weapon was present at the location and, if so, whether any were actually present.[14] Any such firearm or deadly weapon is subject to seizure.

Any firearm or other deadly weapon seized at a "domestic violence" incident must be held by law enforcement for *at least* 48 hours.[15] As discussed below, however, it may take much longer than this to get the firearm back.

## C. Firearm Seizures for Mental Examination

Law enforcement *must* seize any firearms or other deadly weapons owned or possessed by someone who has been detained to examine his or her mental condition, or if that person is someone described in W.I.C. §§ 8100 or 8103.[16]

After seizing the firearm, law enforcement must notify the person of the return procedure.[17] If the person is being kept in a mental health facility, the person in charge of the facility, or a designee, must notify the person of this return procedure.[18] The health facility must also tell the confiscating law enforcement agency when the person is released, and shall make a note that they provided the required notice about the return procedure to that person.[19]

## D. Confiscating Firearms or Deadly Weapons from Gang Members

P.C. § 186.22a allows law enforcement to take firearms or other deadly weapons that are owned or possessed by "criminal street gang" members[20] when those firearms are possessed to commit any of the offenses listed in P.C. § 186.22(e).[21]

---

[14] P.C. § 13730(c)(3).

[15] P.C. § 18265(a).

[16] W.I.C. § 8102(a). *See* Chapter 3 for descriptions of persons covered by W.I.C. §§ 8100 and 8103.

[17] W.I.C. § 8102(b).

[18] W.I.C. § 8102(b).

[19] W.I.C. § 8102(b); *People v. One Ruger .22-Caliber Pistol,* 84 Cal.App.4th 310, 314 (2000).

[20] P.C.§ 186.22(f) defines "criminal street gang" as "any ongoing organization, association, or group of three or more persons, whether formal or informal, . . . [whose] primary activities [include] the commission of one or more of the criminal acts enumerated in paragraphs (1) to (25), inclusive, or (31) to (33), inclusive, of subdivision (e), [of P.C. § 186.22] having a common name or common identifying sign or symbol, and whose members individually or collectively engage in or have engaged in a pattern of criminal gang activity."

[21] P.C. § 186.22a(f)(1).

## E. Seizure of Firearms to Determine Whether They Are Loaded

When a law enforcement officer lawfully comes across a firearm "carried"[22] in most public places, California law allows the officer to inspect it to see if it is loaded.[23] Refusing the inspection gives the officer probable cause to arrest for violating P.C. § 25850(a) – the law against carrying a loaded firearm in public.[24]

These *temporary* seizures may last longer and possibly become permanent if the officer discovers the firearm is loaded. If no criminal activity is suspected, a firearm seizure should end as soon as the officer determines it is unloaded. Otherwise the officer could be violating the Fourth Amendment.[25]

## F. Seizure of Firearms Illegally Used or Possessed

Firearms discovered in public, whether through a lawful search or in plain view, may be seized if probable cause exists to associate the firearm with criminal activity.[26] This means that if law enforcement finds firearms being unlawfully carried openly, concealed, loaded, brandished,[27] used in any other crime, or possessed by someone prohibited from possessing or owning firearms, the firearms may be seized.

## G. Restraining Orders

People prohibited from possessing firearms because they have certain restraining orders[28] against them must either surrender their firearms to law enforcement or sell them to an FFL within 24 hours of being served with the order. These are their *only* two options in this situation. This requirement is for any firearm in, or subject to, their immediate possession or

---

[22] "Carried" generally means when a firearm is on your person (body or attached thereto) or in your vehicle. *See* Chapter 5 for a more detailed definition.

[23] P.C. § 25850(b).

[24] P.C. § 25850(b). This practice arguably violates the Fourth Amendment right against unreasonable search and seizures, but is currently allowed in California. Despite this, officers must still have either discovered the firearm while conducting a lawful search or "pat-down," or the firearm must have been in plain view. *See Terry v. Ohio*, 392 U.S. 1 (1968). Note also that, as explained in Chapter 5, if you are not in a place where loaded firearms are prohibited, then law enforcement is not entitled to inspect your firearm, even under California law.

[25] *United States v. Sharpe*, 470 U.S. 675, 682-683 (1985).

[26] *Payton v. New York*, 445 U.S. 573, 586-587 (1980).

[27] P.C. § 417.

[28] Restraining orders issued pursuant to: C.C.P. §§ 527.6, 527.8, 527.85; P.C. § 136.2; W.I.C. § 15657.03. C.C.P. § 527.9. *See* Chapter 3 for further discussion of these restraining orders.

control because these types of orders prohibit restrained persons from possessing or controlling *any* firearm *for the duration of the order.*[29] Within 48 hours of receiving the order, the restrained person must file a receipt with the court showing that any firearms in, or subject to, their "immediate possession or control" were surrendered to law enforcement or sold to an FFL.[30]

For court orders issued under the Family Code,[31] the requirements are slightly different. These types of protective orders, defined in Family Code § 6218,[32] require any firearm in, or subject to, a person's immediate possession or control to be safely surrendered to a law enforcement officer upon request after being served with the protective order.[33] If law enforcement does not demand otherwise, the restrained person must dispose of his or her firearms as outlined above, *i.e.*, turn in or sell them within 24 hours of being served and show proof to the court within 48 hours of being served.

California statutes do not specifically address how persons should dispose of their firearms once they become prohibited from possessing the firearms by a protective order issued pursuant to P.C. § 646.91. But, P.C. § 29825(d) requires that all restraining orders state that the firearms must "be relinquished to the local law enforcement agency for that jurisdiction or sold to a licensed gun dealer, and that proof of surrender or sale shall be filed within a specified time of receipt of the order." Thus, presumably the same procedure for surrendering firearms for other restraining orders also applies to P.C. § 646.91 orders, unless the order expressly says otherwise.

### 1. Exemption Allowing Continued Possession of a Firearm for an Employment Purpose

In certain specific cases the court may grant an exemption for a particular firearm from the relinquishment requirement of any of the above-mentioned restraining orders.[34]

---

[29] C.C.P § 527.9(a)-(b), (e).

[30] C.C.P. § 527.9(b). Pursuant to C.C.P. § 527.9(g), an individual can sell the firearms in law enforcement's possession to an FFL. Once an FFL presents a bill of sale or receipt showing that all firearms owned by the restrained person have been sold to him or her, the FFL shall be given those firearms within five days of presenting that receipt to law enforcement.

[31] Restraining orders will typically specify under what law the order is issued.

[32] These orders include those issued under Fam. Code § 6320 (enjoining specific abuse), § 6321 (excluding a person from a dwelling), and § 6322 (enjoining other specific behavior).

[33] Fam. Code § 6389(c)(2). This scenario raises serious Fourth and Fifth Amendment concerns because the court is essentially requiring restrained persons to give law enforcement their property without a valid warrant. Family Code § 6389(d) allows those who are served with a Family Code protective order to invoke Fifth Amendment protection and receive "use immunity" (*e.g.*, information provided to law enforcement could not be used against them), but such an invocation of rights is unlikely when a person is faced with a valid court order and armed law enforcement officers are demanding the firearms.

[34] C.C.P. § 527.9(f); Fam. Code § 6389(h). This exception does not appear to apply for orders issued per P.C. § 646.91.

To qualify, the person subject to the order must show that a particular firearm is necessary as a condition of continued employment and that the current employer is unable to reassign the person to another position where a firearm is unnecessary. Or, if the person is a peace officer, he or she may be able to continue to carry a firearm, either on duty or off duty, if the court finds the officer does not "pose a threat of harm."[35]

## H. Limitations on Law Enforcement's Seizing Powers

Sometimes law enforcement asserts that the laws allowing it to seize firearms at a domestic violence incident or mental health commitment also allow it to enter buildings, search for, and seize firearms. This is incorrect. The Fourth Amendment (*i.e.*, warrant) constitutional protections and requirements cannot be bypassed by a state's penal code. People mistakenly allow law enforcement to enter their home and consent to having their property seized for "safe keeping." If the "domestic violence" incident or mental health detention occurred outside of one's home, law enforcement *should not* enter the home and seize firearms without a warrant, permission from an occupant, or via another warrant exception.[36]

Nevertheless, law enforcement officers will often claim it is their "policy" to seize firearms at a "domestic violence" or mental health incident or will ask the owner if they may take firearms for "safe keeping," even after determining no "domestic violence" or mental health incident occurred. You should *never volunteer* to turn your firearms over to law enforcement unless instructed to do so by your attorney. Doing so may subject you to unrelated criminal charges for unknowingly violating a firearm law like possessing an unregistered "assault weapon."[37] Or it may cause you a costly hassle trying to get it back. Just like you should exercise your right to remain silent when questioned by law enforcement, you should not give them evidence that can be used against you unless the law *requires* you to do so.

---

[35] C.C.P. § 527.9(a), (f); Fam. Code, § 6389(a), (h).

[36] *See People v. Sweig*, 167 Cal.App.4th 1145 (2008) *review granted and opinion superseded*, 90 Cal. Rptr.3d 343 (2009). While the *Sweig* case has been de-published (by grant of review to the California Supreme Court), its reasoning that the search of a person's home generally requires a warrant, consent, or an exception to the warrant requirement is sound. "[T]here is no legitimate reason an officer would have thought he could enter a residence without a warrant to confiscate a weapon any more than he could have assumed he could enter a residence to confiscate known contraband absent exigent circumstances." *Cole v. City of Sunnyvale* (N.D. Cal., Sept. 14, 2011, C-08-05017 RMW) 2011 WL 4346510.

[37] *See* Chapter 8 for definitions of "assault weapon."

# III. LAW ENFORCEMENT PROCEDURE WHEN RECEIVING FIREARMS

Whenever law enforcement officers take a firearm into custody, they must give you a receipt that specifically describes the firearm(s) they have taken and lists any serial number(s) or other identifying marks such as the manufacturer and model. This receipt must also tell you where and when the firearm may be recovered and any applicable time limit for its recovery.[38]

Additionally, whenever law enforcement officers seize or receive a firearm, *they* are required to enter the firearm into the AFS.[39] All information entered into the AFS must remain there until the reported firearm has been found or recovered, is no longer under observation, or the record is determined to have been entered in error.[40]

# IV. "NUISANCE" FIREARMS

In some instances, firearms taken or held by law enforcement may be considered a "nuisance." A firearm is considered a "nuisance" under California law when:

- A conviction[41] is secured for any misdemeanor or felony[42] where the firearm was used in the crime (P.C. § 29300(a));
- The firearm was possessed by someone prohibited from possessing or owning firearms due to age, previous conviction, restraining order, or mental health restriction (P.C. §§ 29300, 18000(a));[43]
- The firearm is found being carried concealed unlawfully (P.C. § 25700(a));
- Any firearm in custody for more than 12 months and unrecovered by its owner or lawful possessor will be viewed as a "nuisance." ( P.C. § 18275(a)).[44]

---

[38] P.C. § 33800.

[39] P.C. § 11108(a).

[40] P.C. § 11108(b).

[41] "A finding that the defendant was guilty of the offense but was insane at the time the offense was committed is a conviction for the purposes of this section." P.C. §§ 29300(b), 18000(c).

[42] This includes offenses by juveniles where the court finds the offense would be a misdemeanor or felony if committed by an adult. P.C. §§ 18000(a), 29300(a).

[43] *See* Chapter 3 for an explanation of what persons are prohibited. *See also* 84 Ops. Cal. Atty. Gen. 01-211 (2001) (concluding that a "law enforcement officer may seize a firearm from a person on the basis that the person is the subject of an 'emergency protective order' if the order includes an existing restraining order as specified in Family Code section 6218.").

[44] The exception to this is if the firearm is being used as evidence in a criminal trial; it will not be released until after it is no longer needed. At that point you will have 180 days before the firearm is treated as a nuisance. *See* P.C. § 34000.

"Nuisance" firearms are surrendered to a sheriff, police chief, other head of a municipal police department including the University of California or California State University police chief, or the California Highway Patrol Commissioner.[45]

A firearm that is in the possession of the Department of Fish and Game and was used in the violation of any Fish and Game Code or any regulation thereunder, or forfeited per Public Resources Code § 5008.6 (P.C. §§ 25700(b), 29300(d)), is not considered a "nuisance." Rather, these firearms are automatically forfeited. Nor is a firearm considered to be a "nuisance" under California law even though it would otherwise be a "nuisance" due to a conviction for a crime in which the firearm was used or for possession by a prohibited person, unless the firearm is disposed of per P.C. § 29810 (P.C. § 29300(c)).[46] If the firearm is disposed of like this, the court should provide a DOJ-supplied form to facilitate this kind of firearm transfer.

# V. GETTING BACK SEIZED OR FORFEITED FIREARMS

When law enforcement or courts end up with firearms – whether they were seized, forfeited, or surrendered – constitutional due process entitles the rightful possessor to a way to recover them. Of course, sometimes the law precludes a firearm's return.

## A. Firearm Return Procedure

### 1. General Requirements[47]

If you want your firearm(s) back from a court or law enforcement agency, you have to submit a form called a Law Enforcement Gun Release (LEGR) application to the DOJ to confirm you are not prohibited from possessing firearms.[48] This application is available at http://ag.ca.gov/firearms/forms/pdf/legr.pdf.

---

[45] P.C. § 18000(a). Per P.C. § 18000(b), the California Highway Patrol Commissioner shall only receive weapons confiscated by a California Highway Patrol member.

[46] Though it is generally assumed that firearms used in crimes are immediately forfeited per P.C. § 29300, that assumption may be inaccurate. Subsection (c) suggests that firearms used in a crime or possessed by a prohibited person may be transferred by a defendant. However, since P.C. § 245(e) classifies a firearm used in an assault with a deadly weapon as a "nuisance" if it is owned by the individual convicted, that individual definitely does not have the option of transferring their firearm per P.C. § 29300.

[47] *See* P.C. §§ 33850-33895.

[48] P.C. § 33865. Those prohibited from possessing firearms are discussed in Chapter 3.

LEGR information requirements are explained in P.C. § 33850 and vary with the type of firearm in law enforcement custody. You must list your identifying information and the agency that has the firearm. For *handguns*, you must provide the handgun type (*i.e.*, semiautomatic, revolver, single-shot, etc.) and its serial number, make, model, country of origin, caliber, and barrel length. The DOJ must then record this information in the AFS.[49] For non-"assault weapon" *long guns* and other non-handguns[50] you only need to list your identifying information and the agency that has your non-handguns.[51]

The DOJ generally must process the LEGR within 30 days.[52] Once the DOJ determines whether or not you are prohibited from possessing firearms, you will be sent a letter explaining your legal status. If the DOJ determines you are prohibited from possessing firearms, the firearm cannot be released to you, but, as explained below, you may still have the right to direct the firearm's transfer to someone else. If the DOJ determines you *are* allowed to possess firearms, you will be sent a Law Enforcement Gun Release - Firearms Eligibility Clearance letter (LEGR Letter) that you will then take to the agency that has your firearm.[53] The LEGR Letter is not proof that you are necessarily *entitled* to the firearm's return, only that the agency may lawfully return it to you.

Once you present the LEGR Letter to the agency with the seized firearm(s), if the agency has direct access to the AFS at that time, it is *required* to verify that the firearm is not reported lost or stolen and that it was recorded into the AFS in the name of the person seeking its return – *i.e., you.*[54]

The last requirement above causes a lot of confusion for law enforcement agencies and the DOJ. The DOJ presumes that if a firearm does not appear in the AFS, the person seeking its return is required to show proof of ownership. This practice is incorrect and has unfortunately been passed on to local law enforcement agencies holding peoples' firearms.

---

[49] P.C. § 33865(d).

[50] An "assault weapon" or .50 BMG rifle, as described in Chapter 8, can only be returned to the person listed in the AFS as the registered owner because no one else (other than an FFL with the proper licensing) is allowed to lawfully possess these firearms. P.C. §§ 30910, 30930. If the registered owner is deceased, these firearms can be transferred to an FFL with the proper licensing. P.C. §§ 30915, 30935.

[51] The information required on an LEGR for handguns will apply to all firearms beginning January 1, 2014, per Assembly Bill 809 (2011).

[52] P.C. § 33865(b). Keep a record of the date you submit the LEGR and/or obtain a delivery receipt from the DOJ. This will identify when the 30-day period began if delay becomes an issue. You can also contact the DOJ to find out the reason for any delay.

[53] According to the DOJ, the LEGR Letter is only valid for 30 days from the date appearing on the letter, likely because federal law voids your background check after 30 days. *See* 27 C.F.R. § 478.102(c).

[54] P.C. § 33855(b), *see also* P.C. § 11108. Per P.C. § 11108.5, if an agency identifies a firearm as lost or stolen, it must notify the person entitled to the firearm's possession within 15 days.

Recall from above that whenever law enforcement officers seize or receive a firearm, *they* are required to enter the firearm into the AFS.[55] Therefore, upon returning it, the firearm's information as it relates to you should *already* have been entered into the AFS. This means that when law enforcement officers check the AFS, as they are required to do before they return the firearm, the firearm's information should already be there. But often law enforcement will fail to enter seized or surrendered firearms into the AFS upon receipt. This sometimes creates a situation where they cannot comply with the requirement that they confirm a firearm is in the AFS in the person's name seeking its return.

Moreover the DOJ and law enforcement have, by misreading the AFS check requirement, incorrectly required that firearms be actually *registered* in the AFS to the person, rather than just entered into AFS, without necessarily having a person's name associated with it or with the name of the person seeking the return of the firearm. Thus, even if law enforcement officers recorded the firearm in the AFS upon receipt as they are supposed to do, they may still refuse to release the firearm to you without additional proof of ownership. This is nonsensical because, as discussed in Chapter 4, very few firearms are required to be registered in the AFS in the owner's name.

A handgun will only be "registered" to a specific person if it was acquired through an FFL (though sometimes information is entered into the AFS incorrectly or, albeit rarely, not at all by the FFL), or registered by the individual (following an intra-familial transfer, by a personal handgun importer moving into the state, through voluntary registration, etc.). Handguns brought into the state before the time that handguns were required to be registered will likely not be in the AFS as registered to anyone unless voluntarily registered. And handguns not transferred though an FFL (whether by a PPT before the law required transfers to go through dealers or an illegal PPT transfer after the year 1991) will not be registered in the recipient's name unless voluntarily registered. A safe assumption is, if you did not obtain the handgun through an FFL in California or register the handgun yourself, it probably is not in the AFS registered under your name.

And long gun transfer information is not required to be recorded in the AFS at all, so there is no "registration" information in the AFS for most long guns in California[56] (with the exception of lawfully registered "assault weapons," .50 BMG rifles, or those who voluntarily registered their long guns).

---

[55] P.C. § 11108.

[56] P.C. § 11106(b).

Because thousands of firearms are not required to be registered in the AFS, the DOJ and law enforcement's requirement that firearms be registered in the AFS to the person seeking their return is unworkable, as often is their requiring proof of ownership, receipts, or other documentation. The odd thing about this requirement is that you are not required to keep paperwork on your firearms in the first place. It is a good idea to keep documentation in general, but for almost everyone else in California (excepting FFLs) you are not required to keep paperwork on your firearms. The paperwork requirement becomes even more bizarre when you consider firearms that have been in families for generations. What are the chances of someone still having paperwork for a firearm inherited from a grandfather 30 years ago or more?

Nevertheless some agencies will refuse to return firearms if the person cannot show proof of ownership. And while a firearm's legal owner cannot be required to request a post-storage hearing as a prerequisite to having their firearm released,[57] requesting one may be necessary if the agency so refuses. If this happens to you, contact an attorney.

### 2. Stolen Firearms

Any stolen firearm that is recovered must be returned to the lawful owner as soon as its use as evidence has been served upon the owner's identification of the firearm and proof of ownership and after the agency possessing the firearms complies with P.C. §§ 33850-33895 (*i.e.*, accepts an LEGR Letter, verifies the firearm is in the AFS, etc.). This applies even if the firearm was used by the thief or other person in a way that made it a "nuisance," as long as the owner did not have prior knowledge that the firearm was being used in such a way.[58]

### 3. Firearms Seized at "Domestic Violence" Incidents

As mentioned earlier, law enforcement must keep firearms or other deadly weapons seized from "domestic violence" incidents for at least 48 hours.[59] Subject to a law enforcement petition described below, if a firearm or other deadly weapon is not kept as evidence for a criminal prosecution or considered stolen or "contraband," it must be released to the rightful possessor after the 48 hours and no later than five business days after the rightful possessor demonstrates compliance with P.C. §§ 33850-33895 (*i.e.*, sub-

---

[57] P.C. § 33880(e).

[58] P.C. § 18005(b). This does not apply to "contraband" firearms, which generally cannot be returned under any circumstances.

[59] P.C. § 18265(a).

mits an LEGR to the DOJ and an LEGR Letter to the agency with custody of the firearm, pays all applicable fees, etc.).[60]

## B. Firearm Returns Delayed by Criminal Proceedings

Law enforcement may delay returning firearms to their legitimate owner while waiting to use them as "evidence"[61] in a criminal case.[62] If law enforcement believes the firearm was used in a murder (a crime with no statute of limitations) and the firearm could be used as evidence, the owner may never get the firearm back.[63]

Property used as "evidence"[64] is usually not returned until 60 days after a case is finalized.[65] If an appeal is not filed, criminal proceedings are generally considered final 30 days after the last day to file an appeal.[66] At that time, the court must notify the person from whom the property was taken that he or she may pick up their property *free of charge* within 15 days. Priority is given to the person the property was originally taken from, as long as that person was the lawful possessor at the time the firearms were confiscated. Property may also be released to the person who establishes title or right of possession.[67]

Notwithstanding the rules above, if the owner of a firearm being used as "evidence" in a criminal case is also a defendant in that case and wants to do so, he or she can get the firearm returned faster than as provided in

---

[60] P.C. § 18265(b).

[61] A distinction needs to be made here. In the course of an investigation, a large quantity of firearms may be seized; however, only one or two of the firearms may be considered illegal or associated with a crime. These firearms would be considered "evidence." The other firearms, which are not illegal or allegedly used in the commission of a crime (*e.g.*, a murder weapon or firearms illegally imported, manufactured, etc.), can and should be returned as soon as possible once law enforcement has determined the property is of no evidentiary value and the person is not prohibited from possessing firearms. Often, law enforcement is content to keep all property until the end of a criminal case. But once a criminal case has begun and it is apparent that certain items are not necessary for the case, those items should be requested returned via a non-statutory motion to return property.

[62] P.C. § 11108.5(b).

[63] Because murder has no "statute of limitations," this means the case can be open forever. P.C. § 799.

[64] Property to be used in a hearing or trial is referred to as an "exhibit."

[65] P.C. § 1417.5.

[66] P.C. § 1417.1. A case is also considered final "[w]hen a notice of appeal is filed, 30 days after the date the clerk of the court receives the remittitur affirming the judgment[;] [w]hen an order for a rehearing, a new trial, or other proceeding is granted and the ordered proceedings have not been commenced within one year thereafter, one year after the date of that order. In cases where the death penalty is imposed, 30 days after the date of execution of sentence." P.C. § 1417.1.

[67] P.C. § 1417.5(a)-(b). It should be noted that the provisions in P.C. § 1417.6 states that the provisions in P.C. § 1417.5 do not apply to the release of "deadly or dangerous weapons," and instead prohibits their release – apparently to anyone. It is unclear whether this includes otherwise lawful firearms, but it most likely does *not*. If it did, any time firearms were used as evidence in a crime they would be automatically forfeited, even if it were through no fault of the lawful owner. This does not comport with the vast protections California affords lawful firearms owners to have their firearms returned to them. P.C. § 1417.6 most likely applies to weapons that are generally illegal to possess.

P.C. § 1417.5 by stipulating for its release with the prosecutor, or by asking the court.[68] The owner-defendant may also make a statutory motion for returning a lawful firearm if it is alleged the seizure was improper (*e.g.*, invalid search warrant).[69]

If the owner of a seized firearm is *not* a defendant in a pending criminal action tied to the firearm or its seizure, the owner can still get the firearm back by submitting a non-statutory motion for property return.[70]

Additionally courts must return any property that appears different than what the warrant described or when the court determines no probable cause existed for the warrant in the first place.[71]

## C. If Returning Firearms Is Dangerous

If the agency with custody of a firearm reasonably believes that returning the firearm would endanger either the person seeking its return or someone else, the agency may petition for a court hearing to determine whether the firearm should be returned.

Where a firearm is seized from a "domestic violence"[72] incident, the agency with custody of the firearm must file the petition within 60 days of the firearm's seizure and notify the person seeking the firearm's return of the petition.[73]

If the firearm was seized because its possessor was detained for a mental health evaluation, the agency must file the petition and notify the person of the petition within 30 days of the person's release from the mental health facility.[74] If it does not, the agency must make the firearm available.

For firearms seized from a gang member, there is no specific time limit for the seizing agency to file such a petition,[75] though due process likely demands that any delay be reasonable.

All such petitions require law enforcement to inform the person seeking the firearm's return of the petition by providing written notice to the

---

[68] P.C. § 1417.2. This procedure does not apply to firearms that are prohibited from being released per P.C. § 1417.6.

[69] P.C. § 1538.5(a)(1).

[70] *See generally People v. Lamonte*, 53 Cal.App.4th 544, 549-552 (1997) (although in *Lamonte* it was the defendant who made a non-statutory motion for the return of his property, this procedure is equally available for a person who is not a defendant in a proceeding).

[71] P.C. § 1540.

[72] Pursuant to P.C. § 18250.

[73] P.C. § 18400. The law enforcement agency may request an extension of time but must file the petition no later than 90 days from the date of the seizure. P.C. § 18400(c).

[74] W.I.C. § 8102. An extension to file the petition may be requested in this situation too, but in no case may the petition be filed later than 60 days after the person is released from the health facility. W.I.C. § 8102(c).

[75] P.C. § 186.22a(f)(2).

person's "last known address."[76] The person then has 30 days from receiving the notice to respond and confirm a desire for a hearing to contest the petition. Failure to respond in a timely manner will result in forfeiting the firearm to the agency.[77]

If the person seeking return of the firearm responds to the agency's petition within the allotted time, it is up to the agency to prove that returning the firearm would likely endanger the person's safety and/or that of others.[78] In cases where an agency seizes firearms from a member of a criminal street gang, the "burden of proof" is upon the agency or peace officer to show by a preponderance of the evidence that the seized item is or will be used in criminal street gang activity or that return of the item would be likely to result in endangering the safety of others."[79]

## D. Asset Forfeitures

Both California and federal law allow the government to demand the forfeiture of firearms and other property used in certain crimes or that have been obtained through criminal acts.[80] These cases are usually civil, rather than criminal, have a lower burden of proof, and usually do not require a jury.[81] Forfeitures are usually complicated proceedings that can be time consuming and costly. If you find yourself in this situation, get an attorney if you do not already have one.

## E. When Seized Firearms Cannot Be Returned

The person from whom property is seized is presumed to have a right to have it returned. And once the case is over, "even if the seizure was lawful, the government must justify its continued possession of the property by demonstrating that it is *contraband* or subject to forfeiture."[82]

---

[76] W.I.C. § 8102(e); P.C. § 186.22a(f)(3). Per P.C. § 18405, a person's "last known address" is presumed to be the address the person gives to law enforcement at the time of the "domestic violence" incident. P.C. § 18405(b). If persons who are the subject of a restraining order are prohibited from returning to the address they provided to law enforcement, it is possible they will not receive notice of the forfeiture proceedings.

[77] P.C. §§ 18005(d), 186.22a(f)(6). P.C. § 18405 and W.I.C. § 8102(e) allows the law enforcement agency in these situations to petition for an order of default.

[78] W.I.C. § 8102, P.C. § 18410.

[79] P.C. § 186.22a(f)(5).

[80] 21 U.S.C. § 881(a)(7); 18 U.S.C. § 924(d). *See also* Cal. Health & Saf. Code § 11469 *et seq.* for examples.

[81] *See* Cal. Health & Saf. Code § 11488.4 for examples. *People v. One 1941 Chevrolet Coupe*, 37 Cal.2d 283 (1951).

[82] *United States v. Martinson*, 809 F.2d 1364, 1369 (9th Cir.1987) (emphasis added).

Several justifications exist for the government to retain seized firearms.

## 1.  Illegal Firearms – "Contraband"

If a firearm is "contraband," the owner might not be entitled to its return or compensation because merely possessing such a firearm is a crime.[83] Though not defined in the Penal Code, "contraband" is generally defined as "goods or merchandise whose importation, exportation, or possession is forbidden."[84]

"Contraband is of two types: contraband *per se* and derivative contraband. Contraband *per se* consists of objects which are 'intrinsically illegal in character,' 'the possession of which, without more, constitutes a crime.' "[85] "Courts will not entertain a claim contesting the [seizure] of contraband *per se* because" returning this type of property would be against the law prohibiting its possession in the first place.[86] A typical example of contraband *per se* is an illicit drug like heroine.

"By contrast, derivative contraband includes items which are not inherently unlawful but which may become unlawful because of the use to which they are put . . ." Generally a firearm "is not inherently illegal; its possession, 'without more,' [usually] does not constitute a crime."[87]

This means that firearms are usually *not* contraband *per se*, but can be derivative contraband if they are unlawfully possessed (*e.g.*, by someone prohibited from possessing firearms). Moreover, though possessing an item in a crime does *not* necessarily make that item "contraband" under California law,[88] the use or possession of an otherwise lawful firearm can cause the firearm to be become a "nuisance." But as discussed above, "nuisance" firearms can be returned or released.

Additionally firearms used in violation of the Fish and Game Code may be subject to forfeiture upon conviction of the offense.[89]

---

[83] P.C. § 1417.6(a). *See also Trupiano v. United States,* 334 U.S. 699, 710 (1948); *Chavez v. Superior Court,* 123 Cal.App.4th 104 (2004).

[84] WEBSTER'S SEVENTH NEW COLLEGIATE DICTIONARY (1970 ed.); "The Winston Dictionary (1944 ed.) and the Random House Dictionary (1970 ed.) both define contraband in the same manner." *In re Jordan,* 7 Cal.3d 930, 936 (1972).

[85] *Cooper v. City of Greenwood, Miss.,* 904 F.2d 302, 304 (5th Cir. 1990) (emphasis in original).

[86] *Cooper v. City of Greenwood, Miss.* 904 F.2d 302, 305 (5th Cir. 1990) (emphasis in original) (citing *One 1958 Plymouth Sedan v. Pennsylvania,* 380 U.S. 693, 699-700 (1965)). Even when contraband per se is illegally seized it cannot be returned.

[87] *Cooper v. City of Greenwood, Miss.,* 904 F.2d 302, 305 (5th Cir. 1990).

[88] *People v. Lamonte,* 53 Cal. App. 4th 544, 552-553 (1997).

[89] Fish & Game Code § 12157 *et seq.*

## 2. Prohibited Persons

Likewise, if the person seeking the firearm's return belongs to a class of prohibited persons,[90] the agency with custody of the firearm *cannot* release it to that person. What to do in those situations is discussed below.

## 3. Stolen Firearms

Law enforcement must check the AFS to confirm a firearm has not been reported lost or stolen. Where the firearm has been reported lost or stolen, law enforcement must notify the owner or person entitled to possess the firearms and cannot release the firearm to you if you are not that person.[91] When firearms that were turned in because of a restraining order are found to be stolen, they must be returned to the rightful owner upon identifying the firearm and providing proof of ownership.[92]

## F. Other Options for Owners Who Cannot Receive Their Firearms

### 1. Federal Firearms Licensee (FFL) or Third-Party Transfers

If you are found to be ineligible for the return of your firearms, you may still have the right to have your firearms transferred or sold to an FFL and keep the revenue.[93] People in this situation are supposed to be provided a form for such a transfer by the California DOJ or a court, depending on whether their LEGR was denied or a court convicted them of a prohibiting offense.[94]

# VI. FEES ASSOCIATED WITH FIREARM SEIZURES

California allows the DOJ and local law enforcement agencies to charge storage fees to those recovering seized or surrendered firearms. What the DOJ can charge for, and the permissible fee amounts, are generally governed by P.C. § 33880.

---

[90] *See* Chapter 3.

[91] *See* P.C. § 33855(b)-(c).

[92] C.C.P. § 527.9(e).

[93] P.C. § 33850(b). The law is quiet on whether a person has the right to transfer firearms to an FFL where the agency successfully petitions the court to declare it unsafe for the firearms to be returned. Presumably, since the same due process issues are implicated, such a person should have this option.

[94] P.C. §§ 29810(a), 33865(e).

## A. Local Law Enforcement's Permissible Fees

Law enforcement agencies are allowed to charge administrative costs for firearm seizure, impounding, storage, and/or release as long as they are not more than the agency's actual expense costs.[95] These administrative fees *may* be waived if proof exists that the firearm was reported stolen at the time law enforcement took control of it.[96] If the fees are not waived, any administrative costs must only be charged to the person claiming title to the firearm(s).[97] Fees may not be charged for hearings or appeals regarding the firearm's removal, impound, storage, or release unless the hearing or appeal was requested in writing by the legal owner of the firearm.[98]

## B. Attorneys' Fees

In actions to recover unreturned firearms from a law enforcement agency, reasonable attorney's fees may be awarded to the "prevailing party."[99] A "prevailing party" may be the agency if you lose. Thus, before you bring this action, be aware that you may end up responsible for the agency's attorneys' fees.

## C. Law Enforcement Gun Release (LEGR) Application Fees

The DOJ charges a fee for each LEGR request it handles to recover its processing costs. The fee is $20 for the first firearm (handgun or long gun) and $3 for each additional firearm you are seeking returned.[100] You do not have to pay these fees, if the firearm was reported as lost or stolen *before* law enforcement took custody of it or within five business days after it was stolen.[101]

---

[95] P.C. §§ 33880(a)-(b). Note that P.C. § 1417.5(b) says that an evidence exhibit must be returned "free of charge." Therefore, presumably, if your firearms were used as evidence, you should not be charged any fees for their return, though this appears to contradict the LEGR storage and fee requirements.

[96] P.C. § 33880(c).

[97] P.C. § 33880(d)(1).

[98] P.C. § 33880(d)(4).

[99] P.C. § 33885.

[100] P.C. § 33860.

[101] P.C. § 33855(d).

# VII. DESTROYING SEIZED/SURRENDERED FIREARMS AND ALTERNATIVES[102]

## A. "Nuisance" and Abandoned Firearms May be Destroyed

Law enforcement can destroy any "nuisance" or "contraband" firearm unless the court or district attorney deems it necessary or proper to preserve it.[103]

Law enforcement may also destroy a "non-nuisance" firearm that is otherwise lawful to possess, but only where a court or law enforcement agency has notified the firearm owner that the firearm is available for return and the owner does not claim the firearm within 180 days of being so notified.[104] Likewise, if such a firearm was used as an exhibit in a criminal action or proceeding, the law enforcement agency possessing the firearm can destroy it after 180 days have passed from when it is no longer needed if it is unclaimed or abandoned.[105]

And no stolen firearm that is recovered may be destroyed unless reasonable notice is first given to the owner, if the owner's identity and address can be reasonably ascertained.[106]

If a law enforcement agency has your property, and the matter it is associated with has ended, be sure the agency does not destroy your property. They will often try to contact you at the same address the property was taken from or use the address on your driver's license to send this notice. If you moved or do not use the address on your driver's license for mail, contact the agency holding your firearms and make sure it has a way to contact you. Then follow-up with the agency.

---

[102] Per P.C. § 29300(d), this section does not apply to firearm(s) possessed by the Fish and Game Department, that were used to violate any Fish and Game Code provision or regulation, or that were forfeited per Code of Public Resources § 5008.6. Code of Public Resources is hereafter abbreviated as "C. Pub. Res."

[103] P.C. § 18005(c).

[104] P.C. § 33875.

[105] P.C. § 34000. Per P.C. § 18275(b), however, firearms or other deadly weapons seized or turned over from a "domestic violence" incident that are not recovered within 12 months because of an extended hearing process may *not* be destroyed until the court issues a decision. They may thereafter be destroyed only if they are not ordered returned to the owner. It would seem the owner in this situation should generally be allowed to sell the firearms to an FFL in lieu of their destruction if they were not used in a crime.

[106] P.C. § 18005(d).

## B. Alternatives to Destroying Firearms

When firearms[107] are subject to destruction, law enforcement agencies are not always *required* to destroy them. There are alternatives. The agency may: 1) keep them, or any of their parts, to carry out their official duties; 2) *upon court approval,* release them to any other law enforcement agency for their official duties, or 3) if the firearm would be useful to the National Guard, Coast Guard, or military, with the permission of the city, county, or both, deliver the firearm to the commanding officer of the military unit.[108]

Alternatively law enforcement agencies may sell them to FFLs at a public auction.[109]

Regardless of whether a law enforcement agency keeps custody of a seized firearm or destroys it, the agency must notify the DOJ. This notification must completely describe each firearm, including its "manufacturer or brand name, model, caliber, and serial number."[110]

---

[107] As used here, the term "firearms" does not include "destructive devices," as defined in P.C. § 16460.

[108] *See* P.C. § 34005(a), (b), (d). Per P.C. § 34005(d)(3), "[a]ll firearms released to an academy shall be under the care, custody, and control of the particular academy."

[109] P.C. § 18005(a).

[110] P.C. § 34010.

## CHAPTER 11

# SELF-DEFENSE AND USE OF FORCE

## I. LAWFUL SELF-DEFENSE

**H**omicide is the killing of a human being by another human being.[1] If not legally justified, homicide is among the most serious of crimes. Criminal homicide could be murder or manslaughter. Murder is potentially punishable by life in prison, or even by the death penalty. If done in self-defense (or defense of another), however, a homicide *may* be justifiable.

In evaluating your claim of acting in self-defense, police, prosecutors, juries, and judges will consider many factors, even those which are not legally relevant. This was discussed to some extent in Chapter 1. These factors will include whether your possession of the firearm was lawful, as well as the type of firearm used. Illegal possession of a firearm can place you at a disadvantage in establishing your claim of lawful self-defense. No matter how justifiable a shooting may be, if you illegally possessed the firearm at the time of the shooting, you may still be charged with illegal possession of a firearm. There are, however, some exceptions to this general rule.[2]

The type of firearm, caliber of ammunition, and type of ammunition used will also be considered. Depending on the circumstances, certain types of ammunition and firearms may be difficult to justify, especially if you miss the trespasser in your house and accidentally hit a neighbor inside his home two blocks away, or even a loved one in the next room.

---

[1] The rules of self-defense and defense of others also apply to using force against animals. For example, you have a right to reasonable self-defense if confronted by an aggressive dog. *People v. Lee*, 131 Cal. App.4th 1413, 1429 (2005).

[2] *See People v. King*, 22 Cal.3d 12, 26 (1978), discussed later in this chapter.

## II. THE ELEMENTS OF A "SELF-DEFENSE" DEFENSE

Criminal defendants in murder and manslaughter cases are presumed innocent until proven guilty beyond a reasonable doubt.[3] Prosecutors have the burden of proving beyond a reasonable doubt that a defendant's killing or injury against another was unlawful.

In California,[4] when a defendant relies on the defense of lawful self-defense, the jury will be instructed on the fact that the defendant's actions may have been done in lawful self-defense.[5] If you are the defendant, you will want to show that:

- You reasonably believed that you, or another person, were in imminent danger of being killed or suffering great bodily injury, or in imminent danger of being raped/maimed/robbed or suffering from a forcible and atrocious crime;[6]
- You reasonably believed using immediate deadly force was necessary to defend against that imminent danger; *and*
- You only used no more force than was reasonably necessary to defend against that danger.[7]

Even though showing the above elements will help reduce your likelihood of being convicted of murder or manslaughter, keep in mind that "[t]-he People [or prosecutors] *have the burden* of proving beyond a reasonable doubt that the [attempted] killing was *not* justified. If the People have *not* met this burden, [the jury] must find the defendant *not* guilty of [the offense]."[8]

---

[3] P.C. § 1096. *See also* CALCRIM 220.

[4] Laws governing the use of a firearm for self-defense or defense of others vary from state to state. If you use a firearm in self-defense or defense of others, the laws that govern your actions are dependent on where the shooting took place.

[5] The term "self-defense" refers to lawful self-defense. "Imperfect self-defense" (i.e., unlawful self-defense) and its consequences are discussed later in this chapter. *See also* CALCRIM 505.

[6] In addition to the other situations, if you reasonably believed that you were defending your home against someone who intended to or tried to commit a forcible and atrocious crime or violently, riotously, or tumultuously tried to enter your home intending to commit an act of violence against someone inside, and all of the above-listed elements are met, the homicide should be justified. CALCRIM 506.

[7] CALCRIM 505.

[8] CALCRIM 505 (emphasis added).

# A. Reasonable Belief of Imminent Danger

Using deadly force is legal only if your belief about *imminent danger* to yourself or another is *reasonable*. Threats of serious harm *in the future*, or threats of *non-serious* bodily injury, do not justify using deadly force.[9]

## 1. The "Reasonable Person" Test

When self-defense or defense of others is claimed, a prosecutor can decide to either file charges or settle a case through a plea bargain. If charges have been filed and the case is tried, a jury will be instructed to consider all of the facts and circumstances to determine how a "reasonable person"[10] would act if that person was in the same situation.[11] For use of deadly force to be lawful, you must honestly believe deadly force is necessary and a hypothetical reasonable person in the same circumstances would agree with your decision to use force.

This reasonable person standard is not a precise test. Reasonableness is generally determined by a jury considering all of the known facts and circumstances as they appeared to the self-defending person, while considering what a "reasonable person" in a similar situation and with similar knowledge would have believed. This "what would a reasonable person do" test often leads to problems. Particularly the facts and circumstances may seem different in hindsight to an uninvolved person judging the actions of the person who used deadly force. This person is not under the immediate stress of a survival encounter where seconds mean the difference between life and death and may not appreciate the shooter's position.

But, as long as your beliefs were reasonable, the danger does not need to have actually existed for you to have acted lawfully.[12]

---

[9] Juries may, however, be instructed to consider previous threats a defendant received to determine if the defendant acted reasonably in light of those threats. *See People v. Pena*, 151 Cal.App.3d 462, 475 (1984); *People v. Minifie*, 13 Cal.4th 1055, 1065 (1996).

[10] "Reasonable person" is a phrase used among lawyers and judges. *See* BLACK'S LAW DICTIONARY 1294 (8th ed. 2004) (defining "reasonable person" as "[a] hypothetical person used as a legal standard, esp. to determine whether someone acted with negligence; specif., a person who exercises the degree of attention, knowledge, intelligence, and judgment that society requires of its members for the protection of their own and of others' interests. The reasonable person acts sensibly, does things without serious delay, and takes proper but not excessive precautions."). Like it or not, juries and courts have an emotional response to fact patterns. Your actions will not be considered in a logical vacuum. In fact, jury decisions are often based on emotion and then retroactively justified with logic.

[11] *People v. Humphrey*, 13 Cal.4th 1073, 1083 (1996) (quoting *People v. Moore*, 43 Cal.2d 517, 528 (1954)).

[12] *See* CALCRIM 505. *See also* P.C. § 197 (outlining justifiable homicide), Cal. Civ. Code § 50 (stating the right to repel invasion of rights by force).

## 2.   Imminent Danger

"Imminent danger" is a fear of an *immediate* and inevitable threat of harm. It is *not* a fear that you could be harmed sometime in the future. Previous threats alone do not justify using deadly force, unless the threats were made with an intent to carry them out or they make you "reasonably" believe you will *immediately* lose your life or suffer serious bodily injury.[13] The threat must also make you act defensively out of necessity because you reasonably believe you are in sudden jeopardy or because the danger is so quick that you must act immediately to avoid it.[14]

In other words, if you used deadly force and honestly believed you were in imminent danger, but you actually were not, you have not committed any crime *as long as* a reasonable person would have also mistaken the immediacy of the danger or the existence of the danger itself.[15]

The classic example is where an offender aggressively reaches for his gun and displays an intention to shoot you. Imminent danger seems to exist at that moment, and death or serious bodily injury will likely occur if his actions are not interrupted. The belief that you are, or someone else is, in imminent danger of suffering death or serious bodily injury must be *subjectively held*. That is, you must personally believe that the harm is immediately about to occur. And it must be *objectively reasonable*. That is, a "reasonable person" in the same situation would also believe that the harm is immediately about to occur. So, even if the gun turns out to be unloaded, based on all the circumstances, you must subjectively believe you are in imminent danger of great bodily injury or death and a "reasonable person" should probably agree.

## 3.   Imperfect Self-Defense: Unreasonable but Honest Belief

If you used deadly force and *honestly believed* that you were in imminent danger of death or great bodily harm, but a "reasonable person" would not have acted as you did, you have committed a crime. This is called an "imperfect self-defense."

A person acts in "imperfect self-defense" (or imperfect defense of another) if:

- The person actually believed that he, she, or someone else was in imminent danger of being killed or suffering great bodily injury; *and*
- The person actually believed that the immediate use of deadly force was necessary to defend against the danger; *but*
- At least one of those beliefs was unreasonable.

---

[13] *People v. Scoggins*, 37 Cal. 676, 683-684 (1869).
[14] *People v. Dawson*, 88 Cal.App.2d 85, 95 (1948) (quoting *People v. Hecker*, 109 Cal. 451, 467 (1895)).
[15] *People v. Dawson*, 88 Cal.App.2d 85, 96 (1948).

If you are found to have used deadly force in "imperfect self-defense," you cannot be guilty of "murder" because you did not act with the legally required "intent." In fact, you generally cannot be convicted of a charge more serious than voluntary manslaughter.[16] But a "self-defense" defense is risky. The defense often fails and results in the person asserting the "self-defense" defense being convicted of those more serious crimes.

Additionally you generally cannot use "imperfect self-defense" as a defense if you started the fight. Self-defense is generally not recognized as an excuse if you are the aggressor and created the circumstances in which you were attacked and felt compelled to use deadly force.[17]

## B. Amount of Force That Can Be Used in Self-Defense

Typically you must use the least amount of force necessary to eliminate or stop the threat of danger. The amount of force you can lawfully use to defend yourself or others is also the same amount of force that a "reasonable person" would use in the same circumstances to eliminate the threat of death or serious bodily injury.[18]

If you use more force than necessary to defend against a threat, you may *not* successfully claim self-defense.[19] The use of too much force may, however, be considered a case of "imperfect self-defense" if you genuinely, but unreasonably, believed the amount of force was necessary.

The amount of force used in self-defense can be among the trickiest aspects of asserting a "self-defense" defense. What if the attacker just uses his fists to attack you? Can you use a gun to defend yourself? A knife? The answer will hinge on the reasonableness of the response *under the specific circumstances* as decided by a jury. So if you have something other than a gun that you could use against an attacker, resorting to the gun might be considered unreasonable.

## C. No Use of Deadly Force Once Threat of Danger Ends

When the threat of imminent danger ends, whether your attacker successfully flees or you have eliminated the threat, you no longer have the right to use deadly force. You cannot continue to use force after the threat has stopped just because you may be angry.

---

[16] *In re Christian S.*, 7 Cal.4th 768, 771 (1994).

[17] *In re Christian S.*, 7 Cal.4th 768, 773 n.1 (1994).

[18] CALCRIM 506.

[19] *See People v. Clark*, 130 Cal.App.3d 371, 377 (1982) (referencing *People v. Young*, 214 Cal.App.2d 641, 646 (1963)).

For example, in one case a defendant was convicted of second-degree murder because he continued beating his unconscious attacker. His self-defense claim was unsuccessful because it was unreasonable to believe the unconscious attacker still posed a threat of imminent danger.[20]

## D. Using Deadly Force to Stop Dangerous Felonies

You may also use deadly force if you reasonably believe someone is going to commit a felony or cause great bodily injury.[21] But killing or using deadly force to *prevent* a felony is only allowed if the offense is a "forcible and atrocious crime," such as murder, mayhem, rape, or robbery.[22] These are crimes where the person acting in self-defense or in defense of another is presumed to be in peril.

Other crimes like burglary,[23] however, may *not* create a "great bodily injury" presumption. This is because there are instances when no one is, or is reasonably believed to be, at the scene except the burglar.[24]

Using deadly force to stop a dangerous felony is difficult to justify and can be frowned upon by courts and juries. You may be charged and have to defend yourself in court for doing so.

# III. USE OF NON-LETHAL FORCE IN SELF-DEFENSE

The lawful self-defense requirements or "elements" (*i.e.*, reasonableness, immediacy, no more force than necessary) in situations that do *not* involve the use of deadly force, are almost identical to those circumstances where one needs to defend against death or serious bodily injury. In these cases, if you reasonably believe you or someone else is in imminent danger of *suffering bodily injury* or of *being touched unlawfully*, you may only use the *same* amount of force a reasonable person would use in the same situation.[25] This means using deadly force is generally out of the question.

---

[20] *People v. Shade*, 185 Cal.App.3d 711, 716-717 (1986).

[21] *People v. King*, 22 Cal.3d 12, 26 (1978).

[22] *People v. Ceballos*, 12 Cal.3d 470, 478 (1974). Robbery in California means the "felonious taking of personal property in the possession of another, from his person or immediate presence, and against his will, accomplished by means of force or fear." P.C. § 211.

[23] Burglary is different than robbery because burglary involves entering a vehicle or structure to steal something or commit a felony within. Burglary is not necessarily committed directly against a human being like robbery is. *See* P.C. § 459.

[24] *People v. Ceballos*, 12 Cal.3d 470, 482 (1974).

[25] CALCRIM 3470.

The law does, however, allow you to "brandish" (as defined below) a firearm for lawful *self-defense* purposes under certain circumstances.[26] In order to avoid prosecution for the act of brandishing (an offense that carries with it a mandatory three-month jail sentence[27] and the loss of your firearm rights for 10 years),[28] you must meet the above requirements for self-defense. Defending your *property* is discussed further below.

# IV. NO DUTY TO RETREAT

In California you generally do not have to retreat or attempt to get away if you are being attacked.[29] This is because, where an attack is sudden and imminent, you may increase your danger by retreating. In that case you may stand your ground and face your attacker even if you could have more easily retreated.[30] But consider this: juries don't like it when people don't take an opportunity to retreat if they have one. You will never know what they might hold against you during their deliberations.

If you start a fight, however, you cannot successfully claim self-defense when the other person then responds by attacking you[31] unless you:

- Actually, and in good faith, tried to stop fighting; *and*
- Indicated, by understandable words or conduct that you had stopped fighting; *and*
- Gave the opponent a chance to stop fighting, in cases of mutual combat; *or*
- You started the fight using non-deadly force and the opponent responded with such sudden and deadly force that you could not withdraw from the fight.[32]

An aggressor whose victim fights back in self-defense may not invoke the doctrine of self-defense in response to the victim's legally justified acts.[33] If the aggressor attempts to break off the fight and communicates this to the victim but the victim nonetheless continues to attack, the aggressor

---

[26] P.C. § 417(a)(2).

[27] P.C. § 1203.095.

[28] P.C. § 29805. *See* Chapter 3.

[29] *People v. Clark*, 130 Cal.App.3d 371, 377 (1982) (referencing *People v. Collins*, 189 Cal.App.2d 575, 588 (1961)). *See also* CALCRIM 3470.

[30] *People v. Dawson*, 88 Cal.App.2d 85, 95 (1948) (referencing *People v. Newcomer*, 118 Cal. 263, 273 (1897); *People v. Hecker*, 109 Cal. 451, 463 (1895); *People v. Ye Park*, 62 Cal. 204, 208 (1882); *Beard v. United States*, 158 U.S. 550, 560 (1895)); *see also* CALCRIM 506.

[31] *See* CALCRIM 3472. You do not have the right to self-defense if you provoke a fight or quarrel intending to create an excuse to use force.

[32] CALCRIM 3471. *See also* P.C. § 197(3).

[33] *In re Christian S.*, 7 Cal.4th 768, 773 n.1 (1994).

may use self-defense against the victim to the same extent as if he or she had not been the initial aggressor.[34] Furthermore, if the victim responds with a sudden escalation of force, the aggressor may legally defend against that use of force.[35]

# V. DEFENSE OF PERSONAL AND REAL PROPERTY

## A. Personal Property

California does *not* allow deadly force to be used to protect or defend your personal property. Reasonable *non-deadly* force may be used to protect your *personal* property[36] or that of a family member, guest, master, servant, or ward, from imminent harm.[37] But preserving human life and limb from harm is more important to society than protecting property.[38] This means that when merely personal property is involved, deadly force is *never* reasonable.

Protecting and defending *real* property[39] with deadly force *can be* allowed and is governed by different rules.

## B. Real Property

### 1. The Home Protection Bill of Rights

The "Home Protection Bill of Rights" provides that, when you are confronted by an intruder in your home, the law presumes it is reasonable that you feared imminent death or great bodily injury[40] to yourself or a family member if:

- The intruder unlawfully and forcibly entered or was entering your home;
- You knew or reasonably believed that the intruder unlawfully and forcibly entered or was entering your home;

---

[34] *People v. Trevino*, 200 Cal.App.3d 874, 879 (1988); *see also* CALCRIM 3471.

[35] *People v. Quach*, 116 Cal.App.4th 294, 301 (2004).

[36] Personal property is defined as "[a]ny movable or intangible thing that is subject to ownership and not classified as real property." BLACK'S LAW DICTIONARY 1254 (8th ed. 2004).

[37] CALCRIM 3476.

[38] *People v. Ceballos*, 12 Cal.3d 470, 483 (1974) (quoting *Commonwealth v. Emmons*, 43 A.2d 568, 569 (Pa. Super. Ct. 1945)).

[39] Real property is defined as "[l]and and anything growing on, attached to, or erected on it, excluding anything that may be severed without injury to the land." BLACK'S LAW DICTIONARY 1254 (8th ed. 2004).

[40] As used in this context, "great bodily injury" means "a significant or substantial physical injury." P.C. § 198.5.

- The intruder was not a member of your household or family; *and*
- You used force intended to or likely to cause death or great bodily injury to the intruder.[41]

This statute, sometimes known as the "Castle Doctrine,"[42] creates a "rebuttable presumption" that any person who uses self-defense against an intruder in the person's home did so in lawful self-defense (*i.e.*, acted with reasonable belief of imminent bodily injury or death). Even though the statute is favorable for residents who lawfully use deadly force in self-defense, it is not a "get out of jail free" card for shooting someone inside your home.

That is because a prosecutor can still present evidence to rebut the presumption that your actions were reasonable. For example, the prosecutor could present evidence that the intruder no longer posed an immediate threat or that he surrendered once he saw your firearm. If the prosecutor shows that you still shot the intruder after these acts, the "rebuttable presumption" that you "reasonably" acted in self-defense may be shattered.

## 2. Removing a Trespasser from Your Home

As the lawful owner or occupant of a residence, you have the right to ask trespassers (or anyone, for that matter) to leave your premises. If they do not leave within a reasonable time, you may use reasonable force to remove them. The amount of force you may use is limited to what a reasonable person would believe is necessary to prevent damage to the property or physical injury to you, your family members, and/or guests under the circumstances.[43]

If you are *attacked* or *confronted* by an intruder, the above self-defense principles come into play.

## 3. Prohibited Spring Guns/Booby Traps

Though you can lawfully use deadly force to defend real property, you cannot, under any circumstances, protect it with any type of spring gun or booby trap.[44]

---

[41] P.C. § 198.5; *see also* CALCRIM 3477.

[42] P.C. § 198.5.

[43] CALCRIM 3475.

[44] *See* P.C. § 20110.

# VI. SELF-DEFENSE OUTSIDE THE HOME

The above laws about lawfully using deadly force generally apply in both private and public scenarios. One exception, however, is that, unlike within your home where the law presumes that your fear of imminent serious bodily injury when confronted by an intruder is reasonable, no such presumption exists outside the home. Also, unlike within the home where possessing and carrying firearms is definitively protected by the Second Amendment and is generally unregulated in California, it is very difficult to lawfully possess a firearm in public for self-defense purposes.[45] But a self-defense emergency is one of the instances where you may possess a firearm outside of your home.[46]

Because using deadly force can be legal in public, the old advice that "if you shoot a bad guy outside your house, you should drag him inside" should be ignored. Not only is it unnecessary, but it is illegal and could ruin a valid self-defense claim. And you will get caught. Modern forensics makes it almost impossible to move evidence around without detection, especially a body. The proper procedure in this scenario is to secure yourself from harm and call law enforcement immediately to let them know someone has been shot at your location. Then call your attorney. Your attorney should be with you before you say *anything* about the incident to law enforcement.

# VII. ASSISTING THE POLICE AND CITIZEN'S ARRESTS

There are also self-defense protections when you assist a public officer[47] and when you make a lawful citizen's arrest.

When deadly force is used while you are obeying a public officer's command for aid and assistance, the homicide may be justified if all of the following are met:

- The killing was committed while you were either:
  - taking a convicted felon or felons who had escaped from prison or confinement back into custody; or
  - arresting the charged felon and he was resisting arrest or fleeing from justice; or

---

[45] *See* Chapter 5.
[46] *See* P.C. § 26045.
[47] "Public officer" includes more classes of law enforcement than "peace officers." *In re Frederick B.*, 192 Cal.App.3d 79, 89-90 (1987), *disapproved on other grounds in In re Randy G.*, 26 Cal.4th 556, 567 n.2 (2001).

- overcoming the decedent's actual resistance to some legal process; or
- performing any other legal duty;
- The killing was necessary to accomplish one or more of the foregoing; *and*
- You had probable cause to believe that the decedent posed a threat of death or serious bodily harm either to you or others, or the decedent committed a forcible and atrocious crime that threatened you or others with death or serious bodily harm.[48]

You may also have legal protection where you use deadly force in self-defense while trying to arrest someone for committing a violent felony. The killing would be justified, and not unlawful, if:

- You committed the killing while lawfully trying to arrest or detain the decedent for committing a forcible and atrocious crime (*i.e.*, a felony that threatened death or serious bodily harm), or you suspected the decedent was committing a crime, and that crime threatened you or others with death or serious bodily harm;
- The decedent actually committed the forcible and atrocious felony that threatened death or serious bodily harm or the decedent was suspected of committing a crime, and that crime that threatened you or others with death or serious bodily harm;
- You had reason to believe that the decedent had committed a forcible and atrocious crime (*i.e.*, a felony that threatened death or serious bodily harm), or the decedent was suspected of committing a crime, and that crime threatened you or others with death or serious bodily harm (you have reason to believe the decedent posed a threat of death or great bodily injury or committed, or was suspected of committing, a forcible and atrocious crime and that crime threatened you or others with death or great bodily injury when facts known to you would persuade someone of a reasonable caution to have those beliefs); *and*
- The killing was necessary to prevent the decedent's escape.[49]

---

[48] CALCRIM 507.
[49] CALCRIM 508.

# VIII. PROTECTION FOR HARMING INNOCENT BYSTANDER WHILE ACTING IN SELF-DEFENSE – "TRANSFERRED INTENT"

If you *lawfully* defend yourself or another and accidentally injure or kill an innocent bystander, under the doctrine of transferred intent you should not be held criminally responsible for such injury or death. This is because, for you to be convicted of any crime, you must have the criminal intent to commit a crime. Conversely, if you lacked that criminal intent (for lawful self-defense you are not considered to possess *criminal* intent because your intentional actions were justified) and you subsequently hurt or killed an innocent bystander, you may claim self-defense from criminal responsibility for injuring or killing the innocent bystander.[50]

# IX. SELF-DEFENSE BY A PROHIBITED PERSON USING A FIREARM

As explained in Chapter 3, in *People v. King*[51] the California Supreme Court determined that in limited situations a person prohibited from possessing firearms may be able to possess them briefly. In *King*, a prohibited person, Mr. King, attended a birthday party. Two individuals who were not invited to the party started to cause problems and a fight broke out. The friends of these two individuals attempted to break into the apartment where the party was taking place. The attackers tried to break down the door and climb into the apartment using a balcony. King did not participate in the fight, nor did he attempt to break it up. Rather, he and his disabled friend took refuge in the kitchen of the apartment.

One of the attackers threw a grill through the kitchen window. King and his disabled friend were showered with glass and hit by the grill. After washing the glass out of his eyes, King wheeled his disabled friend into a bedroom for the friend's protection. King returned to the main area of the apartment where one of the residents of the apartment handed him a pistol. King fired three shots into the air and warned the intruders to leave. The intruders retreated briefly but rushed King, believing he was firing blanks. King, believing he was in great danger, fired a few shots over the attackers' heads. One person received a minor gunshot wound.

The laws governing self-defense are some of the oldest on the books. In *King*, the California Supreme Court noted that the laws governing self-

---

[50] *People v. Mathews*, 91 Cal.App.3d 1018, 1024 (1979).

[51] *People v. King*, 22 Cal.3d 12 (1978).

defense date back to 1872 (the year the Penal Code was first enacted) and the code sections for justifiable homicide can be traced back to 1850[52] (the year California became the 31st state). The court identified that there was a conflict between the laws that allow self-defense and the laws that prohibit a person from possessing handguns.[53]

In resolving this conflict the Court etched out a narrow and extremely brief exception to the restriction against prohibited persons possessing firearms for self-defense purposes:

> [T]he prohibition of section 12021 [now sections 29800-29825] was not intended to affect a felon's right to use a concealable firearm in self-defense, but was intended only to prohibit members of the affected classes from arming themselves with concealable firearms or having such weapons in their custody or control in circumstances other than those in which the right to use deadly force in self-defense exists or reasonably appears to exist. Thus, when a member of one of the affected classes is in *imminent peril of great bodily harm or reasonably believes himself or others to be in such danger,* and *without preconceived design on his part a firearm is made available to him, his temporary possession of that weapon for a period no longer than that in which the necessity or apparent necessity to use it in self-defense continues,* does not violate section 12021.[54]

The court's holding essentially means that if you are prohibited from possessing firearms you may *temporarily* possess a firearm for self-defense (or defense of another) when:

- You reasonably believed you or someone else was in imminent danger of suffering a significant or substantial physical injury;
- You reasonably believed that the immediate use of force was necessary to defend against the danger;
- The firearm became available to you without any planning or preparation on your part;
- You possessed the firearm temporarily and only for the time period necessary (or reasonably appeared to have been necessary) for self-defense;
- You had no other means of avoiding danger of injury; *and*
- Your firearm use was reasonable under the circumstances.[55]

---

[52] *People v. King,* 22 Cal.3d 12, 22-23 (1978).

[53] *People v. King,* 22 Cal.3d 12, 23 (1978). The firearm restriction for felons was only limited to handguns at the time of the *King* case.

[54] *People v. King,* 22 Cal.3d 12, 24 (1978) (emphasis added).

[55] CALCRIM 2514.

# X. AVOIDING PROSECUTION FOR CRIMINAL OFFENSES INVOLVING FIREARMS

If your use of a firearm does *not* qualify as lawful self-defense, you can be convicted of a serious crime. Aside from the obvious crimes of murder, attempted murder, and manslaughter, you can be charged for illegally using a firearm even if you do not physically injure anyone.

## A. Assault with a Deadly Weapon

The term "assault" does not require any actual physical contact, but is rather an unlawful *attempt*, with a present ability, to commit a violent injury on someone else.[56] Anyone who commits an assault with a firearm against another person may be punished with a felony, misdemeanor, and/or a fine of up to $10,000.[57]

Assault with a "machinegun," "assault weapon," or .50 BMG rifle is a felony with a state prison sentence of either four, eight, or twelve years. Assault with a semiautomatic firearm is a felony with a sentence of three, six, or nine years.[58] Who the victim is can also affect the severity of the charges and sentences.[59]

## B. Brandishing a Firearm

Except for in lawful self-defense, drawing or showing any firearm, whether loaded or unloaded, in a rude, angry, or threatening manner or unlawfully using a firearm in any manner in someone else's presence, or in any fight or quarrel, violates California law.[60] The type of firearm used, where you brandish it, and who you brandish it at are all factored into whether the offense is a felony or a misdemeanor and what type of sentence you can receive.

For example, it is a felony to threateningly draw or show a firearm to anyone in a car that is on a public street or highway in a way that would cause a reasonable person to fear bodily harm,[61] while it is a misdemeanor to threateningly draw or show an imitation firearm[62] to another in a way that would cause a reasonable person to fear bodily harm.

---

[56] P.C. § 240.

[57] P.C. § 245.

[58] P.C. § 245(a)(2)-(3), (b).

[59] P.C. § 240 *et seq.*

[60] P.C. § 417.

[61] P.C. § 417.3.

[62] As discussed in Chapter 9, an imitation firearm is any "BB device," toy gun, firearm replica, or other device that is so substantially similar in color and overall appearance to an existing firearm that a reasonable person would think it *is* a firearm. P.C. §§ 417.4 and 16700.

## C. Vehicle Forfeiture for Discharging or Brandishing of Firearms

In most cases where motor vehicles are used in murder, manslaughter, attempted murder, assault with a deadly weapon, or where someone unlawfully discharges or brandishes a firearm from or at an occupied vehicle where a victim is killed, attacked, or assaulted on a public street or highway, the motor vehicle must be forfeited to law enforcement and possibly sold or destroyed.[63]

However, the motor vehicle may not be sold if:

- It is a stolen vehicle (unless the identity of the legal and registered owner cannot be obtained); or
- It is owned by another person, or co-owned by a spouse of the defendant, and the vehicle is the only vehicle of the immediate family.[64]

# XI. WHAT TO DO AFTER USING DEADLY FORCE IN SELF-DEFENSE

If you ever have the misfortune of having to shoot an aggressor in self-defense, there are some essential steps you should consider taking to avoid potentially being charged criminally or sued civilly by the aggressor or a survivor of the aggressor.

Once you and others, if any, are secure, call 911 as soon as possible. Unjustified delay in making this call may be seen as the cause of the aggressor's further injury or death and may increase your risk of liability. When you call 911, assume your call is being recorded. Remain as calm as possible. Give basic factual information so the 911 dispatcher can get help on its way to you while you complete the call. Make clear that an ambulance should be sent immediately. Tell the dispatcher that a shooting just occurred. Give your name and a description of yourself. Give the address where you are. If the shooting took place inside your home, explain that you are the resident there. Mention if others are present and if they are injured. Give their names and specify if they are residents in your home or innocent bystanders if you are in public. Don't elaborate beyond this information.

Call your attorney immediately after calling 911. Your attorney will assist you with presenting your claim of lawful self-defense.

---

[63] P.C. § 246.1.
[64] P.C. § 246.1(f).

Put the gun in a place where police can see it but won't feel threatened by it. Do not alter the scene of the shooting in any other way. Don't pick up shell casings. Don't move the body. Don't clean up anything. Modern forensics can detect these types of efforts, and you will only arouse suspicions that you acted illegally or have something to hide.

When the ambulance and the police arrive, remember that you have no duty to talk to the police. In fact, I recommend that you should *not* explain the details of the shooting without your attorney present. But this is a close call, particularly in a shooting that is obviously justified. "Lawyering up" is seen by some police as a sign of guilt. It may help if you tell the police you would like to give them more information, but you read a book (this one) that suggested you shouldn't.

Your reactions after a use of force in self-defense can be twisted by politically inclined authorities, can be misinterpreted by police, prosecutors, and juries, and may be understood differently in Texas or Los Angeles.

The appropriate response to being forced to use deadly force to defend yourself is resigned regret and righteous remorse. Not guilt, remorse. As in: "I value all life, even the criminal's. I hated to have to use force that might deprive another person of life, but I had no choice. It's tragic that the guy left me no choice. He forced me to do what I had to do. If I hadn't done what I did, I thought he would kill me."

How to articulate that sentiment unambiguously is the tricky part. I have seen several people, after killing in completely righteous self-defense, burst into tears when they see the dead body and realize what they have done. This is understandable, because even taking the life of a "dirt bag" who "deserves shooting" is very, very sad. No matter how righteous, it's sad. But crying can be made to look like you realize you did something wrong, regret your mistake, and are upset about it. And this can hurt you.

To avoid feeling that sadness, I have also seen people respond with psychological defense mechanisms, putting up emotional walls and hardening their feelings so they don't feel sorrow for the event or the criminal, or second guess themselves and their actions. And you will second guess yourself if you have even a shred of humanity in you. You will replay the incident in your head and wonder how it might have been different.

That response, both the emotional walls and the second guessing, can hurt you legally if articulated to authorities because that reaction can also be misconstrued. It can come across as demeaning the criminal, insensitive, and inhumane if it comes across as a casual attitude like, "Screw him, he got what he deserved; I don't care."

As appropriate as that might be in reality, the Dirty Harry tough-guy response is often perceived by a jury, when spun sympathetically by a prosecutor, as cavalier. It can make you look impulsive and trigger happy – you could have avoided the incident but were in a hurry to judge and execute the criminal. Save the self-doubt for the psychologist who you should absolutely see if you have to use deadly force and save the hard-ass self-righteousness for your lawyer in private.

Probably the best reaction is to sit down, say nothing, look sad, and tell them you read a book that said that after an incident like this you should say nothing and ask for a lawyer, so that's what you are gonna do. Then ask for the lawyer and say you intend to remain silent. If they keep asking you questions, just keep asking for a lawyer. Don't take the bait. Police are great at getting people to talk, especially after a stressful event. It's natural to want to talk. But in the heat of the moment it's easy to say things that can be taken out of context, misconstrued, and spun to make you look like you did something wrong, or worse, that you knew it was wrong when you did it.

Depending on these and some other very specific circumstances that police investigators will pick up on, the police may or may not be on your side. If they think you acted suspiciously or unlawfully, they may look for more information and evidence to confirm their suspicion. No matter how justified your actions were, speaking with the police without your attorney can result in incriminating yourself and can get you into deeper trouble.

If you are taken to the police station for further questioning, so be it. No matter what you say, a trip to the station is statistically likely. Be aware that there are hidden audio recorders in most police cars. And any phone calls you make from the station or jail will be recorded. So do not discuss the facts of the shooting at anytime, or with anyone, until your attorney is present and says it's okay. Inform any person you call that you were arrested and where you were taken, and ask them to please call your lawyer as well.

# APPENDIX A:
# "ASSAULT WEAPONS" LISTED BY NAME[1]

## Combined Listing of Category 1 and Category 2 "Assault Weapons"

Italicized models are Category 1 "assault weapons" and were required to be registered on or before March 31, 1992. Non-italicized models are Category 2 "assault weapons" and were required to be registered with the Department of Justice on or before January 23, 2001. Category 3 "assault weapons" are not included in this listing.

## Rifles

**American Arms**
AK-C 47
AK-F 39
AK-F 47
AK-Y 39

**American Spirit**
ASA Model

**Armalite**
AR 10 (all)
*AR-180*
Golden Eagle
M15 (all)

**Arsenal**
SLG (all)
SLR (all)

**B-West**
AK-47 (all)

**Beretta**
*AR-70*

**Bushmaster**
*Assault Rifle*
XM15 (all)

**Calico**
*M-900*

**Colt**
*AR-15 (all)*
Law Enforcement (6920)
Match Target (all)
Sporter (all)

**Daewoo**
*AR100, AR110C*
*K-1, K-2*
*Max 1, Max 2*

**Dalphon**
B.F.D.

**DPMS**
Panther (all)

---

[1] This list is from the CALIFORNIA ATTORNEY GEN., CALIFORNIA ASSAULT WEAPONS IDENTIFICATION GUIDE 82-84 (3d ed., 2001), *available at* http://ag.ca.gov/firearms/forms/pdf/awguide.pdf (last visited July 31, 2012).

**Eagle Arms**
EA-15 A2 H-BAR
EA-15 E1
M15 (all)

**Fabrique Nationale**
*308 Match, Sporter*
*FAL, LAR, FNC*

**Frankford Arsenal**
AR-15 (all)

**Hesse Arms**
HAR 15A2 (all)
Model 47 (all)
Wieger STG 940 Rifle

**HK**
*91, 94, PSG-1*
*93*

**IMI**
*Galil*
*Uzi*

**Inter Ordnance -
Monroe, NC**
AK-47 (all)
M-97
RPK

**J&R ENG**
*M-68*

**Kalashnikov USA**
Hunter Rifle / Saiga

**Knights**
RAS (all)
SR-15 (all)
SR-25 (all)

**Les Baer**
Ultimate AR (all)

**MAADI CO**
*AK 47*
*ARM*
MISR (all)
MISTR (all)

**Made in China**
*56*
*56S*
*84S*
*86S*
*AK*
*AK47*
*AKM*
*AKS*

**Made in Spain**
*CETME Sporter*

**MAS**
*223*

**Mitchell Arms, Inc.**
AK-47 (all)
AK-47 Cal .308 (all)
M-76
M-90
RPK

**Norinco**
*56*
*56 S*
81 S (all)
*84 S*
86 (all)
*86 S*
AK-47 (all)
Hunter Rifle

MAK 90
NHM 90, 90-2, 91
Sport
RPK Rifle
*SKS w/ detachable
magazine*

**Ohio Ordnance Works
(o.o.w.)**
AK-74
ROMAK 991

**Olympic Arms**
AR-15
Car-97
PCR (all)

**Ordnance, Inc.**
AR-15

**Palmetto**
SGA (all)

**Poly technologies**
*AK47*
*AKS*

**Professional Ordnance,
Inc.**
Carbon 15 Rifle

**PWA**
All Models

**Rock River Arms, Inc.**
Car A2
Car A4 Flattop
LE Tactical Carbine
NM A2 - DCM Legal
Standard A-2
Standard A-4 Flattop

**RPB Industries, Inc.**
*sM10, sM11*

**SIG**
*AMT, PE-57*
*SG 550, SG 551*

**Springfield Armory**
*BM59, SAR-48*

**Sterling**
*MK-6*

**Steyr**
*AUG*

**SWD Incorporated**
*M11*

**Valmet**
*76 S*
*Hunter Rifle*
*M62S, M71S, M78S*

**Weaver Arms**
*Nighthawk*

**Wilson Combat**
*AR-15*

**WUM**
WUM (all)

## Pistols

**Advance Armament Inc.**
*M11*

**Bushmaster**
*Pistol*

**Calico**
*M-950*

**Encom**
*MP-9, MP-45*

**IMI**
*UZI*

**Intratec**
*TEC-9*

**MARS**
Pistol

**Military Armament Corp.**
*M-11*

**Professional Ordnance, Inc.**
Carbon 15 Pistol

**RPB Industries Inc.**
*sM10, sM11*

**Sites**
*Spectre*

**Sterling**
*MK-7*

**SWD Incorporated**
*M11*

## Shotguns

**Cobray**
*Streetsweeper, S/S Inc., SS/12*
*Striker 12*

**Franchi**
*SPAS 12, LAW 12*

# ABOUT THE AUTHOR

C.D. "Chuck" Michel is Senior Counsel and owner of Michel & Associates, P.C., a boutique law firm employing 15 attorneys located in Long Beach, California. The firm's practice focuses on litigation, both civil and criminal. Areas of practice include firearms law, constitutional law, civil rights advocacy, business litigation, land use law, employment law and environmental law. The firm's website is www.michellawyers.com.

Mr. Michel has been litigating civil and criminal firearm cases since 1991. His clients include the National Rifle Association (NRA), the California Rifle and Pistol Association (CRPA) Foundation, *FFLGuard*, gun manufacturers, wholesalers, retailers, and individual gun owners. He has represented thousands of individuals and companies charged with violating California's confusing firearms laws. He has been trial counsel in scores of jury trials, many of which were high profile and attracted state and national media attention. He has litigated hundreds of firearms cases involving constitutional issues, including Second Amendment challenges, in both state and federal trial and appellate courts. As an attorney for the NRA, Mr. Michel has been a stakeholder in drafting legislation to protect California gun owners and an advocate in opposing ill-conceived legislation that restricts their rights. Since 2002, Mr. Michel and his law firm have donated over 1.5 million dollars worth of *pro bono* legal work to the NRA and the CRPA Foundation.

Among many other victories, Mr. Michel won the NRA-sponsored lawsuit that struck down Proposition H, the San Francisco law that would have banned the civilian possession of handguns in the city. He also led the successful CRPA Foundation lawsuit that struck down Assembly Bill 962, an anti-gun politician's attempt to severely restrict and require registration of all ammunition purchases. Mr. Michel filed prestigious, influential, and unprecedented *amicus* briefs on behalf of dozens of California district attorneys in both the 2008 *District of Columbia v. Heller* and the 2010 *McDonald v. Chicago* Supreme Court gun-rights cases. He has been honored with numerous awards for his legal successes, including awards for his civil rights advocacy, trial advocacy skills, writing skills, and *pro bono* work.

Mr. Michel has served as a spokesperson for the NRA, CRPA, other civil rights group clients, and for individual clients. He has appeared on dozens of television and radio interviews and been quoted in thousands of newspaper articles. He publishes a monthly column, *Legal Front Lines*, and a blog at www.calgunlaws.com. He has had articles and editorials published in the *Los Angeles Times,* the *Los Angeles Daily Journal,* and other state and national newspapers and magazines.

"Professor" Michel also teaches classes in Firearms Law and Law Practice Management as an adjunct professor at Chapman University School of Law in Orange, California.

Mr. Michel graduated near the top of his classes from both Rutgers University in New Jersey in 1980 and from Loyola Law School in Los Angeles in 1989. He began his legal career with a coveted judicial clerkship for U.S. District Court Judge William J. Rea in Los Angeles. He worked as a criminal prosecutor for the Los Angeles County District Attorney's Office and several Southern California cities and as an advocate with the Los Angeles Federal Public Defender's office. Mr. Michel also practiced environmental and general civil litigation as an attorney at the renowned international law firm of O'Melveny & Myers, LLP. While at O'Melveny, Mr. Michel represented clients ranging from individuals to multinational corporations. Among many other cases and clients, he represented Exxon in connection with the Exxon Valdez oil spill and served as a staff counsel to the "Christopher Commission" which investigated the Los Angeles Police Department after the Rodney King incident.

Mr. Michel grew up in what used to be rural New Jersey at a time when neighbors wished him luck as he walked out his back door and into the woods behind his house to go rabbit hunting before high school. (These days the neighbors would call the SWAT team on a high school student with a gun.) His father was a businessman who loved teaching others, including his three sons, the shooting sports as an NRA instructor. Some of the author's fondest childhood memories are of backyard plinking contests with his entire family. The author is striving to pass this firearm heritage along to his own sons and hopes that they will be able to pass it on to future generations of free Americans.

# NATIONAL RIFLE ASSOCIATION
## MEMBERSHIP APPLICATION

NRA RECRUITER ID#
## XP025815

## STEP ONE: Provide Personal Information

NAME: Mr./Mrs./Ms. _____

ADDRESS: _____

CITY/STATE/ZIP: _____

E-MAIL: _____

PHONE: _____ BIRTHDATE: _____

## STEP TWO: Select Membership Type

| | |
|---|---|
| __ 1 YEAR | $35 |
| __ 3 YEAR | $85 |
| __ 5 YEAR | $125 |
| __ JUNIOR (15 years & up) | $15 |
| __ ASSOCIATE (no magazine) | $10 |
| __ REGULAR LIFE MEMBERSHIP | $1,000 |
| __ JUNIOR LIFE MEMBERSHIP | $550 |
| __ DISTINGUISHED LIFE MEMBERSHIP – Age 65+ | $375 |
| __ EASY PAY LIFE MEMBERSHIP* | $25 (minimum) |

\* Easy Pay for Life Membership: minimum $25 down payment,
then minimum $25 quarterly payments until total dues are paid.

__ Foreign Postage (per year: $5 Canadian – $10 other) ____

**CALCULATE TOTAL AMOUNT DUE   $ _____**

## STEP THREE: Select One Magazine

(Junior Members under age 15 receive Insights digital* magazine,
15 and older choose magazine) *E-mail address required for digital version.

| AMERICAN RIFLEMAN | AMERICAN HUNTER | AMERICA'S 1ST FREEDOM |
|---|---|---|
| __ Digital __ Print | __ Digital __ Print | __ Digital __ Print |

## STEP FOUR: Provide Payment Information

__ CHECK PAYABLE TO NRA: Check # _____ enclosed

__ CHARGE TO:   __ AMEX   __ VISA   __ MC   __ DISCOVER

ACCOUNT # _____

EXPIRATION DATE: _____

SIGNATURE: _____

## STEP FIVE: Please Read The Following:

Contributions, gifts, or membership dues made or paid to the National Rifle Association of America are not refundable or transferable and are not deductible as charitable contributions for Federal income tax purposes.

Please allow 4 to 6 weeks for delivery of membership credentials and materials.

Call NRA at 800-672-3888 for more information about membership programs, or visit us at **www.NRA.org.**
Manage your membership online at **www.NRAMemberServices.org**

## STEP SIX: Mail this application with payment to:

National Rifle Association of America
c/o Recruiting Programs
11250 Waples Mill Road
Fairfax, VA 22030

You can also sign up on the internet through the "Join NRA" badge on www.calgunlaws.com.

# WHY JOIN THE NRA?

800-392-VOTE • www.NRAILA.org

## NRA Membership Benefits

These basic membership benefits are automatically included with your NRA Annual Membership or Life Membership, along with special members-only discounts and services.

- An official NRA Membership ID card - showing your Membership ID number and expiration date or Life Member status. You should carry this card with you at all times.
- With all regular memberships, you will get a choice of subscription to American Rifleman, American Hunter, or America's 1st Freedom.
- Junior members receive a subscription to Insights.
- Annual members receive $5,000 of Accidental Death and Dismemberment coverage at NO COST to you. The plan covers accidents at, or to and from, an NRA event; and accidents that occur during the use of firearms or hunting equipment while hunting. Insurance must be activated at time of renewal. (Does not include Junior membership.)
- Life members receive $10,000 of Accidental Death and Dismemberment coverage at NO COST to you. The plan covers accidents at, or to and from, an NRA event; and accidents that occur during the use of firearms or hunting equipment while hunting. Insurance must be activated at time of upgrade to Life member status
- Law Enforcement Officers, that are NRA members, killed in the line of duty will have $25,000 in coverage.
- $2,500 of ArmsCare coverage with your NRA membership. This plan covers insured firearms, air guns, bows and arrows against theft, accidental loss, and damage. Insurance must be activated.

  For purposes of insurance, NRA members must be current active members of the NRA whose name appears on the NRA membership list. Activation is required.

- New and Enhanced insurance coverages through the NRA Endorsed Insurance Programs. Enroll on-line for Life, Health and Accident and Individual Property and Liability insurance or call Toll free 1-877-NRA-3006 (1-877-672-3006.) New Commercial Property Liability Insurance Program for NRA Affiliated Clubs and Business Alliance Members, visit on-line or call Toll Free 1-877-487-5407.

- The most important benefit of NRA membership, however, is the defense of your Constitutional right to keep and bear arms, both nationally and in California. NRA-ILA tracks the issues and alerts members about legislation involving firearms and hunting at the federal, state and local levels of government. Successful legislative action begins with you -- the individual member. For information regarding legislative action or to become an ILA grassroots volunteer, call 1-800-392-8683.

- NRA Institute for Legislative Action representatives are your voice on Capitol Hill and in Sacramento.

- Your NRA Membership dues payment receipt allows you to immediately enter NRA registered tournaments.

For real American values, shop NRAstore.com,
where 100% of the profits go directly to support vital NRA programs
Request a catalog • 888-607-6007 • Shop online: www.NRAstore.com